T0399999

THE HISTORY AND PHILOSOPHY OF SCIENCE

This book provides an in-depth analysis of the history and evolution of the major disciplines of science, which include the basic sciences, bioscience, natural sciences and medical science, with special emphasis on the Indian perspective. While academic interest shown in the history and philosophy of science dates back to several centuries, serious scholarship on how the sciences and the society interact and influence each other can only be dated back to the twentieth century. This volume explores the ethical and moral issues related to social values, along with the controversies that arise in relation to the discourse of science from the philosophical perspectives.

The book sheds light on themes that have proved to have a significant and overwhelming influence on present-day civilisation. It takes the reader through a journey, on how the sciences have developed and have been discussed, to explore key themes like the colonial influences on science; how key scientific ideas have developed from Aristotle to Newton; history of ancient Indian mathematics; agency, representation, deviance with regard to the human body in science; bioethics; mental health, psychology and the sciences; setting up of the first teaching departments for subjects such as medicine, ecology and physiology in India; recent research in chemical technology; and even the legacy of ancient Indian scientific discoveries.

A part of the *Contemporary Issues in Social Science Research* series, this interdisciplinary work will be of immense interest to scholars and researchers of philosophy, modern history, sociology of medicine, physical sciences, bioscience, chemistry and medical sciences. It will be of interest to the general reader also.

Nandan Bhattacharya is currently Assistant Director of UGC-Human Resource Development Centre, Jadavpur University. Dr Bhattacharya received his MSc (Zoology) in 1992 and PhD (Zoology) degree in 2004 from Vidyasagar University. He has so far published several articles in reputed journals and delivered lectures in different national and international colleges and universities. He has experience in coordinating and designing the course curriculum of orientation programmes, workshops and short-term courses especially meant for college and university teachers/librarians under the UGC guideline. He is interested in ecology, education, communication skill development, science and art connection, theatre in education, forum theatre, etc. as research fields. Dr Bhattacharya is also an acclaimed stage actor and director.

Contemporary Issues in Social Science Research

Series editors: Rajat Acharyya and Nandan Bhattacharya

UGC-Human Resource Development Centre,
Jadavpur University, India

Contemporary Issues in Social Science Research is a series dedicated to the advancement of academic research and practice on emerging 21st century social and cultural themes. It explores fresh perspectives on a legion of interdisciplinary social science themes connecting subject areas that have hitherto been unexplored, underdeveloped or overlooked. This series aims to provide scholars, researchers and students a ready reference for the new and developing in social science academia which has come into the fore as focal points of debate and discussion today.

The History and Philosophy of Science
An Indian Perspective
Edited by Nandan Bhattacharya

Peace and Conflict Studies: Theory and Practice
Edited by Shibashis Chatterjee and Anindya Jyoti Majumdar

For more information about this series, please visit https://www.routledge.com/Contemporary-Issues-in-Social-Science-Research/book-series/CISSC

THE HISTORY AND PHILOSOPHY OF SCIENCE

An Indian Perspective

Edited by Nandan Bhattacharya

Routledge
Taylor & Francis Group

LONDON AND NEW YORK

Cover image: Getty Images

First published 2023
by Routledge
4 Park Square, Milton Park, Abingdon, Oxon OX14 4RN

and by Routledge
605 Third Avenue, New York, NY 10158

Routledge is an imprint of the Taylor & Francis Group, an informa business

British Library Cataloguing-in-Publication Data
A catalogue record for this book is available from the British Library

ISBN: 978-0-367-46311-3 (hbk)
ISBN: 978-0-367-47106-4 (pbk)
ISBN: 978-1-003-03344-8 (ebk)

DOI: 10.4324/9781003033448

Typeset in Bembo
by Apex CoVantage, LLC

*This volume is dedicated to those noble martyrs
who sacrificed their lives for Science*

CONTENTS

FIGURES

TABLES

CONTRIBUTORS

Sudipa Bandyopadhyay is Associate Professor in the Department of Sanskrit, Vidyasagar College, Kolkata. Since 2007, she is Guest Faculty in the Department of Sanskrit, University of Calcutta. She is the supervisor of MPhil and PhD programmes at the University of Calcutta since 2009. She is working on the area of history, epigraphy and palaeography of ancient India. The thrust area of her research project is science and technology, that is metallurgy, surgery and medical treatment, numismatics, iconography, painting and sculpture, art and architecture, social science as revealed in the glorious civilisation of ancient India. Some of her publications – *Dharma and War Policy of Ancient India*, *War: Elements of Science in Ancient India, Influence of Sentiments (Rasa) in Ancient Indian Painting'*, '*Iconography and Religious Tolerance'* and so on. She was awarded the Shiksha Ratna Award by the Government of West Bengal.

Manika Pal Bhadra is an eminent and well-reputed scientist in India. She is presently the chief scientist at the Applied Biology Division, CSIR-IICT-Hyderabad. She was awarded PhD degree in advanced cytology and molecular genetics from Calcutta University. She pursued postdoctoral studies at the University of Missouri, Columbia. She has expertise in RNAi and epigenetics, nanotechnology, drug discovery and authored 120 publications in several international journals. Owing to her exceptional contribution, she has been bestowed with several prestigious awards like Young Scientist Award 1991, Welcome Trust Fellow 2005, IICT Roll of Honour 2007, NASI Reliance 2012, and IICT Best Women Scientist, 2012.

Santanu Biswas is Professor of English at Jadavpur University, and a psychoanalyst practising in Kolkata. He is the first psychoanalyst belonging to the 'Lacanian' orientation in India. He has been affiliated to the Lacan Circle of Australia (a chapter of the World Association of Psychoanalysis) since 2005. He has lectured on psychoanalysis at numerous institutions in India and abroad, and has written extensively on the theory and practice of psychoanalysis. He is a member of the advisory boards of some of the leading journals of Lacanian psychoanalysis in France, England, USA, Australia, and Slovenia.

Susanta Kumar Chakraborty, Professor of Zoology, and former Dean, Faculty of Science at Vidyasagar University, has research specialisation in ecology and environmental management. He has been teaching in the postgraduate level for more than three decades. He has so far published around 200 research papers, supervised 40 PhD candidates, written a number of textbooks, completed 15 research projects and visited several countries as part of his academic commitments. He is the recipient of several awards in recognition of his academic and research contributions.

Bijan Das was educated at the University of North Bengal, Darjeeling and Saha Institute of Nuclear Physics, Kolkata. He carried out advanced research at the University of California, Berkeley, USA; Universitaet Karlsruhe, Germany; and Saint Francis Xavier University, Antigonish, Canada. He has been Professor of Chemistry at Presidency University, Kolkata, since 2012. Previously, he was Professor of Chemistry at the University of North Bengal for six years, where he served as a member of the faculty of the department of chemistry from 1989 to 2012. His research interests include physical chemistry of surfactants, electrolytes, polymers and biopolymers. He has so far published more than 100 research articles.

Samantak Das is Pro-Vice-Chancellor and Professor of Comparative Literature, Jadavpur University. He is also Director of the School of Cultural Texts and Records (SCTR) at Jadavpur University. Samantak has written and lectured on nineteenth-century literature, translation, the relationships between the biological sciences and literature, environment, ecology, rural development and education in journals, magazines and newspapers in India and abroad, including *The Times Higher Education Supplement*, *Economic and Political Weekly*, *Interventions: International Journal of Postcolonial Studies*, *The Times of India*, *The Statesman*, *The Telegraph*, *The Indian Express*, *The Hindu*, *Biblio*, among others. He has led, or jointly led, several national and international projects including on language learning, digitising ephemera, creating databases and so on.

Somnath Gangopadhyay is Professor in the Department of Physiology, University of Calcutta. He is actively involved in extensive research activities, with more than 250 research publications of his work in national and international peer reviewed journals and books. He has been conferred FABMS title by the Indian Association of Biomedical Scientists. He has been conferred Fellow, Chartered Institute of Ergonomics and Human Factors and awarded Chartered status title by Chartered Institute of Ergonomics and Human Factors, United Kingdom. Presently, he holds the post of the secretary of scientific committee of International Commission on Occupational Health.

Pradip Kumar Ghosh was former Lecturer at Maharaja Manindra Chandra College. He completed his PhD work in theoretical physics on 'Stochastic Quantization and Some Aspects of Supersymmetry' in 1991. Then he switched to academic administration by joining Bangabasi College in Kolkata, and then Jadavpur University as registrar. After retirement, he was appointed Pro-Vice Chancellor of Jadavpur University.

During his entire career he published a number of papers in theoretical physics in different journals of repute. Besides, he has written articles on philosophy of science and academic administration. Also, he has participated as a resource person in national and international seminars and in UGC-organised orientation and refresher courses and visited different universities.

Bichitra Kumar Guha was Professor of Physics at IIEST, Shibpur, Kolkata, where he was former Dean, Faculty of Science. He stood first and third in BSc and MSc respectively. His research interest is in electronic ceramic materials, especially ferroelectric materials. He introduced a new technology for chemical doping of niobium in barium titanate. He proposed a material having very high dielectric constant of about 105. He also found out the exact dopant concentration of niobium at which a material undergoes transition from semiconductor to insulator. He has published books with several reputed and international publishers.

Deepak Kumar has worked and published on science and society links in the context of colonial India for more than four decades. Apart from several edited books, he is known for his *Science and the Raj* (1995), *The Trishanku Nation* (2016) and a recent book in Hindi titled *Atam Khabar: Sanskriti, Samaj aur Hum* (2022).

Pradip Kumar Majumdar is former Professor of Indian Astronomy, Rabindra Bharati University and Department of Mathematics, Kalyani University. He is Fellow of Asiatic Society. He was awarded Ganit Bhushan, Ganit Acharya, Ganit Ratna, and Jnan Chandra Ghosh national award. He is the author of 27 books, including *A Dictionary of Sanskrit–English Technical Terms: Mathematics Volume I, A Dictionary of Sanskrit–English Technical Terms: Astronomy Volume II, A Bibliography of Islamic Mathematics, M.A.S.S. Mathematics of Ancient India*, among others.

Manjusha Majumdar (Tarafdar) is Professor, Department of Pure Mathematics, University of Calcutta. Her area of teaching and research is geometry. She has examined more than 25 PhD theses so far. She has published 43 articles, books, chapters, attended 44 conferences and invited lectures and shared many administrative responsibilities. She is a reviewer of several national and international journals. She has been included in Who's Who in the World (USA), the World Who's Who of Women (USA), Who's Who in Science and Engineering (USA), and nominated for 1999 Woman of the Year (American Biographical Institute).

Sankar Kumar Nath was former Professor, Department of Oncology, R.G. Kar Medical College, Kolkata. He is President of Oncolink Cancer Centre. His field of research includes history of medicine, astronomy and cancer. He has published many articles in different reputed journals and written and edited 15 books. He was awarded Rabindra Puroshkar by Government of West Bengal.

Sarmistha Sen Raychaudhuri graduated from Presidency College, Kolkata, and obtained both her Masters and PhD degrees from the University of Calcutta. She was awarded the ISCA Young Scientist Award in the year 1987. In the same year she went to the Queen Mary University of London, for postdoctoral research. She was awarded Uma Kant Sinha Memorial Young Scientist Award (ISCA). She was a visiting scientist at the Yale University, USA. She has published many research articles in reputed journals. She has guided many students for doctoral degree. At present she is a professor at the University of Calcutta.

Samir Kumar Saha obtained his Bachelor's, Master's and PhD degrees, all in mechanical engineering from Jadavpur University, specializing in thermal engineering. His teaching career spans a period of 40 years in the mechanical engineering department at Jadavpur University and five years at MCKV Institute of Engineering. He has guided several PhD and postgraduate candidates. He has international and national journal publications as well as conference proceedings publications. Prof. Saha has authored a book *Engineering Education in India* (2012). He was a visiting faculty in USA at Virgina Polytechnic and also co-investigator of an international project on sustainability transition with Eindhoven University, the Netherlands. He also attended an international seminar on philosophy of science at Lille, France, in 2019. He is a fellow and life member of several reputed organisations.

SERIES EDITOR'S NOTE

Academic interest shown regarding history and philosophy of science dates back to several centuries but solemn efforts have been taken since the twentieth century onwards. Integrated History and Philosophy of Science (HPS) has set forth a programme for considering it as a unified discipline. Today, almost all the leading universities across the globe have their research units in this field. In India, Jadavpur University, University of Calcutta, Jawaharlal Nehru University and several others regularly practise research on the mentioned fields comprising copious number of faculty members, scholars and students. Therefore, this book will be an input and contribution to the international academia about the history and philosophical thoughts regarding various fields of science. This book will provide a detailed understanding of history and evolution of different major disciplines of science including basic sciences, biosciences, natural science and medical science with special emphasis on Indian perspectives. It also intends to focus on the philosophical views regarding the disciplines, as well as to explore the issues related to ethical, moral and social values. The volume will make an effort to bring to light the philosophical point of view on controversies arising in relation to use of science for civilisation. The respective chapters are based on the selected lectures delivered by experts from Jadavpur University, Calcutta University at several UGC-sponsored orientation programmes and refresher courses organised by the UGC-Human Resource Development Centre, Jadavpur University during 2012–2022. These courses were targeted for and attended by teachers and librarians working at different colleges, universities and institutes in India. Potential target reader groups of this volume are assumed to be teachers of concerned subjects in different colleges and universities, research scholars of concerned fields and libraries of different academic institutions. Students of undergraduate as well as postgraduate courses like basic disciplines of science such as mathematics, physics, chemistry and biosciences, sociology, education, anthropology, philosophy and history from different colleges and/or universities are also supposed to be the readers of the volume.

February 2022
Nandan Bhattacharya

ACKNOWLEDGEMENTS

The editor deeply acknowledges the authors for their valuable contribution. Heartiest thanks are extended to the officials, colleagues and staff of Jadavpur University and UGC-Human Resource Development Centre, Jadavpur University, for their support, enthusiasm and logistic support they provided without which this volume would not have been completed. The editor is also thankful to University Grants Commission for its kind allotment of the programmes on the basis of which the content was selected.

INTRODUCTION

Nandan Bhattacharya

Each and every civilisation has its own unique contributions to the overall human civilisation. This is not and should not be an issue of competition and superiority of a particular civilisation but a matter of understanding the great past to move forward for a greater future as a whole. Simultaneously, it is not also praiseworthy to claim blindly the metaphysical or pseudoscientific ideas of the past to be "scientific". Academic researchers on the contrary should focus on past inventions and discoveries in a materialistic and truly scientific vista. Indian civilisation, similar to other great cultures like The Mesopotamian, Egyptian, Chinese or Mayan, has its noble contributions to mankind. One may list the contributions which are still used and practised today in the fields of astronomy, mathematics, medicine, metallurgy, geography, etc. (Uttpal and Soni, 2018; Singh and Kaur, 2014). Another fact should be kept in mind that like other parts of the world, ancient Indian science also is interwoven with philosophical backdrop. Therefore, talking about history of science automatically encompasses philosophy of science. While exploring the past, it is also required to look simultaneously into the future. Hence, the recent trends in scientific discoveries in India should be considered with due weight. Though numerous studies are there involving these issues, a compilation of history and philosophy of science and future trends with special emphasis to Indian context is necessary. Keeping this in mind, the present edited volume comprises 15 chapters from eminent scholars and specialists to serve the quest of students and intelligentsia of the world.

Sarton said,

> I am convinced that the historical method is the best to convey scientific facts and ideas to unprepared minds and to make them thoroughly understandable, – at least that is so in the case of grown-up people.

DOI: 10.4324/9781003033448-1

On the other hand, the genius minds of scientists whose discoveries and inventions created paradigm changes in human civilisation have influenced philosophy as well, or the scientists borrowed their ideas from philosophical stores. Thus, without discussing history and philosophy the study of science is incomplete as these three components are entwined from their beginning. Therefore, this volume tries to explore the history and philosophy of science from three main points of view in three parts. The first part of the book addresses the historical aspects of scientific evolution. The second part deals with the philosophical aspects, and the third one is dedicated to the emerging issues in biomedical sciences and healthcare from their historical and philosophical perspectives like ergonomy, psychoanalysis and RNA interference, with special focus on the discussion of Indian contribution to science. Thus, in brief overview, the volume not only tries to travel around the world history and philosophy of different disciplines of science with their counterparts in India, but also highlights the unique contribution of Indian intellects.

In the first chapter, "History of Science", **Prof. Samir Kumar Saha** gives a brief outline of the journey of science. "The history of science is the study of the development of science just as one studies the development of a plant or an animal from its very birth", said Sarton (1916). Professor Saha therefore describes the very basic ideas of scientific evolution. He starts from the emergence of science and then points out the milestones of discoveries and inventions of science in different eras and in different countries or continents. A brief description of notable philosophers and scientists and their discoveries which have changed the course of scientific evolution at a particular period of history is given in a nutshell. The chapter depicts the scientific evolution of ancient civilisations like India, China, Arabia, and Greece. At the end of the chapter the contribution of modern Indian scientists is portrayed. As a whole, this chapter will serve as a text of history of science.

Modern science is no doubt an endowment of colonialism. **Prof. Deepak Kumar** intends to find out the detailed background of colonial influence on science in India. The chapter describes the glorious past of Indian intellects and their contributions. While during the eighteenth and nineteenth centuries, Europe developed and flourished their science remarkably and used its fruits for their business purpose. Bridges between continents were laid, and the era of ruthless colonialism started. But wherever they stepped they brought their crown in one hand and science on the other. The new trends and practices which the East observed were institutionalisation, the adhesion of government and science, science in education, the modern scientific research techniques, technological imperatives and many others. As a whole, the philosophy of Indian scientific tradition and culture was transformed. This raises a discourse of modernity as well because it "kills and nourishes almost simultaneously". Thus, this chapter, in a nutshell, finds out the whole story of modern Indian science and will be one of the most important discussions in the field of history of science from Indian perspective.

Goethe once said, "If we look at the problems raised by Aristotle, we are astonished at his gift of observation. What wonderful eyes the Greeks had for many things!" Indeed, another ancient civilisation which, like India, has changed the course of journey of science in a different era is the Greek civilisation. Both ancient and modern science of other civilisations are indebted to Greece. Quite a lot of milestone discoveries and inventions have their roots in ancient Greek science. Einstein remarked that development of Western science is based on two achievements, namely "formal logical system" (Euclidean geometry) and "to find out the causal relationships by systematic experiment". This volume therefore tries to explore the history of science in Greece. **Prof. Bichitra Kumar Guha** surveyed the journey from Aristotle to Newton in Chapter 3, which covers in detail the development and evolution of physics, mathematics, astronomy and other fields where Greek philosophers planted their flags. At the same time, he also discusses the social perspectives of the discoveries, the role of the Church, the tarnished Inquisition etc. The chapter deals with the glorious struggle and martyrdom of scientists like Galileo and Bruno to hold the banner up in even the most crucial dark age of irrationality in the name of religion.

Peter Gobets of ZerOrigIndia Foundation states, "The Indian (or numerical) zero, widely seen as one of the greatest innovations in Human History, is the cornerstone of modern mathematics and physics, plus the spin-off technology". Besides, India enlightened the world with other blessings of science like *sulya sutras*, astronomy, algebra, trigonometry and analysis and so on. More important is that ancient Indian science and Indian philosophy always progressed hand in hand. The very concept of *Byom* (*Mahashunya*) was the unique contribution of Indian philosophy. This perception of eternity and entity of nothingness or devoid was described in several religious and philosophical texts of ancient India. In Chapter 4, **Prof. Manjusha Majumdar (Tarafdar)** traces the origin and evolution of these ideas and concepts chronologically, beginning from the Vedic period onwards. A link to other civilisations regarding exchange of ideas and comparison between them with regard to the concepts is also the focus of the chapter.

Ancient Indian medical science started its journey from Ayurveda (science of life) from where eight branches originated among which surgery (*Śalyatantra*) was one of the important fields of research. **Dr Sudipa Bandyopadhyay** touches upon the history of surgery in ancient India. But before that, one must have a clear concept of the Ayurveda. Since the second century BC, Ayurveda flourished in the ancient schools of Hindu philosophical teachings called *Vaisheshika* (inferences and perceptions obtained about a patient's pathological condition for treatment), the school of logic named as *Nyaya* (extensive knowledge of the patient's condition and the disease condition before proceeding for treatment). It is related to the manifestation framework, well known as *Samkhya*. Later, *Vaisheshika* and *Nyaya* schools worked together and jointly founded the *nyāya–vaiśeṣika* school. Like other such materialistic and scientific ideas, Ayurveda also is said to have divine origin from Lord Brahma, who framed the process for the well-being of mankind. The first *Shlokas* were found in the *Vedas* complied by the sage Atreya (Ninivaggi, 2008). Agnivesha compiled the knowledge which was edited by mainly Charaka (*Charaka Samhita*). *Charaka Samhita* describes all aspects of Ayurvedic medicine, and *Sushruta*

Samhita describes the science of surgery. The Ayurvedic practice requires the full involvement of the patient. It is an interactive system and educational. It encourages self-empowerment of patient. It is a system for empowerment, freedom and long life (Pandey et al., 2013). Thus, the whole system is beyond just medical practice and reaches the philosophical horizon from where it originated. During the last few decades, Ayurveda has been going through paradigm changes. Lots of interdisciplinary works are now carried out regarding Ayurveda. A new discipline called "Ayurgenomics", developed recently, "bridges this gap between genomics and Ayurveda and serves as an aid in understanding of inter-individual differences in responses to therapies in various diseases" (Gupta, 2015). The basic concept of Ayurveda, the *Prakriti*, is now interpreted from the standpoint of body mass index (BMI) (Rotti et al., 2014). Rotti et al. (2015) reported "classification method for human population, with respect to DNA methylation signatures" based on *Prakriti*. Thus, this traditional Indian heritage is now supplemented with new flow of knowledge from other streams of sciences, and at the same time it also ramifies itself into other disciplinary tributaries. Like Ayurveda, as stated earlier, surgery also has its long past in Indian medicine.

Tipton, describing about Sushruta, says that he (Sushruta) opined about the main and true nature of a physician as a preventer of disease rather than invest efforts in curative medical procedures. Now, when under the severe effect of viral attack this volume is being processed, this statement seems to be the preamble of medical science. The development and evolution of medical science in India, is also presented in a chronological manner. One of the most important aspects put forward by Sushruta was perhaps the amalgamation of religious ideas and empirical studies. In his *Sushruta Samhita* he said,

> The different parts of the body as mentioned before the skin, cannot be correctly described by one who is not well versed in anatomy. Hence, anyone desirous of acquiring a thorough knowledge of anatomy should prepare a dead body and carefully observe, by dissecting it, and examine its different parts.

This *Shloka* indeed depicts the progressive mindset of the early Indian medical scientists, vast knowledge and the great heritage of India. This chapter (Chapter 5) will surely draw the attention of researchers to understand the medical history of India.

In Chapter 6, **Dr Sankar Kumar Nath** deals with rather recent past. His focus is on the establishment of India's first medical college, Medical College of Bengal on 28 January 1835, affiliated with the London University.

> Prior to this college a few medical schools were there in India offering mostly insufficient and to some extent unscientific medical education to the students. Dr Mountford Joseph Bramley (1803–1837) was appointed as the first Principal of Medical College of Bengal,

says Dr Nath. After colonisation, British rulers in India started reforming education, science, law and all other infrastructure and superstructures in line with their
own system, as they did in other parts of the world where their colonies were
established. The Western medical footprints were first recorded in around AD 1600,
with the arrival of British medical officials in India. The first medical department
was established in AD 1764 (Mushtaq, 2009). Finally, in the year 1835, after the
opening of the first medical college, Indian Medical Service (IMS) was opened for
the natives. Bramley, one of the pioneer figures of modern Indian medical science,
is as much an important name as any other British legends like Beaton, Long or
others. Therefore, this volume should have the duty to rediscover him and not
to leave him "fallen into oblivion in the history of medical science in India" as
Dr Nath says.

The term "Science" is just a newcomer in the field of academics when Willium
Whewell first coined the term scientist. Previously, science was included under the
broad spectrum of philosophy. Earlier ancient scholars of Greece were called natural philosophers not analogically the same as modern scientists. The great minds of
the "Age of Renaissance" like Descartes, Galileo or of the "Age of Enlightenment"
like Newton were considered as philosophers rather than as "scientists". Newton's
book is named as *Philosophiae Naturalis Principia Mathematica* (simply as *Principia*).
After the nineteenth century, different disciplines emerged as subjects of sciences,
such as biology and physics, and the researchers started to be addressed as biologists or physicists respectively. Still, the relation of science with philosophy never
departed. Rather, new issues are coming up as science progresses. For example
bioethics is one of the most recent issues dealing with the human genome project
and cloning. Philosophy of science deals with the ultimate purpose of science, its
trajectories, boundaries, reliabilities of scientific theories, relationship of science
and truth, etc. Particularly, the last one is important in the sense that should science aim to determine the ultimate truth or some question would be there forever
unsolved. Therefore, without discussing the philosophy the discussion of sciences
is incomplete. Keeping this in consideration, in the second part of this volume
philosophy of sciences is discussed.

"Philosophy always asks questions on justification. To decide: Is there any absolute Truth and Will science be able to arrive at it?" Keeping this in mind, **Dr Pradip
Kumar Ghosh** tries to encompass the brief overview of philosophy of science in
Chapter 7, by focussing on Western philosophy. He starts with the origin of modern
science pointing out the radical theories which have shaken the world of science.
Then comes the issue of evolution of philosophical thought, the difference between
science and pseudoscience, the debate of science and similar science. As described
earlier, the relation of science and truth is one of the chief issues of philosophy of
science. Prof. Ghosh naturally touches upon the concern. Also, he focuses on the
history of this journey, pointing out issues such as inductive and deductive reasoning, logical positivism, and so on. The philosophies of David Hume, Karl Popper,
Imre Lakatos, Kuhn and others are considered. The long existing debate of scientific
realism is another topic emphasised in the discussion on philosophy of science, and

he concludes the chapter with this issue. Thus, in brief, induction, explanation, realism and scientific changes, empiricism, realism and naturalism, conflict of science and religion are taken into consideration.

The famous werewolf legend which even took the lives of several innocent people in ancient times due to superstition was eventually found to be the Ambras syndrome or hypertrichosis (growth of abnormal hair on body). Once, after discovery "Supermale" or XYY karyotype of human genomic structure was a misnomer postulation claimed to be linked with criminal activities. Later on, it was proved to be just a chromosomal aberration like other such kinds, for example Down and Klinefelter syndromes, and no such scientific evidences supporting the claim were found. But this fact, during the 1960s, evoked once more the philosophical and ethical issue of relationship between human anatomy, physiology or genetics with the characteristic feature of human being that is either good or evil nature. Not only in criminology but in biology, physiology or in politics, philosophy, literature, human body has always been a prime focus of attention for thousands of years. Even in recent days the Human Genome Project still raises many philosophical debates from the ethical point of view. **Prof. Samantak Das** in his chapter, Written on the Body: Agency, Representation, Deviance, intends to shine the light on one of such classical issues which has been a matter of discourse in history and in the contemporary times also.

In Chapter 9, **Prof. Pradip Majumder** discusses Āryabhata I and his method of "Continued fraction to find out the integral solution of indeterminate equation of the type by asrc" and the discussion enters into specific problem. This chapter surely opens a new window of research that is to review and search in depth any particular issue.

Psychology is nowadays a very much important field and day by day it is gaining more emphasis in daily life due to increasing mental disorders as a result of increasing complexity of the fast and complex modern life. The World Health Organization (WHO) (2019) reports that every 40 seconds, there is a case of suicide. So, the subject with its details needs to draw the attention of the academic field also. As a discipline it was closely related to philosophy for several centuries. The soul, the mind and other concepts were discussed in Hindu, Greek and Chinese philosophies in the ancient era. In 1890, William James first defined psychology as "The Science of mental life, both of its phenomena and their conditions". Psychoanalysis is one of the major wings of psychology. Sigmund Freud established this discipline in 1890, and soon it attracted people's attention. Though today science has described much sophisticated and developed theories and therapies regarding psychoanalysis, Freudian technique still retains its crown. **Prof. Santanu Biswas** in Chapter 10 deals with "The Death Instinct in Psychoanalysis", an important part of the Freudian theory.

In the third part of the book, the recent advances of sciences in different fields are taken into consideration with special emphasis on Indian perspective. India not only has a great heritage but after Independence, the country has taken quite a big leap in science. Apart from conventional disciplines, research is pursued on several specialised areas of modern science, such as space science, computer science, specialised branches of biosciences and bioengineering such as ergonomics. India has a long heritage regarding conservation of nature and its bioresources. But it is also one of the leading countries in the world so far as the modern techniques and strategies are concerned. The principal objective of this part is to point out the current advancements on those issues. This part intends to focus on rather specialised attempts of sciences to enhance the quality and magnitude of welfare and well-being of mankind through scientific discoveries. In this regard, authors emphasise on the various types of research carried out in Indian laboratories by Indian intelligentsia.

Prof. Bijan Das addresses the very fundamental question of mankind in Chapter 11: how did life originate on Earth? Indeed, this question has intrigued scientists as well as philosophers from the beginning of human civilisation thousands of years ago, and it still remains unsolved. New researches are coming up with new discoveries every day. Though so many doctrines are there from the point of view of ancient religions (e.g. the Bible, Upanishads), folk beliefs and even tribal postulations (e.g.) on origin of life, materialistic or scientific investigation was started nearly 2,000 years back by Aristotle. Prof. Das tries to start with the early "scientific" notion of Aristotle and then takes a journey of discoveries up to recent works on it.

RNAi or RNA interference is one of the most current techniques and researches are ongoing in this field from only the past two to three decades. It gains its importance not only for its role in further research to understand genetic phenomena further in detail but also for its use in drug production (Kim and Rossi, 2008). After facing a lot of challenges involving "safety and potency" during August 2018, there was a paradigm shift when US Food and Drug Administration finally approved Patisiran, the first RNAi-based drug. Thus, the science of RNAi has now gained significance as a noble scientific research field for human benefit along with its academic importance. **Prof. Manika Pal Bhadra** with her fellow researchers works in this contemporary and sophisticated field at CSIR-Indian Institute of Chemical Technology, one of the leading institutes in India. In their chapter, they discuss the origin and journey of the works done on RNAi, its mechanism, ethics, applications (in agriculture, in healthcare, e.g. cancer and HIV) and RNAi-based therapeutics and its advent and evolution. Chapter 12 thus seems to be one of the most valuable chapters of this volume.

According to WHO the number of people with diabetes rose from 108 million in 1980, to 422 million in 2014. The global prevalence of diabetes among adults over 18 years of age rose from 4.7% in 1980, to 8.5% in 2014 (WHO, 2016). Between 2000 and 2016, there was a 5% increase in premature mortality due to diabetes. According to the National Diabetes Statistics Report, 2020, 10.5% of the US population are suffering from diabetes. "The mean of amount of money spent on the current visit was 553.15 INR. The direct cost of healthcare for diabetic individuals was 553 INR, among them medicines accounted for the largest share", says Sandhya Rani Javalkar (2019). These statistics show the severity of the disease.

Therefore, it can easily be assumed how much benefit the rural and/or poor people of India would have if low-cost medicines are available in the market. Numerous researches are being conducted around the world to mitigate this silent killer. **Prof. Sarmistha Sen Raychaudhuri** and her fellow scholars worked on *Momordica charantia* L., an antidiabetic medicinal plant, at the Department of Biophysics, Molecular Biology and Bioinformatics, University of Calcutta. This plant, with antidiabetic factor charantin, can be propagated through somatic embryogenesis, an *in vitro* technique by which plant propagation can be achieved by exploiting its inherent property of totipotency. Their work certainly creates possibilities for further research in this field and hope for betterment of crop production and in turn betterment of human life (Chapter 13).

The concept and attempts for better user-friendly work tools and places date back to several millennia. It is assumed to be first exercised in the hominid evolution in *Australopithecus prometheus* when they invented handmade tools from stone. Other civilizations also practised "occupational health and safety" and productivity. But ergonomics as a well-defined and theorised science has only a few decades of existence in academic arena, and it is very much a specialised one. Though the term ergonomics has been coined in 1857, it came into being as a separate subject during the 1940s, and finally took a definite shape in 1949, with the establishment of The Ergonomics Society. In India, it started its journey during the late 1950s, and it was first taught as a subject in the physiology department of Presidency College, Calcutta. This is a growing discipline and is still taught in only a few colleges and universities for Bachelor's and Master's degree courses. The importance of this subject is proved time and again, as even during the current pandemic situation the Chartered Institute of Ergonomics and Human Factors (CIEHF) and its members are regularly providing consultation and guidance with their professional and scholarly expertise. **Prof. Somnath Gangopadhyay** presents an overview of the subject, its role and importance in Chapter 14.

Scrupulous focus has already been given to the conservation of bioresources and sustainable development of them as severe damage is being done due to rapid and voracious progress of human civilisation and population explosion of mankind. The whole concept and research comes under the purview of the subject ecology. Though the term ecology took birth a few decades ago, the very concept prevails through several thousand years. It is flourishing and gaining more importance steadily with the increasing degradation of nature by human civilisation. So, considering the importance, the subject deserves a space in this volume. **Prof. Susanta Kumar Chakraborty** in Chapter 15 talks about the origin and evolution of the subject with special emphasis on the issue of biodiversity which also is a blazing matter today.

The legacy of ancient Indian scientific discoveries on which modern science still depends includes medicine, mathematics and metallurgy. Examples such as the value of pi, the concept of zero are well known and widely described. But there are a few more which have not been taken into consideration in regular literature. Metallurgy is one of these heritage topics. Prof. Cyril Stanley Smith has remarked that usually man assays metals. Metals can just as well be used to assay the progress of mankind. Srinivasan and Ranganathan (1997) discuss in detail the field which interested readers may go through for further research.

References

Gupta, P. (2015). Pharmacogenetics, pharmacogenomics and ayurgenomics for personalized medicine: A paradigm shift. *Indian Journal of Pharmaceutical Sciences*, 77, 135–141.

Javalkar, S. R. (2019). The economic burden of health expenditure on diabetes mellitus among urban poor: A cross sectional study. *International Journal of Community Medicine and Public Health*, 6(3), 1162–1166. DOI: http://dx.doi.org/10.18203/2394-6040.ijcmph20190604

Kim, D. H. and Rossi, J. J. (2018). RNAi mechanisms and applications. *Biotechniques*, 44(5), https://doi.org/10.2144/000112792

Mushtaq, M. U. (2009). Public health in British India: A brief account of the history of medical services and disease prevention in colonial India. *Indian Journal of Community Medicine: Official Publication of Indian Association of Preventive & Social Medicine*, 34(1), 6–14. https://doi.org/10.4103/0970-0218.45369

Ninivaggi, F. (2008). *Ayurveda: A Comprehensive Guide to Traditional Indian Medicine for the West*. Rowman and Littlefield Publisher, Inc., Lanham, MD.

Pandey, M. M., Rastogi, S. and Rawat, A. K. S. (2013). Evidence-based complementary and alternative medicine. Article ID 376327, 12 pages. http://dx.doi.org/10.1155/2013/376327.

Rotti, H., Mallya, S. and Kabekkodu, S. (2015). DNA methylation analysis of phenotype specific stratified Indian population. *Journal of Translational Medicine*, 13, 151.

Rotti, H., Raval, R. and Anchan, S. (2014). Determinants of prakriti, the human constitution types of Indian traditional medicine and its correlation with contemporary science. *The Journal of Ayurveda and Integrative Medicine*, 5, 167–175.

Sarton, G. (1916). The history of science. *The Monist*, 26(3), 321–365.

Singh, T. and Kaur, R. (2014). Scientific and technological developments in Indian Heritage: A review. Proceedings of The National Seminar on Indian Heritage: Perspectives AND Prospects, January 10–11.

Srinivasan, S. and Ranganathan, S. (1997). Metallurgical Heritage of India. In *Golden Jubilee Souvenir, Indian Institute of Science*. Indian Institute of Science, Bangalore, 29–36. https://www.tf.uni-kiel.de/matwis/amat/def_en/articles/metallurg_heritage_india/metallurgical_heritage_india.html

Uttpal, A. and Soni, S. (2018). A glimpse of science, technology, and mathematics in ancient India: Social and cultural perspective. *Journal of Social and Political Sciences*, 1(2), 225–231.

WHO (2016). Global report on diabetes. https://apps.who.int/iris/bitstream/handle/10665/204874/WHO_NMH_NVI_16.3_eng.pdf

WHO (2019). Suicide: One person dies every 40 seconds. News Release. 9 September 2019. https://www.who.int/news/item/09-09-2019-suicide-one-person-dies-every-40-seconds

PART I
History of Science

1

HISTORY OF SCIENCE

A Brief Overview

Samir Kumar Saha

This chapter outlines the importance and origin of science. Advances in modern science have been dealt with briefly including a section on Indian science.

The Scientific Method

Any kind of scientific method takes the following steps. It starts with observation and asking questions. After this comes the study of background works related to the problem. Now formulation of a hypothesis can be done and then arises the need for testing of hypothesis by experimentation. Experimentation, in turn, is of two types, namely physical and thought experiment (logical/mathematical). This is followed by analysis of data and only then a conclusion can be drawn which genesis of a law or theory. Then is the time to communicate the results (books, papers).

Why History of Science?

It is better to recall the definition and concept of history. History is a continuous interaction between the historian and his facts, an unending dialogue between the past and the present (What is History, Carr, P-35). History has also been defined as the knowledge of the man's past, verifiable knowledge (Marron, 1966). History of science is important for many reasons as mentioned here.

First, we will understand about the methods of science. It includes:

(i) Observation to theory (Newton's laws, Darwin's theories of evolution etc.);
(ii) Theory from fact, observation, experiment (Einstein's general theory of relativity, 1907–1922);
(iii) Logical ideas of deduction, induction – general to particular and particular to general.

DOI: 10.4324/9781003033448-3

Second, we will learn about new ways of thinking; for example Poincare, Einstein, measurement of time to relativity.

Third, we learn about men/women who thought out of the box and went against conventions. It teaches that going against convention is not always wrong as Galileo went against the Aristotelian concept after almost 2,000 years.

Fourth, we learn how the social transformation of the world took place. There are several great leaps which took place during the course of human history as a result of revolutionary advancements in science; for example stone age to metal age, agriculture to industry, steam engine to Industrial Revolution, electricity (Faraday, Davy to J.C. Maxwell), IT, computers (theories of Shanon, Weiner Von Neuman, Alan Turing, Bardeen and Shockley's invention of transistors (1930–1940). Earlier Babbage's analytical machine with, Ada Lovelace) and of course War and birth of Big Science.

Fifth, history of science places scientific discoveries in the context of other historical (and social) events. There are lots of scientific principles which have influenced and been utilised in social events. Archimedes' principle brought about a radical development in ship industry and global trade. Manhattan Project is well known for its influence on atom bomb and the Second World War. Classical mechanics of Newton in fact changed the whole world of technological civilisation qualitatively.

Sixth, history of science brings history alive to people with a humanities inclination. It is important to know Shakespeare, but it is also important to know the second law of thermodynamics (C.P. Snow, Two Cultures, 1956). Likewise, knowing Tagore is obviously important but never to forget M.N. Saha and J. C. Bose. Learning about science in the context of society at that time helps to understand segments of history. Therefore, teaching of history has to be made interesting. The important scientific discoveries of any specific time period of human evolution should be incorporated during teaching of history.

Seventh, it is true that learning about the history of science differs somewhat from conventional history in the sense that it is actually learning about people observing the physical/natural world or physical phenomena. Hence, it is not just a chronology of events and trends in society and their analysis. It makes clear the difference between history of ideas and social history. The human adventure is incorporated.

Eighth, we also understand through the history of science how science influences culture and trade or economics and sustainability. We learn also how culture influences science. How, say for example, religion influences science. The long-inherited discourse on science and religious conflict and controversies is a very significant chapter in the history of science. *History of the Conflict Between Religion and Science* by J.W. Drapier (1874) is an important book in this context.

Often, the history of science has been overlooked, particularly in literature. More emphasis has been given to love, war or family affairs, but natural catastrophes have been less talked about in literature leaving people less aware of environmental or scientific issues like climate change problems (see, for example, *The Great Derangement* by Amitav Ghosh, Penguin Books, 2016).

No less important than all the above is that the history of science makes us learn about scientific revolutions. There are many important eras where scientific achievements produced qualitative changes in society. Some of them are history's most important eras, such as the Industrial Revolution, IT revolution, biotechnology revolution (that is mapping of human genome), global warming (anthropogenic catastrophic fuel burning) and climate change.

The Emergence of Science

Science originated about 4,000 years ago. There are debates about where it originated. The reason behind it is that recorded history of those times is really scarce. Though we now know, historians of science agree that most of science originated in Mesopotamia/Babylon (Tigris/Euphrates Valley), Mohenjodaro-Harappa (Indus Valley) and Egypt (Nile Valley). Archaeological evidence shows the exchange of knowledge between these places. The means of such transport were probably canoes and ships. Travel by land was also undertaken on a regular basis (Gordon Childe, 2016).

Babylonian/Mesopotamian Science

Babylon was about 70 miles south of the present-day Baghdad. Science originated mostly from observing the sky and recording the movements of celestial bodies. They recorded their findings on clay tables. So, these have survived till today. Cuneiform was the script. They were the first to divide time into units of "sixty". Astronomical data of Babylonians were transmitted to the Greeks via Egypt (Fara, 2009).

Egyptian Science

Egyptians worked on astronomy, mathematics and medicine. They recorded on papyrus. Their script was hieroglyphics. Unfortunately, records being on papyrus did not survive with time. However, the link of Egypt with Mesopotamia, India, and Greece in ancient times is well established. Pyramids of Egypt are about 3,000 years old and still remains as a sign of great geometrical and technical achievement (S.N. Sen, BijnarerItihas, Vol 1, 2nd Ed, 1962).

Mohenjodaro and Harappa (Indus Valley)

The notable achievements were large irrigation systems, which prove their expertise on mathematical measurements. The concept of arithmetic, zero and decimal system originated during that time. Pythagorean geometry may have been partially inspired by Hindu models (G. Sarton, Introduction to History of Science, Vol I, P-74). Ayurveda originated in about 3000 BC to 2500 BC (Sushruta). Records of this great civilisation also are not well available.

Science in China

Professor of Cambridge Joseph Needham's work confirmed that understanding science's history means thinking about social environments, not just chronicling great discoveries and theories. In China, astrologers, calendar makers and physicians first observed patterns in nature and applied their knowledge to obtain practical results. Compass and gunpowder were invented in China (Morus, I. R., Ed., Oxford Illustrated History of Science, Oxford University Press: UK, 2017).

Islamic or Arabic Science

Islamic or Arabic science dates back to AD 780–850, when Khwarizmi first used algebra with words, not symbols. He lived in Baghdad, and his major contribution was to help establish the wide use of the Hindu–Arabic number system. During AD 1000, *Book of Optics* by Ibn-al-Haytham was published. However, the works were done mostly during the medieval period (Morus, I. R., Ed., Oxford Illustrated History of Science, Oxford University Press: UK, 2017).

Greek Science: Comprehending Nature

The Ionians

The important input the Greek science gave was the Naturalistic Explanation. No place for arbitrary gods or demons was there and no place for design. They believed that order comes out of chaos through the processes of nature and chance. The noteworthy contributors were as follows.

Thales (ca. 625–545 BC): He tried to explain the world from observation and common sense. His postulation about the origins of the world was from water from natural processes.

Anaximander (ca. 611–547 BC): He first stated the four elements of nature viz. earth, water, air and fire. According to him, these elements are layered in "Natural Order" and the earth formed through fire acting on the elements.

Anaximenes (ca. 550–475 BC): He focused on processes. His doctrine was based on three principles. According to him, the "First Principle" is "Mist" and every change is through refraction and condensation.

Heraclitus (ca. 550–475 BC): His focus was on change and contrary to Anaximenes his opinion was that fire is "First Principle" and everything is in "Tension" (like the string of a lyre).

The Atomists

Two important thinkers in this school of thought were Leucippus (fl.c.400 BC) and Democritus (fl.c.420 BC). Democritus was a materialist. He explained the world in terms of an infinite number of hard, indivisible particles ("Atoms"). He opined that "Qualities" are really the effects that materials have on our senses. Another major conjecture was "Nothing is created out of nothing".

Up to this era is called the pre-Socratic era and comprised three major schools of philosophy, namely Ionians, Pythagoreans and Atomists. They provided the first basic outlines of the core concerns of science and demonstrated the range of possible approaches.

Plato, Aristotle and the Order of Things

Aristotle, a pupil of Plato, was the most influential of all Greek philosophers. He has pioneered several fields of science like observation of nature, classification of species, important correlations, embryology and so many other domains. He was the first to propose the hierarchy of nature and placed living beings into the bottom top order as plants [vegetative soul] > animals [animal soul] > humans [rational soul].

Aristotle's "Causes": Explaining Things Unlike Plato, Aristotle believed that it was possible to explain Nature. To explain something was to discover its "Causes". The causes of things are of four kinds: (1) material, that is what something is made of; (2) formal, that is the design or form of something; (3) efficient, that is the maker of something; and (4) final, that is the purpose of something.

For example when applied to a pot of clay, the material would be clay, formal would be the design of the pot, efficient would be the potter and final would be the purpose (such as for drinking wine or water).

Motion: The phenomenon of natural motion was also discussed by Aristotle. Describing this, he inferred why something falls. The answer is "Gravity". So, what is "Gravity"? Describing gravity, he said "The tendency of heavy bodies to fall to the Earth". The problem of non-natural motion was also answered by him. He argued that "Displacement" is the reason behind something that moves before falling to the Earth.

The Classical Contribution to Technology

The classification table (Table 1.1) will help us understand the contribution to technology. Although disdaining technology, Plato and Aristotle freely used observations of craftsmen at work.

Archimedes (287–212 BC): He was a mathematician and natural philosopher who worked on statics and hydraulics. He was in one sense an inventor.

The New World: the Spread of Printing

Johannes Gutenberg: He was able to tackle problems of Molding Standard Type, organising Composition ("Cases"), formulating Ink and designing useful

TABLE 1.1 The classification table of observations of craftsmen at work

	Greece	Rome
The place of technology in the classical world	Great philosophical but modest technological achievements	More noted for technologies – particularly for organisation, mobilization and building
Greek attitudes toward technology	"The Arts" – The Work of Slaves	Xenophon on the Crafts "The Mechanical Arts Carry a Social Stigma and are Rightly Dishonored in Our Cities". Workers "Are Looked Upon as Bad Friends and Bad Patriots"

Press. The result was complex, artistic work. The first book published was The Great Bible (1455–56). Rapid spread of printing produced 30,000–35,000 different volumes, and 15–20 million volumes were printed between 1450 and 1500.

Printing and Technology: The Renaissance and the Technological Imagination The Machine Books: Technology becomes a subject not only of reporting but also of the imagination. New methods were introduced to make clear technical information. Leonardo da Vinci worked on machinery and flying machines.

The Origin of Modern Astronomy

Scientific Revolution

The idea of "Scientific Revolutions" deals with the discourse that science changed by "revolutionary" jumps. Thomas Kuhn proposed the structure of scientific revolutions as normal science, paradigms, anomalies, revolution, all leading to a new paradigm.

Then came the Aristotelian background: the problem of planets. Planets are "Wanderers". They are heavenly bodies that move in apparently irregular patterns against the background of the "fixed stars". The cosmic geometry of Claudius Ptolemy – "Geostatic" – on the other hand, considered the Earth is in the centre and five planets, Sun, Moon and Stars that circle the Earth.

Copernicus, in his book De Revolutionibus Orbium Coelestium (1543), wrote on the revolutions of the celestial spheres. His theory, the Copernican system, was "Heliostatic": the Sun stays still, near the centre, and the planets (including the Earth) orbit around the Sun while other stars are stationary outside the planetary orbits.

Tycho Brahe (1546–1601) was the best observational astronomer. His theory is called Tychonic system. It states that the cosmos is "Geostatic" but "Heliocentric".

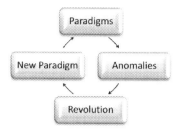

FIGURE 1.1   Idea of Thomas Kuhn of the structure of scientific revolutions as normal
science, paradigms, anomalies, revolution all leading to new paradigm

Johannes Kepler (1571–1603) was a mathematician and astrologer. He combines
mystical with respect for observation (worked with Tycho Brahe) and accepted
Copernican System. Kepler's laws of planetary motion comprised three laws.

First law: The planets orbit in ellipses, with the Sun at one focus.
Second law: Planets sweep out equal areas in equal times (and thus are travelling
faster when near the Sun).
Third law: The ratio of squares of periodic times or orbits is proportional to the
ratios of the cubes of the mean distances from the Sun.

Galileo Galilei (1564–1642) was a great radical of the scientific revolution who
worked on several aspects of physics and astrology. He supported the Copernican
system with telescopic observations. He was the first to differentiate the stars in
the Milky Way. He contributed on the phases of Venus, mountains on the Moon
and the bulges of Saturn (not distinct enough to see the rings). He discovered the
moons of Jupiter, which was the most startling and important of his discoveries.
The radical publications of Galileo were *Siderius Nuncius* in 1610, where he published his first findings, and his "Great Defence of Copernicus" in 1632, was a
dialogue on the two great systems of the world.

The scientific revolution broadens further the astronomical revolution by Copernicus, Kepler, Galileo etc. The distinction between heaven and the Earth is challenged. Moreover, new directions in the language and rules of science were prepared.
Galileo Galilei (1564–1642) was the greatest radical of the scientific revolution who
insisted on making science accessible, as a result of which he was convicted by the
Inquisition in 1633.

Rene Descartes (1596–1649) was another rebel against authority who said that
everything can be explained in terms of matter and motion. He classified the types
of matter as: (a) primary – subtle, fills all spaces, makes the Sun and the stars;
(b) secondary – celestial space, in constant motion, swirling in vortices and
(c) tertiary – gross, earthly matter (also the Moon and planets). His physical observations and formulations were the conservation of momentum (colliding billiard
balls), inertia (stated in the modern form), the optical laws (especially, law of sines
in describing refraction) and "The Mechanical Philosophy", which stated that the

world was to be described as a great machine, completely comprehensible in terms of only its various parts (matter) and their movements (motion).

Francis Bacon (1561–1626) was famous for his inductive method, published in the *Novum Organum* (The "New Means to Knowledge") in 1620. He worked on interferences in human understanding and idols of the tribe (weaknesses of human nature and the senses), idols of the cave (weaknesses of the individual, due to education, personality or talents), idols of the marketplace (weaknesses in society, especially language and its misuse). *New Atlantis* (1627), an incomplete utopian novel of Bacon, was published after his death. In this novel, "Solomon's House" was a research establishment on the island. Bacon discussed there that the glory of the state lies in the promotion of knowledge and "Useful Arts". He was the inspiration for scientific societies in the seventeenth and eighteenth centuries. Bacon was one of the chief contributors on the quarrel of the Ancients and the Moderns (French: *querelle des Ancienset des Modernes*). The measure of the human condition was discussed in the debate.

The Newtonian Age

Experimentalists

This era can be called the era of mechanisation of the world and was characterised by the clockwork universe, the search for systems and the need for a new paradigm. Experimentalists believed in "The Experimental Philosophy". They were promoted by scientific societies. "Baconianism" or the importance of the "Inductive Method" influenced several scientists like Evangelista Torricelli (1608–1647), Robert Boyle (1627–1691), Robert Hooke (1635–1703) and Isaac Newton (1642–1727). It is worthy to mention that Newton's "Miracle Year" (Annus Mirabilis) was 1665–1666.

Newton's mathematical principles of natural philosophy were discussed in the book *The Principia* (1687), the key book in synthesising a new physics. The key elements of *The Principia* are as follows.

1   It stated the definitions of mass, velocity, force etc.
2   It described the laws of motion:

    (i) Every body continues in a state of rest or straight-line motion unless compelled to change by force.

    (ii) The change of motion is proportional to the force impressed, perpendicular in direction.

    (iii) For every action there is always an equal reaction, in the opposing direction.

Newton was the first scientist to discover the laws of universal gravitation, according to which (i) gravitation is proportional to the masses of the attracting bodies; and (ii) inversely proportional to the square of the distance separating them.

3   Calculus ("Method of Fluxions") though it was also claimed by Gottfried Leibniz (1646–1716).

As a whole, *The Principia* accounts for orbit and period of the Moon, Kepler's laws, parabolic paths of comets, the tides and the nature of gravity:

> To tell us that every species of thing is endowed with an occult specific quality by which it acts and produces manifest effects is to tell us nothing. But to derive two or three General Principles of Motion from phenomena, and afterwards to tell us how the properties and actions of all Corporeal things follow from these Manifest Principles, would be a very great step in Philosophy, though the causes of These Principles were not yet discovered; Therefore, I scruple not to propose the Principles of Motion above mentioned, they being of very general extent, and leave their causes to be found out.

Twentieth-Century Dissolution in Physics

The twentieth-century dissolution of Newtonian physics was marked by the following inventions and discoveries.

Quantum Theory

Looking into the inside of matter

1 Cathode rays by William Crookes
2 Electron by J.J. Thomson (1897)
3 X-rays by Wilhelm Röntgen (1895)
4 Radioactivity by Henri Becquerel (1896)
5 Radium by Marie Curie (1902)
6 Radiation – alpha and beta – by Ernest Rutherford (1899)
7 Alpha-particle scattering, that is model of the atom by Niels Bohr (Bohr's model of the atom)
8 Quanta by Max Planck and Planck's constant
9 Wave–particle duality, that is light may behave like a wave or a particle
10 The Uncertainty Principle by Werner Heisenberg Indeterminancy – Uncertainty – and the status of science. The world is inherently unknowable

Relativity

Albert Einstein proposed the special theory of relativity (2005). Its postulations are as follows.

1 The laws of nature are the same for observers in any inertial frame of reference.
2 The speed of light (c) is the same for all such observers. Conclusions were drawn that observers in two different frames of reference will find contractions of the Fitzgerald–Lorentz kind in each other's frame, in both space and time.

3   "Time Dilation". The observable mass of an object seems to increase as it goes faster (approaching infinity as it approaches c). It is theoretically possible to state an equivalence between mass and energy [$E = mc^2$]. Two great hypotheses were elimination of absolute space and absolute time and elimination of the ether.

4   General theory of relativity. Extending relativity to "Non-inertial" (accelerating) frames of reference.

Thermodynamics: From Practice to Theory

The renowned figures in this field are Thomas Savery (1698), Danis Papin (1708), Thomas Newcomen (1712), who patented his atmospheric engine. James Watt worked and patented (1765–1782) on the current form of steam engine. He worked under Joseph Black, professor at Glasgow University and father of calorimetry. Heat was considered a fluid "Caloric" then. The scientific work on heat needed the knowledge of thermometry, measurement of temperature as an indicator of hotness and coldness. Originators of thermometers were Galileo (1592), thermoscope; Jean Rey (1631), water thermometer; Tuscany's Duke (1641), alcohol thermometer; Farenheit, a Dutch scientist, Farenheit scale (1724); and Celsius (1742), Celcius scale.

The theoretical work started on this aspect with notable contributions from Fourier (*Analytical Theory of Heat*, 1822), Sadi Carnot (Reflexions on the Motive Power of Fire and on Machines *Fitted to Develop That Power*, 1824), Bajamir Thomson (canon boring experiments establishing that work and heat are equivalent, 1798), J.R. Mayer, J.P. Joule, Alexandar Von Helmholtz, Lord Kelvin and others. The first law of thermodynamics, the equivalence of heat and work as forms of energy, was established by J.R. Mayer in 1844. After experimenting during 1840–1848, J.P. Joule found the value of mechanical equivalent of heat, "J". Alexandar Von Helmholtz stated the first law of thermodynamics in 1847. In his book, *The Dynamical Equivalent of Heat*, published in 1851, Lord Kelvin gave due recognition to Mayer, Joule and Helmholtz. Thereafter, Rudolph Clausius (1854–1912) formalised the second law and deduced the concept of entropy in 1865, after deducing Clausius integral in 1862. And then, Max Plank in 1897, Poincare in 1908, and Carathedory in 1909, formalised the science of thermodynamics as it is taught now. More names like Walther Nernst (for third law of thermodynamics, 1906), J.C. Maxwell (for kinetic theory of heat, 1866), J.W. Gibbs (for the first book on statistical thermodynamics, 1901) and Prigogine (for irreversible thermodynamics, 1950) must be mentioned here.

Information Technology, Computer and the World Wide Web

As early as in the first half of the nineteenth century, Charles Babbage, educated in Cambridge, invented the analytical engine – the mechanical computer (1840).

Ada Lovelace, daughter of poet Byron, translated Babbage's work in 1843. It took almost 100 years to develop the modern electronic computers (Claude Shannon, 1948).

On the other hand, Shannon (1948) worked on computable numbers and Norbert Weiner (1948) on cybernetics or control and communication in the animal and the machine and his PhD student, Amar Bose et al. (2009), on theories of computation. Transistor was invented in 1947, by Bardeen and Shockley at Bell Lab, New Jersey. During 1931–1942, Vannever Bush and Atanasoff completed a partially working computer with 300 vaccum tubes. Von Neuman worked on ENIAC at Pennsylvania and completed the modern computer UNIVAC in 1952, in Princeton. Later on, in 1952, the IC chip was developed. In 1968, Noyce and Moore formed INTEL. The development from ARPANET to the World Wide Web was performed by Tim Berners-Lee. In 1971, Ray Tomlinson introduced the email. In 1998, Google was started by Larry Page and Sergey Bin. In 2001, Wikipedia was launched, and the story goes on.

The Tree of Life

The first name to be mentioned here is probably Galen (AD 130–199). He worked on anatomical procedure and on Medical Experience. He wrote over 400 treatises to analyse the function of the spinal cord.

Andreas Vesaliusin (1543) researched on the fabric of human body, made dissections and reported on the changes in physiology and anatomy. William Harvey, in 1682, reported on the motion of blood and the workings of the heart. He described the heart and its role in blood circulation. Gregor Mendel (1865, 1869) published two papers in the *Proceedings of the Natural Science Society of Brono*, Czechoslovakia. His eight years' experiment on peas resulted in the laws of heredity.

Meanwhile, Charles Darwin came up with his theory of evolution. In his voyage on "Beagle" to South America, he researched at the Galapagos Island, and after returning to England in 1836, he started formulating his study, which was finally published in 1859, as *On The Origin of Species* and then in 1871, as *The Descent of Man*. August Weisman (1834–1914) contributed on the interconnected sciences of embryology, genetics and evolution. His famous book is *Studies in the Theory of Descent*.

On the other hand, studies in molecular biology and genetics had started in parallel by three groups: Rosalind Franklin and Wilkins at University College of London; Crick and Watson (got Nobel Prize) postulated the double helix structure of DNA in 1957, at Cambridge University; and Linus Pauling at CalTech. Genetics and genome mapping changed the face of life science.

Modern Indian Science

I will conclude the chapter by documenting significant contributors to modern Indian science.

C.V. Raman (1889–1970) was the first (and only) Indian to win the Nobel Prize (1930) for science. He worked mainly at the Indian Association for Cultivation of Science and Calcutta University and later in Bangalore. He discovered the "Raman Spectrum" from the analysis of light scattering.

J.C. Bose (1858–1937) started his carrier with Tripos from Cambridge and a BSc degree from London. J.C. Bose returned to India in 1884. He produced and experimented with wavelength of 5 centimetres, but his main work was on wireless transmission (probably before Marconi), 1895–1899. He got his MA degree from Cambridge University and DSc degree from London in 1896. He then transited to research on similarity of responses in living and non-living systems. He was awarded knighthood and became Fellow of Royal Society. Bose was an intimate friend of Rabindranath Tagore all through his life. He was reputed for his great writings in Bengali literature.

P.C. Ray (1861–1944) got his BSc degree from Edinburgh University in 1885, and DSc degree in 1887. He returned to India in 1888, but remained unemployed till 1889. Then he started teaching at Presidency College, then at Calcutta University Science College. His main achievements were the discovery of mercurous nitrate, the book *History of Hindu Chemistry* (in which the history of Indian chemistry was well chronicled), establishment of Bengal Chemical and Pharmaceutical Work – one of the first swadeshi industries in Eastern India – and building up a great school of chemistry teachers. He also got the knighthood.

Srinivasa Ramanujan (1887–1920) A movie *The Man Who Knew Infinity* based on a book by Rebert Kanigel was based on the life of Ramanujan. Ramanujan did not have a formal degree, but such was his work in number theory that he was called to Cambridge University by G.H. Hardy. His notebooks were filled with many original works on mathematics, particularly number theory and infinite series. He was the second Indian to be elected Fellow of Royal Society. He came back to India, where he died at a young age because of ill health. Still, much research is being done on his mathematical notes.

S.N. Bose (1894–1974) His main research was on statistical thermodynamics. He derived Planck's constant independently. Einstein translated his article and helped publish it. From his work, the particle Boson was conjectured, the existence of which has been proved now. He also became Fellow of Royal Society.

M.N. Saha (1893–1956) Coming from a poor family he was very ill-treated by fellow students. He got his DSc degree from Calcutta University in 1918. Then he went abroad and worked in Nerns't laboratory. He developed Saha's ionisation equation. He wrote *A Treatise on Heat* when he was at Allahabad University. He established Saha Institute of Nuclear Physics. He wanted a science academy in India, and played a significant role in establishing two of them viz. the Indian National Science Academy (INSA), New Delhi and the National Academy of Sciences (NASI), Allahabad.

P.C. Mahalanobis (1893–1972) was a polymath. He did his Tripos in physics at Cambridge University. He joined Presidency College and shifted his research to statistics. He played a key role in establishing the Indian Statistical Institute. He also became Fellow of Royal Society. Most notably, he was considered to be the father of India's five year plans. The second Five Year Plan was drafted by him. Like other scientists of that era, he was also very close to Tagore and drafted the constitution of Visva Bharati.

Besides these famous names, others like H.J. Bhabha, S.K. Mitra, D.M. Bose made significant contributions to Indian science. At present Amal Roy Chowdhury and Asoke Sen are still contributing in String Theory.

References

Bose, D. M., Sen, S. N. and Subbarayappa, B. V. Eds. (2009). *A Concise History of Science in India*. Universities Press, Indian National Science Academy, New Delhi.

Drapier, J. W. (1874). *History of The Conflict Between Religion and Science*. Reprint: Create Space Independent Publishing Platform (November 13, 2014).

Fara, P. (2009). *Science: A Four Thou-sand Year History*. Oxford University Press.

Gordon, C. (2016). *What Happened in History?* Aakar Books (1st ed.).

Johnston, S. F. (2009). *History of Science: A Beginner's Guide*. Oneworld Publications.

Sen, S. N. (1962). *BigyanerItihas*. Indian Association for Cultivation of Science (2 vols).

Shannon, C. (1948). A mathematical theory of communication. *The Bell System Technical Journal*, 27, July/October.

Turing, A. M. (1950). Computer machinery and intelligence. *Mind*, 49, 433–460.

Further Reading

Anderson, R. S. (2010). *Nucleus & Nation*. University of Chicago Press.

Bernal, J. D. (1969). *Science in History*. Penguin (4 vols).

Gleick, J. (2011). *The Information: A History, a Theory, a Flood*. Pantheon Books, New York.

Greene, J. E. (1967). *100 Great Scientists*. Washington Square Publisher.

Isaacson, W. (2014). *The Innovators: How a Group of Hackers, Geniuses, and Geeks Created the Digital Revolution*. Simon & Schuster Limited.

Weiner, N. (1948). *Cybernetics: Or Control and Communication in the Animal and the Machine*. John Coiley and Sons, New York and the Technology Press, MIT.

2

SCIENCE, SOCIETY AND GOVERNANCE IN COLONIAL INDIA

Deepak Kumar

Science and Society in Colonial Period

> Our spirit rules the world. Our wisdom enters into the composition of the every-day life of half the globe. Our physical as well as intellectual presence is manifest in every climate under the sun. Our sailing ships and steam-vessels cover the seas and rivers. Wherever we conquer, we civilize and refine. Our arms, our arts, our literature are illustrious among the nations. We are a rich, a powerful, an intelligent and a religious people. No place is too remote for our enterprises or our curiosity. We have an insatiable energy, which is of the utmost value to the work. We have spread ourselves over all regions.
>
> The Illustrated London News, Vol. XIII, no. 327, 22 July 1848

The aforementioned powerful claim captures the spirit of colonialism, a great historical process that shook and overtook almost the whole planet in the eighteenth and nineteenth centuries. In the twentieth century, it gradually disintegrated but not without effecting profound changes in both the colonizing and the colonized world. The Indian society also fell under its spell. It was never xenophobic and had seen many ups and downs in its civilizational journey. It had a fair share of science and scientific thinking in its repertoire. In the realm of astronomy, medicine, and mathematics, it had made significant contributions. Panini, Charaka, Susruta, Vagbhatta, Aryabhatta, Brahmagupta, and Bhaskara are well-known names. A tenth-century Moorish text hails India as the fountainhead of knowledge. In ancient texts, one finds numerous references to *yukti* (reason), *tarkavidya* (science of reasoning), *anvikshki* (investigation), *anumana* (intelligent inference), *pramana* (proof), and *hetusastra* (dialectics). The celebrated *Charaka Samhita* talks of *yuktibheshaj* (rational medicine). It says, 'any success attained without reasoning (*tarka*) is as good as sheer accidental success'. Neelkantha (AD 1444–1545) argued, *etatsarvamyukti-mulam,*

DOI: 10.4324/9781003033448-4

evanatva agama-mulam (all this is rooted in reason, not in the dogmas). But not everyone believed in this. A vast majority preferred *anubhuti* (experience) to *tarka* (logic). This 'experience' along with creative imagination and some rationale was codified into sacred texts which gradually acquired canonical status. To question or challenge a canonical text or knowledge (*sastra-sammatjnan*) has never been easy in any society. Many perished in the process and a vast majority had to compromise. The result was that a keen observer, Al Beruni, found in the Indian knowledge system gems mixed with cow-dung!

Even the arrival of Islam and the establishment of Muslim rule in India could not effect the desired change. It was itself in the grip of Gazzalian orthodoxy. Trade flourished, new cities were established, beautiful mosques and tombs came up but no new knowledge, no glass-grinding, and no horology. The period saw remarkable socio-religious reformers, saints, and sufis. But the Indo-Islamic knowledge, though rich and varied within its own sphere, was no match to what was happening in Western Europe.

So, when in the eighteenth century, the European travellers and merchants knocked at the Indian royal courts, the difference and decline were obvious. During the post-Renaissance epoch (that of Descartes and Newton), Western Europe had begun to outdistance all other culture areas. In the eighteenth century, this distance became virtually unbridgeable. For India, this century proved unique in the sense that it saw the decline of pre-colonial systems as well as the inauguration of systematic colonization. During this period, the rise of modern science itself coincided with the rise of merchant capitalism and colonial expansion. Probably, they grew in tandem, feeding each other. Some nations, now ruling the waves, came in, and through their trading companies chalked out large areas. Their sails, guns, and training were substantially different. They had 'new' knowledge behind them.

Colonization was never a linear or smooth process; it had its own hazards. It involved knowing the local terrain, its inhabitants, and their knowledge systems. The colonizers could condemn the local knowledge and its practices but could never ignore them. In fact, in some cases the local knowledge of the indigenous population gradually became universal knowledge, and in many cases, the universal knowledge was internalized by the locals with open heart. Similarly, rejections also took place with great disdain. Of course, a lot must have been lost in the process of translation and delivery, but the different societies developed their own strategies and mechanisms to deal with this process.

Institutionalization

Ideas and artefacts cannot hover in air. They need to be housed and transacted. Under the East India Company, perhaps for the time in Indian history, the state had emerged as the producer of knowledge and the sole arbiter of what was to be delivered and to whom. The recipients had limited options and a limited access. Moreover, they had their own prejudices and requirements, which were not always congruent with those of the rulers. Rather, they differed greatly. It is in the realm of education that cultural encounter takes place and unfolds the complications of civilizational interactions. To establish their complete supremacy, British colonizers had first to dethrone and delegitimize several pre-colonial symbols and totems, both political and cultural, and then present their ideological and material wares in a form that would appear attractive, if not always superior, to at least a section of the indigenous population. The colonial state thus had the most important role to play, even though it was controlled by a trading company. Trade also depends on knowledge, and every economy is a knowledge economy! Can the same be said of every society?

Scientific institutions are modern icons. These came to India as part of the colonial baggage and soon became the carriers of new ideas and in fact symbolized modernity itself. As the conquest began, new forts, ports, and cities were established. Thus came into being the new port cities of Calcutta, Bombay, and Madras. These were to witness a distinct break with the past. In the new cities, new institutions were to be established, not in the older cities of Delhi, Hyderabad, or Lahore; some of these institutions were to become the carriers of new knowledge. It is not easy to see in them as sites for exchange of knowledge as it involves a two-way process, which colonial conditions would seldom permit. They mostly functioned as sites for dissemination and also contestation. The transfer of knowledge, though purported to be osmotic, was not really a one-way simple process; it sparked debates and produced cross-currents.

Against this background of the colonial onset, William Jones founded the Asiatic Society in 1784. This society soon became the focal point of all scientific activities in India. This was a unique experiment, probably the first such in Asia. The scope and objects of its enquiries were 'Man and Nature; whatever is performed by the one, or produced by the other (Fermor, 1935)'. What could be colonial in such magnificent objectives! Nothing. The difference lay in practice. Though the criteria for its membership were nothing more than 'a love of knowledge and zeal for promotion of it', Indians were not taken as members until 1829, and no Indian made any scientific contribution to its journal till the 1880s.

The roots of professional and scientific colonial literature from the viewpoint of science can be traced back from the publication of the *Asiatic Miscellany* (1785). It soon flowered into *Asiatic Researches* (1788–1839) and the *Journal of the Asiatic Society* (*JAS*). Between 1784 and 1839, the Asiatic Society published 20 volumes. The demand for the publication was such that in 1798, a pirated edition was brought out in England. It is impossible to look at the *JAS* without considering the role played by Orientalism in its development. Orientalism led to the study of Eastern civilizations by scholarly Europeans. The literary researches of the 'Orientalist' scholars complemented scientific investigations in colonial India. Orientalism had its most visible manifestation in the nineteenth century and is symbolized in India, by the development of the Asiatic Society. It had its supporters and detractors. On the one hand, it can be said that it rediscovered the history and culture of the subject people and cast it in a modern idiom and promoted global awareness of diverse civilizations. On the other hand, going by the critiques of Edward Said, orientalism was the vehicle by which Western civilization penetrated into the civilizational hearts of its subject and functioned as an inseparable handmade of imperialism. Both the defence and critiques of Orientalism would also apply to the mindset and the body of thought and action that gave rise to these journals (Sinha, In press). There is equally an element of self-interest as well as reform in their study of natural resources, topography, sociocultural traits, diseases, etc. in the native milieu.

The Asiatic Society suffered and prospered simultaneously but remained a beacon of knowledge for long. It was the sole organ of research in Asia. Whatever was done in geology, meteorology, zoology, and botany was done through the Society. Gradually, all these branches developed in line with their own and blossomed into separate departments. The society multiplied by fission, like the 'philoprogenitive sponge' and gave birth at successive epochs to the Geological Survey of India, the Indian Museum, India Meteorological Department, the Botanical Survey of India, and the Linguistic Survey of India (Risley, 1904). As *Nature* noted in 1907,

> Like all the scientific organizations in the East, it has suffered vicissitudes. The short and broken residences of Europeans in the country, pressure of official work, lack of native co-workers, want of libraries of reference, and last, not least, the indifference of the Indian Government, which prefers that its servants should devote their spare time to the judgements of the High Courts or the circulars of the Board of Revenue rather than to the science and literature of the country, have at times interrupted its progress.
>
> *(The Asiatic Society of Bengal, 1907)*

Another important scientific society was the Calcutta Medical and Physical Society, established in March 1823. The objectives of this society were twofold – first to collect original papers relating to discoveries in medicine and surgery and in the branches connected with them, as researches in anatomy, physiology, botany, chemistry for the advancement of professional knowledge, for the mutual benefit of the members, more particularly, with reference to Indian diseases and treatment – the papers would be presented, read, and discussed at regular appointed meetings and afterwards published under the title *Transactions of the Society*. And the second objective was the formation of a select and extensive medical library for the use of its members. It broke the social and professional isolation of doctors, and, without any government aid, it was able to publish its *Monthly Circular and Selections* regularly (Medical Selections, 1833). The Medical and Physical Society of Calcutta elected four Indians – Radhakant Deb, Ramcomul Sen, Madhusudan Gupta, and Raja Kalikrishna Bahadur – as corresponding members in 1827, and they did produce a few papers on indigenous drugs (Transactions of the Medical and Physical Society of Calcutta, 1827–1831). India being a predominantly agrarian economy, the formation of the Agricultural and Horticultural Society, in 1818, was no less significant. Its proceedings (still preserved in its Alipore office) show what a pioneer this society was in terms of introduction of new seeds, plants, and livestock. It was not a mere seed or plant distribution centre but served educational purpose by organizing agricultural fairs.

These societies rendered invaluable services, particularly through their journals whose standard compared very favourably with that of European ones. It was no mean achievement that Calcutta, with a public of a little more than 2,000, could produce and support scientific journals like the *Gleanings in Science* and *Calcutta Journal of Natural History*. The latter even attempted to establish, in 1841, the Indian Association for the Advancement of Natural Science (Calcutta Journal of Natural History, 1841) on the pattern of the British Association for the Advancement of Science.

Government and Science

Colonial expansion required knowledge of the terrain, its people, its resources etc. No domination could be established without this knowledge. And this knowledge could not be obtained without scientific surveys. Next to the guns and ships, survey operations were the most potent tools in the hands of a colonizing power. Through them it could afford to know unknown people, chart untrodden paths, and estimate local resources. So the East India Company encouraged surveys and as the requirements came, it established the topographical surveys, geological surveys, botanical surveys, and, of course, revenue surveys were a regular feature. As a survey pioneer rightly noted,

> Whatever charges may be imputable to the managers of the Company, the neglect of useful science, however, is not among the number. The employing of geographers, and surveying pilots in India; and the providing of astronomical instruments, and the holding out of encouragement to such as should use them, indicate, at least, a spirit somewhat above the mere consideration of gain.
>
> *(Rennell, 1788)*

The surveyors were the forerunners of scientific exploration. They came from the military and it is from their ranks that we find early geologists, meteorologists, and astronomers emerging. Another set of early scientists came from a medical background, trained in the universities of Edinburgh, Glasgow, and other north European universities. They became the early botanists and zoologists. They were knowledge-seekers, no doubt, but they also knew that their knowledge was crucial for control over alien lands and people. They were a talented and dedicated lot. They were the men on the spot who largely determined what was advantageous to both trade and the country. Also they enjoyed certain amount of flexibility and autonomy. The East India Company, for which they worked, would be largely unobtrusive. There were tremendous difficulties but also enormous opportunities to sight and discover new things. Support from metropolitan scientists added to their confidence and their agenda was not entirely derivative; they too influenced metropolitan discourses (for example on the deposition of coal-seams, nature of cholera etc.). Sometimes, the periphery could and did alter the terms of the centre (Kumar, 1995; Chakrabarti, 2004)!

Trigonometrical and geological surveys were the most favoured ones and were pretty centralized. Botanical surveys were deliberately kept decentralized. The flora was so varied and of such great economic advantage that every region required different care and handling, and the provincial governments also did not want to lose their grip over agriculturally and economically advantageous knowledge. Science administration in colonial India mirrored colonial administrative policies in general; top-heavy structure, inner-contradictions (e.g. imperial vs provincial claims), and professional jealousies were reflected everywhere. The Government of India had its own limitations. Financial demands, as those of administrative expediency, hindered the growth of a well-knit and integrated scientific department. A few branches which were of military and instant economic significance (e.g. the Survey of India and the Geological Survey of India) could manage to develop. On the whole, the efforts remained ad hoc, sporadic, and provincialized. The local civilian administrators wanted the scientific staff to be provincial rather than imperial; they wanted practical results rather than research papers. An excessive administrative control exercised at different levels (that too, by more than one centre of power) ensured that the colonial scientist would always dance to the official tune. But at the same time, this bred dissatisfaction, often demoralization, among them. Some found themselves saddled with administrative responsibilities more than research while others resented their hopeless dependence on bureaucracy for every minor favour. They had little faith in the civil administrator and very often felt insecure. The latter, on their part, could seldom understand the complexities of scientific investigations and, in their zeal for immediate practical returns, bungled with whatever opportunity and funds they had.

Science in Education

The importance of education was realized early, no doubt. The colonizers would first use brute power to colonize and then tried to 'civilise' through education. As Kipling wrote,

> They terribly carpet the earth with dead,
> And before their cannons cool,
> They walk unarmed by twos and threes
> To call their living to school.

As the cannons cooled, schools came up. Education was no less potent a weapon. It gave them legitimacy, some relief from guilt, and what is more, a large number of collaborators. There was another requirement too. In the process of consolidating its rule, the East India Company also needed to know the people it had the luck and fortitude to win and govern. Education in science was not the priority. The very purpose of education was formulated as 'character formation'. Literary education was thus more suited for this purpose. As a Bengali journal, *The Bengal Hurkaru* (28 April 1838), claimed that 'more useful knowledge is to be gained from the study of one page of Bacon's prose, or Shakespeare's poetry, than from a hundred pages of Euclid Calcutta Monthly Journal, 1838)'. Scientific courses were introduced in the 1850s, but degrees in sciences could come only in the 1880s. Yet, medical colleges were established, in 1835 and 1845, in Calcutta and Bombay respectively. These colleges pioneered medical education in India, while engineering education began at Roorkee in 1847, and then at Shibpur in 1854. Western medicine and engineering were projected as a humanitarian rationale for the British rule.

The medical college in Calcutta began with a bang. Its student Madhusudan Gupta became the first Indian to break a centuries-old taboo by dissecting a human corpse – an event to commemorate which the Fort William had even boomed a 21-gun salute and in opposition to which a prominent local *vaidya* left the city as it had been rendered impure! When the Grant Medical College was opened in Bombay in 1845, the government expected a good response. But very few students turned up for admission; the Brahmins refrained probably because the new medical school required them to touch and dissect dead bodies. For several successive years the seats remained vacant, so the principal wrote to the DPI of Bombay asking for permission to admit students from the lower classes (castes). The DPI shot back, never do this.

> 'The lower-class people once they get this new higher education will earn more when they return to the society and will thereafter demand higher social status. This would upset the social balance. We have come here to rule, not to cause social upheavals,' the DPI rightly warned and made the forecast, 'the Brahmins would come once they see money in modern medicine'
> *(Report of the Board of Education, Bombay, 1850–51).*

This is exactly what happened later.

But the urge to comprehend the modern knowledge and tools that the colonizers had brought, and to assimilate them, was definitely there. This urge came from within, and the acculturative influence of European thought and Christian liberalism strengthened it. The new *bhadralok* interlocutors did put a premium on alien rule and in a sense idolized it and supported downward filtration. They had to do this the more so because initially they could think of no other effective way to deal with the serious ills their society was suffering from. They experienced a dual alienation from the traditional and later from the colonial life and system (Panikkar, 1986). They could to some extent anticipate the distortions the colonial medium was likely to produce. But the realization was slow and diffident. Perhaps, this explains why Rommohun Roy (1772–1833, Calcutta) looked to both Vedanta and the West (Joshi, 1975). Ishwarchand Vidyasagar (1820–1891, Calcutta), an admirer of Western knowledge, wanted the Indian students to study their own 'false system' also (Sen, 1975). Bal Shastri Jambhekar (1802–1846, Bombay) commenced his science popularization activities in both Marathi and English (Jambhekar, 1950), and Master Ramchandra (1921–1980, Delhi) began his mathematical treatise from a twelfth-century Indian text, Bhaskar's *Bij-Ganita* (Raina, 1992). The soil was being prepared for cross-fertilization, and the seed was a cross-breed.

The latter half of the nineteenth century is a period of consolidation and institution-building. These institutions not only 'imported' knowledge, but they imparted and, to some extent, generated knowledge. But did they diffuse new knowledge and to what extent? Telegraph and railways were the high-technology areas of those days. Telegraph remained a purely governmental exercise while the railways, raised on guaranteed profits, depended on wholesale import from Britain. Even its great repair-cum-manufacturing establishments like the Jamalpur work-shop proved to be enclavists. No technological spin-off could emerge, much less galvanize, from the neighbourhood of a railway colony. Mechanical engineering came late and remained a poor distant cousin of the public works engineering. Irrigation and later hydraulic engineering definitely benefitted, thanks to the large irrigation works. The Roorkee Engineering College was closely linked to Caut-ley's Ganges canal. Whether the generation or refinement of irrigation technology at Roorkee, or Guindy, reduced or increased the economic dependency of India, is rather arguable and a matter of several statistical debates. These enterprises were basically technology projects with specific aims and not technology systems with a wider canvas and greater results. A geographical relocation of technology (as in the case of railways) was possible and was achieved but a cultural diffusion of technol-ogy is so different and much more complex. Moreover, the professional colleges were so controlled that they could not induce changes at a perceptible or faster pace. The medium of instruction was also a factor. The Japanese had insisted on their own language. The result was modern knowledge and scientific spirit that could percolate down to the lower level of the masses. But, in India, the colonial education had widened the gulf and accentuated the age-old divide.

Research in Science

In the early phase of colonial science, the opportunities were immense; so much new to explore, and the colonial scientists like surveyors, medical men, and explor-ers were amazed with their findings and reported enthusiastically to their men-tors and colleagues in England and Europe. But fundamental research was simply out of question. Till 1890, research remained an exclusive government exercise and was carried out mostly through survey and military organizations. No doubt, surveyors and explorers very often were more than surveyors and contributed sig-nificantly to scientific research. But the fact remains that the choice and charac-ter of their research were heavily influenced by the economic requirements of the then government. A colonial scientist was expected not only to discover new economic resources but also to advise on their most efficient use. He was not a mere 'explorer'; he was now a 'settler'. This explains why plantation research was the most encouraged activity. Next came survey operations in geology and meteorology. Then the importance of medical knowledge was always recognized because the survival of the army, the planters, and others were at stake.

Botanical experiments were vital for plantation works. The flora had to be explored and classified. Botanists like Roxburgh, Wallich, Giffith, Clarke, and King rendered distinguished service to the scientific and economic aspects of botany. As late as in 1899, the Government of India complained that 'scientific research has hitherto been confined mainly to the classificatory or systematic stage of science' (India Agriculture, 1869–1921). Early geological works were coal and mineral oriented, this was the need of the time. But this does not mean that stratigraphical classification and map-making were ignored. Within their pressing economic explorations, they won worldwide recognition of the importance of deposits formed on land and also the significance of the Permian glacial epoch. In the *Memoirs* and *Records of the Geological Survey of India* are enshrined the achievements of a handful of geologists spread on different parts of India. These botanists and geologists were expected to perform a dual role – as explorers working for the benefits of the colonizers and at the same time as scientists busy in advancing the frontiers of scientific knowledge in their respective subjects.

This duality had created certain practical difficulties; it was not easy to mark clear demarcation between practical economy-oriented works and those of scientific value. As a noted geologist, T.H. Holland wrote,

> In the preparation of our annual programme, we are not wholly free to follow the line which we think is best for the country in the long run; questions of economic importance sometimes cannot be postponed without immediate loss and inconvenience whilst an un-surveyed area, about which nothing certainly is known, is neglected from one field season to another . . . India cannot, perhaps, afford to rank itself beside the more thoroughly developed European countries, where pure science is so richly endowed; and the practical difficulty here Is to discover *the profitable mean course* in which scientific research, having a general bearing will, at the same time, solve the local problems of immediate economic value.
>
> *(Holland, 1905)*

Health issues and medical research were of paramount importance for a tropical country like India, which was virtually a pathological reservoir of immense proportions. Till the mid-nineteenth century, both the Western and Indian medical systems had almost similar medical epistemologies; both believed in humoral imbalance and miasma. But they were not willing to collaborate and the final rupture came with the emergence of the germ theory of disease. New bacteriological investigations made a paradigm shift. The aetiology of the disease had to be sought out. The cholera epidemic of 1861, made the colonial medical men think in terms of cause of a disease and then new remedies like vaccine. Health-related laboratories were established in Pune, Agra, Mukteswar, Kasuali, Coonoor, and later in Madras. Medical commissions like cholera commission, leprosy commission, plague commission, and malaria commission were formed to deal with these terrible diseases at different points of time. they were no doubt honest attempts, but their recommendations were mostly shelved by the government as their implementation would involve huge costs. When faced with epidemics, segregation and vaccination were undertaken, but these remained of limited value and could not prevent massive casualties. In the midst of several public health disasters, one can still notice individual sparks. A German bacteriologist confirmed his discovery of the cholera bacillus in Calcutta, in 1884. Two such examples deserve special notice.

The first example is that of a zoologist of Jewish origin W.H. Haffkine, who tried vaccines on cholera and plague patients during the 1890s. He had administered about 70,000 injections, inoculating more than 40,000 Indians. He prepared the vaccines 'while traveling by train, in the dusty passenger carriages, or at the railway stations, or else in rooms temporarily placed at my disposal and transformed for a day or two into a laboratory' (Haffkine, 1908). By the time Haffkine took to research, two distinct schools had clearly emerged. The German school, led by Koch, concentrated on the isolation and exhaustive study of individual bacteria and thus laid the foundations of several highly specialized branches of bacteriology. The French school, led by Pasteur, concentrated on the problems of prevention of infective diseases by calibrated inoculation and thus developed the science of immunology (Bulloch, 1983; Newman, 1932; Geison, 1994; Brock, 1988). Haffkine chose to follow Pasteur in letter and spirit. Right from the beginning of the plague outbreak, Haffkine differed from the schemes of disinfection, segregation, and forced hospitalization which the government medical officials had launched. To him, the only plausible method to combat the epidemic was individual preventive treatment. This remains relevant in the wake of the Corona virus pandemic in 2020! This was apparently not liked by the government officials.

The second remarkable example is that of Ronald Ross, who worked under very difficult circumstances on the relationship between mosquitos and malaria. He was the first to delineate the life cycle of the malarial plasmodium and also show that the larvae of the Indian *Anopheles* do not float head downward like those of culex but float on the surface like sticks. Ross gave credit for the second observation to his Indian assistant, Muhammad Bux (Ross, 1899). Ross was not interested in vaccine; probably he knew that it was not possible. A successful malaria vaccine eludes us even now! He strongly advocated mosquito control by destroying or treating their breeding areas. This was a practical and preventive approach, but it involved large-scale sanitary measures, which the colonial government found too expensive to be pursued.

While dealing with the question of scientific researches, one needs to keep in mind that colonialism is not philanthropy and a colonial government would only go up to a point and not beyond. Theoretical research at par with the metropole was not possible until a few absolutely determined and brilliant people emerged at the turn of the century. Yet under the limited opportunities, a great deal was achieved as mentioned earlier, at least when compared with other colonies in the world.

Technological Imperatives

Colonization would not have been possible without the guns, sails, and the power of steam. New tools played a remarkable role. When steam ships appeared on the Ganges, a captain noted:

> Some of my servants on board had never before seen such a thing as a steamer, and their wonder and admiration were infinite, as was their curiosity, to have explained to them the means by which the *angun-jehaz* (fire ship) was made to go against the stream of the mighty Ganga, without sail or peddle. This I endeavoured, as well as I could to explain; and further told them of steam carriages and also of balloons.
>
> Only a few days subsequently to this conversation on my arrival in Calcutta, Sahaduk and his companions had an opportunity of witnessing the ascent of Mr. Robinson, the aeronaut. Sahaduk came to me and said, 'Sir, you are right; the English are, indeed, gods; we have nothing in India which can be compared to this. Can your countrymen survive at the bottom of the sea?' I told him of the diving-bell, and his disbelief was again beginning to display itself when suddenly he exclaimed – 'No, if you can fly in the heavens like an eagle, surely, you may live in the sea. You are gods'.
>
> *(Bacon, 1837)*

Along with brute force, colonies were built upon this sense of awe. Telegraph was another great tool. A colonial chemist, W.B. O'Shaugnessy experimented upon it in the late 1830s, and within 20 years, Calcutta was connected with Attock, and this telegraph line not only boosted commerce but also saved the British rule from almost extinction at the Revolt of 1857. No wonder very soon the newly emergent Indian middle class began to demand technical training and new industries. The quest for a techno-scientific knowledge in the last two decades of the nineteenth century had brought in people belonging to different walks of life – people who realized that the limitations of being colonized also meant that no scientific curriculum was introduced in the schools and colleges with practical applications in mind. The science interlocutors therefore questioned the purpose of scientific knowledge as disseminated through a mechanized educational system, which failed to adopt a 'holistic' view of education.

The Great War had brought to fore the inability of India to support the war-efforts through industrial productions. India could provide only soldiers as cannon fodders. So, an industrial commission was appointed during the progress of the War itself. In its deliberations the question of education, particularly technical education, came up. One of its members, Madan Mohan Malaviya, gave an exceptionally critical dissenting note (Visvanathan, 1985). Like his cultural predecessors who had rejected rationality as a Western import, Malaviya presented a nationalist critique of British economic policies in India, and stressed that India had remained deindustrialized. He knew that industry was no longer a mere tool of domination, it had become a discipline and, therefore, technical schools (with new curriculums) had become more important than factories. The British model was inadequate. The new icons were Japan and Germany, and the new watchword was science-based technology. At the same time, demands were raised to induct more Indians in technical and medical services, Indianization was another watchword.

An interesting characteristic of the period is the cautious yet firm demands for industrialization. In industrialization lay salvation, the nationalists believed; but it was also thought necessary to avoid the pitfalls of blind imitation and crude industrialization. Efforts were to be made not to lose human, nay Indian, face. The colonizers had talked about moral regeneration for a long time. This the nationalists viewed as propagandist in nature. Instead, they dwelt upon a 'synthetical' economic and industrial regeneration. This regeneration was not to be achieved at the cost of peasants and artisans. Whether it was the *Dawn Society Magazine* of Calcutta or the *Kayastha Samachar* (later the *Hindustan Review* of Allahabad), or the *Swadeshmitran* of Madras, the tenor was the same – industrialization was in the national interest and should be conducted on national terms Native Newspaper Reports published during 1900–1930 for similar demands in the vernacular press. Benoy Kumar Sarkar, an important interlocutor of the period, used interesting terms like 'mistrification' and 'factorification' (*mistri* refers to technicians) (Sarkar, 1946). The importance of artisans and technicians was thus brought into focus. The demand for chemical industries was ably advocated and pushed by scientists like P.C. Ray (Ray, 1923). All this had been preceded by a vociferous demand for techno-scientific education. There was to be no diminution in that. Rather, the new argument was that science should be taught in a scientific way and not by the literary method (Patel, 1921). The overall picture that emerges is of an all-embracing 'socio-cultural transformation'.

Individual Pioneers

The aforementioned transformation would not have been possible without the exertions of some gifted and dedicated individuals. The nineteenth and early twentieth century saw so many luminaries with remarkable scientific temper and spirit. One such indefatigable crusader for modern science was Mahendralal Sircar (1833–1904). Sircar was a product of modern medical education, and in 1869, he wrote a pamphlet on 'the desirability of a national institution for the cultivation of sciences by the natives of India'. He wanted to show that the Indians were capable of original research, provided they get the necessary encouragement. To inculcate the virtues of self-reliance, he wanted this institution to be entirely under Indian management and control. With great difficulty, he raised funds through public appeals and in 1876, an institution called the Indian Association for Cultivation of Science (IACS) was opened. In his travails, Sircar symbolized dissatisfaction as well as hope. He was very clear about his objective and he would not allow it to be confused with the demand for technical education. This movement for the cultivation of science had an enormous psychological impact. It symbolized the search for a distinct

Indian identity in the world of science. A whole generation of Indian scientists was inspired by Sircar's thoughts and initiatives. India's first and only homespun Nobel laureate in science, C.V. Raman worked at IACS.

A few years earlier, Syed Ahmed (1817–1898), who tried to reform the Muslim society post-Mutiny, had formed a scientific society at Aligarh. Its idea was not promotion of scientific research but its popularization to fight the prevalent superstitions and to develop some sort of scientific temper. Sir Syed's idea was to reform the tradition-bound Muslim society from within. He attempted a synthesis. Here is the crux of Syed Ahmed's belief: 'the real purpose of religion is to improve morality'. Let scientific truths be established by observation and experiment, he says, and not by 'attempting to interpret a religious text as a book of science'. This articulation was very significant. It defended new knowledge from obscurantist attacks in the name of religion and tradition and at the same time protected the indigenous culture and beliefs from the colonial and evangelical onslaught. Sir Syed's associate Munshi Zakaullah was even more emphatic. He wrote, 'God has given human beings the ability called reason (*aql*) to discover and comprehend the real world, and the application of this ability by the human beings leads to the creation of knowledge'. To drive home the point he added, 'reason is to knowledge what sun is to light and eye to vision' (Habib, 2000).

In the last decades of the nineteenth century, some of the individual 'native' scientists gathered sufficient strength to differ with their metropolitan peers and fight the colonial bureaucracy. For J.C. Bose (1858–1937), a creative physicist, it was a lifelong struggle and a multi-pronged fight against his scientific peers abroad for recognition, the colonial bureaucracy for fair treatment and facilities, and, to a lesser extent, his own scientific compatriots. Initially, he was engaged in the construction of compact apparatus for the generation of short electromagnetic waves and the study of their optical properties. Also, he carried out signalling through space by means of his apparatus. This preceded the wireless technology patented by Marconi. But he did not continue with this line of physical research, and during 1898–1905, Bose gradually shifted from physics to plant physiology. Like Darwin, he could deal with thousands of apparently unrelated facts and show that they were but manifestations of some universal law (Jacob, 1958; Nandy, 1980; Dasgupta, 1999; Lourdusamy, 2004).

A far more courageous and socially conscious scientist was Prafulla Chandra Ray (1861–1944), a chemist and teacher of great repute and standing. As early as 1885, while on a Gilchrist scholarship at Edinburgh, Ray published a pamphlet, *India: Before and After the Mutiny,* in which he asked, 'Is there no golden mean between stubborn denial . . . and humiliating surrender?' It was during the 1890s, that his work on mercurous nitrite won laurels. He was a multitasker, so around the same time he began thinking about chemical industry. He knew that industry based upon empirical knowledge had always preceded science. After all, glass-making, dyeing, and metallurgical works were done centuries before the chemical reactions involved in making them were understood. With the advantage of the new scientific knowledge, such industries could generate more employment and improve the then-impoverished economy. The industrial progress made in Europe and America, he wrote, 'is a history of the triumph of researches in the laboratory'. In contrast, Bengal lacked not only the spirit of entrepreneurship, even orthodox culture came in the way. He established a chemical industry and also researched on the alchemical history of India. As a teacher, Ray was peerless and around him grew an invisible college of chemistry. The unique surge of scientific brilliance (unrivalled even a century later) that Bengal saw during the first half of the twentieth century owes a great deal to him. He was the father figure, indeed a patron saint.

Thanks to the foundation laid by these pioneers, during the 1920s and 1930s, India could see a kind of scientific efflorescence. The works of scientists like C.V. Raman, S.N. Bose, and M.N. Saha were and still remain simply matchless. Raman's initial publications were on acoustics. His experiments on Huygens's secondary waves attracted the notice of the Western scientific community. In 1913, he was offered Palit Professorship of Calcutta University. He continued to work at the IACS, and in collaboration with some young and bright students and colleagues, he could do many outstanding research in physical optics, molecular diffraction of light, crystals, colloids, X-ray scattering of liquids, and so on. In 1928, he published a paper titled 'A New Radiation' in the *Indian Journal of Physics*. This came to be known as the Raman Effect, which won him a Nobel Prize in 1930 (A Century, 1976; Singh, 2005). Sir C.V. Raman, till date, remains the only homespun Noble laureate in Indian science.

S.N. Bose and M.N. Saha were students of mathematics and began their career as lecturers in the applied mathematics department of Calcutta University in 1916. Both of them were destined to make fundamental contributions in their respective fields of their choice. Saha gave the theory of thermal ionization, which explained the physical conditions in stellar bodies. It is considered one of the ten major discoveries in astrophysics. Bose formulated Bose Statistics, which still plays a very vital role in the study of modern physics, in the field of elementary particles, and in the field of superconductivity (Chatterjee and Chatterjee, 1976). S.N. Bose was attracted to the new wave in physics called quantum theory as formulated by Max Planck in 1901 and 1906. Scientists found it irreconcilable with the laws of classical electrodynamics. Planck had been looking for the justification of quantization not in free but in interacting systems. In contrast, Bose considered a free quantum gas; he argued that 'the light quanta are particles which must be treated relativistically; they are massless; their number is not conserved; and, most important, the light quanta must be treated as being indistinguishable' (Mehra, 1975). In June 1924, Bose sent this paper to Einstein, who immediately recognized its significance, translated it by himself into German, and published it. Thus, was born the boson. Boson is a particle that follows Bose–Einstein statistics. It is a force-carrying particle, as opposed to a matter particle (Fermion). Bosons can be piled on top of each other without limit. Examples include photons, gluons, gravitons, weak bosons, and the Higgs boson. It encourages identical bosons to crowd into one quantum state.

Meghnad Saha was both a thinker and a fearless man of action. His interests were vast and varied. He worked on stellar spectra, thermal ionization, selective radiation pressure, spectroscopy, radio waves in ionosphere, solar corona, radio emission from the Sun, beta radioactivity, water dam technology, calendar reform, and even the age of the rocks! (Kothari, 1960). His research papers were the result of intensive theoretical studies and frugal instruments. The year 1930 was a watershed in Saha's life. He was attracted towards the discovery of neutron, and in 1936, he wrote on the origin of mass in neutrons and protons. Thus was sown the seeds of what came to be known as the Saha Institute of Nuclear Physics. Around the same time, he decided to emerge from his 'ivory tower of research and laboratories'. He now wanted to correlate science with the social needs of his time. For this purpose, in 1935, he founded a journal called *Science and Culture* (Visvanathan, 1985). In the very first issue of this celebrated journal, while appreciating Gandhi's 'genuine sympathy with the victims of an aggressive an selfish industrialism', he firmly refuted the claim that 'better and happier conditions of life can be created by discarding modern scientific technique and reverting back to the spinning-wheel, the loin cloth, and bullock cart (Science and Culture, 1935)'.

Gandhi's own political heir and independent India's first Prime Minister, Jawaharlal Nehru himself begged to differ with his mentor. For Gandhi, the individual, the society, and technology formed one whole in a similar manner as did religion, politics, and constructive work. Keeping them separate or autonomous was to him inconceivable. In a letter to Nehru, in September 1945, Gandhi talked about the necessity to escape the 'moth-like circling'. 'When the moth approaches its doom it whirls round faster and faster till is burnt up' (Young India, 1925). To this Nehru replied:

> I do not think it is possible for India to be really independent unless she is technically advanced country. I am not thinking for the moment in terms of just armies but rather of scientific growth. In the present context of the world we cannot even advance culturally without a strong back ground of scientific research in every department.
>
> *(Nehru)*

Such was the milieu in which independent India woke up. Science and technology were taken seriously. These were to make a new India. There was enormous enthusiasm which was used by some to serve their own professional or even selfish interests. Several excellent scientists took up administrative responsibilities. Committees became more important than classrooms. J.B.S. Haldane, who made India his home, was worried about how to organize science in India:

> [T]he first thing to do is to utilise the scientists whom we have got. That is to say they should be given time for research and teaching and as far as possible not asked to do anything else. If I am asked to spend a day listening to platitudes by politicians and administrators, this means insult to me. (Haldane, n.d.)

But Haldane had few takers. The post-colonial state was no less powerful than the colonial state. The concepts of state science and state scientists now had a permanent place both in Indian system and psyche.

Conclusion

The motto of the Imperial College of Science and Technology, established in London in 1907, reads: 'Scientia Imperii Decus et Tutamen' – 'Science is the Pride and Shield of Empire'. This encapsulates the science and colonization relationship. Yet, a colonial enterprise (and science itself) should not be seen in monolithic terms. Its objectives and machinations might have some kind of uniformity, but it elicited variegated responses and produced both desired and undesired results. The organs of colonialism did differ in their views and implementation programmes. But these differences were not of a very basic nature. They differed in matters of detail and execution. That is why the implementation part appears ad hoc and half-hearted, but when one looks at the policy pronouncement, particularly at the higher levels, one is struck by its generosity and utilitarianism. Full trust or emphasis on them, however, could be misleading, for they tend to hide the 'real' requirements and intentions of a colonial power.

The establishment of scientific institutions and journals was dictated not so much by the diffusion of scientific knowledge *per se* as by the local management of the complex resources of the colony. The government, that too of a trading company, would naturally be guided by economic considerations. But there was no guarantee that scientific excellence would bring economic benefits. So, science came to be valued more as a cultural activity. The government asked its officials to undertake such pursuits only in 'leisure' time. Researches thus were individualistic and esoteric, the only binding cord being the scientific 'clubs'. Some institutions lost their sheen sooner than expected, some survived. Ideas do not float in a vacuum; they need to be housed; so institutionalization was necessary. But they also move through networks, both formal and informal. Despite slow communication channels, the colonial scientists tried to remain in touch and exchanged papers and publications. But these networks were not idyllic nodal points of exchanges. If the colonizers and the colonized mobilized and transformed their specialized practices for the common resolution of problems, this does not mean that they participated equally in this dialogic process in an idyllic 'commonwealth of letters' (Raj, 2000). In most cases, the exchange was unequal and the results uneven. Also, this led to the emergence of some kind of scientocracy, and independent India continues to pay a heavy price for this bureaucratization of science.

Like colonialism, modernity is also janus-faced; it kills and nourishes almost simultaneously. Both succeeded to a large extent and dominated but not without resistance. These were powerful historical forces but no monoliths. There were punctures and disjunctions all around. The very nature of historical construction invites one to look at cross-currents and fluidity. A point to be noted here is that the practice of science remained largely alienated from its social context. In fact, one may ask, was it culturally divisive? Some found cultural dependence quite unavoidable while others rejected all that colonialism represented and searched for identity in indigenous traditions. The spread of modern science required the penetration of indigenous science and culture by Western science. Many residents of the Presidency and other big towns responded enthusiastically. Was it because the *bhadralok* wanted to legitimize their newly won status or was it a true craving for knowledge and improvement? The truth perhaps lies somewhere between the two.

References

Bacon, T. (1837). *First Impressions and Studies from Nature in Hindostan*. London, 7 (II vol).

Brock, T. D. (1988). *Robert Koch: A Life in Medicine and Bacteriology*. Science Tech. Publications, Madison.

Bulloch, W. (1983). *The History of Bacteriology*. Oxford University Press, London, 255.

Calcutta Monthly Journal, XLVIII, October 1838, 206.

A Century. (1976). Centenary Publication of the Indian Association for the Cultivation of Science, Calcutta.

Chakrabarti, P. (2004). *Western Science in Modern India: Metropolitan Methods, Colonial Practices*. Permanent Black, New Delhi.

Chatterjee, S. and Chatterjee, E. (1976). *Satyendra Nath Bose*. National Book Trust, New Delhi, 23.

Cited in, Habib, S. I. (2000). Reconciling science with Islam in 19th century India. *Contributions to Indian Sociology*, 34(1), 63–92.

Dasgupta, S. (1999). *Jagadish Chandra Bose and the Indian Response to Western Science*. Oxford University Press, New Delhi.

Fermor, L. L. (1935). *Year Book of Asiatic Society of Bengal for 1934*. Calcutta, 16 (I vol).

Geison, G. L. (1994). *The Private Science of Louis Pasteur*. Princeton University Press, Princeton.

Haffkine to Secretary to GOI, July 31, 1908, Haffkine Papers, f. 408, Hebrew University Archive, Jerusalem.

Haldane, J. B. S. Papers, 20626, n.d. p. 39, Scottish National Libhaldanrary, Edinburgh.

Holland, T. H. (1905). Revenur Dept. Agriculture Branch, Proc. No. 3, August, File 127, National Archive of India (emphasis added).

Jacob, K. T. (1958). *Acharya Jagadish Chandra Bose Birth Centenary Volume*. Bose Institute, Kolkata, 40–41.

Jambhekar, G. G. Ed. (1950). *Memoirs and Writings of Bal Gangadhar Shastri Jambhekar*. G.G. Jambhekar, Poona (3 vols).

Joshi, V. C. Ed. (1975). *Rammohan Roy and the Process of Modernisation in India*. Vikas Pub., New Delhi.

Kothari, D. S. (1960). Meghnad Saha. *Biographical Memoirs of Fellows of the Royal Society*, 5, February, 217–236.

Kumar, D. (1995). *Science and the Raj*. Oxford University Press, New Delhi.

Letter from R. Ross to G. F. Nuttal, 28 April 1899, Ross Papers, Mss. 02/229, London School of Tropical Medicine Library.

Lourdusamy, J. (2004). *Science and National Consciousness in Bengal*. Orient Longman, Hyderabad, 92.

Medical Selections, I, Calcutta, 1833, III–IV.

Mehra, J. (1975). Satyendra Nath Bose. *Biographical Memoirs of Fellows of the Royal Society*, 21, November, 128.

Miscellaneous Reports, India Agriculture, 1869–1921, f. 105, Royal Botanic Garden Archive, Kew.

Nandy, A. (1980). *Alternative Sciences*. Allied Publishers, New Delhi.

Native Newspaper Reports Published During 1900–1930 for Similar Demands in the Vernacular Press.

Nehru, J. *Selected Works* (14 vol) 554–557. Seventy years later now to some it has become a habit to berate Nehru. But it will be like missing woods for trees!

Newman, G. (1932). *The Rise of Preventive Medicine*. Oxford University Press, London.

Panikkar, K. N. (1986). The intellectual history of colonial India: Some historiographical and conceptual questions. In Bhattacharya, S. and Thapar, R. (Eds.) *Situating Indian History*. Oxford University Press, New Delhi, 402–432.

Patel, R. D. (1921). *The Claims of Science in National Life*. Surat, ix.

The Asiatic Society of Bengal (1907). *Nature*, 75, 511. https://doi.org/10.1038/075511a0

The prospectus of this Association was published in the *Calcutta Journal of Natural History*, 1841, 8–14.

Raina, D. (1992). Mathematical foundations of a cultural project or Ramchandra's treatise through the unsentimentalised light of mathematic. *Historia Mathematica*, 19, 371–384.

Raj, K. (2000). Colonial encounters and the forging of new knowledge and national identities: Great Britain and India, 1760–1850. *Osiris*, 15, 134.

Ray, P. C. (1923). *Convocation Address*. Jamia Millia, Aligarh, 58.

Rennell, J. (1788). *Memoir of a Map of Hindustan*. London, 15.

Report of the Board of Education, Bombay, 1850–51, 10–15, Maharashtra State Archive.

Risley, H. H. (1904). Presidential Address, Proc. of the Asiatic Society of Bengal, 26, January 6.

Sarkar, B. K. (1946). *Education for Industrialisation*. Chatterjee & Sons, Calcutta, 3.

Science and Culture. (1935). 1, June, 3–4. This Editorial Was Repeated in June 1942.

Sen, A. (1975). Ishwarchandra Vidysagar and his elusive milestones. Occasional Paper No. 1, CSSS, Calcutta.

Singh, R. (2005). *Nobel Laureate C. V. Raman's Science*. Philosophy and Religion, Bangalore.

Sinha, S. D. (In press). *The Indian Medical Gazette: Mirror of Medical Thoughts and Practices*. Manohar Pub., New Delhi.

A successful malaria vaccine eludes us even now!

This remains relevant in the wake of the corona virus pandemic in 2020!

Transactions of the Medical and Physical Society of Calcutta, III–V, 1827–1831.

Visvanathan, S. (1985). *Organising for Science: The Making of an Industrial Research Laboratory*. Oxford University Press, New Delhi, 39–96, 97–132.

Young India. (1925). To industrialise India in the same sense as Europe is to attempt the impossible. *Young India*, 6 August 1925.

3

EVOLUTION OF IDEAS FROM ARISTOTLE TO NEWTON

A Journey Towards the Unification of the Earth and the Heavens

Bichitra Kumar Guha

Introduction

There is a well-known story about Sir Isaac Newton which is widely popular amongst school children. It goes like this: one fine morning, Newton was relaxing under an apple tree when a ripe apple decided to get detached from the branch of the tree. That it did and fell on Newton's head. The impact of the apple induced Sir Newton to think about why it fell down and not gone up and he discovered gravitation!

This story really does injustice to the genius of Newton. The theory of universal gravitation with all its mathematical details as constructed by Newton was a colossal achievement, and it was definitely not merely the result of a falling apple. This story also does injustice to his predecessors. It cannot be true that nobody before Newton gave any thought as to why heavy bodies left to themselves unsupported at an altitude always fall down and never go up. In later life, Newton had remarked: if I can see further, it is because I stand on giant shoulders. The giant shoulders are of course the great thinkers who preceded Newton and who contemplated about the workings of nature. With the passage of time, ideas changed, ideas evolved, new ideas bloomed and slowly patterns emerged out of confusion and complexities resulting in the progress of modern science that began its journey with the advent of renaissance in Europe.

In this chapter we will present a brief account of the evolution of ideas about our world that took place from ancient times to the beginning of modern science.

Ancient Greece

To appreciate our story, we have to mentally go back in history by about 2,500 years and forget about modern times. We must remember that in those days there was

DOI: 10.4324/9781003033448-5

no electricity, no motor cars, no spaceships, no cell phones and in fact no science in its present form except some primitive technologies. We are going to talk a little about the ancient Greek civilization. It is because what the Greeks achieved in the purely intellectual realm, apart from their excellence in art and literature, continued to influence the future European civilization for generations to come.

The ancient Greece of that time consisted of independent city states like Sparta, Athens, Miletus, and so on. It was a society where the manual labours like tilling the land, breeding cattle, works in the mines or small workshops were all left to the slaves and slavery was thought to be natural and not a matter of shame. The slaves were mostly acquired in battles where the vanquished was made slave of the conqueror. They were denied of all human rights, were not considered to be citizens but only the property of their owners. The citizens had the privilege to live on the labour of the slaves. It was remarked by Aristotle that the goal of a citizen was to attain the life of leisure.

While slavery, a deplorable practice, prevailed in Greece, it had its other side also. A section of the citizens, who did not have to toil for food and got ample spare time, utilized the leisure to cultivate art and literature and also to improve their intellectual skill through development of rational and critical thinking, elevating their mental prowess. Thus, ancient Greece produced generation after generation of great thinkers who went on enriching the civilization.

The most ancient form of world outlook that dates back to the dawn of civilization was mostly mythology, an imagined reflection of reality which arose in the consciousness of primitive man, who thought that there was spiritual life in the surrounding nature. The origin and workings of nature were ascribed to the gods and spirits. It was the Greek thinkers who tried a rational explanation of the world as opposed to the myth-steeped religious consciousness. These thinkers were called the philosophers. The word philosopher was coined from two Greek words: *phile* (love) and *Sophia* (wisdom). There is a legend that Pythagoras of Croton, a great thinker and mathematician was the first person to use that word showing a sense of modesty. He used to comment: man should not be so audacious as to claim that he possesses wisdom, but any rational human being can be a lover of wisdom, that is a philosopher.

Thales of Miletus (585 BCE) is acclaimed to be the first philosopher. He predicted occurrence of a solar eclipse which was not a novel thing, as such predictions could be done by ancient Egyptian priests long before Thales. The importance of Thales's prediction lies in the fact that he described the eclipse as a naturally occurring phenomenon, not originated by the working of a demon and that the eclipse would be over naturally, not requiring any chanting of sacred hymns by the priests. Thales was followed by a great many philosophers, but in this chapter, we are concerned chiefly with the last of the famous three of Athens: Socrates, his disciple Plato and his disciple Aristotle.

If you ask a school-going child whether he or she knew who Aristotle was, you are most likely to get a fragmented answer like he was the private tutor of Alexander the Great or that he was the father of biology. But actually, this man has contributed tremendously to many fields of knowledge: sociology, politics, poetry, logic, rhetoric, philosophy of mind, ethics, metaphysics, natural science, science of living beings, etc. The twentieth-century great philosopher and mathematician Bertrand Russell paid his tribute to Aristotle with the remark:

> He came at the end of the creative period in Greek thought, and after his death it was two thousand years before the world produced any philosopher who could be regarded as approximately his equal.

So, the ideas of Aristotle prevailed and went on influencing future generations not for decades or centuries but for millennia. But it is also true, as Russell has observed, that the authority of Aristotle became almost unquestioned and created hindrance to progress. Ever since the beginning of the seventeenth century, almost every intellectual advance had to begin with an attack on some Aristotelian doctrine.

Aristotle was probably born in 384 BCE in the Macedonian region of northeastern Greece in the small city of Stagira. He came to Athens for study when he was 17 years old and joined the academy of Plato. He was a brilliant student and stayed at the academy for nearly 20 years till the death of Plato in 347 BCE. Aristotle then left Athens, probably being a little bit disheartened as he was not given the charge of the academy after Plato's death, but its control passed over to Plato's nephew Speucippus. Aristotle was invited by Phillip, king of Macedonia to tutor his 13-year-old son Alexander, and Aristotle went to Pella, the capital of Macedonia, for this purpose. After about three years, Alexander went on to conquer the world. Aristotle came back to Athens in 335 BCE and founded his own academy called Lyceum where he preached his students and went on writing in the form of notes and dialogues about his doctrines. His works were later compiled as treatises and there were nearly 200 such treatises. Most of them are either lost or damaged and only some 30 odd have survived. After the death of Alexander in 323 BCE, there was a resurgence of anti-Macedonian sentiment in Athens. Aristotle was denounced for impiety and he left Athens. Aristotle had remarked that he saw no reason to permit Athens to sin twice against philosophy. He was referring to the execution of Socrates in Athens, and he did not want himself to be dealt with in this manner. Aristotle died the next year in 322 BCE.

It has been mentioned that about 30 treatises of Aristotle have survived till date. As we are interested in the evolution of ideas on natural science, the following account will be based on three of the treatises written by him: *Phusis* (Physics), *De Caeloet Mundo* (On the Heavens) and *De Generationne et Corruptione* (on Generation and Corruption).

Aristotle divides the universe into two distinct layers: everything from the Moon upward was the *supralunar* region and everything below the Moon and on Earth belongs to the *sublunar* region. He opined that nature works *completely differently* in the two regions, and this idea took a strong root in the minds of later thinkers and could be wiped out only after Newton published his monumental work known popularly as *Principia*.

Elements

It appears that reductionism has been the trend of thought throughout the history of mankind. The idea is the following: the varieties of matter that we see around us, the wood, the stone, the clay, the flower, etc. are different in appearance but are really consisted of a few fundamental substances that combine in different proportions, giving rise to such varieties. Thales thought that the fundamental substance is water while Anaximenes preferred air to be the basis of all substances. It was Empedocles who advanced the idea of four fundamental substances: earth, water, air and fire. It was Plato who first used the term *element* to describe these fundamental substances.

Aristotle, in his *Generation and Corruption*, upheld this idea by ascribing certain qualities to them: the element earth was cold and dry, water was cold and wet, air was hot and wet and fire was hot and dry. According to Aristotle, all matter in the sublunar region are made of these four elements and they are corruptible, that is subject to change. We see around us stones breaking, earth cracking, seeds growing into plants, decay of flesh after death and so on.

Aristotle tried to demonstrate the combination of elements to form substances in the following way. Take a piece of wood and ignite it. You will see smoke coming out of it, indicating there was air in it. If you touch it, you will feel hot, indicating that there was fire in it. After burning out, there will remain ashes, showing that there was earth in it. If you consider the human body, the flesh and bones are mostly made up of earth; blood, perspiration and urine are made up of water. As we inhale air during breathing, there must be air in the body and a living human being feels warm when touched, showing that there is fire in the body.

But in the supralunar region, we, with naked eyes, do not observe any change in the stars and other celestial bodies except change in their location and brightness. So, Aristotle thought of a fifth element called aether that built up *the* heavens. This fifth element, also called *quintessence*, literally meaning 'fifth element' was incorruptible, unchangeable and existed as it is for eternity. The idea of aether, in a different form, continued to exist till the nineteenth century. When James Clark Maxwell put forward his theory of electromagnetic waves, he thought that an all-pervading medium called aether existed throughout the universe, and undulations in this medium gave rise to the electromagnetic waves. Only after the advent of the special theory of relativity proposed by Einstein, scientists have been able to drive out the idea of such a hypothetical medium.

The idea of these four elements of the Earth was prevalent in the Zoroastrian philosophy, in ancient and medieval China, and elsewhere in the world. In ancient India, in the classic text of the *Vedas*, however, five elements have been mentioned: *khshiti* (earth), *ap* (water), *tej* (fire), *marut* (air) and *byom* (space or vacuum). According to the *samkhya* philosophy, space was considered to be the seat of sound. In passing, it may be mentioned that Aristotle denied the existence of vacuum and he had his own logic for doing so which we will discuss shortly.

It may be mentioned again at this point that the idea of element has undergone a complete change from the beginning of the seventeenth century when John Dalton came up with his atomic theory.

Phusis

One of the great treatises of Aristotle was *Phusis*, which later became physics in English. The word *phusis* literally means "nature", not in the sense that it describes the scenic beauty surrounding us such as the forest, ocean or mountains. Here, the word nature signifies *"an inner principle that decides something to be what it is"*. It is not very difficult to understand what it means. Let us give an example. Suppose Mr X was passing through the marketplace where a beggar was asking for alms. Mr X looked haughtily at him and went by. We say that "by nature" Mr X was arrogant or miserly or cruel. It is something inside him that prompted him to be what he was. Animals also have such nature. It is the nature of the dog to go for a piece of bone.

But the importance of Aristotle lies in the fact that he ascribed such "nature" not only to living beings but also to inanimate objects, and this idea prevails in modern science also. Aristotle said that it is the *nature of the elements to be at rest*. And if we examine the first of the great three laws of motion enunciated by Newton, we observe that it begins with the words "Every body continues to be at rest". The later part of the law was of course a tremendous advance on Aristotle's theory.

Such nature of inanimate objects was not uncommon in ancient India also. There, people talked about *dharma* meaning property. It was the *dharma* of water to flow from a higher level to a lower level.

Aristotle not only said that the nature of elements was to be at rest, but he also fixed the natural places of rest for the elements. Heavy elements like earth and water sought the centre of the universe lying deep below the surface of our planet Earth. So, the natural place of rest of the element earth was at the bottom-most position. Above earth, there should be water, above water air and above air the natural space is that of fire. It was demonstrated in the following way:

Take a vessel filled with water. Put some sand in it and with a stirrer, stir the content well and then allow it to settle down. What shall we observe? The sand, made up of earth, settles at the bottom and above it lies the layer of water. Now blow some air through the water by a pipe and it is clearly seen that air bubbles rise through the water. Then ignite a stick in air. The flame of fire will rise through air, thus justifying his conjecture.

Now what will happen if we displace a body made up of some element from its natural place of rest and leave it to itself? Naturally, it will try to seek its natural place of rest and move towards that place. So, if a stone made up of the element earth is elevated to an altitude and then left unsupported, it will seek to move to its natural place of rest, that is towards the bottom-most position, which is the ground. That explains the falling of the stone or for that matter, an apple.

So, according to Aristotle, *up and down motions on the Earth are natural motions.* It may be noted that it is a very simple explanation involving just the nature of the elements, whereas the explanation of Newton through his theory of gravitation is quite complicated indeed. That theory involves attraction of the stone by not only the planet Earth but everything in this universe, including distant stars, and the resultant of all such forces creates a downward acceleration of the stone. But, of course, that explanation is the correct one and that proposed by Aristotle was not.

But apart from the natural up and down motion, we also observe horizontal motion on the Earth. How is it caused? From the everyday experience, we find that to initiate such a motion, we need to push or pull the body to be moved. May be a horse is tied by a rope to a carriage and using his muscular power, the horse will pull the carriage, making it move. This muscular power we loosely call force. So, horizontal motion is caused by the use of force, and Aristotle called such a motion as *violent* motion. In modern language, we may say that according to Aristotle, force is the cause of horizontal motion. This idea ultimately was changed completely by Newton, and now we know that *force is not the cause of motion but the cause of change in motion.* The change may be in its speed or direction.

But, even then, a question was raised regarding a particular type of motion. Suppose an arrow is released from the bow by using the power of the hand. Or, for that matter, consider a stone thrown horizontally. At the time of throwing, force is used by the hand. But as soon as the arrow leaves the bow, or the stone leaves the hand, there is no more physical contact between the hand and the stone and no force is therefore applied on it. So, the stone must now execute its natural motion and just fall down vertically. But we see the stone moving for some time in air before falling down. Doesn't it contradict Aristotle's theory? Aristotle came up with an explanation. As the stone is hurled, it drags some air with it. Dragging of the surrounding air creates a partial vacuum behind it. Aristotle said that nature abhors vacuum. So air from its neighbourhood will rush in to fill this vacuum and this rushing air provides the impetus for the stone to move forward. It will fall down when the impetus of air is exhausted.

Nowadays, we know that air has nothing to do with such motion and the stone will describe a curved trajectory after leaving the hand even in vacuum. In those times, it was thought that the stone moves for some time horizontally and then falls vertically. But that it is a curved trajectory was brilliantly demonstrated by Galileo centuries later. We will come back to him in due time.

Atomism and Aristotle

We have remarked earlier that Aristotle denied the existence of vacuum and he had his own reasons for doing so. This is intimately connected with the atomistic theory of matter, which Aristotle did not accept.

Our senses suggest that matter is continuous. The air that surrounds us appear to be continuous as we are not bombarded by individual particles of air. The water that we drink seems to be continuous as we do not take discrete particles of water.

But about a century before Aristotle, Leucippus and Democritus advanced the atomistic theory of matter. It will not be out of context to quote Democritus at this juncture:

> By convention sweet is sweet, by convention bitter is bitter, by convention hot is hot, cold is cold, by convention colour is colour. But in reality there are atoms and the void. That is, the objects of sense are supposed to be real and it is customary to regard them as such, but in truth they are not. Only the atoms and the void are real.

These words have some deep philosophical implications. Suppose I look at a piece of cloth and call it blue. Then I look at a painting and also call it blue. So will another person. Why? The piece of cloth creates some impression in our minds through the sense organ known as the eye. But I do not know what sort of impression it creates in another person's mind. But I know that the piece of cloth and the painting both create more or less the same impression in me, and another person will agree that both create similar impressions in him also. We then "agree" to call this kind of impression as "blue". The same is the case with sweetness or bitterness where the sense organ involved is the tongue. So also is the case with heat or cold where the sense organ involved is the skin. Thus, colour or taste or feeling of hot and cold are conventions depending on the perceptions of the senses. If we say that such perceptions are "real", we are making a mistake. Because if there be no human being or for that matter no living being, there will be no meaning of colour or taste. But the world outside our consciousness will continue to exist. So, according to Democritus, the "true" or reality is not the sensory perceptions, but the objective reality is only the existence of atoms and void.

Leucippus thought of breaking a substance into finer and finer particles. Is this process never ending? Both Leucippus and Democritus said that this process of breaking will finally come to an end. We will ultimately reach a stage when the particle cannot be broken any more and such an ultimate particle was called atom, coined from two Greek words: *a thomos*, meaning unbreakable. These atoms, according to Democritus, were solid and homogeneous and all apparent changes in matter result from changes in the groupings of atoms.

Now, the world cannot be fully packed with atoms because we notice matters to move. So, space or vacuum is needed for movement of atoms. Hence, the true realities of the world are atoms and the void.

Aristotle denied this atomic structure and said that matter was continuous and made from the four elements mentioned earlier. He denied the existence of atoms because he denied the existence of void or vacuum. The logic behind his denial of vacuum is the following.

We see heavy bodies falling through a medium. But the same body falls rapidly through air and slower through water. It means that the speed of fall of a body increases as the density of the medium of fall decreases. In modern language, we may say that the speed of fall is inversely proportional to the density of the medium of fall. If we mentally go on decreasing the density of the medium, the speed of fall will go on increasing and as we reach vacuum having zero density, the speed of fall will be infinity, which is a physical impossibility. Hence, there cannot be any void and so the atomic theory is wrong.

What Aristotle missed out completely, and in fact for thousands of years people were not aware of the fact that the falling body actually accelerates, is that its speed goes on increasing as it falls. The concept of acceleration was first introduced by Galileo, and now we know that the role of the medium is not to change the so-called speed of fall but to change the acceleration of fall due to the resistance it offers.

The atomic structure of matter was proposed by ancient Indian philosophers also, notably by *Kanada,* who probably lived in the second century CE and was the proponent of the *Vaishesika* school of Indian philosophy. The followers of the school put forward a logic for establishing the hypothesis of unbreakable particles in the following manner.

Let us assume that matter is continuous so that the process of breaking a piece of matter is never ending. Now consider a piece of stone. If we go on breaking and subdividing it, the process is unending. So the piece of stone may be supposed to be consisting of infinitely many particles. Now consider the Himalayan mountain. In a similar fashion, the process of subdividing the mountain is never ending. Thus, the mountain is also consisted of infinitely many particles. Thus, it is possible to construct the huge mountain range of the Himalayas with a single piece of stone which is an absurdity. Hence, the initial proposition is wrong. Matter is not continuous but consists of finite number of unbreakable particles or *anu*, as *Kanada* called them. The number of atoms in the piece of stone is much less than that in the mountain.

We have discussed in brief the salient points of Aristotelian mechanics in the sublunar region, and now let us look up to the heavens.

On the Heavens

To appreciate the thought and ideas of the ancient philosophers, first we have to admit that it is the witness of the eye that dictated all the conjectures of the yesteryears. Even now, we use the phrase "to see is to believe".

As we look up to the firmament, we see a hemisphere full of glittering lights in the night and the bright Sun warming us in the day. We also see the whole firmament with all those sparks of light revolving round us in a regular manner.

Now to describe this revolution, one needs to fix up what are called the directions. And the directions cannot be judged by just looking at the rising and setting Sun and calling their directions as the east and the west because these directions vary throughout the year. To be precise, we can proceed by setting up a pole vertically on a flat and open ground. And let us perform this exercise in the northern hemisphere. The shadow of the pole is longest at the time of rising or setting of the Sun. If we look at these long shadows of the pole at the time of the Sun rising or setting, we will notice their directions change over the year from one extreme to another, meaning that the directions of the rising or setting Sun also vary with time and so the rising or setting Sun cannot be the yardstick for identifying the east or the west accurately. But if we concentrate on the shadow of the pole at exactly the midday, when the Sun is overhead, the shadow will be shortest. Day after day, the direction of this shortest shadow will not vary. If we extend the shadow for miles after miles and again set up the vertical pole, we will notice the direction of this midday shadow still remains the same. This direction has therefore some significance and we call the direction towards the tip of the shadow from the base of the pole as the north. The opposite direction will be the south and a line drawn perpendicular to it will point towards east in the right and west in the left. An imaginary vertical plane drawn through the north–south line is called the meridian plane that divides the heavenly hemisphere into two halves.

Incidentally, the shadow of the pole at the time of the Sun rising will be found to move from an extreme point towards the north of west to another extreme point towards the south of west. And the shadow at the time of the Sun setting will move from some extreme point in the south of east to another in the north of east.

If we look at the stars, night after night, we will notice them moving along circles around some imaginary pole situated in the meridian plane. A star situated on this pole, when extended into space, will not appear to move at all and we call it the pole star.

Now, while the whole of the sky appears to revolve around the Earth from dawn to dusk and then from dusk to dawn, there are a large number of stars, may be about 2,000–3,000 visible to the naked eye, that maintain their relative positions in the sky the same day after day. For example consider the well-known constellation of seven stars known as the Great Bear. The constellation really looks like a question mark when the stars are joined by imaginary lines and the length and orientations of these lines never change. Such stars were called the fixed stars. But in the background of fixed stars, a few are found to move slowly across the sky. For example if we look at a star in the eastern horizon when the Sun is setting in the west and observe this star day after day, we will find that after some days, the star is already high up in the sky when the Sun is setting in the west. This indicates that though the heavens rotate with all the fixed stars, the Sun moves a little slower than them losing one complete circuit of the heavens in about 365 and 1/4 days. If we divide this span of time into 12 segments and call each of them a month, we observe the Sun to cross one stellar constellation each month. A constellation is an apparently closely spaced assembly of stars. Such constellations were given names by the ancients according to the imaginary figures they presented when the member stars were joined by imaginary lines. One was called libra, another virgo, another pisces and so on. They have come to be known as the zodiac signs and at this point, what is known as astrology as opposed to astronomy crept into the society. As if the fate of a person is governed by the movement of the stars. If somebody is born in a month when the Sun crosses a certain zodiac sign, his future is decided by that sign.

But forgetting about astrology, the Moon is also seen to undergo a similar movement in the background of the fixed stars. It appears to cross one star every night and completes its journey in about 27 and 1/3 days. In Indian mythology, the 27 stars so crossed by the Moon were considered to be the wives of the Moon god and that he spent one night with each of them.

Apart from the Sun and the Moon, five more celestial bodies visible to the naked eye were also found to move in the background of the fixed stars. They were named Mercury, Venus, Mars, Jupiter and Saturn. In Egypt, the priest-astronomers classed these five bodies together with the Sun and the Moon. All were "wanderers" in the background of the fixed stars. Later, they came to be known as "planets" which is another Greek word, meaning the wanderers. In that way, the names of the days of the week had their origin. Saturn, Jupiter, Mars, Sun, Venus, Mercury and the Moon: this was supposed to be the order of decreasing distance from the solid ground of the Earth. The ancient astronomers could guess the relative distances of the planets, but of course not their exact magnitude. It was guessed on the basis of their relative brightness and the time taken by them to describe a certain arc in the sky. The planet at a smaller distance had to move through a small distance in describing an angle and so took a smaller time while the planet at a greater distance had to move through a larger distance to describe the same angle and thus took a longer time.

Interestingly, Indian mythology talks about *nabagraha* (nine planets). Apart from the seven mentioned earlier, two more entities have been conferred the status of planets. They were called *Rahu* and *Ketu*. As per Indian mythology, these two entities are demons who try to gulp up the Sun and the Moon which causes the solar and lunar eclipses. Actually, it was a single demon who was very angry at not getting the elixir of life and tried to harm the creation. Fortunately, Lord *Vishnu* severed his head from the body and so even though the head gulped the Sun or the Moon, they could come out of the demon through the opening below his head. The head was called *Rahu* and the body *Ketu*.

But, in reality, what are these entities? The apparent orbit of the Sun round the Earth was called the ecliptic which does not lie in the same plane as the Moon's orbit. So, in space, these two orbits would intersect at two imaginary points. They are called the nodal points and in Indian mythology these two imaginary points in space were referred to as the *Rahu* and *Ketu*. During its orbital motion, when the Moon comes roughly within an angle of 18° around the two points, the Sun, the Earth and the Moon lie in the same straight line and eclipses occur. This phenomenon has prompted the astrologers to predict dark and ominous effect of these two so-called planets on the life of a man.

It now remains to discuss how the ancient philosophers tried to explain the motion of the stars and the planets.

As already mentioned, Aristotle proposed that the heavenly bodies from the Moon upward were made up of a fifth element called aether which was incorruptible and unchangeable. At this point, it may be mentioned that by the term "motion" Aristotle meant any kind of change in one of the ten categories that can be used to describe matter. He classified them as being "said of" and "being present in". We need not discuss all these difficult terminologies but suffice it to say that he thought of ten categories under which a being can be described. For example substance, quantity, quality, relation, place or location, time, posture, possession, action and affection. The growth of a seed into a plant is a change in quantity and hence is motion. Setting a chair upright from a lying position is a change in posture and so is a motion. Motion, according to Aristotle, is actuality of potentiality. A piece of stone has the potentiality to become a sculpture, which is the actuality of its potentiality. Now, when Aristotle mentions that aether is unchangeable, he actually means no change in any of the categories except location or place for we see the stars and planets moving round us, continuously changing their position.

Since aether is perfect, its natural motion should also be perfect and according to the ancient Greeks, a perfect geometrical figure is a circle since all the points on its circumference are equidistant from the centre. Aristotle upheld this view and said that the natural motion of aether is along circular paths as opposed to the up and down natural motion on Earth. Thus, according to Aristotle, the Earth and the heavens were different on the following major aspects.

(i) They are made up of different elements; the four elements making matter on Earth are subject to change, growth or decay; but the fifth element aether making up the heavenly bodies is eternal, not undergoing any change.

(ii) On Earth, there are two kinds of motion, natural in the vertical direction and violent in the horizontal direction while the heavenly bodies have only a natural circular motion which is perfect. Also, it was presumed that the heavenly bodies circle round the Earth, the centre of the universe being in the depths below the surface of the Earth.

Now the question remains about how and why such natural circular motion of the celestial bodies takes place. This was contemplated in Aristotle's *Metaphysics*.

Metaphysics

Aristotle discussed what is known as "being qua being", that is what it is for something to exist and what types of existence there are, in his *Metaphysics*. The nomenclature is not due to him. The work consisted of 14 books, and Aristotle called it the first philosophy, in the sense of its being the chief or most important philosophy. A first century BCE editor of his works, possibly Andronicus, compiled these works and since these works followed the earlier work on physics, he named it *ta meta ta physika*, meaning beyond or after physics. We are concerned here with his cosmological theory as found in this work.

Eudoxus, a student of Plato, developed a planetary model using concentric spheres for all the planets. Each planet was supposed to be associated with a set of crystal-like spheres, and it was embedded in the innermost of them. The spheres revolved round the Earth. Twenty-six such spheres were needed for him to describe the motion of the seven planets. Callippus later modified the theory and suggested 33 spheres. Aristotle based his theory on the model of Eudoxus. In his model, the Earth was at the centre of the universe and the planets are moved by either 47 or 55 interconnected spheres that formed a unified planetary system. The planetary spheres were followed by a stellar sphere containing the fixed stars.

Now, the question is how these spheres are made to move. Aristotle's fundamental principle is that everything that is in motion is moved by something else. So, the innermost sphere of the Moon might be moved by the next sphere of Mercury with which it is connected. The sphere of Mercury may be moved by the next outer sphere of Venus and so on. But why should these spheres be moved at all? And also there cannot be an infinite series of moved movers. If B moves A, then B must be moved by C and so on, but there has to be an end of this series. It must come to a halt at some X that is a cause of motion but does not move itself – an *Unmoved Mover*.

This unmoved mover is an eternal substance for it causes motion of the heavens which is everlasting. It cannot come into existence and go out of it by turning into something else. Also, it must lack potentiality. The heavenly bodies have potentiality to move from one place to another; but the unmoved mover cannot have it, for then it will cause a change in itself and cannot be called unmoved. It can only be a pure actuality (*energeia*). How will it then cause motion? Because the act of causing motion will change it. So Aristotle's conclusion is that it can act as a final cause only by being an object of love, for being loved does not change the beloved. The stars and the planets, out of their love for this perfect being, will try to imitate it by moving about the Earth in circles, the most perfect of shapes. Of course, for feeling love, the planets must have souls which we may call angels.

Can this unmoved mover be capable of thinking? The answer by Aristotle is "yes". The delight that a human being takes in the sublime philosophical thoughts must be present in the unmoved mover in a perpetual state. He must be thinking; otherwise, he is no better than a sleeping man. But if He thinks of something other than himself, he would be somewhat degraded. So He must think of himself, the supreme being and his existence is that of a thinking of thinking (*noesisnoeseos*).

At this point we ask ourselves whether Aristotle was referring to God, the creator as was later described in the Bible. It appears from his discussions that he was not. The delight of thinking is the only attribute of this unmoved mover. And according to the Greek thinkers, the reason and rationality of philosophical thoughts is the supreme form of thinking. So, this unmoved mover of Aristotle may point to pure reason and rationality that is driving the stars and the planets.

In Figure 3.1, Aristotelian universe is presented schematically. The innermost shell of the Earth contains the element earth, above it in succession lie the shells of water, air and fire which are their natural places of rest. The shell of fire extends up to the Moon. From the Moon upward are the celestial spheres containing the planets and the outermost sphere has fixed stars embedded in it. Beyond this sphere lies the Unmoved Mover. There is a controversy regarding the number of unmoved

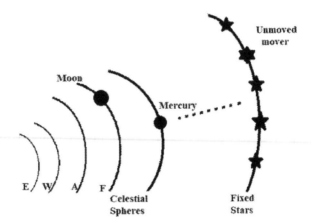

FIGURE 3.1 Schematic representation of Aristotelian universe

movers. Aristotle might have thought about a number of unmoved movers, not just a single one.

Ptolemy's Universe

In the period 127–151 CE, in Alexandria, Claudius Ptolemy summarized and codified the knowledge and accepted belief in astronomy and trigonometry. His classic treatise is known as the *Syntaxis*, or alternatively, *Almagest*. The latter name originates from the fact that the work has come down to Europe mainly through its Arabic translations done in the ninth and tenth centuries. It appears that in Book 2 of his *Planetary Hypothesis* he replaced the spheres of the earlier period by thick circular discs. These discs are the deferent and epicycles. Let us elaborate this point a little more.

Already there was a problem regarding circular motions of the planets round the Earth. In general, the five planets, apart from the Sun and the Moon, move from west to east in relation to the fixed stars; but once in each year, there is for each a phase of retrogression, when the apparent motion is in the reverse direction. In a simple circular motion, the planet should move always in the same direction and it is difficult to explain their retrogression. Also, the rate of retrogression varied from planet to planet. To overcome this difficulty, Hipparchus had already introduced the concept of deferent and epicycles. There is a circular motion of a sphere or disc round the Earth, but the planet is not moving along this circular path. It is moving on a smaller circle whose centre lies on the periphery of the bigger circle. The bigger circle is known as the deferent and the smaller one as the epicycle. It has been demonstrated in Figure 3.2.

The motion of the deferent is slower compared to that of the epicycle. When the planet is at the top of the epicycle, both the motion of the deferent and the epicycle are from left to right and the planet also appears to move that way from the Earth denoted by E. But when the planet is at the bottom-most position of the

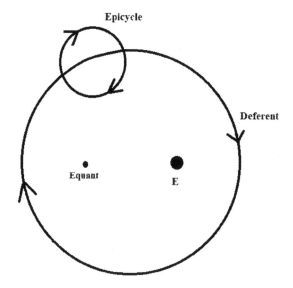

FIGURE 3.2 Schematic representation of Ptolemy's universe

epicycle, it is moving rapidly in the backward direction while the motion of the deferent is slower in the forward direction. So, from the Earth, the planet would appear to move backward.

It may be seen that the Earth has not been drawn at the centre of the defer-ent. The off-centre position of the Earth was necessary to describe the planetary motion. Ptolemy introduced the concept of the equant, which is a point from which the motion of the planet appears to be uniform. But to describe the motion of even a single planet, one epicycle and an eccentric Earth was not enough. It was necessary to mount one after another smaller and smaller epicycles on the inner ones. Ptolemy undertook an extremely tedious and complicated calculation to describe the observed motion of the planets accurately. He found that 78 epicycles were needed for the purpose and the calculations were so cumbersome that he had remarked: it is easier to drive the planets than to explain their motion.

So, the basic structure of Ptolemy's cosmos did not differ much from Aristotle except in the details of calculations and the introduction of epicycles and deferent.

Aristarchus and Heliocentricity

Though all great philosophers of that time agreed on the geocentric model and assumed circular revolution of the heavenly bodies around the Earth, there were people who held an unorthodox view. Notable among them was Aristarchus of Samos who lived during 310–230 BCE. The only book written by him that has survived till date is *On the Distance and Sizes of the Sun and the Moon*, which does not say anything about his heliocentric model. The book is important because here he has described how he measured the distance of the Sun and the Moon from the Earth and also their sizes by examining the shadow cast by the Earth on the Moon during a lunar eclipse. He could not of course estimate the exact values of the parameters, but he rightly concluded that the size of the Sun is much bigger than that of the Earth and that it is at a great distance.

His doctrine about the heliocentric model is found from later works by Archimedes and Plutarch. He put forward the hypothesis that the Sun and not the Earth was at the centre of the universe and that the Earth, along with other planets revolved round it. He guessed that the distant stars are just like the Sun. The conclusion would be that the size of the universe would be much bigger than what was thought at that time. His doctrine was rejected by stalwarts like Hipparchus and slowly forgotten. The objections to his heliocentric model can be summarized as follows.

1   If the Earth moves round the Sun, the apparent diurnal motion of the heavens, the occurrence of the day and night necessarily requires the Earth to rotate around its axis once per day. But it is our everyday experience that if we ride a rotating body like a merry-go-round, we feel a tendency to be thrown away and to maintain our position we must hold on to a support. So, a rotating Earth would result in all the objects on its surface to be thrown in the space and the Earth itself would fly apart.

2   If the Earth moves from west to east, then a stone which is allowed to fall vertically from a height should not reach a point which was vertically below it at the time of start, because during the time of fall the Earth would have moved through a certain distance.

3   Stellar parallax should have been observed which was not. Stellar parallax is demonstrated in Figure 3.3.

Suppose the Earth was at the extreme right of its orbit round the Sun at some time. The orbit is the horizontal circle. At that point, a star A appeared to be vertically overhead. After six months, the Earth would have travelled to the position

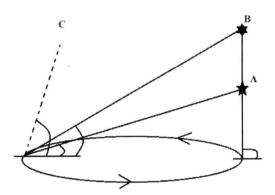

FIGURE 3.3   The stellar parallax

extreme left of its orbit, and the same star should not appear to be vertically over-head but at an angular elevation less than the right angle. But naked-eye obser-vation at that time revealed no such parallax and the star always appeared to be vertically overhead. The paradox can be explained if we consider the distance of the star from the Earth to be enormous as is really the case. If we consider a star at B at a greater distance than A, it is seen from the figure that its elevation at the extreme left point of the Earth's orbit is greater than that of A. If we increase the distance of the star more and more, the elevation will increase more and more and as the star be at an enormously large distance, the elevation will tend to a right angle making it appear to be vertically overhead to the naked eye. That the cause of not observ-ing the parallax with naked eye is the enormous distance of the stars was guessed by Copernicus about 2,000 years later. It may be mentioned, however, that such parallax can be and has been observed in recent times using powerful telescopes.

The explanation of the other two objections was clarified with works of Galileo and Newton about which we will discuss shortly.

The Medieval Europe

Ever since the Roman emperor Constantine (280–337 CE) adopted Christianity as the state religion, the Church gradually grew in stature. With passage of centuries, the Church started influencing the politics of the kingdoms apart from purely reli-gious matters. We find no significant advance in the realm of intellectual thoughts regarding the natural science in this period. The world was supposed to be gov-erned by the scriptures and no other conjectures were encouraged. The philoso-phers in this period were mostly dealing with theology. A very influential catholic philosopher was St. Thomas Aquinas (1225–1274 CE). He was very much familiar with Aristotle's works and interpreted his metaphysics in line with the scriptures. For example he proposed five ways to prove the existence of God and concluded that the Unmoved Mover of Aristotle was in fact God. It was found that the cos-mological model of Aristotle and Ptolemy was consistent with the preaching of the Bible except, probably, the assumption of a spherical Earth, while the scripture preached it to be flat. The universe must be geocentric, since God loves man, his greatest creation, and must have fixed a privileged place for him to live which is the centre of the universe. If we suppose that the Earth is just one of the planets mov-ing round the Sun, which is just one of an enormous family of stars, man loses his place of importance, thereby resulting in the loss of importance of the clergy also. So, the authority of Aristotle now became unquestioned and it created hindrance to progress. Anybody questioning the validity of the cosmology of Aristotle and Ptolemy would invite the wrath of the Catholic Church.

Nicholas Copernicus

Nicholas Copernicus (1473–1543 CE) was a Polish ecclesiastic of unimpeachable orthodoxy. He studied mathematics at the University of Cracow, law at Bologna, and medicine at Padua. In 1505, he returned to his native Poland, and spent the rest of his life in ecclesiastical duties. In Italy, he had sensed the excitement of the reawakening of the spirit of critical enquiry in Europe: the doctrine of Aristotle and Ptolemy was at last subject to fresh scrutiny. He had become convinced that in cosmology a much simpler system can be developed in which the spherical bodies rotated because of their sphericity and in which the Sun, not the Earth, was at the centre of things.

After his return to Poland in 1505, and for seven years, as a physician to his uncle the bishop of Ermeland, he had time to mature his ideas, but they were not fully committed to paper for another 18 years and not published for 31 years. Possibly, fear of ecclesiastical censure delayed publication of his views though he allowed them to become known. Finally, at the insistence of George Joachim, a professor of mathematics at Wittenberg, who devoted four years of his life as Copernicus's disciple, Copernicus allowed the publication of his celebrated work *De revolutionibus orbium celestium* (On the revolution of celestial orbits) in 1543. The first printed copy came from the press only a few weeks before he died. It was dedicated to the Pope and contained a preface by his friend Osiander saying that the heliocentric theory was put forward only as a hypothesis and not claimed to represent reality.

We find in his work that Copernicus advanced the model of the solar system with the Sun at the centre and planets, including the Earth, revolving round it. But he stuck to the Aristotelian belief of circular motion of the planets which necessarily needed epicycles and the eccentric deferent. But he showed that with the Sun at the centre, the calculations became much simpler and instead of Ptolemy's 78 epicycles, only 33 were now required to describe the motion of the planets. This simplification of calculations was his justification for his heliocentric model, which, as mentioned earlier, he claimed to be only a hypothesis and not representing reality. It is doubtful whether he really meant it, for it appears from his earlier works that he was convinced about the reality of this system and possibly talked about a hypothesis so as not to incur the wrath of the Church.

It may be mentioned at this point that Copernicus had at his disposal, the observational data used by Ptolemy and it was insufficiently detailed to sustain the heliocentric model. Fifty years later, Tycho Brahe, the Danish noble, made and recorded the necessary observations. He made a star catalogue and noted the positions of the planets throughout many years.

The Inquisition

The Inquisition was a powerful office set up by the Catholic Church to root out and punish heresy throughout Europe and America. It started its activities in the late twelfth century and continued for several hundred years, ruthlessly executing any dissenter. The inquisitors used to arrive in a town, announcing their presence and gave the citizens a chance to admit to heresy. Those who confessed were punished by pilgrimage or whipping and those who did not were tortured mercilessly and executed. In 1307, inquisitors were involved in the mass arrest of 15,000

Knights Templar in France, resulting in dozens of executions. Joan of Arc, burnt at stake in 1431, is the most famous victim of Inquisition. The Spanish Inquisition was infamous for its brutality and abuse of power.

In 1542, Pope Paul III created the Supreme Sacred Congregation of the Roman and Universal Inquisition to combat Protestant heresy. The Roman Inquisition did not spare the freethinkers who tried to challenge the old cosmological doctrines of Aristotle and Ptolemy.

Giordano Bruno

The Catholic Church did not show any intolerance or adverse reaction to the treatise of Copernicus, possibly ignoring it as just a mathematical exercise to simplify calculations and not claiming the heliocentric universe to be a physical reality. But it was not so with Giordano Bruno.

He was born as Filippo Bruno in February 1548, at Nola, about 17 miles north of Naples, and he entered the Dominican Convent of San Domenico Maggiore of Naples at the age of 17, assuming the name Giordano. He became a priest in 1572, and formally obtained his doctorate on theology in 1575. Bruno refuted Aristotle's natural philosophy, notably the idea that sublunary elements occupied or tried to return to their natural places of rest which are the elemental spheres at the centre of the universe. He also refuted Aristotle's contention that supralunar regions are made up of incorruptible aether that circled the Earth. Bruno asserted that the universe was infinite having no centre. The Earth was a planet revolving round the Sun like other planets and the universe was populated by innumerable solar systems. All the stars are just like our Sun and each of them has its own system of planets. He also thought that life might exist in any place of these worlds just like ours on Earth. His philosophy is known as the *cosmic pluralism*. Not only did Bruno defy Aristotle, but he also denied the divinity of Christ in line with what was known as the Arian heresy. As a result, a trial for heresy was prepared against him by the provincial father of his order.

Bruno fled from Naples, went first to Rome, and after wandering in northern Italy, he went to Geneva. He was now a fugitive from his order and excommunicate. Over the next 14 years or so, he moved from one city to another. He moved to France. Then in succession to Switzerland, England, Germany, and Bohemia. He was a brilliant teacher and an orator, but everywhere he invited trouble because of his unorthodox views. He mostly wrote on his cosmic views while in England, in 1584. Notable among his books were *La Cena de le Ceneri* (The Ash Wednesday Supper), *De la Causa, Principio et Uno* (On Cause, Principle and Unity) and *De l'infinito, Universo e Mondi* (On the Infinite, Universe and Worlds).

In 1591, he fatefully returned to Venice, on an invitation from the local patrician Giovanni Mocenigo. Bruno tried for the position of the chair of mathematics at the University of Padua but failed to get it. Then he spent a couple of months in Venice, before announcing his intention to leave for Germany. At this point, Mocenigo betrayed him and handed him over to the Venetian

Inquisition, charging him with blasphemy and heresy. It was 22 May 1592. After a year, Bruno's case was transferred to the Roman Inquisition, and Bruno was kept in imprisonment while his trial went on for seven years. The charges brought against him included denial of divinity of Christ, denial of holiness of Mother Mary, denial of eternal damnation and the Holy Trinity and so on. But topping them all was the charge of heresy for advocating plurality of worlds, removing the Earth from its privileged place at the centre of the universe. There have been attempts to underplay this charge by many scholars, but the fact remains that Pope Gregory XIII's corpus of canon law clearly stated that having the opinion of innumerable worlds was indeed heresy.

The judges, most prominent of whom was Cardinal Bellarmine, demanded a complete recantation from Bruno. Bruno denied the charges of blasphemy and refused to recant. *He neither needed nor wished to recant and did not know what he should recant.* On 20 January 1600, Pope Clement VIII ordered that Bruno be sentenced as an impertinent and pertinacious heretic. On 8 February 1600, the bench of judges passed a sentence of death against Bruno. It is said that Bruno, after hearing the sentence, addressed the judges and told them: *Perhaps your fear in passing the judgement on me is greater than mine in receiving it.*

He was handed over to the secular authority. On 17 February 1600, Giordano Bruno was marched to the Campo de' Fiori, the market square of Rome, naked and hands tied behind, his "wicked" tongue incapacitated with a metal plate clamping it. He was tied to a stake and, accompanied by the chants of the Confraternity of the beheading of St. John, was burnt alive.

A statue of Bruno has been erected in Campo de' Fiori in the nineteenth century after Rome was freed from the fear of the Inquisition. Bruno is now hailed as a martyr for science, a martyr for the freedom of thought.

1609, a Memorable Year

The cruel and awful end of Giordano Bruno could not suppress the voice of the freethinkers. Once the challenge to the old order starts, breaking the shackles of dogma, no power can ultimately subjugate it. The challenge itself becomes the order of the day and slowly the new order arises.

Hans Lippershey, a Dutch eye glass-maker, applied for a patent for the invention of telescope on 21 December 1607. In 1608, he claimed that the device made by him could magnify objects three times. A professor, holding the chair of mathematics at the University of Padua in Italy, heard about this invention, trained himself to grinding of lenses and made his own telescope. His telescope was an improvement upon the Dutch one because it produced an erect image of distant objects as opposed to inverted images in the Dutch telescopes, and also the magnification was 20 and not three. By the term magnification, one should not think that the actual size of the Sun or the Moon is magnified 20 times. It is the angle subtended by the Sun or the Moon or any other object at the eye which is magnified so that apparent diameter of the disc of the Sun or the Moon is magnified 20 times. Naturally, the details of the surface of the Sun or the Moon could now be observed that was impossible to be noted by the naked eye.

Now, this professor of mathematics at Padua set up his telescope in the garden of his house and looked up at the heavens through it on the night of 30 November 1609, as noted in his diary. The name of this professor was Galileo Galilei, and this event proved to be of epoch-making significance. Commemorating 400 years of observational astronomy by telescope, the year 2009 was declared by the United Nations as the International Year of Astronomy.

What did Galileo observe through his telescope? He observed that

1   The sunspots move on the surface of the Sun, they appear and disappear;
2   The surface of the Moon is just like that of the Earth, populated with mountains. Galileo drew analogy of these mountains with those at Bohemia;
3   Four moons of Jupiter circled round it periodically;
4   Venus has phases just like that of the Moon.

The sunspots, as we know today, are dark regions on the surface of the Sun whose temperature is less than that of the surroundings. They are created due to concentration of the magnetic field that inhibits convection. All these things were not known at the time of Galileo, but the temporary existence of the sunspots, their appearing and disappearing, clearly contradicted Aristotle's theory of the incorruptible and unchangeable aether of which the heavenly bodies were supposed to be made of. The argument became stronger when the surface of the Moon was found to be exactly like that of the Earth. Galileo started arguing that matter was not different in the sublunar and supralunar regions but had the same character everywhere.

The four moons of Jupiter proved to be another blow to the myth that the Earth was at the centre of the universe and everything revolved round it. For, here was another centre, Jupiter, about which four celestial objects revolved.

The phases of Venus strongly indicated the validity of the heliocentric model of the solar system as proposed by Copernicus. Because such phases could be explained only if Venus is placed between the Earth and the Sun and both the Earth and the Venus are allowed to revolve round the Sun.

Galileo started talking about his observations at dinner parties and in public debates in Florence. He thought that observation through telescopes would make the educated and learned people believe in the heliocentric system. But his attempts were in vain as the learned people from the Church or academics mostly refused even to look through the telescope. They passed remarks to the effect that the telescope was a devil's instrument and anything could be shown to be true by it.

Galileo did not react very kindly to such allegations. We find in a letter written by him in 1610, to Johannes Kepler, the German astronomer, the following text:

My dear Kepler, I wish that we might laugh at the remarkable stupidity of the common herd. What do you say about the principal philosophers of this academy who are filled with the stubbornness of an asp and do not want to look at either the planets, the moon or the telescope even though I have freely and deliberately offered them the opportunity a thousand times? Truly, just as the asp stops its ears, so do these philosophers shut their eyes to the light of truth.

Galileo and the Inquisition

To reach a bigger audience, Galileo started to write about his findings. In 1610, he published his book *Siderius Nuncius* (Starry Messenger) in which he wrote about his observations and conclusions in a direct and simple way, as opposed to the pedantic turgid manner of a university professor.

In 1613, he brought about another book, *Letters on the Sunspots*, in which he openly defended the Copernican heliocentric model. As Galileo wrote in Italian language, unlike the pedantic scholars who used to write in Latin, his writings became very popular and drew the attention of the clergy. Father Lorini complained to the Roman Inquisition against Galileo, charging him with heresy in preaching the heliocentric universe. The scripture clearly points to the fact that the Earth is at the centre of the universe and everything is moving round it. Any other opinion amounts to heresy. Particularly, a letter from Galileo to his disciple Castelli was mentioned in which Galileo remarked that the words of the scripture may not be taken literally and may be reinterpreted if it is found not to conform to reality. The Church appointed a group of "qualifiers" to assess the validity of the heliocentric system. The qualifiers opined that the heliocentric model was foolish and absurd and formally heretical. Pope Paul V directed Cardinal Bellarmine to summon before him the said Galileo Galilei and admonish him to abandon the said opinion, to abstain altogether from teaching or defending this opinion and even from discussing it.

The dictate of the Church forced Galileo to keep silent about the Copernican system. But he was encouraged to bring it again into the open when, in 1623, Cardinal Maffeo Berberini was elected Pope assuming the name Pope Urban VIII. The new Pope had long interactions with Galileo and Galileo thought that he would be sympathetic to the new doctrine if he could be convinced about its truth.

Galileo undertook to write a voluminous treatise of 500 pages which, after much dilly-dallying, was published in February 1632. The title of the book was *Dialogue Concerning the Two Chief World Systems*. It was written in the form of a dialogue between three people: Salviatti, a sublime intellectual who supported the Copernican view; Sagredo, a Venetian noble man who was open-minded to accept rational arguments and Simplicio, a stubborn defender of the Earth-centred universe. Needless to say that, through the dialogues the heliocentric system emerged victorious, and Simplicio was made to look like a fool with his bland arguments. But what annoyed the Pope was that the arguments put in the mouth of Simplicio were *the* arguments that he himself had advanced earlier to Galileo.

The machinery of the church swung into action. Galileo was summoned to appear before the Inquisition in September 1632. Galileo, a septuagenarian old man with frail health, came to Rome in February 1633. His trial began and went on for weeks. Galileo was interrogated while threatened with physical torture. A panel of theologians reported that the *Dialogue* taught the heretical Copernican view. Galileo was found guilty and the majority of the cardinals demanded that Galileo be made to abjure, even under the threat of torture in a plenary assembly of congregation and then be imprisoned.

On 22 June 1633, the judgement was pronounced by the Inquisition. Galileo was found "vehemently suspect of heresy", having held the opinion that the Sun lies motionless at the centre of the universe, that the Earth is not at the centre and moves and having defended such opinion even after it has been declared contrary to the Holy Scripture, and hence he was required to abjure, curse and detest those opinions.

The sentence continued as,

> and so that you will be more cautious in future and as an example for others to abstain from delinquencies of this sort, we order that the book Dialogue of Galileo be prohibited by public edict. We condemn you to formal imprisonment in the Holy Office at our pleasure. . . As a salutary penance, we impose on you to recite the seven penitential psalms thrice a week.

The old man could not bear the threat of physical torture. After hearing the judgement, he knelt to recite his abjuration:

> Desiring to remove from the minds of your Eminences, and of all faithful Christians, this strong suspicion, reasonably conceived against me, with sincere heart and unfeigned faith I abjure, curse and detest the aforesaid errors and heresies and generally every other error and sect whatsoever contrary to the said Holy Church and I swear that in the future I will never again say or assert verbally or in writing anything that might furnish occasion for a similar suspicion against me.

According to popular legend, Galileo had, after his abjuration, muttered the rebellious phrase "*Eppursimuove*" (And yet it moves).

Not only that his book *Dialogue* was banned, in an action not announced at the trial, publication of any of his works was forbidden, including anything that he might write in future.

His imprisonment was later commuted to house arrest for life and he spent the rest of his life at his villa at Arcetri near Florence.

Galileo's Mechanics, Beginning of the New Science

During the period of his house arrest, Galileo undertook to commit to writing, his findings on mechanics through the extensive experiments that he performed in his earlier life. Thus was composed the book *Discorsi e dimostrazioni matematiche intorno a due nuove scienze* (*Discourses and Mathematical Demonstrations Relating to Two New Sciences*), which was possibly the first such treatise to affirm the importance of controlled experiments and drawing correct conclusions from them logically.

Though publication of any work by Galileo was prohibited by the Church, *nullo excepto*, he managed to get the manuscript of this book smuggled to neighbouring Holland, where it was published in 1638. Galileo went blind by this time and died in 1642, at the age of 77.

This *Discoursi*, much in the same manner as his earlier *Dialogue* on two world systems, was written in the form of conversations between the same three characters, namely Salviatti, Sagredo and Simplicio.

The two new sciences referred to in the title are related to kinematics and strength of materials. Kinematics is a division of mechanics that is concerned with description of motion. It is not possible to discuss all the aspects of kinematics that have been dealt with in this dialogue. But we will mention a few, that about falling bodies and inertia, which changed the Aristotelian way of looking at the nature once and for all.

We may recall that according to Aristotle, up and down motions in the sublunar region are natural motions, as the elements tend to seek their natural places of rest. Materials made of the element earth tend to go down, seeking the centre of the universe lying below the surface of the planet Earth. Aristotle also asserted that bodies of different weights fall through the same medium with different speeds, speeds which are proportional to their weights.

Let us see the classic argument that Salviatti advanced to disprove this proposition.

SALVIATTI: Tell me Simplicio, whether you admit that each falling body acquires a definite speed fixed by nature, a velocity which cannot be increased or diminished except by use of force or resistance.

SIMPLICIO: There can be no doubt. . .

SALVIATTI: If then we take two bodies whose natural speeds are different, it is clear that on uniting the two, the more rapid one will be partly retarded by the slower, and the slower will be somewhat hastened by the swifter. Do you not agree with me in this opinion?

SIMPLICIO: You are unquestionably right.

SALVIATTI: But if this is true, and if a large stone moves with a speed of say, eight while a smaller moves with a speed of four, then when they are united, the system will move with a speed less than eight, but the two stones tied together make a stone larger than that which before moved with a speed of eight. Hence the heavier body moves with less speed than the lighter, an effect which is contrary to your supposition. Thus you see how, from your assumption that the heavier body moves more rapidly than the lighter one, I infer that the heavier body moves more slowly.

At this point, Simplicio says that he is at sea and cannot understand how the smaller stone tied with the larger one increases its weight but decreases its speed. Here,

Salviatti makes a very important observation that it is necessary to distinguish between heavy bodies in motion and the same bodies at rest. A large stone placed on a balance will acquire additional weight even if we place a handful of hemp on it, but if we tie the hemp with the stone and allow them to fall freely, the hemp will not be able to press down upon the stone and so its weight will not increase, if they fall with same rapidity. It would be the same as *trying to strike a man with a lance when he is running away from you with a speed which is equal to that with which you are following him.*

Salviatti then disproves another supposition of Aristotle that the speed of fall of a body is inversely proportional to the density of the medium through which it is falling. We may recall that from such an argument, Aristotle denied the existence of vacuum saying that the speed of fall through vacuum would be infinity, its density being zero. Salviatti says, let us assume that a wooden ball falls through air with a speed of 20 and that the density of water is ten times that of air. Then, as per Aristotle, the wooden ball should fall through water with a speed of two. But, in practice, it is seen not to fall at all but rise though water. Simplicio objects by saying that Aristotle did not talk about such material which falls through air but rises through water but about such materials which fall both through air and water. The next discourse was as follows:

SALVIATTI: Since the wooden ball does not go to the bottom, I think you will agree with me that we can find a ball of another material, not wood, which does fall in water with a speed of two.

SIMPLICIO: Undoubtedly we can, but it must be of a substance considerably heavier than wood.

SALVIATTI: That is it exactly. But if this second ball falls in water with a speed of two, what will be its speed of descent in air? If you hold to the rule of Aristotle you must reply that it will move at the rate twenty; but twenty is the speed which you yourself have already assigned to the wooden ball; hence this and the other heavier ball will each move through air with the same speed. But now how does the philosopher harmonize this result with the other, namely that bodies of different weights move through the same medium with different speeds, speeds which are proportional to their weights?

Through such decisive and razor-sharp arguments, Galileo, through Salviatti makes Aristotle contradict himself in all points regarding terrestrial motion. Salviatti finally remarks that the difference of speed between bodies of different specific gravities is most marked in those media which are the most resistant as can be readily observed. In a medium of quicksilver (mercury), gold sinks to the bottom more rapidly than lead but all other metals and stones not even sink but rise to the surface. But in air, the variations of speed between balls of gold, lead, copper etc. are very slight and falling from a certain height, all of them reach the ground almost simultaneously. Salviatti says: *Having observed this, I came to the conclusion that in a medium totally devoid of resistance all bodies would fall with the same speed.*

We will now describe briefly the experimental set-up used by Galileo to arrive at the laws of falling bodies. This is important because it will show how Galileo introduced the method of controlled experimentation in science for establishing a theory, not just depending on the mental exercise of making intelligent conjectures, as has been the practice of the Greeks.

To establish that all bodies fall with equal rapidity in a medium devoid of any resistance, it was first necessary to measure the time of vertical fall of a body from a reasonable height. Let us just forget the myth that Galileo established his theory by letting fall a heavy and a light body from the top of the leaning tower of Pisa. It is very much doubtful how such attempts would succeed in verifying the proposition. But Galileo describes clearly how he did it in the laboratory, which is nothing but a big room.

From a small height, a body falls very rapidly to the ground, and Galileo did not have a watch to measure such times very accurately. There was of course no electronic stopwatch and not even the pendulum clocks were developed. But the time to fall down an *inclined plane* would be somewhat greater since to describe a certain vertical height, the distance covered along the inclined plane would be greater and the body would roll down the plane less rapidly than in a vertical fall. So, Galileo measured the time of fall along the inclined planes, described in the following.

> A piece of wooden moulding or scantling, about 12 cubits*long, half a cubit wide and three finger breadths thick, was taken; on its edge was cut a channel a little more than one finger in breadth; having made this groove very straight, smooth and polished, and having lined it with parchment, also as smooth and polished as possible, we rolled along it a hard, smooth and very round bronze ball. Having placed this board in a sloping position, by lifting one end some one or two cubits above the other, we rolled the ball, noting the time of descent . . . for the measurement of time, we employed a large vessel of water placed in an elevated position; to the bottom of this vessel was soldered a pipe of small diameter giving a thin jet of water, which we collected in a small glass during the time of each descent, whether for the whole length of the channel or for a part of its length; the water thus collected was weighed after each descent on a very accurate balance; the differences and ratios of these weights gave us the differences and ratios of the times of descent.

From this description, it transpires what is meant by controlled experiment. In an experiment, we ask some specific questions to nature. To get the answer, we have to eliminate any stray effect that might interfere with the result, which is the answer we want from nature. The aim of Galileo was to see whether bodies of any weight fall with equal rapidity through a medium which is totally devoid of resistance. To make the channel on the edge of the board as devoid of resistance as possible, it was made smooth and polished and lined with parchment paper. Let us now see what Galileo did with the inclined planes.

*Cubit was used as a unit of length, being equal to the length of the arm from the elbow to the tip of the middle finger, measuring approximately 45 cm.

Let AC be the inclined plane and two balls of different sizes but of same material were rolled down this plane. The balls would obviously be of different weights. The times of descent of both balls were measured and found to be almost the same. The experiment was repeated by changing the inclination of the plane. As shown in Figure 3.4, the plane may be shifted to the position AD having a different inclination. But whatever be the inclination of the plane, the times of descent of both the lighter and heavier balls were always found to be almost the same. The conclusion was that the time of fall of both balls would be exactly equal if the little resistance of the plane could be completely eliminated and that *the equality of the time of descent of both balls does not depend on the slope of the inclined plane*. A vertical fall in vacuum is nothing but rolling down a completely smooth plane of inclination 90° to the horizontal. Hence, *all bodies fall in vacuum with equal rapidity*.

Now the time of fall of a ball along the whole length was compared to its time of fall through a part of the length of the board. On repeating the experiment many times, and for many fractions of the length, it was found that *the distance covered by a body in descent was proportional to the square of the time taken for the descent*. And since this result was valid for any slope of the plane, it must be valid for vertical fall also.

The dependence of the distance covered on the square of the time of descent could be explained only if the ball descended *not with uniform speed but with a speed that changed proportionally with time. So, falling was an accelerated motion*.

Thus, for the first time in science, the concept of acceleration was introduced. The free fall of a body was an accelerated motion and the role of the medium was to alter this acceleration according to the resistance it offers.

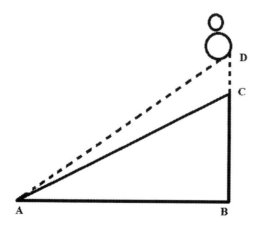

FIGURE 3.4 Galileo's experiment with the inclined planes

Anticipating Inertia

Galileo was the first person to anticipate the law of inertia but could not quite arrive at it. Again, he performed experiments with inclined planes, which were the wooden planks as already described. Let us examine the following diagram shown in Figure 3.5.

AO is an inclined plane whose vertical height is AB. CO is another inclined plane of the same vertical height and the two planes are facing each other. A round bronze ball is rolled along AO. The junction at O is made a little roundish so that the ball may not find much resistance in climbing up the plane OC from O after rolling down the plane AB. It is observed that the ball more or less rises to the same vertical height along OC from which it climbed down. It may be inferred that had there been no resistance, the ball would have climbed to exactly the same vertical height. Now, if we make the second plane less steep and keep it in the position, say, OD, we will again observe that the ball, after descending through AO, has climbed to the point D having the same vertical height. It is thus clear that the ball after reaching the foot of the first plane will always seek to attain the same vertical height along the second plane, whatever be its inclination.

But in attaining the same height, the ball has to describe a greater distance along the second plane if its slope is less. The distance OD is greater than OC. If we go on making the second plane less and less inclined to the horizontal, the ball will have to traverse greater and still greater distances in attaining the height and in the limit when the second plane becomes horizontal, the ball will seek to attain the same height but will never be able to do so and will therefore continue to move along the horizontal plane forever.

We get the first glimpse of inertia of motion. If there be no force acting in the horizontal direction, a body would naturally go on moving in that direction. But after this brilliant experimental procedure, Galileo somehow loses the actual perspective. He is thinking about the unending horizontal motion as horizontal only locally. He says that this horizontal path is a small part of the big circle that goes along the Earth and completes a round trip along its spherical surface. Thus, Galileo came to the wrong conclusion that without any force, a body would naturally move along a circle.

However, with the concept of inertia of motion along a locally horizontal path in the absence of any force, Galileo brilliantly demonstrated why a ball dropped

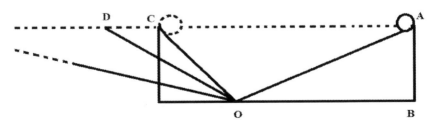

FIGURE 3.5   Galileo's experiment with the inclined planes to anticipate the law of inertia

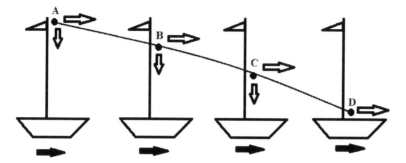

FIGURE 3.6 Galileo's experiment with the ship and the ball

from the top of the mast of a ship moving with uniform speed will reach exactly the bottom of the mast (See Figure 3.6).

Let the ball be dropped from A. At the time of dropping, the ball was moving with the same horizontal velocity as that of the ship. As there is no force acting on the ball in the horizontal direction (neglecting the small air resistance), both the ship and the ball will move equally in the horizontal direction and describe the same horizontal distance in a certain interval of time. But due to some gravitating force downward, the motion of the ball will be accelerated in the vertical direction, Thus, as shown in the figure, at points B, C or D, the ball and the ship would have the same horizontal location, but the ball will move vertically downward relative to the ship and finally reach the bottom of the mast.

With this demonstration, the second objection against the heliocentric model as enunciated in the section **Aristarchus and heliocentricity** could now be resolved. If a stone be dropped vertically from a height above the surface of the Earth, the stone and the Earth will have the same horizontal velocity and would move through the same horizontal distance during the time of fall. A person on Earth then will see only the vertical motion of the stone and so it will reach a point vertically below the starting point.

It may be noted that here we have not considered the spinning motion of the Earth. Taking that into consideration, the stone will be found to be deviated slightly from the exactly vertical path due to pseudo forces like the Coriolis force and the centrifugal force.

It is also to be noted, examining the diagram of the moving ship and the falling ball, that a person standing on the shore will observe both the horizontal and the vertical motion of the ball, as if the ball has been projected horizontally with the velocity of the ship and from the figure, it is clear that to the observer, the trajectory of the ball would be a curved path. Throughout the previous centuries, people thought that a stone thrown horizontally will move exactly horizontally for some distance due to the impetus provided by the rushing air behind it and then move exactly vertically down which is its natural motion. This idea of Aristotle was also negated by Galileo.

Tycho Brahe and Johannes Kepler

The story of evolution of ideas in the field of celestial mechanics will remain incomplete unless the contribution of the two persons mentioned in the heading is discussed. Tycho Brahe, a Danish nobleman was born three years after the publication of Copernicus's *De Revolutionibus*. He was fortunate in being able to follow academic studies in different centres of learning like Copenhagen, Leipzig, Wittenberg, Rostock, and Augsburg. Before he was 30, he secured the patronage of the king and set up an observatory at Uraniborg, with as many instruments as possible.

Brahe made a thorough and systematic observation of the heavens and prepared an accurate chart of the location and movement of the fixed stars and the planets. Copernicus had at his disposal the old charts prepared during the time of Ptolemy and lacked accuracy. Tycho Brahe corrected all the data. He was indeed the greatest observer of the pre telescopic era. In his *De nova stella* (On the new star) of 1573, he refuted the Aristotelian claim of an unchanging celestial world through his observation of the brightness of the supernova that appeared in November 1572. He also observed the great comet of 1577, and correctly inferred that this object was not a member of the sublunar world. Brahe tried to theorize his observation by combining the geometry of Copernicus with the philosophy of Aristotle. He concluded correctly that the Moon was orbiting the Earth, and the planets were orbiting the Sun, but he incorrectly thought that the Sun, with its planets was orbiting the Earth, which was at the centre of the universe.

Brahe left Denmark in 1597, after the death of his patron King Frederick II and on invitation of the Bohemian king and Holy Roman Emperor Rudolph II, he settled near Prague and reassembled his equipment to set up an observatory at the castle of Benatky. Tycho died in 1601, and the vast material compiled by him was left to his successor Johannes Kepler.

Kepler was born in 1571, at Weil der Stadt, Wurttemberg, Germany. His parents were ill educated and not well off. His father left the family when Johannes was five years old, and his mother was a healer and a herbalist. When Kepler was nearly 50 years old, his mother was arrested for practising witchcraft and Kepler had to exert all his influence to secure her release.

All schooling in Germany, as elsewhere, was under the control of church institutions – Roman Catholic or Protestant. Local rulers used the churches as a means of consolidating the loyalty of their populations. One way of achieving this was a system of scholarships for the poor boys, who, after their training period is over, would be completely faithful to the local ruler. Kepler was a beneficiary of the ducal scholarship, which enabled him to attend the seminary at the University of Tubingen. Kepler had planned to become a theologian, but his life did not work out quite as he expected. At Tubingen, the professor of mathematics was Michael Maestlin, who, privately, was an adherent of the Copernican theory and introduced Kepler to it. In the Copernican theory, Kepler saw a divine planning. He always held that God created the universe to be governed by certain rules and wanted man, a creation in his own image, to comprehend it. Kepler used to remark that he was thinking God's thoughts.

In 1596, Kepler published a dissertation in which he described a complicated figure. He took five regular polyhedra: octahedron, icosahedron, dodecahedron, tetrahedron and a cube. Now, the figure was so constructed that the circumscribed sphere of the octahedron was the inscribed sphere of the icosahedrons; the circumscribed sphere of the icosahedron was the inscribed sphere of the dodecahedron and so on. He claimed that the radii of these spheres from the centre outwards were in proportion as the mean distances of the five planets from the Sun. This essay in geometrical mysticism brought him the gratifying reward of correspondence with Galileo and Tycho Brahe.

In 1598, the archduke Ferdinand issued a decree of banishment against the Protestant professors. Although Kepler was spared immediate exile, he was happy to accept Brahe's offer of appointment as his personal assistant at the observatory at the castle of Benatky. After the death of Brahe in 1601, the emperor Rudolph II appointed Kepler to succeed Brahe. From this time, until his death in 1630, at least he had no lack of observational material on which to work and against which to test his hypothesis.

Tycho Brahe had systematically observed the motion of the planets and the stars throughout the whole year, and year after year continually. He had observed the apparent motion of Mars in this way for 13 years, and Kepler was advised to concentrate on these data for his formulation. Kepler did that painstakingly and it was nearly ten years before he achieved what he wanted. After postulating one shape after another for the orbit of Mars, at last he fitted its trajectory with that of an ellipse and concluded that the planet moves along an elliptical path round the Sun with the Sun at one of its foci. Similarly, after postulating one law of velocity after another, finally he could formulate the law of area, that is the straight line joining the Sun and the planet sweeps out equal areas in equal intervals of time. This automatically implies that the velocity of the planet is not constant. It is maximum when it is nearest to the Sun (perihelion) and minimum when it is furthest from the Sun (aphelion). He tested his assumptions on the Earth and found them satisfactory. He did not wait to confirm that the motion of the other planets could be similarly described. He assumed that the two laws must be true for all planets and time proved him to be right.

In 1609, he published his work titled *Astronomia Nova* (*New Astronomy*) containing the first two laws, that of elliptical orbit and the law of area for the planetary motion. It took him nine more years to formulate the third law, which in the modern language reads as: the square of the periodic times of the planets are in the ratios of the cubes of their mean distances from the Sun. This third law was described in his book *Harmonices Mundi* (*Harmony of the World*), published in 1619. By this time, Kepler has consolidated the observations of Brahe on more distant planets, Jupiter and Saturn and also on Venus and Mercury, verifying the first and second laws for them.

Kepler formulated the geometry of planetary motions but could not describe it in terms of cause and effect. He had an idea that the Sun had a motive power to move the planets, but he was influenced by Gilbert's theory of magnets and thought that the Sun is forcing the planets to move by magnetic attraction and repulsion.

A word about the retrograde motion of planets. The reader may recall that in the background of the fixed stars, the planets move slowly from west to east, but the distant planets like Jupiter, Mars or Saturn are seen to move backward for some time before again moving forward. In the geocentric model of Ptolemy, such retrograde motion was accounted for by complicated epicycles and the eccentric deferent. But once we put the Earth along with other planets in elliptical orbits round the Sun, there is no need to take help of such complicated figures. The Earth is moving round the Sun with a speed greater than far-away planets. Suppose, during its journey, the Earth is approaching Jupiter. Jupiter will appear to move in the same direction as the Earth till the Earth overtakes it. At the time of overtaking, Jupiter would appear to move backward as it would be left behind while the Earth advances. But after some time, when both planets have advanced sufficiently, again the Earth would be approaching Jupiter and Jupiter would appear to move forward.

Kepler breathed his last in 1630. In passing, it may be mentioned that he contributed significantly to the field of optics through his books *Astronomia pars optica* (*Optical Part of Astronomy*) and *Dioptrics* in which he explained the inverse square law of intensity of light, properties of double convex and double concave lenses, designed an astronomical telescope with two convex lenses and also discussed how inverted image was cast on the retina by the eye lens.

Rene Descartes

Rene Descartes, born in 1596, at La Haye of France, has been considered as the founder of modern philosophy, according to Bertrand Russell. Russell has also remarked that "he is the first man of high philosophic capacity whose outlook is profoundly affected by new physics and astronomy".

As a philosopher, his methodology for arriving at the truth was scepticism. One has to doubt everything and judge everything in the light of reasoning. He is quite famous for his statement *cogito, ergo sum*, meaning "I think, so I exist". Thus, his ontological argument is that thinking is the final proof of existence since it cannot be doubted that thinking is inseparable from being.

In the field of mathematics, Descartes is known for developing the subject of coordinate geometry, where one can discuss geometrical figures in terms of algebra. Here his original contribution was the way to locate a point in space by means of its distances from mutually perpendicular fixed straight lines called the Cartesian coordinates. Most of his philosophical and scientific works were done during his 20 years of residence in Holland, from 1629 to 1649.

He had planned to publish a book titled *Le Monde* (*The World*) in which he would discuss his views on the universe. But he withheld its publication in 1633, when he heard of the trial of Galileo, as he has advocated the heliocentric theory and the theory of many worlds. His fear seems to be a little unfounded, for Holland was the place where freethinking was allowed and nobody had to fear the Inquisition.

However, Descartes put forth his views on metaphysics and science in the books *Discourse on the Method of Rightly Conducting One's Reason and Seeking Truth in the Sciences* published in 1637, and in *Principia Philosophiae* (Principles of philosophy) published in 1644. Descartes advanced a mechanistic view of the world, saying that motion or any other change takes place according to some fixed laws of nature and that God, while creating the world, wished it to behave in that fashion. This idea is in direct contradiction to Aristotelian view that every motion, that is change occurs to serve some purpose. Let us examine the laws of nature that Descartes proposed.

> Law I states that each thing, as far as in its power, always remains in the same state, and that consequently when it is once moved, it always continues to move.
>
> Law II states that all movement is, of itself, always along straight lines.
>
> Law III states that a body upon coming in contact with a stronger one, loses none of its motion; but that, upon coming in contact with a weaker one, it loses as much as it transfers to that weaker body.

Descartes was no experimentalist. He conceived his laws of nature through pure thinking and considering the data about collision of bodies available at that time. But one may note that his first two laws combined together resemble strongly Newton's first law of motion. He recognized that a motion, once started, will continue forever in a straight line and cannot stop by itself without an external influence. He said that rest and motion are opposite to one another and that nothing moves by its own nature towards its opposite or its own destruction. On this aspect, he was erroneous and Newton put the state or rest or of uniform motion in a straight line on the same footing, not taking them in opposition to one another. But Descartes must be given his due credit for almost hitting upon the correct principle of inertia and may be considered to be the immediate predecessor of Newton in this regard.

Regarding the third law, which deals with collision or impact of one body with another, Descartes talks about a quantity called motion. He defined motion as the *product of the size and speed of each impacting body.* He also remarked that *when God created the universe, a certain fixed amount of motion was transmitted to its material occupants; a quantity that God continuously preserves at each succeeding moment.*

It may be noted that in the hands of Newton, the quantity of motion was correctly changed to what we now know as the *momentum*, which is the product of not the size and speed but the product of mass and velocity of a body. But it is quite transparent that Descartes was talking about a principle, the principle of the conservation of motion in his third law, a predecessor to the principle of conservation of momentum as enunciated by Newton.

Descartes also recognized what nowadays we know as the centrifugal force. If one stands on a rotating body, one feels a tendency to fly outward. If we whirl a stone in a circular path by tying a rope to it, the stone pulls on the rope in the outward direction. Descartes called it as a centre-fleeing tendency but erroneously thought that if the rope is cut, the stone would fly radially outward which is not true; it would move tangentially out of the circle, since at the time of detachment, its velocity was in the tangential direction and after detachment, no force would be acting on it to change that direction.

Descartes also tried to give his theory about celestial motions. But he denied the existence of vacuum and was much preoccupied with some vortices round the Sun, by means of which the Sun is forcing the planets to move round it.

The philosophy and science of Descartes highly influenced later masterminds like Newton, Leibnitz, Bacon, Locke, Hobbs and Spinoza.

Galileo fought the Aristotelian dogma regarding both the terrestrial and the celestial phenomena. In the sublunar region, he anticipated the law of inertia, though not to its final form. He found the laws of falling bodies and talked about relativity of motions. In the celestial sphere, he supported the heliocentric universe on the basis of his telescopic observations and also concluded that matter is not different in the sublunar and supralunar regions. All are subject to change. Kepler, based on observations of Tycho Brahe, finally established the correct laws related to orbits of the planets round the Sun. Through him, ultimately the ghost of "perfect circular motion" of planets left the arena of science. Descartes has more or less pronounced the law of inertia and dethroned Aristotelian teleological argument for motion. According to him, nature works as per some definite laws, which are fixed and they do not serve any so-called purpose. He has also recognized what nowadays we know as the centrifugal force. The stage was now set. The world was ready for the appearance of a genius who would synthesize the existing knowledge and light up the true path along which science would progress.

Annus Mirabilis

The Latin phrase *Annus Mirabilis* literally means "the miraculous year". "Annus Mirabilis" was a poem written by John Dryden to celebrate the victory of the English fleet over the Dutch in 1666, and also the survival of the city of London, from the great fire of that year. But the same term was used later to celebrate Newton's great achievements during the same year and was called Newton's miraculous year.

Galileo died on 8 January 1642 and Newton was born in the same year on 25 December. However, this date is as per the old Julian calendar. According to the new calendar, the modified date would be 4 January 1643. He was born at the manor house of Woolsthorpe, Licolnshire, and his father had died before he was born. His maternal uncle looked after his education and after the initial schooling at the King's School at Grantham, he went to Trinity College, Cambridge in 1661, as an undergraduate. In August 1665, the institute was closed down as the Great Plague broke out as an epidemic in London. Newton came back to his manor house at Woolsthorpe, and he spent the two subsequent years there before coming back to Cambridge in April 1667. In later years, Newton recapitulated his years at Woolsthorpe and wrote:

> *In the beginning of the year 1665 I found the method of approximating series & the rule for reducing any dignity of any Binomial into such a series. The same year in May I found the method of tangents . . . & in November had the direct method of fluxions & the next year in January had the Theory of colours & in May following I had entrance into the inverse method of fluxions. And in the same year I began to think of gravity extending to the orb of the Moon & having found out how to estimate the force with which a globe revolving within a sphere presses the surface of a sphere: from Kepler's Rule of the periodic times of the Planets being in sesquialterate proportion of their distances from the centre of their orbs, I deduced that the forces which keep the Planets in their orbs must be reciprocally as the squares of their distances from the centres about which they revolve & thereby compared the force requisite to keep the Moon in her orb with the force of gravity at the surface of the Earth, & found them answer pretty nearly. All this was done in the two plague years of 1665 and 1666. For in those days, I was in the prime of my age for invention and minded Mathematics and philosophy more than at any time since.*

The language used by Newton may seem to be a bit tough to present-day readers. In modern language it means that at the age of 23, what Newton achieved in the plague years were the following.

1   He developed the mathematics of generalized binomial theorem. The binomial theorem is a series expansion of the expression $(1+x)^n$, and Newton found the series for any exponent n, be it an integer or a fraction.
2   He developed a direct method of fluxions, which is nowadays known as the differential calculus.
3   Then he formulated his theory of colours, that is he found that white light can be decomposed into its constituent seven colours and the seven colours may be combined to produce white light.
4   Next, he developed the inverse method of fluxions, that is integral calculus.
5   Then he started thinking about the Earth's gravity regulating the orbit of the Moon. He found out how to calculate the force "with which a globe revolving within a sphere presses on the surface of the sphere" which is actually the centrifugal force, the outward force that we feel if we ride a carriage that revolves. Then, from Kepler's third law of planetary motion, stating that the periodic times of the planets are in the ratio of "sesquialterate" of their distances from the centres of the orbit (meaning that the time period T varies as $R^{3/2}$ where R is the distance of the planet from the centre of the orbit), he deduced that the forces necessary to keep the planets in their orbits vary inversely as the squares of their distances from the centre of the orbits. Finally, he says that with this inverse square dependence of gravitational force, he

compared the force required to keep the Moon in its orbit and the force that a body feels while resting on the surface of the Earth and that his calculations tallied fairly well with observations.

All these were achieved by a young man at a time when no formal science existed at all, apart from intelligent conjectures and attempts to grasp the truth. Even a single discovery of this level would earn anybody a global recognition and eternal fame. No wonder people thought it befitting to name the year 1665–1666 as the "miraculous year of Newton".

I would like to draw the attention of the reader to point 5 mentioned earlier. Newton says that he started to think about the Earth's gravity extending to the orbit of the Moon and that he has compared the force required to keep the Moon in its orbit and the force that is exerted on a body at rest on the surface of the Earth. This clearly demonstrates that Newton was already fairly convinced that the same law of gravitation worked on the surface of the Earth as well as at the orbit of the Moon. However, he did not publish his results for 21 years and kept silent. We will come back to this point a little later. But let us first examine what Newton did in the field of mechanics.

It is well known that Newton formulated three laws of motion that are supposed to govern the motion of *everything* in this universe, be it a disc rolling on the ground or be it a planet moving round a star. In his celebrated treatise, *Principia*, Newton stated these three laws along with eight definitions and six corollaries. After Galileo and Descartes, Newton finally hit upon the correct law of inertia which is his first law of motion.

> A body continues to be in the state of rest or of uniform motion in a straight line except so far as it be compelled by an external impressed force to change that state.

The tendency of a body to continue to be at rest or uniform rectilinear motion has been defined as inertia, and the external action that changes or tends to change such states has been defined as force. It is to be noted that this mechanical definition of force does not conform to our everyday idea of the term, since we are accustomed to think about force as a muscular power with which a living being pushes or pulls a body, and we also understand that application of such a force needs a contact or link between the driver and the driven. Inanimate objects can also apply force but only at the time of an impact or collision. But after Newton, such ideas had to be changed. We have to infer the existence of a force only by looking at a body whose velocity is changing. If the velocity of the body increases, decreases, or its direction of motion is changed, we have to infer that the body is acted upon by a force. The cause of this change, that is the force, is originated outside the body. We may recognize some external agent to be responsible for applying this force, but it does not matter if this agent and the body be in contact or not, nor does it matter if they are not linked by a chain or rope-like mechanism. It is not impossible for one inanimate body to exert force on another inanimate body from a distance, without any link. Newton did not bother about finding the mechanism of application of force, it was sufficient to find a mathematical expression for it.

In light of this concept, the law of universal gravitation is to be examined. According to this law, enunciated by Newton, *every particle of matter in the universe attracts every other particle with a force that acts along the straight line joining them and is proportional to the product of their masses and inversely proportional to the square of the distance between them.*

One cannot but feel amazed by the sheer depth and universality of this law. It connects *every* particle of matter with every other particle in the universe. It truly unifies the terrestrial and the celestial worlds. The same force that causes a piece of unsupported stone to fall down near the surface of the Earth also causes a planet to move round the Sun.

If one feels a bit disturbed and thinks that if the Sun attracts the planet in the same manner as the Earth attracts a stone, then the planet should head towards the surface of the Sun and fall down on it instead of revolving round it, then one may examine the diagram shown in Figure 3.7.

If a stone is projected at an angle with the horizontal from the surface of the Earth, it describes a curved path and falls down due to the force of gravity. If it is projected with a higher speed, it will fall down at a point further away. If the speed of projection be increased beyond a certain limiting value, the stone will try to fall but now it cannot find a point on the spherical surface where to touch down. It will continuously fall, that is go on revolving round the Earth.

The point is that if a body is already in motion at an angle with the direction of the attracting force, the force will not pull the body towards the centre of attraction but will change its direction of motion and cause it to describe a curved path. So the planets must have been initially in motion and the Sun's attraction simply changed their directions of motion and kept them in their orbits.

Aristotle's natural circular motion of the heavenly bodies did not remain natural any more. The circular motion is a forced motion, the force being required continuously to act on the body to change its direction of motion.

Newton of course could not know the theories advanced by later astronomers for formation of planets. There are many such theories. As per the tidal theory,

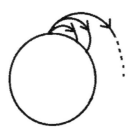

FIGURE 3.7 The stone-throwing experiment

bulks of masses were ejected at a high speed from the Sun when a massive star passed by it (just like a stone thrown at an angle with the horizontal from the surface of the Earth with a very high speed) and so they went on orbiting the Sun. As per the nebular hypothesis, the Sun and the planets were formed by gravitational collapse of a giant molecular mass. But whatever be the mechanism for formation of the solar system, the basic fact arising out of Newtonian mechanics remains valid, that the gravitational attractive force of the Sun simply changes the direction of motion of the planets continuously to keep them in their orbit.

At this point, we intend to provide an explanation for the first objection against the heliocentric doctrine proposed by Aristarchus. The objection ran like this: if the Earth moves round the Sun, it must also spin about its own axis to explain the occurrence of day and night. But on a spinning Earth, we will feel the outward force, that is the centrifugal force, and will be thrown into space. Now, Newton has calculated this centrifugal force and also the gravitational force that binds a body on the Earth's surface. It is now known that at the equator, the gravitational attraction of the Earth will be more than 300 times stronger than the centrifugal force, and so it is no wonder that we are not thrown out into the space from the surface of the Earth.

We have slightly digressed from the discussion of the nature or mechanism of the gravitational force. As per the mechanical definition of force, we have to conclude that a force is acting on a planet since its direction of motion is changing. We may search for the external agent which is applying this force and identify the Sun as the origin of the force. But the Sun is not a living being, having no muscular power, and the Sun is not in contact with the planet nor is it tied with the planet by some rope. How can it apply the force then? Newtonian physics provides no answer. In later life, Newton has remarked: *it is inconceivable that a brute matter (i.e. the Sun) can act at a point (i.e. the site of the planet) where it is not*. But Newton did not try to make any conjecture as to how it was possible. He has only described the observed phenomenon. He uttered his famous phrase in this regard: *hypotheses non fingo* (I make no hypothesis). In an essay titled "General Scholium", appended to the second edition of *Principia*, he wrote:

> I have not as yet been able to discover the reason for these properties of gravity from phenomena and I do not make any hypothesis. For whatever is not deduced from the phenomena must be called a hypothesis and hypotheses . . . have no place in experimental philosophy.

We have been discussing the nature of the gravitational force in the light of the mechanical definition of force arising out of the first law of motion. The first law of motion defines inertia and force and the second law shows how to measure the force. It states that *the rate of change of momentum of a body is proportional to the external impressed force and takes place in the direction of that force*. Naturally, it was now necessary to define the quantity, momentum. Newton defined it in two steps. First, he defined mass: mass is the quantity of matter or mass is the measure of it given by the product of the measures of density and volume. Next, he defined momentum: the quantity of momentum of a body is the measure of it given by the product of the measures of its velocity and its mass. We need not discuss all these definitions in detail. In fact, the definition of mass is a little vague. It is not clear what is meant by quantity of matter. But we can think of it as a measure of inertia. More massive a body is, more inert it is, that is more is its resistance to any change in the state of rest or uniform motion.

What I would like to emphasize is that the laws clearly recognize the directionality of quantities like the velocity, force or momentum as is evident from the statement of the second law . . . *and takes place in the direction of that force.* The law of gravitation also specifies the direction of the gravitational force, stating that it acts along the straight line joining the attracting bodies. Newton thus distinguished between scalar and vector quantities and gave rules for addition of vectors that have both magnitude and direction.

In the miraculous year, Newton developed the mathematics of differential and integral calculus. The whole of his treatise *Principia* dealt with application of calculus. The very term "velocity at an instant" cannot be conceived of without the idea of infinitesimals. And the structure of Newton's dynamics could be developed only with the application of calculus. Thus, Newton also invented the mathematical tools necessary for describing his physics.

To complete the discussion of his three laws of motion, let us state the celebrated third law: *To every action, there is an equal and opposite reaction.* This law, in fact, gives us a method to compare the masses of two bodies. If we let the two bodies collide, they will exert equal and opposite forces on one another and hence a simple mathematics shows that their accelerations will be in inverse proportion of their masses.

At this point, let us also note that Newton distinguished between the concepts of "mass" and "weight". The mass that he defined as the quantity of matter and is the measure of inertia of a body is called the inertial mass. On the other hand, the mass to which the gravitational force is proportional is called the gravitational mass. There is no reason why they should be equal, but they are, and Newton realized it. Their equivalence was later verified experimentally. The weight of a body, as distinct from mass, is actually the force with which a body presses down upon a platform due to the attraction of the Earth. It is thus a force and is given by the product of the mass and the acceleration of fall.

While developing the theory of gravitation, we have mentioned in reference to his miraculous year that he understood how to calculate the force required to maintain the Moon in its orbit and compared it with the force required to support a body at rest on the surface of the Earth. Actually, he compared the accelerations of the Moon and a body near the surface of the Earth with his assumption of inverse square law of the force of gravity and calculated the time period of revolution of the Moon round the Earth in terms of the radius of the Earth, the distance of the Moon from the Earth and the acceleration due to gravity on the Earth. He had remarked that "*found them answer pretty nearly*". In fact, the calculated time period of the Moon differed from the then-available data by about 16%, which should have been much less, and though Newton was convinced about the validity of the law of gravitation, he refrained from publishing it.

There was one more reason for him to keep silent. To find the gravitational attraction of the Earth on a body on its surface or on the Moon, it was necessary to assume that the force exerted by the Earth on a body outside it would be the same if the whole mass of the Earth be supposed to be concentrated at its centre. This Newton could not prove at that time. It shows his concern for developing a theory free of any flaw that cannot be challenged or criticized. Till the required perfection was achieved, he chose not to publish his theory.

Newton renewed his thinking about gravitation again around 1680. Jean Picard had made a fresh determination of the radius of the Earth in 1669, and using his value, the time period of the Moon calculated by Newton came to within 1.6% of the measured value, which was quite acceptable. Meanwhile, Newton was able to prove very elegantly his proposition that while calculating the gravitational force exerted by the Earth on an external body, its whole mass may be supposed to be concentrated at its centre.

The time was now ripe for a final publication of his works, especially because at that time quite a few fellows of the Royal Society were discussing the issue of gravity at length. Robert Hooke claimed that he had full solution of the problem but did not publish anything of interest. Edmond Halley, famous for the comet named after him, was very much interested in the problem of gravitation and as Hooke did not commit anything to writing, he approached Newton and Newton assured him that he had solved the problem of gravitation in full details several years earlier. On the insistence of Halley, Newton started writing his work in three volumes, and the manuscripts were completed in two years. Halley took the responsibility to publish it, and in July 1687, *Philosophiae Naturalis Principia Mathematica* (*Mathematical Principles Of Natural Philosophy*), popularly known as the *Principia*, was published, a quarto volume of 500 pages, bound in calves' leather. At a price of nine shillings a copy, the men of science were able to acquire, in all its original magnificence, a most profound and remarkable contribution that a single man could make in the learning of his generation.

Our discussion so far may mislead the reader a little, for it may appear that we have taken the Sun to be at rest and the force acting on a planet is solely due to the Sun. This is not true and according to the law of gravitation, a planet is acted upon by gravitational forces of all other planets apart from the Sun, and the planets also attract the Sun. Actually, the system of the Sun and a planet rotates about a common centre of mass of the system. But this is a matter of detailed calculation, and for all practical purposes, the Sun may be supposed to be at rest due its tremendous mass. But the motion of a planet is definitely modified by the attraction of other planets as was verified with amazing accuracy long after the death of Newton.

The planet Uranus was discovered in 1781, by William Herschel and by 1830, it was clear that its path deviated from the orbit predicted by Newtonian mechanics. It was thought by many that this perturbation was caused due to attraction of a yet-undiscovered massive planet further away from the Sun. John Couch Adams calculated the mass and the location of a new planet that could cause this perturbation and sent his findings to Sir George Airy, the Astronomer Royal at Greenwich on 21 October 1845, but Airy seems not to have taken any interest in it. Meanwhile, completely unaware of the findings of Adams, U.J.J. Leverrier of France, wrote to J.G. Galle at Berlin observatory to search for a new planet whose mass and location he has calculated that may cause the observed perturbation in the orbit of Uranus. On the night of 24 September 1846, this new planet was observed exactly at the same location predicted by Leverrier on the basis of Newtonian mechanics. The discovery of this new planet, named Neptune, was the final triumph of the theory of gravitation as formulated by Newton.

Newton, in his later life, got engaged in some unfortunate conflicts. One was with the German polymath and philosopher Gottfried Wilhelm Leibnitz regarding the development of calculus. It appears that Leibnitz had developed this method and published works on it in 1674, but Newton did not publish any account of his method till the publication of *Principia*. But Leibnitz was accused by some people of plagiarism, saying that he used Newton's private communications to develop calculus. It was more unfortunate that the Royal Society, in 1712, gave a verdict in favour of Newton and denounced Leibnitz for plagiarism. It was of course true that Newton started developing his mathematics way back in 1665–1666, but he did not publish it. It is seen from the works of both men that they developed the method of calculus from two different aspects and their notations were different. It is more or less agreed nowadays that both invented calculus independent of one another.

Another such conflict was with Robert Hooke, who accused Newton of plagiarism regarding the theory of gravitation. But from written records, it is clear that though Hooke might have an idea about mutual gravitational attraction between the Sun and the planets and that the force of gravitation decreased with distance, he definitely did not hit upon the law of universal gravitation nor did he develop the full mathematical theory from which elliptical planetary orbits of Kepler could be deduced.

In passing it may be noted that apart from mechanics, Newton did a lot of work on optics and also developed the reflecting telescope, though his corpuscular theory of light did not stand the test of time. Moreover, he formulated the law of viscosity. Fluids obeying his law are called Newtonian fluids. Newton theoretically calculated the velocity of sound in air, and his theory was modified later by Laplace. Newton formulated the law of cooling regarding the rate of decrease of temperature of a hot body radiating out heat.

We have talked about the miraculous year of Newton. After the plague years, Newton went back to Trinity College at Cambridge in April 1667, and became the Lucasian Professor of Mathematics in 1669, at the age of 27 only. He became the Fellow of the Royal Society in 1672, and served as its president from 1703, till his death. He became the Master of the Royal Mint in 1699, and contributed in exercising his authority to reform the currency and punish clippers and counterfeiters. He breathed his last on 20 March 1727 (as per the old calendar and on 31

March 1727 as per the new calendar) in London, and was buried in the Westminster Abbey. The famous English poet Alexander Pope wrote an epitaph on Newton that reads:

> Nature and Nature's laws lay hid in night,
> God said: Let Newton be! And all was light.

Long after the death of Newton, his private papers have been published which reveal Newton's attachment to alchemy. Alchemy refers to the occult practice of search for the philosopher's stone that could transmute metals into gold. It seems that actually Newton experimented with chemicals and also possibly had some fondness for magic. It is sometimes said about him that he was the first man of the age of reasoning but he was also the last of the age of magic.

A Few Observations

There is no doubt about the fact that Newton, almost single-handedly, built the edifice of physics by bringing order out of chaos, by properly synthesizing the existing knowledge and recognizing the correct laws of nature. It is not easy to find a law of nature. A law cannot be proved by reasoning, nor can it be formulated just from existing experimental data. It needs deep insight to extrapolate the existing data to ideal situations and also needs intuition to guess the correct law. A law has to stand the test of time. If a single instance is found that violates a law, it has to be rejected. A law must have inherent in it the possibility that "it might have been otherwise also". Take, for example, the first law of motion. It is not possible to find any real situation where a body is not acted upon by any force. At least gravitational force must act on it due to the presence of matter in the universe. But Newton had the insight to guess what would happen to the state of motion had there been no force acting on a body. Of course, experiments of Galileo or conjectures of Descartes helped, but it was Newton who could correctly synthesize them.

In my opinion, the two most important contributions of Newton to the field of thought are the following.

1   Newton's laws of motion and the law of gravitation finally wiped out the 2,000-year-old concept advanced by Aristotle that the terrestrial and the celestial worlds are different and follow different laws. Newton ultimately unified them by demonstrating that both follow the same set of laws and put his theory on firm mathematical footing. After Newton, the Sun, the Earth, the planets or the stars – all were to be regarded just as matter, without attaching any angels or souls to them.

2   The mathematical formulation of his laws of motion resulted in the deterministic view of the world. It is a matter of school-level mathematics to write down the differential equation of motion of a body on the basis of the laws of motion. Now, provided we know the functional form of the force acting on

the body and the initial values of its position and velocity, the solution of this differential equation will give the trajectory of the body at any instant of time in future. Thus, a knowledge of the force enables a scientist to predict, at least theoretically, the future of the universe with unlimited accuracy. Accordingly, during the 200 years after the death of Newton, the aim of science was concentrated on recognizing different types of forces operating in nature. Thus, apart from the gravitational force, the electromagnetic force was discovered in the nineteenth century and the strong and weak forces operating at the nuclear level were discovered in the twentieth century.

We may, at this point, comment on the difference in the situations in which Galileo and Newton wrote their immortal books, the *Dialogues* of Galileo and the *Principia* of Newton. Galileo had to fight against all sorts of oppositions, chiefly the Church which was not tolerant of any idea that contradicted the scripture and Aristotle. Newton lived in the protestant England, that had severed its ties with the Catholic Church long ago, and he did not have to fear the Inquisition. So, as remarked by Whitehead:

> [I]n 1632 Galileo is arguing with the past, while in 1687, Newton . . . ignores all adversaries and dissensions, and looking wholly in the future, calmly enunciates definitions, principles and proofs which have ever since formed the basis of physical science. Galileo represents the assault and Newton the victory. Whitehead also remarked that there can be no doubt but that Galileo is the better reading. It is a real flesh and blood document of human nature which has wedged itself between two austere epochs of Aristotelian Logic and Applied Mathematics. It was paid for also in the heart's blood of the author.

Epilogue

For about 200 years since Newton's death, science and technology advanced on the basis of Newtonian physics. We have talked about the final triumph of Newton's theory of gravitation, which was achieved with the discovery of the planet Neptune. That happened in 1846. But by the end of the nineteenth century, with more sophisticated instruments, it was found that the orbit of Mercury round the Sun was not a closed ellipse, but its long axis slowly rotates in space. This causes rotation or precession of the perihelion of Mercury, and Newtonian gravitation was unable to explain a slight discrepancy in its precession. The discrepancy was just 43 arc seconds per century, which is really small because an arc of a second is 1/3,600th of a degree. But nevertheless, this discrepancy was there.

It was finally resolved by Albert Einstein in 1915, through his general theory of relativity, which replaced the concept of the Newtonian force by curvature of a four-dimensional space–time continuum and postulating that bodies move along "straight lines" in this curved universe. Nowadays, any study in cosmology or astrophysics is done in the light of Einstein's theory or its modified versions. His theory also predicted bending of light rays while passing by massive bodies like the Sun and it was verified experimentally.

Newton's deterministic physics also underwent a drastic change with the advent of quantum mechanics in the twentieth century. Heisenberg's principle of indeterminacy rules out the possibility of determining with unlimited accuracy both the position and the momentum of a body.

Does it mean that Newton's theory was all wrong? No. Not at all. The level of experimental measurement possible in his time completely justified his physics and on the basis of it, civilization progressed for more than 200 years. There is no such thing called absolute truth in science. Truth is modified according to discovery of new phenomena that require new theories to explain. Newton's physics served its purpose and still serves the purpose of everyday life without any problem. But with advancement in sophisticated instrumentation, newer observations are made and hitherto unknown phenomena may be discovered, like the precession of the perihelion of Mercury. Such new phenomena call for newer theories of which the older ones would be only special cases. Like Newtonian mechanics was a special case of relativistic mechanics when we think of speeds extremely small compared to that of light and Newtonian determinism holds pretty good for macroscopic large-scale objects and the indeterminacy becomes significant only for subatomic particles.

In short, with advancement of technology, new theories are developed which are an improvement on old ones, leading to a deeper understanding of nature. This process is dynamic and will proceed without an end, for if it be really possible to completely unveil the mystery of nature, progress will be stalled; no further discovery will be needed and civilization cannot develop into a still better future. So, with passage of time, we will come more and more nearer to the truth but will never reach it; actually we will be approaching the truth asymptotically.

At this point, let us take leave from the reader by visiting the tomb of Sir Isaac Newton at the Westminster Abbey and his statue and the monument therein. We pay homage to this great soul with the words inscribed on his monument which, translated in English, reads as *Mortals, rejoice that there existed such and so great an ornament of the human race.*

Further Reading

Extensive help has been taken from the following texts in preparing this article:

Beiser, A. (1960). *The World of Physics*, ed. McGraw-Hill Book Company, for quoting excerpts from *Dialogues on Two New Sciences* by Galileo Galilei, translated by Henry Crew and Alfonso de Salvio, Dover Publications.

Cohen, I. B. (1971). *Introduction to Newton's Principia*. Harvard University Press, United States of America.

Encyclopaedia Britannica (Chapters on Aristotle, Ptolemy, Aristarchus, Giordano Bruno, Copernicus, Tycho Brahe, Kepler, Galileo and Newton) (https://www.britannica.com).

Feather, N. M. (1963). *Length and Time*. Penguin Books (Originally published by Edinburgh University Press, 1959).

Medley, D. M. (1983). Teacher effectiveness. In Mitzel, H. E. (Ed.) *Encyclopedia of Educational Research*. The Free Press, New York (4 vol), 1894–1903.

Rapport and Wright. (1964). *Physics*, ed. New York University Press, for quoting excerpts from *The First Physical synthesis* by Alfred North Whitehead originally published in *Science and Civilization*. Mervin, F. S. Ed. Oxford University Press, Oxford.

Russell, B. (1964). *A History of Western Philosophy*. Simon and Schuster, Touchstone.

Stanford Encyclopedia of Philosophy (Chapters on Aristotle, Ptolemy, Aristarchus, Giordano Bruno, Copernicus, Tycho Brahe, Kepler, Galileo and Newton) (https://plato.stanford.edu).

4

HISTORY OF ANCIENT INDIAN MATHEMATICS

Manjusha Majumdar (Tarafdar)

Introduction

Little is known about the achievement of ancient Indian mathematics and very few have been printed so far. The contribution can be divided into the following categories.

1 Zero and the place value notation for numbers
2 Vedic mathematics and arithmetical operations
3 *Sulya sutras*
4 Astronomy
5 Algebra
6 Trigonometry
7 Analysis

The number zero

Indian mathematicians have taken "0" as the base a long time ago. Greeks had no terminology above 10^4. Romans had no terminology above 10^3. But in around first century BC, in a Buddhist work "Lalitavistara", we have the terminology 10^{14}. Even in "Yajurveda", in its description of rituals, in "Mahabharata" and in "Ramayana", in the description of statistics and measurements, we have the terminology of the base 10^{13} and more.

The number "zero" is the subtle gift of antiquity by the Indians to mankind (BhanuMurthy, 1992; Dutta and Singh, 1962; Hooda and Kapur, 1996). The concept itself was one of the most significant inventions. In Sanskrit "sunya" is the word for zero. Europe came to know through Arabs, when Muhammed Musa of Baghdad explained it around AD 820, and for this reason, it is called Indo-Arabic

DOI: 10.4324/9781003033448-6

numerals. The exact time and name of the inventor are not known. A European book (in French) first used "zero" in 1275.

Arithmetic

"Patiganita" is the word for arithmetic in Sanskrit. Actually "Pati" means board in English, and "ganita" means the science of calculation. In Buddhist literature, it has been mentioned that there are three classes of *Ganita*, namely "mudra" (finger arithmetic), "ganana" (mental mathematics) and "Samkhyana" (higher arithmetic). Indians/Hindus made remarkable contributions in these fields by saying that there are eight fundamental operations. They are addition, subtraction, multiplication, division, square, square-root, cube and cube-root. The names of the great ancient mathematicians whose contributions are remarkable are Āryabhata I (b. AD 475), Bhaskara I (b. AD 528), Brahmagupta (b. AD 598), Āryabhata II (b. AD 950), Bhaskara II (b. AD 1114) (BhanuMurthy, 1992; Colebrooke, 2010; Dutta and Singh, 1962; Hooda and Kapur, 1996; Joseph, 1995).

"Sulya Sutra" (Geometry)

From the times of Vedas, the ritual literature, which gave directions for constructing sacrificial fires, dealt with the measurement and constructions of different kinds of "Vedi" (altar), thus giving rise to "sulya sutra"(geometry). The three most important books are *Bodhyana*, *Apastamba* and *Katyayana*. They are written between 800 BC and 500 BC, and *Bodhyana* is the oldest and the biggest. In these books, we have the instructions for the construction of squares, rectangles, parallelograms and trapeziums. In "Bodhyana", we have the Pythagorean theorem in a different manner. A remarkable achievement was the discovery of the square root of 2, which is mentioned as 1.4142156 . . . (Dutta and Singh, 1962) "Katyayana" remarkably exhibits the geometrical knowledge of the human body. Moreover, some of the geometrical statements have been mentioned without proof. Nowadays, we call them axioms.

Astronomy

The contribution of Indian mathematicians is so great in the field of astronomy that it mesmerises the whole world. In Sanskrit, "Jyotisa" is the word for astronomy. Ancient Hindu mathematicians gave 27 formulae by applying which one can say about the exact time, while watching the position of stars Krishnamurthy (1998) (Hooda and Kapur, 1996). Āryabhata I in his famous book "Aryabhaterya" (AD 499) mentioned that the diurnal motion of the heavens is due to the rotation of the Earth about its axis (Hooda and Kapur, 1996). A famous astronomer and astrologer, Varaha Mihira wrote a book "PanchSiddhartika" in AD 505. He gave the accurate value of precession of equinoxes. We are indebted to him for the correct version of the Indian calendar.

Algebra

Ancient Indian mathematicians mentioned "bijaganita" for algebra. They said *bijaganita* deals with symbols which are "avyakta" (unknown). They started studying it separately from arithmetic in the beginning of the seventh century. Āryabhata I was the first one to give the method for solving quadratic equations and first degree in indeterminate equations. He mentioned the approximation value for π as 3.1416 and gave the formulas $1^2 + 2^2 + \ldots + n^2$ and $1^3 + 2^3 + \ldots + n^3$. But the remarkable contribution was done by Brahmagupta, whose book "Brahma-Sphuta-Siddhanta" (AD 628) was translated by the Arabs in AD 770. Bhaskara II called him "ganita-churamoni". He termed "Kuttaka" (pulveriser) as algebra. He was the first one to mention that a triangle connected by $a^2 + b^2 = c^2$ is a right-angled triangle. All the results in cyclic quadrilaterals, which are taught in high school, are the contributions of Brahmagupta. He pointed out that $a+0=a$, $a-0=a$, $a\times0=0$, $\sqrt{0}=0$. His outstanding contribution was the solving of the indeterminate equation. He was also the first one to give a rule for interpolation with data at equal intervals (BhanuMurthy, 1992; Colebrooke, 2010; Dutta and Singh, 1962; Hooda and Kapur, 1996; Joseph, 1995).

Bhaskara II wrote a book "Siddhanta-Siromoni" in AD 1150. The arithmetic part of this book is the famous book "Leelavati", which was translated into Persian by Fyzl, brother of Abul Fazl, under the command of the great Mughal emperor Akbar in 1587. The algebra portion of this book was also translated into Persian by the command of Akbar in 1634. The other two portions of this book relate to astronomy where he gave the formula of sin $(A\pm B)$ and sin 18 and many more rules for mensuration.

Trigonometry

Āryabhata I, in his book written in AD 499, was the first one to give the table of sine or the concept of sine. He first introduced $r\sin\alpha$, $r\cos\alpha$, where r is the radius of the circle and α is the angle at the centre (Hooda and Kapur, 1996).

Another Indian mathematician Madhaba (circa AD 1340–1425) was the first one to develop infinite series approximation for a range of trigonometric functions, which has today come to be known as mathematical analysis, well ahead of Newton, who later developed this, 300 years after Madhaba.

Let us hope that the new millennium will spread the mathematical knowledge conceived by Indian-born mathematicians.

References

BhanuMurthy, T. S. (1992). *A Modern Introduction to Ancient Indian Mathematics.* Wiley Eastern, New Delhi, Bangalore, Bombay.

Colebrooke, H. T. (2010). *Algebra with Arithmetic and Mensuration from the Sanskrit of Brahmagupta and Bhaskara.* John Murray, Albemarle Street, London.

Dutta, B. and Singh, A. N. (1962). *History of Hindu Mathematics*. Asia Publishing House, Bombay (2 vols).

Hooda, D. S. and Kapur, J. N. (1996). *Aryabhata – Life and Contributions*. New Age International, New Delhi.

Joseph, G. G. (1995). *The Crest of the Peacock – Non-European Roots of Mathematics*. Princeton University Press, Princeton and Oxford.

Krishnamurthy, V. (1998). The clock of the night sky. K. K. Birla Academy Monograph No. 2, UBSPD.

5

SURGERY IN ANCIENT INDIA AND *SUŚRUTA*-SAṂHITĀ

Sudipa Bandyopadhyay

The glorious civilization of ancient India, develops its medicinal practices, eventually leading to a medical system called *Āyurveda,* a system that attracted the attention of even foreign lands both in the West and the East, from the very beginning of human civilization. *Āyurveda* means a science dealing with the varied aspects of ill health, its preventive as well as curative measures to ensure a healthy and long life. That is why *Āyurveda*, a codified medical system comprises eight branches such as Śalyatantra (surgery), Śālākyatantra (ophthalmology and ENT), *Kaumārabhṛtya* (paediatrics, obstetrics and gynaecology), *Agadatantra* (toxicology), *Rasāyana* (geriatrics and nutrition), *Vājīkaraṇa* (Sexology), *Bhūtavidyā* (psychiatry and demonology) and *Kāyacikitsā* (internal medicine). Each of these branches has presented them under its own different heads. Along with the other seven branches of the *Āyurveda*, Śalyatantra had reached the zenith of achievement at an early stage of Indian history. The word Śalya (arrow) indicates that the arrow of the enemy was regarded as the most common and dangerous of foreign objects causing wounds, giving rise to pain and misery that required surgical treatment.

Thus, *Śalyatantra* embraces all such sources of knowledge which aim at the removal of factors producing pain and misery to the body or the mind. Even the removal of excessively vitiated morbid factors responsible for causing a disease, pain and misery would come within the domain of Śalyatantra.

The earliest record of the treatment of wounds by herbs is found in the *Vedas*. There is a mention in the Vedic literature about *Aśvinau* (the twin surgeons) who are capable of transplanting metallic femur, implanting different organs including the eye.[1] Management of *garbhasaṅga* (obstructed labour), *mūtra-saṅga* (urinary obstruction) and the description of pathological organisms (*kṛmis*) have been dealt with in the *Atharvaveda*. The use of drugs like *visaṅka* and *lākṣa* have been advised to check bleeding in the *Rāmāyaṇa*. The story of Hanumāna fetching *Sañjīvanī* to treat and revive Lakṣmaṇa, who was critically injured in a battle with Meghanāda,

DOI: 10.4324/9781003033448-7

son of Rāvaṇa, is well known. In the *Mahābhārata*, Bhīṣma is said to have been attended by a band of army surgeons when he was wounded during the war.[2] It is said that even every soldier used to carry with him honey, ghee, bandages as first aid materials. Literary sources of Buddhist period, such as *Mahāvagga*, *Bhoja-Prabhandha* and *Navanitakam*, allude to famous Jīvaka (circa 5th century BC), who performed operation for *antra samurcana* (intestinal obstruction), *kapālamocanī* (craniotomy) and even operations on the eyeball. Treatments of wounds and abscesses as well as various diseases by bloodletting were performed.

In this point of view, it is said that in spite of such developments of surgical treatment the credit for providing a systematized approach goes to Suśruta since he was the earliest to make elaborate efforts to keep it on a sound, footing so far as his age is concerned in practice as of imparting practical knowledge. Though it is difficult to identify the exact time of Suśruta, it may be said that his period existed just after Pāṇini and just before Buddha, sometime around 8th–6th century BC. Instrumentology also developed during his time since this has a greater potential for success in this field. Plastic surgery and rhinoplasty described by Suśruta have been acclaimed even today as the greatest of the surgical techniques and they may be treated as important landmarks in the fields of surgery. Cataract crouching, amputation of limbs, abdominal operation, setting of fractures and dislocations, treatments of haemorrhoids and fistula, treatment of hernia etc. and the basic principles behind these numerous operations which were described by Suśruta are as much valid today as it was then. The present work is a humble attempt to point out the fundamental conceptions of surgery from the perspective of Suśruta.

Although all the eight branches of *Āyurveda* have been detailed in the *Suśruta-saṃhitā* the main calibre of the book lies in the description of surgical concepts and procedures. Suśruta undoubtedly made dissections of the human body. He devised a novel method of dissection of the human body which scrupulously avoided touching of the dead body by the hand of the dissector. The dead bodies were left lying in shallow running water for a week, after which the macerated skin and flesh was scraped off in layers with the help of whisk brooms and the structures thus exposed were examined, no hand ever actually touching the body. According to him the study of anatomy continues with embryology. He describes in good detail all the parts and sub-parts of visceral organs, muscles, tendons and ligaments and classifies joints into eight types and bones into five types. The original *Suśruta-*saṃhitā consisted of 186 chapters spread over five sections – *Sūtrasthāna* = 46, *Nidānasthāna* = 16, *Śañrasthāna* = 10, *Cikitsāsthāna* = 40, *Kalpasthāna* = 8 and an *Uttaratantra* = 66 chapters. The entire compilation has been divided into 6 *sthāna*s (volumes).

1 ***Sūtrasthāna*:** Deals with the fundamental concept of surgery and also includes knowledge about various herbs and drugs used as medicines.
2 ***Nidānasthāna*:** Deals with the diagnostic aspects of different diseases – Surgical and Para Surgical.

3 **Śarīrasthāna:** Deals with the anatomical, physiological and also embryological aspects, including obstetrics, pre-natal and post-natal care of the mother and child care.

4 **Cikitsāsthāna:** Deals with treatment, both medical and surgical, including operative techniques, prognosis and complication of various diseases amenably to surgery or Para Surgery. It also provides an account of preventive medicine, the science of nutrition and geriatrics (*rasāyana*), reproduction and virility (*vājīkaraṇa*), therapeutics (*pañcakarma* i.e. five measures for cleansing the system from morbid factors to achieve homeostasis).

5 **Kalpasthāna:** Deals with poisons and toxicological consideration.

6 **Uttarasthāna** (or **Tantra**): Deals with the rest of the eight specialties of *Āyurveda* as follows:

Śālākya (ophthalmology and oto-rhino-laryngology)
Kaumārabhṛtya (paediatrics and gynaecology)
Bhūtavidyā (psychotherapy) and
Kāyacikitsā (internal medicine, personal and social hygiene including dietetics)

Suśruta-saṃhitā includes two small but important chapters describing the basic tenets of experimental operative surgery for surgical training and codes and regulations for a new surgeon entering into the profession. The text emphasizes the great need of such training and describes the methods of experimental surgery using artificial objects for learning the operative procedures using appropriate principles and instruments.

It must be observed that every subject is classified and explained in a scientific manner in the form of groups and sub groups, divisions and sub divisions. Such classifications were possible because of wide practical experience, close observation and logical interpretation. These have made Suśruta's work stand on a firm footing even today. As regards surgery, his observation and inference are so thorough and complete that nothing else is known beyond them even after 2000 years since Suśruta practiced surgery.

During recent years, though technological knowledge has made advances, there are many areas where the basic approach of Suśruta in dealing with surgical problems has more utility and practicability. That is why Suśruta mentioned sixty types of management[3] i.e. *Apatarpanam* (restriction in diet), *Ālepaḥ* (medicated plastering), *Upanāham* (poultice), *Raktavisravaṇam* (blood-letting) and others, related to the total surgical treatment.

In the *Suśruta-saṃhitā*, the dressing of a wound has been described in detail. Bandages and their indications as well as the materials to be used for stitching a traumatic wound have been well documented. The emphasis on protecting the wound from flies, contamination and maggot formation is an ample proof of Suśruta's power of observation at such an early time, when Bacteriology as a science had not even been born, nor was the theory of asepsis and anti-sepsis thought of anywhere in the world. Moreover, he advocated that the wound should be kept dry and clean for early healing.

Suśruta opines that a surgeon's fight against diseases may not be a thorough one, unless he or she is well versed in the knowledge of accessories and their proper handling. Instrument, medicaments and bandages are the criteria of evaluation of the knowledge or a good surgeon is indeed essential and Suśruta's contribution in this direction is noteworthy. According to him, the surgical instrument should be of good quality, made of superior metal and appropriately designed for the purpose of their **use**.[4] In this case, two types of instruments, i.e. sharp and blunt, are mentioned **properly**.[5] Besides that, the systematic classification of instruments into 20 types of *Śastras* (sharp instruments) and 101 types of *Yantras* (blunt instrument), the methodology of naming them, their size, shape and indications in different surgical procedures, their maintenance as well as sterilization were the contribution of Suśruta to the art of surgery over 2000 years ago. According to Suśruta, sharp **instruments**[6] are *Maṇḍalāgra* (circular knife), *Karapatra* (bone-saw), *Vṛddhipatra* (scalpel, dissecting knife, bistoury), *Nakha-śastra* (nail parer), *Mudrikā-śastra* (finger knife), *Utpalapatra* (lancet, phlebotome), *Ardhadhāra* (single edged or half edged knife), *Kuṭhika* (axe shaped knife, chisel), *Vetasapatra* (scalpel), *Sūcī* (needle and others). These instruments were used for operative procedures (Figure 5.1).

1. **Sharp instruments for excision and incision (*bhedanam*)**: To cut deeper into the tissues, the following sharp instruments were designed which could also be used to cut at the dermal level apart from their use for cutting into the deeper tissues. *Maṇḍalāgra, Karapatra, Vṛddhipatra, Nakha-śastra, Mudrikā-śastra, Utpalapatra* and *Ardhadhāra* are all used for incision.
2. **Sharp instruments for scraping, scarification or cutting (*lekhanam*)**: To make clean, smooth or for levelling the tissue, *Maṇḍalāgra* and *Karapatra* were designed for the purpose of scraping or curetting.
3. **Sharp instruments for puncturing or tapping (*vyadhanam; dāraṇam*)**: The instruments that were long, pointed and could pierce into the tissues were designed for puncturing the veins, abscesses or accumulated fluid.
4. **Sharp instruments for probing (*eṣaṇam*)**: For probing the sinuses and non-healing ulcers having a foreign body inside, Suśruta designed three types of cutting probes with sharp margins.
5. **Sharp instruments for extraction (*āharaṇam*)**: Different types of sharp hooks resembling the fish-hook for the extraction of a foreign body, dead foetus from the uterus or a scybalum from the anus were designed. Similarly, a tooth scaler with a curved end was used for the extraction of a tooth.
6. **Sharp instruments for the drainage of fluids or vitiated blood (*visravaṇam*)**: Suśruta advised the use of *Kuśapatra* (knife, straight bistoury), *Atimukha* (lancet), *Sararimukha* (pair of drainage scissors), *Antarmukha* (curved bistoury), *Trikūrcaka* (a tiny instrument having three sharp bristles) and *Sūcī* (needles).
7. **Sharp instruments for suturing (*sīvanam*)**: Suśruta designed different types of needles for suturing superficial or deeper tissues. Such needles were either round-bodied or triangular, curved or straight.

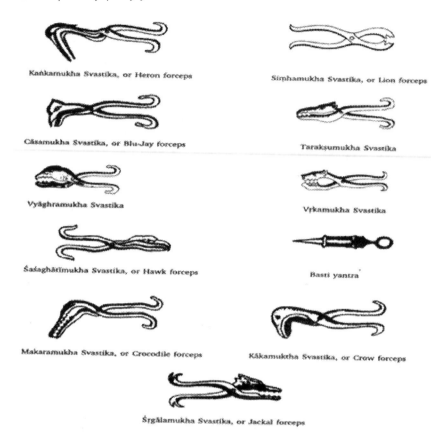

Kaṅkamukha Svastika, or Heron forceps

Siṃhamukha Svastika, or Lion forceps

Cāsamukha Svastika, or Blu-Jay forceps

Tarakṣumukha Svastika

Vyāghramukha Svastika

Vṛkamukha Svastika

Śaśaghātīmukha Svastika, or Hawk forceps

Basti yantra

Makaramukha Svastika, or Crocodile forceps

Kākamukha Svastika, or Crow forceps

Śṛgālamukha Svastika, or Jackal forceps

FIGURE 5.1   Some of the sharp and blunt instruments (*śastras* and *yantras*) as mentioned in the *Suśruta-saṃhitā*.

Source: Subbarayappa, B.V. *Medicine and Life Science in India*, Vol. IV, Part 2 of History of Science, Philosophy and Culture in Indian Civilization, Chattopadhyay, D. P. (Gen. ed.). Centre for Studies in Civilization, New Delhi, 2002.

Similarly, different blunt instruments[7] related to the surgical procedure are *Svastika* (cruciform instruments), *Sandaṃsa* (gripping instrument, pincers), *Tāla* (scoops, disc-shaped instruments) and *Śalāka* (rod shaped instruments).

i) **Svastika (cruciform instruments):** This type of instrument has a fulcrum at the centre and around which its cross-action blades act to achieve the function of extraction of a foreign body from the superficial or deeper tissues especially from the bone. Suśruta had named them after animals or birds. The bone forceps, dental forceps, Ferguson's lion-jaw forceps, dental hawk-bill forceps used in the modern surgical armamentarium can be grouped under this category. The artery forceps designed to catch the bleeding vessels and the needle-holder used for holding the suturing needle in modern surgery are examples of the *Svastika Yantra*.

ii) **Sandaṃśa (gripping instruments; pincers):** Suśruta has described two types of such instrument – one with a handle and another without any handle. They were used for extracting a foreign body from the soft tissues. The dissecting forceps with or without teeth now used in modern surgery, belongs to this category of instruments.

iii) **Tāla (scoops, disc-shaped instruments):** This type of instrument was used for removing foreign bodies from the ear and nose.

iv) **Nāḍi (tubular instruments):** These types of instruments were hollow inside and of different types, used for different purposes. Some of them were used for the extraction of a foreign body, some were meant for diagnostic purposes, some were for suction and others were for facilitating the operation. It must be said that *Suśruta* described a large number of tubular instruments which are nowadays known as catheters for the evacuation of the urinary bladder. Thus, the credit for initiating such techniques for diagnosing a lesion, using tubular instruments goes to *Suśruta*, which ultimately led to the development of a wide range of endoscopes used today.

v) **Śalākā (rod-shaped instruments):** These were used for different purposes and they differed in their sizes and shapes; but a common feature was that they were not hollow inside nor sharp. Suśruta has given an account of eleven types of rod-shaped instruments and Vāgbhaṭa added four more.

Suśruta also mentioned categories of other accessories of *Upayantras* and *Anuyantras*. Such instruments that could not be categorized in any of the aforesaid groups were classified separately as *Upayantras*: they are *Rajju* or *Sūtra* (thread), *Veṇika* (twine), *Paṭa* (bandages), *Carma* (hide), *Antarvalkala* (barks), *Latā* (creeper), *Vastra* (cloth), *Asthilaṣma* (round pebble), *Mudgara* (hammer), *Pāṇitala* (palm), *Padatala* (foot), *Aṅgulī* (finger), *Jihvā* (tongue), *Danta* (tooth), *Nakha* (nail), *Mukha* (mouth), *Śākha* (branch of a tree), *Kṣāra* (medicinal caustics like alkalis), *Bheṣaja* (medicaments) and others.

In this connection, it should be noted that Suśruta happened to be the surgeon to evolve a sound method of training in surgical skills. For that reason, he advocates the dissection of the human body to gain a first-hand knowledge of the human anatomy. The detailed descriptions of all the anatomical parts, including their numbers, shapes and arrangements appear in the *Śarīrasthāna* of the text. Suśruta has identified 107 vital points (*marmaḥ*).[8] A thorough knowledge of these anatomical spots was essential for a surgeon because, any trauma or injury to these spots could lead to shock and various other lesions including death of the patient.

According to *Suśruta*, each surgical procedure was a phased program (*trividha karma*) of three stages.[9]

Pre-operative measure (*Pūrvakarma*)
Operative measures (*Pradhānakarma*)
Post-operative measures (*Paścātkarma*)

Pre-operative measures (*Pūrva karma*): preparation of a patient and keeping ready of the instruments are partly similar to the measures that are essential for safe operation and uneventful recovery. Over and above these measures, *Suśruta* advocated different procedures to bring the body to an ideal state of health as possible. They are *Apatarpaṇam* (restriction of diet or starvation), *Ālepaḥ* (local application of medicated pigments etc.), *Pariṣekaḥ* (local irrigation by liquids), *Svedanam* (sudation or fomentation), *Vimlāpanam* (resolution), *Upanāham* (poultices for preventing suppuration), *Pācanam* (poultices to bring about suppuration), *Snehanam* (internal administration of medicated oils, ghee), *Virecanam* (purgation), *Visravanam* (letting out blood) and *Vamanam* (emesis).

Operative measures (*Pradhāna karma*): Suśruta has provided detailed descriptions of the main surgical procedures which are eight in number encompassing all types of surgical manoeuvres. According to the necessity and choice of a surgeon, more than one technique could be followed in the procedure. The eight types of surgical procedures[10] are as follows:

> *Chedanam* (excision)
> *Bhedanam* (incision)
> *Lekhanam* (scraping)
> *Eṣanam* (probing)
> *Āharaṇam* (extraction)
> *Vyadhanam* (puncturing)
> *Visravaṇam* (drainage)
> *Śivanam* (suturing)

Post-operative measures (*Paścāt karma*): After the completion of a surgical procedure and till the patient is completely cured of the diseases, a careful and minute follow-up regarding appropriate bandaging, antiseptic fumigation, dietetics and rest should be undertaken as post-operative measures. In this context it must be mentioned that Suśruta has described 14 types of bandages, covering their indications on all parts of the body.[11] Flannel or wool, cloth, silk, leather, bark of tree, bamboo etc. were used for bringing about correct bandaging. The types of bandages and their locations are as follows. *Kośa* (sheath bandage) for fingers and toes; *Dāma* (quadruped arm-sling) for painful arm and hip, *Svastika* (cross or spica) for shoulder and other joints, *Anuvellita* (spiral) for limbs of uniform girth, *Pratoli*, penile or cervical, *Maṇḍala* (circular) over the chest, *Yamaka* (twin bandages) for two wounds adjacent to each other. *Khaṭvā* (four-tailed) for chin, face and jaws, *Cina* (eye bandage), *Vibandha* (many-tailed) for back, abdomen, chest, *Gophanā* (sling or t-bandage) for perineum, chin, nose, lips etc. *Pañcāṅgī* (five-tailed) and others.

Suśruta also discussed about the tissue due to heat or burns.[12] He mentioned four categories depending upon the tissues burnt according to the degree of signs and symptoms, they are *Pluṣṭa* (partial epidermal burn or first-degree burn), *Durdagdha* (dermo-epidermal burn or second-degree burn), *Samyagdagdha* (whole skin-thickness burn or third-degree burn) and *Atitdagdha* (fatty and muscle layer burn or fourth, fifth and sixth-degree burns). He also described special kinds of burns and scalds, *Dhūmopahatadagdha* (asphyxiation by hot fumes), *Uṣṇavātātapadagdha* (sun-stroke), *Śītavarṣāniladagdha* (frost-bite and chilblain), *Atitejasādagdha* (burn by extremely hot objects) and *Indravajrāgnidagdha* (burn by lightning). Suśruta had observed that the damage of tissues produced by subnormal temperature as in frost-bite and chilblain were identical in nature to those produced by high temperatures as far as the signs and symptoms in patients were concerned.

Suśruta has classified the skeletal injuries into two broad groups,[13] (i) injuries of skeletal origin involving joints, i.e. dislocations, which he termed *sandhi-bhagna* or *sandhi-muktam* and (ii) skeletal injuries without any involvement of joints i.e. fractures, which he termed *asthi-bhagna* or *kāṇḍa-bhagna*.

Suśruta clearly differentiates the treatment of such bone injuries as *savraṇa-bhagna* (compound fracture) and *avraṇa-bhagna* (simple fracture).

Suśruta prescribes following principles that are highlighted to indicate the height of development of Indian surgery before the Christian era i.e. (a) the prognosis of a case of skeletal injury depends on age of the patient, size of the injury, type of injury, status of the bone and of the patient and seasonal variation (b) complications of skeletal injuries like malunion resulting from improper reduction and suppuration may occur locally. It is also said that the systematic complications may also occur in advanced cases. Suśruta prescribed four types of management of skeletal injuries, such as traction, manipulation by pressure, reduction or apposition and immobilization. He has used *Madhūka* or Indian butter tree, *Udumbara* or cluster fig, *Aśvattha* or sacred fig, *Vaṃśa* or bamboo, *Vaṭa* or banyan tree etc.

Suśruta is recognized by scholars as the originator of plastic surgery in ancient India. The cosmetic part of plastic surgery is also given its due consideration viz. measures to elevate the depressed scar tissues. Similarly, to depress the raised scar tissue, restoration of the normal colour of the skin, hair etc. have been dealt with in detail and these are collectively termed *Vaikṛtāpaha cikitsā*.

Suśruta has described fifteen varieties of repairing torn or defective earlobes,[14] such as *Nemi-sandhānaka* (when both flaps are equal in size, thick and wide), *Āsaṅgima* (when inner flap is longer), *Gaṇḍakarṇa* (when outer flap is longer), *Nir-vedhima* (when flaps are absent, but have tiny base), *Kapāṭasandhika* (uneven flaps, with small outer flap), *Ardhakapāṭasandhika* (outer flap is long with small inner flap), *Kākauṣaka* (when the lobule is devoid of muscle and is tiny).

Principles of Rhinoplasty (*Nāsāsandhānam*) are exactly what present day plastic surgeons name as pedicle grafting. A patch of living flesh including the skin, sub-cutaneous tissue along with the circulatory attachment is raised from the adjacent portion of the body and transferred to the scarified portion of the nose. This attachment must be maintained until a new circulation has developed from the nose of the recipient site. Care should be taken to insert two pipes into the nostrils to facilitate breathing.[15]

Suśruta also discussed about Labiaplasty (*oṣṭhasandhānam*) for severed lips, which is a similar operation like rhinoplasty but no pipe is required in Labiaplasty.[16]

Thus, it is realized that the treatise of Suśruta laid emphasis on the study of every sphere of medical and surgical fields along with embryology, biology, cosmology,

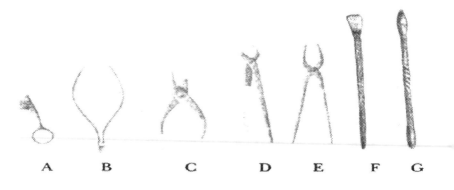

A   B   C   D   E   F   G

Some trade objects of iron and copper excavated from Taxila
A.   Fragment of a scissor
B.   Forceps
C.   Tongs
D.   Tongs
E.   Tongs
F.   Stylus
G.   Kohl rod

FIGURE 5.2   Some trade objects of iron and copper excavated from Taxila

Source: The Surgical Instruments of the Hindus by G.N. Mukhopadhyaya, included in *Medicine and Life Science in India*, Vol. IV, Part 2 of History of Science, Philosophy and Culture in Indian Civilization.

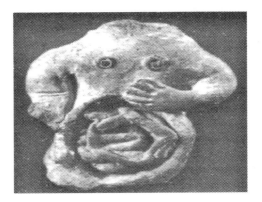

FIGURE 5.3   Terracotta from third to fourth century CE showing dissected abdomen

Source: Naqvi, Nasim H. *A Study of Buddhist Medicine and Surgery in Gandhara*, Motilal Banarsidass Pvt. Ltd., Delhi. First edition, 2011.

physiology, toxicology and a number of subjects which have relevance to the study of medical science. In conclusion, it must be said that considering the age in which Suśruta lived, and the success that the surgeons of his time seemed to have, as recorded in our ancient texts, one wonders if the acumen in surgical skill reached by ancient Indian surgeons was ever surpassed by any other physician of any ancient nation. The crown of the "Father of Surgery" must therefore be on the head of

Suśruta, who rid the science of medicine of priestly domination, and paved the way for independent rational thinking and sound scientific training of a surgeon.

List of Abbreviations

Cikitsā   Cikitsāsthāna
Mbh   Mahābhārata
ṚV   Ṛgveda
SS   Suśrutasaṃhitā
Sūtra   Sūtrasthāna

Notes

1 *ṚV* X. 39-40
2 *Mbh* VI. 121, 55-56
3 *SS. Cikitsā*, 2. 4
4 *SS, S?tra*. 8.14
5 *Ibid.*, 8.3
6 *Ibid.*, 8.4
7 *Ibid.*, 8. 15-18
8 *Ibid.*, 8. 16-24
9 *Ibid.*, 5.3-19; 19.3-37; 17.16-17.
10 *Ibid.*, 5.5
11 *SS.Sūtra.*18.18-19
12 *SS.Sūtra.*12.15-18
13 *SS.Ni.*15.4.
14 *SS.Sūtra.*16.10
15 *SS.Sūtra.*16.49-53
16 *SS.Sūtra.*16.54

References

Primary Sources

Atharvavedasaṃhitā. Whitney, W. T. (1962). Ed. and Eng. Trans. Motilal Banarsidass Publishers, New Delhi.
Maharṣivedavyāsapraṇīta-Mahābhārata. Pandeya, R. S. (1999). Ed. and Hindi. Trans. Gita Press, Gorakhpura (I–VI vol).
Ṛgvedasaṃhitā. Griffith, T. H. (1973). Ed. and Eng. Trans. Motilal Banarsidass Publishers, New Delhi.
Suśrutasaṃhitā. Singhal, G. D. (2007). Ed. and Eng. Trans. Chaukhamba Sanskrit Pratish- than, New Delhi (I–III vol).

Secondary Sources

Deshpande, P. J. (1984). *Surgical in Ancient India with Special Reference to Āyurveda*, Banaras Hindu University, Varanasi.

Prasad, G. C. and Udupa, K. N. (1976). *Suśruta's Contribution to Surgery*, Indological Book House, Varanasi.

Singhal, G. D. and Singh, R. H. (1979). *Non-operative Considerations in Ancient Indian Surgery*, Chaukhamba Surbharati, Varanasi.

Subbarayappa, B. V. (2002). *Medicine and Life Science in India* (IV vol), Part 2 of History of Science, Philosophy and Culture in Indian Civilization, Chattopadhyay, D. P. (Gen. ed.). Centre for Studies in Civilization, New Delhi.

Suggested Readings

Vālmīki-Rāmāyaṇa. Chakravarty, D. (1996–97). Ed. and Beng. Trans. (I–II vol). New Light, Calcutta.

6

DR M.J. BRAMLEY (1803–1837), THE FIRST PRINCIPAL OF CALCUTTA MEDICAL COLLEGE

Sankar Kumar Nath

On 17 March 1836, the principal of Calcutta Medical College was delivering the "Introductory Address" at the present site of the college, nearly 13.5 months after its foundation. (In fact, the college had initially started in a house opposite to the present Calcutta Sanskrit University.) A part of the lecture goes as follows.

> Finally, I would fain say no less to you, my young friends, than to natives of every denomination; you may believe me when I assert, if ever than was a truly wise and liberal measure adopted, by authority, for your good, it is that which has called into existence amongst you an Institution for instructing you in Medical Science. . .
>
> A celebrated writer has asserted, in substance, that were the British to-morrow to quit India for ever, they would leave behind them no lasting monument of good, – no features of general improvement on the face of the country, – no durable effect of beneficent power. In his day that assertion might have been correct; but I deny its applicability to ours, in which, strange to say, it has been repeated with equal confidence, though by men less eminent.
>
> Can it be maintained, I ask, that if we were now to quit India, we should indeed leave behind us no durable monuments of good Government, – no lasting effects of philanthropic exertion, – no features of general improvement in the country? No! I will venture to say, that were there no other fact to which we could appeal in contradiction of such an unqualified assertion, the Hindoo and Medical Colleges would alone go far to supply an ample refutation of it. You may rely upon it, that, with whatever other faults our tenure of this country may be changeable, that posterity will gratefully acknowledge the noblest of all our acts: The enfranchisement of native

DOI: 10.4324/9781003033448-8

intellect from the darkness of ignorance, and the yoke of superstition which is ever its concomitant.

It can scarcely be expected of me in this place, or on this occasion to appeal to any specific evidence of the cheering fact I have now stated. If any were required indeed– this institution, established by Government in a spirit of liberality, worthy of the noble cause to which it is devoted, might supply it; while the presence here this day of the distinguished noble man now at the head of this administration, may be justly regarded as an indication of his recognition of this enlightened policy; and as a proof of the interest he takes in your improvement, – a mark of condescension, which should stimulate you, as I sincerely hope it may, to renewed and unceasing exertions in your important and most interesting studies.

(Bramley, 1836)

The speaker was none other than Dr Mountford Joseph Bramley, the first principal of Calcutta Medical College.

It was the first great meeting or assemblage since the foundation of Calcutta Medical College on 28 January 1835. A vivid description of this meeting was given in *The Calcutta Monthly Journal* of 1836 as a news item.

We repaired to the Native Medical College on Thursday morning the 17th March, full half an hour before the time appointed for the commencement of the proceedings of the day, but found the Theatre already nearly filled, and eventually we learned that about 580 persons were assembled in it. We observed among the distinguished members of society present, the Members of Council, of the Law Commission, who were already in the Theatre when we entered it, the Secretaries of Government, &c. &c. &c. and the attendance of the faculty was very full. At about ¼ past 11, the Right Honourable Lord Auckland was ushered into the Theatre by Principal Bramley, attended by Professors Goodeve and O'Shaughnessy; and soon after the worthy Principal commenced his address.

(Bramley, 1836)

It was an eventful lecture where Dr Bramley sketched the progress of medicine amongst the ancient people in terms of scientific accounts as professed by Aesculapius and his sons, the Asclessiadae. He spoke of Hippocrates, Celsus and Galen thereafter.

He called upon the public to come forward in support of Calcutta Medical College with a view to giving thrust to its welfare. He particularly alluded to the wealthy and influential members of the native community.

Dr Bramley concluded by paying tribute of high praise to the great persons to whom India was indebted for the foundation of the first medical college in the country, to Lord William Bentinck and Charles Metcalfe.

Let us see what the *Calcutta Monthly Journal* wrote after the lecture of the principal was over.

> At the close of this impressive address, the speaker was greeted with loud plaudits which lasted for several seconds, and immediately afterwards Lord Auckland walked round the table and cordially shook the worthy Principal by the hand, expressed his thanks to him and intimated the deep interest he felt in the welfare of this noble institution. His Lordship then familiarly conversed with Principal Bramley for several minutes on subjects connected with the institution, and afterwards proceeded to inspect the arrangements of the building, the anatomical figures, the chemical laboratory, the room appropriated for the library, etc. and with all these his Lordship expressed himself very much pleased.

The Bengal Hurkaru writes in this context,

> Principal Bramley, Professors Goodeve and O'Shaughnessy are all enthusiastic in the discharge of their duties and their performance of them is a labour of love to them. Their talents are highly estimated by all who have had an opportunity of appreciating them – their system is good and their pupils are making rapid progress. In short the highest credit is due to these gentlemen individually and collectively – they have proved themselves worthy of the honorable posts they fill, and under their auspices we have no doubt the College will realize the most sanguine expectations of Lord William Bentinck who founded it.
>
> *(Bramley, 1836)*

Dr Mountford Joseph Bramley was born on 16 April 1803. He became an assistant surgeon on 29 August 1829. He was in Medical Charge of Body Guard from 20 April to 6 October 1830, on which latter date he was appointed to the medical duties of the Residency at Khatmandhoo (Hodson, 1910).

Calcutta Medical College was established on 28 January 1835, as per government order No. 28 dated 28 January 1835, after having accepted the recommendations of the report of a committee formed by the then-Governor-General of India Lord William Bentinck, the committee being consisted of J. Grant, J.C.C. Sutherland, C.E. Trevelyan, T. Spens, Ramcomul Sen and M.J. Bramley (University of Calcutta. Medical College, 1934).

The *Calcutta Courier* on 4 February 1835, wrote,

> An important order of Council appears in this day's Gazette, by which the Sanscrit College Medical Class, the Medical Class of the Madrussa, and the Native Medical Institution, are abolished and, in their place, a new college

is to be formed, of which Dr. Bramley is made superintendent, "for the instruction of native youths in various branches of medical science".

(Native Medical Institutions, 1835)

At the same time, the reformer (Native Medical Institutions, 1835), with all good wishes to Dr Bramley as the head of the institution to break the prejudices regarding dissection of human dead body for the cause of medical education, wrote,

> We are much rejoiced to hear that the superintendence of this newly-created institution has been intrusted to a very talented and zealous member of the faculty, Dr. Bramley. Much of its success will depend on his exertions, and the method he may adopt of conveying instruction to the Hindoo youth. Our young men of the higher castes unfortunately entertain a great abhorrence of anatomical dissections, without which it is next to impossible that they can become practically useful.
>
> *(Native Medical Institutions, 1835)*

In the article "India: Past, Present, and Future", published in Macphail's Edinburgh *Ecclesiastical Journal* in March 1857, it was mentioned that it had been due to Drs Bramley, Goodeve and O'Shaughnessy, the introduction of dissection could be possible at Calcutta Medical College, and it was done first by Pundit Madhusudan Gupta (Macphail's Ediburgh Ecclesiastical Journal, 1857).

Dr Bramley joined Calcutta Medical College on 28 January 1835, as superintendent, as already said. But soon the post of superintendent was abolished and Dr Bramley was made the first principal of the institution, thus becoming the first principal of any medical college in India. A report of Fort William, General Department, 5 August 1835, was released, which read:

> The Hon. The Governor-general in Council has been pleased to appoint Dr. W.B. O'Shaughnessy to be a professor at the new medical college. With reference to general orders in the military department dated the 28th Jan. and 11th Feb. 1835, the former appointing Mr. Assist. Surg. M.J. Bramley to be superintendent of the new medical college, and the latter, Mr. Assist. Surg. Goodeve, M.D., to be the assistant to the superintendent; the Governor-general in Council is pleased to sanction the following alteration in the designation of those appointments: Mr. Assist. Surg. Bramley to be principal of the new medical college. Mr. Assist. Surg. Goodeve, M.D., to be a professor at ditto.
>
> *(The Asiatic Journal, 1836)*

Dr Bramley was attached to different organisations while he was working in India, such as the Asiatic Society of Bengal, the Medical and Physical Society of Calcutta and the Agricultural and Horticultural Society of India.

Dr Bramley was, indeed, a very hard-working man in all respects. Several research works were done by him in his short tenure of life. I will cite one such here. In the journal of *Transactions of the Medical and Physical Society of Calcutta* Vol-VI, 1833, his much discussed article, "Some Account of the Bronchocele of Nipaul, and of the cis and trans-Himalayan Regions" was published. Later on, one observer of the "Waldie's Select Circulating Library" of 17 February 1835 issue, wrote,

> Perhaps bronchocele is a disease confined to the lesser altitudes; an opinion held by members of the faculty of the first eminence on the continent, as I find from a paper in the transactions of the Medical Society of Calcutta, by Dr. M.J. Bramley, of the Bengal army.
>
> *(Select Circulating Library, 1835)*

Detailed reviews of this paper of Dr Bramley were published in different medical journals such as *The London Medical and Surgical Journal* in 1836 (The London Medical and Surgical Journal, 1836) and in *The British and Foreign Medical Review* in July 1839 (The British and Foreign Medical Review, 1839).

In 1836, a book having 99 pages and containing the Bengali version of the lectures of Dr Bramley was published by Uday C. Adea. The name of the book is *Bramly Baktrita*. Rev. J. Long reviewed this book as

> a discourse at the opening of the Medical College, by Dr. Bramley. Treating of the nature and cause of diseases and the European mode of treating them. Some of the best writers in Bengali have been the Vaideas or medical caste.
>
> *(Long, 1855)*

Dr M.J. Bramley died on 19 January 1837, in Calcutta, at the age of 34 years. Till death, he was the principal of Calcutta Medical College. But it is worth mentioning here that the death-news of Dr Bramley, published a few days after his death in *The Calcutta Monthly Journal*, 1837, goes as,

> Death of Dr. Bramley:- Principal Bramley, of the New Medical College, died at mid night on the 17th of Jan. His remains were entered in the 19th instant, attended by a numerous assemblage of friends.
>
> *(The Calcutta Monthly Journal, 1838)*

This news regarding the date of death is not correct because, it is seen from the account book of the medical college that Dr Bramley withdrew his salary till 18 January 1837. Dr Bramley was buried in the North Park Street Burial Ground at Calcutta, and an inscription thereof reads as "Sacred to the Memory of Mountford Joseph Bramley, late Principal of the Medical College of Calcutta, who departed this life on the 19th of Jan. 1837, aged 34 years" (Holmes and Co., 1851).

It is a matter of regret that this sacred grave can never be found in Calcutta, because the North Park Street Burial Ground remains buried under the high-rise buildings of today.

Later on, a tablet bearing the following inscription was erected to his memory in the theatre of the medical college. Now it can be seen beside the college library entrance.

> In memory of Mountford Joseph Bramley, late principal of the Medical College of Calcutta, this tablet is erected by his grateful pupils to record their sense of the zeal and ability with which he watched over their private interests and those of their country, & the courtesy & kindness with which he won their affections, while he improved their minds. Aged 35 years, died January 19, 1837. "Why has worth so short a date – while villains ripen grey with time".
>
> *(Hodson, 1910; Bose et al., 2009)*

After the death of Dr Bramley, the civil appointments by the then-governor-general was announced as follows (this news was published in the *Asiatic Journal* in 1837).

> Medical College – Feb. 1. The following additional lecturers and establishment appointed to Medical College, consequent on demise of the late principal, Mr. Assist. Surg. M.J. Bramley: Mr. Assist Surg. C.C. Egerton to be professor of surgery and clinical surgery. N. Wallich, Esq., M.D., superintendent of Botanic garden, to be professor of Botany. Mr. Assist. Surg. T. Chapman, M.D., to be lecturer on clinical medicine. Mr. Assist. Surg. McCosh to officiate for Dr. Chapman during his absence from presidency. Mr. R. O'Shaughnessy to be demonstrator to dissecting room in Medical College, and to give assistance to chemical lecturer. Mr. David Hare to be Secretary to institution.
>
> *(The Asiatic Journal, 1837)*

The Englishman, 3 February 1837, issue, stated as,

> We hear that Government has determined not to nominate another Principal to the Medical College, but to appropriate the salary of that office to two new Professorships. We believe Drs. Egerton and Chapman are to be the additional professors.
>
> *(The Asiatic Journal, 1837)*

I will conclude with Dr Bramley's obituary article as published in *the Englishman* on 21 January 1837,

> Dr. Bramley had been but a few years in this country, before his natural acuteness, aided by patient investigation, satisfied him of the feasibility of

an attempt, which he had an honest confidence in his own ability to carry through – namely, the introduction of the regular English school of medicine and surgery among the natives, instruction being conveyed through the medium of the English. The mass of prejudice he had to overcome was of course, immense; he set forth to work out his system, at first, alone, but soon saw its practical adoption, with the aid of highly talented and energetic fellow-labourers, whose powers his tact and penetration enabled him to discover and appreciate. His success was, to all, wonderful. With unwearying diligence – by kindness, by admirable patience, and constant attention, he vanquished, one by one the difficulties which opposed him in the institution of the Calcutta Medical College.

(The Asiatic Journal, 1837)

References

175 Years of Medical College Bengal, Commemorative Volume, Ed. By Dr. D. Bose, Dr. S. K. Nath, Dr. J. K. Das, 2009, 27.

The Asiatic Journal, XIX, 1836. London, 135.

Bramley, M. J. (1836). Introductory address delivered at the opening of the Calcutta Medical College, March 17, 1836. *The Calcutta Monthly Journal*, for 1836, 1, 107, 109.

The British and Foreign Medical Review, VIII, 1839, 103.

The Calcutta Monthly Journal, for 1837, 74, 1838.

Hodson, V. C. P. (1910). *Historical Records of the Governor-General's Body Guard*. W. Thacker & Co, London, 285.

Holmes and Co. (1851). *The Bengal Obituary*, 194.

The London Medical and Surgical Journal, III, 1836, 364.

Long, J. (1855). *A Descriptive Catalogue of Bengali Works*, 33.

MacPhail's Edinburgh Ecclesiastical Journal, March 1857, 73.

Native Medical Institutions. (1835). *The Asiatic Journal*. London, 1837, 225, 226, 229.

Select Circulating Library, Part I, 1835, 116.

University of Calcutta. Medical College. (1934). *The centenary of the Medical College, Bengal, 1835–1934*. Calcutta. 285.

PART II
Philosophy of Science

7

THE PHILOSOPHY OF SCIENCE

A Brief Understanding

Pradip Kumar Ghosh

Introduction

Scientific investigations in ancient and medieval times were dominated by Aristotle. According to him, all earthly bodies are composed of just four elements: earth, fire, air and water. The modern era of science started with Nicolas Copernicus's (1473–1543) Sun-centric model, refuting Ptolemy's idea of the solar model. Sir Isaac Newton gave the theoretical and mathematical explanation of Copernicus's universe. The essence was that the physical world consists of inert particles of matter. Their interaction and collision are governed by certain laws, which hold the key to understanding the structure of Copernicus's universe. It discarded the Aristotelian concept. This era believed in determinism and treated mass as the reason of extension, which is valid for all branches of science. In the early twentieth century, revolution in science occurred again through the theory of relativity of Albert Einstein and the introduction of quantum mechanics by Bohr and others.

We are indebted to science for the intellectual achievements reached by the society at large. Popularisation of science courses became universalised with such feats. People are also motivated to pursue science as a profession. In fact, we are obtaining the fruits of study and research in science when it is translated to technology. We observed such applications in technology till the end of the nineteenth century with the Newtonian concept and enormous technological applications for the betterment of mankind from the early twentieth century after the introduction of quantum mechanics and relativity. Biological science and social science added many more to the society. But, while studying specific science, we have to face some unsolved questions on the nature of science and how it works.

Philosophy of science, a rapidly developing branch of philosophy, occupies a key note in understanding the development of science in the contemporary philosophical domain. Though its development got momentum in the twentieth century,

DOI: 10.4324/9781003033448-10

this branch has an old history. We may recall from ancient period the "Greek Atomistic" which falls under the philosophy of science. Aristotle contributed in this area through his inductive–deductive method and his analysis of scientific explanation. He maintained that the scientist should induce explanatory principles from the phenomena to be explained and then deduce statements about the phenomena from premises which include these principles. In this chapter, I will try to introduce some basic understanding of the subject, keeping in mind readers from different backgrounds.

Origin of Modern Science

Let us begin with some of the developments in the field of science since Copernicus's Sun-centric model. At this age, we are enjoying the fruits of science in the form of technological advances – whether it is computer and its allied aids or nuclear energy or genetic engineering or high-temperature superconductors or sophisticated spacecraft to know the universe and beyond. These have been achieved by using basic science researches, which have a long history. But this journey is long. Rapid scientific development occurred in Europe, between the years 1500 and 1750. But it did not come from nowhere. Here, I am not going into ancient history of science, which may be treated as a separate branch of study.

There were many scientific investigations in ancient and medieval times, and the dominant world was that of the Aristotelians. But it was based on belief to some extent. According to him, all earthly bodies are composed of just four elements: earth, fire, air and water.

The modern era of science started with Nicolas Copernicus's (1473–1543) Sun-centric model refuting Ptolemy's idea of the solar model, where the Earth is a mere planet. Johannes Kepler (1571–1630) advanced it with a theory of three empirical laws of planetary motion based on astronomical data collected by Tycho Brahe. At that juncture, Galileo Galilee (1564–1642) invented the telescope and established the concept of mechanics. He also introduced that all freely falling bodies will fall towards the Earth at the same rate irrespective of their weight. To explain this, he used the language of mathematics of the French philosopher, mathematician and scientist, Rene Descartes's (1596–1650) radical mechanical philosophy.

The essence was that the physical world consists of inert particles of matter. Their interaction and collision are governed by certain laws which hold the key to understand the structure of Copernicus's universe. Though Galilean ideas discarded the Aristotelian concept, he retained Aristotle's view of scientific enquiry as a two-stage progression from observations to general principles and back to observations.

Finally, all the theories and observations on motion of inert particles and Copernicus's universe got theoretical and mathematical confirmations by Sir Isaac Newton's (1643–1723) laws of motion and law of gravity. It also established the use of Calculus – a mathematical technique. The scientific world of this era believed in determinism and treated mass as the reason of extension, which was valid for all branches of science, viz. in the study of physical science, in the fields of chemistry, optics, energy, thermodynamics and electromagnetism. Lots of developments with the idea of Newton took place to utilise the natural resources for the development of mankind. Scientists started rethinking to go beyond macroscopic objects in a different way after the discovery of electron though they had the idea of atoms and molecules as microscopic unobservable objects.

In the early twentieth century, the revolution (known as the modern era of physics) in science occurred again through

(a) Theory of relativity by Albert Einstein
(b) Introduction of quantum mechanics by Niels Bohr, Heisenberg, Schrodinger and Dirac

These are radical theories and they raised questions on deterministic sciences that were followed till then. Their emergence caused considerable conceptual upheaval not only in physics but also in other branches of science. For example in non-physical science, Charles Darwin introduced the theory of evolution by natural selection in his famous book, *On the Origin of Species*. It states that all species of organisms arise and develop through the natural selection of small inherited variations that increase the individual ability to compete, survive and reproduce. His theory led to challenge the orthodox concept of living beings as "all are creatures of God".

A revolution in biology, though yet an incomplete one, took place in 1953, with the discovery of the structure of DNA by James Watson and Francis Crick. It is an acid molecule called deoxyribonucleic acid, which carries the genetic instructions for development, functioning and reproduction of all known organisms and many viruses. It led to the development of molecular biology and also removed the wall between physical and biological sciences.

Similarly, significant development of cognitive science in the last 30 years reveals the remarkable study of various aspects of human cognition such as perception, memory, learning and reasoning. This leads us to wonder – "Whether we will be able to reveal about the workings of the mind".

Evolution of Philosophical Thought

Let us now discuss what is science and how the very definition of science raises a few questions which become the subject of philosophy of science. The common man's queries on science are the key to philosophy of science. Queries may be assembled as follows. What's the difference between science and pseudoscience? When is a scientific generalisation justified? How do we distinguish between coincidence and natural laws? Does science describe reality or is it just a tool? Are quarks, electron etc. real or hypothetical entities? Is science objective or does it have an inherent perspective? Is everything reducible to physics? Is everything reducible to a few rules?

At this point, we must be aware that philosophy deals with the basic problems of life and the world, while philosophy of science deals with the basic problems of science, its methods, invention, certainty, practices etc. In this context, we may note from M.H. Salmon (1992): "Philosophy of Science is the name given to the branch of Philosophy that reflects on and critically analyses science. As a discipline it tries to understand the aims and methods of science, along with its principles, practices and achievements".

Moreover, in scientific queries, the frequently asked question "why" is used to understand different natural phenomena, like why the Sun looks red during sunrise or sunset, or why sugar dissolves in water but sand does not. They require explanation. To find explanation for such queries, we need to understand the following terminologies which philosophy of science deals with.

First is the debate on what science is and which is similar to science. Atomism of Greek philosophy and atomism of the modern era of Dalton are obviously not similar. Two factors went against any widespread acceptance of the classical version of atomism, that is atomism of Greek philosophy. The first factor was the uncompromising materialism of this philosophy. They tried to challenge man's self-understanding while explaining the cause of sensation and even reason of motion of atom. That atomism seemed to leave no place for spiritual values. In fact, the values of friendship, courage and worship cannot be reduced to the platform of atoms. The second factor was the ad hoc nature of the atomists' explanations. Their idea to explain through a process of offering a picture-preference method, a way of looking at phenomena, but in the process, they never tried to check the accuracy of the picture. We can cite an example of dissolving of salt in water. The strongest argument advanced by classical atomists was that the effect could be produced by dispersal of salt atoms into the liquid. However, the classical atomists could not explain why salt dissolves in water whereas sand does not. Of course, they could say that salt atoms fit into the interstices between water atoms whereas sand atoms do not. But this way of "explanation" would be dismissed by another way of saying that salt dissolves in water whereas sand does not. There is no doubt that the discussion on the history of science developed "similar" to science. That is why the science that developed from the seventeenth century through institution-based research is a subject of philosophy of science.

Second, methodology is another aspect that is dealt with in philosophy of science. According to Peter Kosso, "Science enjoys a lot of respect these days, if not always for the social values of its result than at least for the rigor and precision of method". As there are different branches of science like physics, chemistry, mathematics, biology and geology, there are also different methods like deductive, inductive, synthetic and analytic. Members of Vienna Circle, Karl Popper and Paul Feyerbend are the pioneers in the twentieth century's methodological discussion. In fact, the members of Vienna Circle introduced "Logical Positivism". The question that may arise however is whether there is any method distinctive of science. As mentioned, there are many methods used in science and they become discoveries or applications in science. So, in that sense there is no priori methods. A simple idea that a naive intuitivist follows is to look into the problem, to observe. If there is well-established regularity, then we have to take them to a law or causal connection. But this is not as simple because a discovery also needs justification. According to Karl Popper's view on method – a process of coming up with a hypothesis – conjecturing is an exercise of imagination. But at the same time, he introduced the concept of falsification, which we will discuss at a later stage. The methods followed by Imre Lakatos, Carl Hemple and Thomas Kuhn also are discussed later.

Third, a reasonable expectation of science by using different methods is "Certainty", and it is thus the subject of philosophy of science. Aristotle's idea may be stated here. Statements like "all men are mammals", for instance, are necessarily true, and whereas the statement "all ravens are black" are only accidentally true. Aristotle would say that although a man could not possibly be a non-mammal, a raven might well be non-black. Although Aristotle did give examples of this kind to contrast "essential predication" and "accidental predication", he failed to formulate a general criterion to determine which predications would be essential. Aristotle bequeathed to his successors a faith that, because the first principles of the sciences, mirror relations in nature which could not be other than they are, is incapable of being false. To be sure, he could not authenticate this faith as certainty. Despite this, Aristotle's position that scientific laws state necessary certainty towards truths has been widely influential in the history of science. Scientists collect data and information of a subject matter to reach that certainty.

Fourth, causality is another important issue in the domain of knowledge of science. The principle of causality says that every event has a cause, and in identical situations, the same cause will produce the same effect. Causality is also thought to be the key to unlock the secret of explanation. The natural concept of causality is found at the borderline between physics and philosophy. It was considered in the early work of Aristotle. It was also followed by Renée Descartes, and finally we find continuation of the idea of causality in the modern view of David Hume and Immanuel Kant. In considering the explanation of scientific theory "Causality" is considered as an alternative by many philosophers. In scientific explanations we come across – why are there one or more laws? Sometimes, we claim that scientific explanation is causal explanation. So, scientists search for causes to provide explanation. All this is because science seeks explanation as this enables us to control and predict phenomena. A general view of empiricists is that the causation consists of law-governed sequence. The empiricists' account of causation holds that the relation of cause and effect obtains only when one or more laws subsume the related events. When a vase is broken by a child due to fall from a table on to a marble floor, the general notion of the cause is the act of child, but the scientific cause of breaking the vase is based on some law(s). Here we find the role ofscience. But we should not consider causation as mere regular succession but much more to relate the events. To explain in scientific language the temperature of ideal gas is obtained by knowing its pressure and volume at equilibrium. But the actual cause that explains the reason of temperature and pressure of gas in a container, according to kinetic theory of gases, is the effect of motion of molecules of the gas. Here, a discussion is required whether notion of causality would be independent of determinism or it became also the consequence of quantum theory because of its probabilistic nature. From the twentieth century, with the introduction of quantum mechanics, "Question raised on the role of 'causality'; whether it has any relevance? What does it actually mean?" We may quote Karl Popper here: "As to controversy over 'Causality', I propose to dissent from the indeterminist metaphysics until recently in vogue among physicist is not so much its greater lucidity as its greater sterility".

Fifth, whenever a scientific discovery takes place, scientists take it as the truth. The general aim of science is to give us an accurate description and other representations of what reality is like. But interestingly, there may be lots of different representations of a same issue by different scientists. For example the building up of the Sun-centric model, conceptual development of theory of light and many others prove that truth is not absolute as expected by scientists. Some philosophers think that the main goal for a realist is truth. We know the philosophical theories on truth are authority, coherence, correspondence and pragmatism. Aristotle claimed that genuine scientific knowledge has the status of necessary truth. He maintained that the properly formulated first principles of the sciences, and their deductive consequences, could not be other than true. The goal of philosophy of science is also to determine the position of scientific truth in light of these theories.

Sixth, to know about nature and life, scientists apply their acquired knowledge without discussing the nature of knowledge. Questions may arise, such as "What is knowledge?", "When does a statement acquire the status of knowledge?" Epistemology is one of the important parts of philosophy. It discusses the sources, criteria and validity of knowledge. One important aspect of epistemology is to deal with knowledge and belief and how knowledge is distinguished from mere belief. There are different doctrines of knowledge – authoritarianism, empiricism, rationalism and intuitionism. In developing science, information is required. Philosophy of science comes into focus when this information turns into knowledge. We may recall that Hume's denial of the possibility of a necessary knowledge of nature was based on three explicitly stated premises:

(a) All knowledge may be subdivided into the mutually exclusive categories "relations of ideas" and "matters of fact";
(b) All knowledge of matters of fact is given in, and arises from, sense impressions;
(c) A necessary knowledge of nature would presuppose knowledge of the necessary connectedness of events.

Next, in dealing with science, we need to conceptualise what makes a problem "philosophical". Hundreds and hundreds of problems haunted us since the beginning of our civilisation which are dealt by philosophy with a central concern on ethics, epistemology and metaphysics. Modern development of the subject also includes more in this study like aesthetics, logic and many more. Metaphysics involves the examination of concepts that play the key role in different areas other than philosophy such as:

(i) To identify the "true nature" of things by going beyond nature and try to understand the essence of it and reasons of its being.
(ii) It tries to study basic structure of existence and reality.
(iii) It is concerned with things which might not belong to existing space and time.

We are aware of the distinction between laws, regularity and intuition (mainly using mathematical logic) to explain what is happening around us. There are laws which generalise between events of regularities. But there are certain regularities termed as laws, for example certain genes (segregation-distorters) that do not obey the genetic law of random segregation. They are termed as ceteris paribus laws. The frequently used example – all ravens are black – also falls in this category. In that sense, many laws of social science fall under this category. Laws are understandable through the concept of causation, necessitation and explanation. While dealing with regularity, we find law and sometimes, it becomes universal – as for example the law of gravity of Isaac Newton which explains not only planetary motion but many more with mathematical intuition. This leads to a new terminology "Laws of Nature". But David Hume observed that "all events seem entirely loose and separate. One event follows another but we never can observe any link between them". In the example of heat produced by fire, we feel heat after the occurrence of fire, but there is no connection between the two. Here we do not expect mysterious connection between events – no metaphysics to cope with. Metaphysics is also termed as "After Physics". Metaphysics is the discussion on those subject matters which are beyond this physical world, the ultimate nature of reality. As stated, science deals with physical world. So twentieth-century philosophers found some contradictions between science and metaphysics. Logical Positivists of Vienna Circle always considered metaphysics as nonsensical. But Karl Popper, who was sceptic about induction, could not assert on the opinion that metaphysics had no value for empirical science. According to him "it cannot be denied that along with metaphysical ideas which have obstructed the advance of science there have been others – such as speculative atomism –which have aided it". He also expressed that despite the fact that a faith is completely unwarranted from the point of view of science yet scientific discovery was impossible without faith in ideas, where in many cases they are of purely speculative kind. This according to him is "metaphysical".

Theories and Reasoning

Consider the following.

1 Biologists tell us that we are closely related to chimpanzees.
2 Geologists have established that Africa and South America were once joined together.
3 Cosmologists tell us that the universe is expanding.

If we ask, "whether these are in the imagination of common man", the answer will be "no". Scientists have established them by a process of reasoning or inference. All logically correct arguments fall into two types: deductive and inductive. They are fundamentally different from each other. In a valid deductive argument, all the content of the conclusion is present in the premises and if premises are true, then the conclusion entails premises. Induction is ampliative. Even the argument based on true premises conclusion may be false, and it does not entail premises. In deductive patterns of reasoning, premises of the inference entail conclusion. But in inductive reasoning, premises do not entail conclusion. However concrete the deductive reasoning is, in nature, mankind depends on inductive reasoning and so the scientist. Popper was the believer of deductive inferences, but most philosophers believe that inductive reasoning is more acceptable to a scientist. Though induction may not be universally accepted, it is one of the standards we use to decide whether the claims about the world are justified or not. Here we may refer to the Cambridge philosopher Frank Ramsay's conclusion – "Ask for a justification of induction is to cry for the moon". As mentioned earlier, we always ask "why" to understand nature, which is an important role of philosophy of science. Naturally, such explanation demands argument.

Let us consider the following four examples.

1   All humans are mortal.
    Galileo is human.
    Galileo is mortal.

2   All observed crows are black.
    All crows are black.

3   First five eggs in a bucket are found rotten.
    The eggs are to be used before a particular date.
    So, the sixth egg will also be rotten.

4   All colitis patients are anaemic.
    Mr Ghosh is a colitis patient.
    Mr Ghosh is also anaemic.

In example 1, the conclusion entails from true premises, but in examples 2 and 3, conclusion does not entail premises as we have not checked all the crows, and as all eggs may not be rotten within the date. The fourth example, though it is deductive in nature, explanation is required for the trueness of premises.

If we consider another example:

"Eating of cheese cube by mouse"
A cheese cube on a shelf has disappeared apart from a few crumbs.
Scratching noises coming from the area is high.
So, the cheese was eaten by mouse.

It is again non-deductive as the premises do not entail conclusion. Rather, there may be other conclusion(s) to the example. We may explain it from a different perspective. We may say it is an act of dishonest maid in the house who ate it when a boiler was running at night. The maid mischievously kept a few crumbs and the cracking sound is from a nearby boiler. There is no doubt the first explanation is simple and fits the incident correctly.

The inductive inference discussed so far has similarity like "as all x's that are examined so far is y, the next x reexamined is also y". It is similar to doctors' prediction that all colitis patients are anaemic based on their observations. Popper in fact questioned this; he emphasised whether we could allow inference which takes us from examined to unexamined. Such inference is not only used in science but also widely used in our daily life.

However, if we examine Darwin's argument on anatomical similarities between the legs of horses and zebras, or the explanation of Brownian motion of Einstein, they give us another common type of non-deductive inference that does not fit this pattern. In case of similarity, we have to distinguish between the explanations: *God created both horses and zebras separately or both are descended from a common ancestor.* Brownian motion is another interesting example in this regard. Though several explanations were suggested to explain the Brownian motion – the motion of particles suspended in a fluid discovered in 1827, by the biologist Robert Brown – the final explanation was obtained in 1905, by Albert Einstein by considering random motion of molecules of fluids and their constant impact with suspended particles. This also convincingly established the existence of atoms and molecules.

The role of natural laws in explanation is quite significant. If A is the explanation of B, then we have to know the content law of A. Similarly, if in some case the cause X is incomplete to explain Y, we need to find the law which will be able to explain Y with other condition(s). This clearly indicates that for explanation we need to have the knowledge of laws which are essential for explanation. This is nothing but human participation of using knowledge of explanation to explain certain facts using some knowledge of law and its causal connection, if any.

"Inference to the Best Explanation" is used extensively in science. We have given a few of them already. One classical example of it is the phlogiston theory (a complete metaphysical entity) of eighteenth century to explain the theory of combustion. In this theory phlogiston is the central explanatory entity. The irrelevance of phlogiston in this theory of combustion is now well established with the modern concept of combustion in Lavoisier's theory, where combustion is a result of reaction between the burning substance and the gas oxygen present in the atmosphere. Similarly, we recall the journey of theory of light in explaining different optical phenomena from the age of Newton to the age of quantum mechanics. In the time of Newton, light was treated as particle in his "corpuscle theory" to explain the property of propagation of light and the same was able to explain optical phenomena like reflection and refraction. When phenomena like interference and diffraction of light were observed, Huygens was forced to introduce wave theory of light by the prediction of presence of a fictitious fluid medium – ether, which pervades the universe (another metaphysical idea) – to explain the propagation of optical wave. The explanation of all wave phenomena, till date, then found realistic explanation through Maxwell's electromagnetic theory. This was able to explain additionally the transverse nature of light wave and yet another new optical phenomenon – polarisation. But, finally, quantum mechanics introduced the dual character of photon, a type of elementary particle, which not only explained all the phenomena of optics but also explained the interaction of light with metal observed in photoelectric effect, Compton scattering etc. Source of light also got an explanation. According to quantum mechanics, photon is the quantum of electromagnetic field including electromagnetic radiation such as light and radio waves and the force carrier for the electromagnetic wave. This also helped us to understand scientific realism.

The main criticism of Inference to the Best Explanation (IBE) is that we expect that simplicity or unwillingness to accept the explanation is somewhat subjective (we may refer to the example of eating the cheese cube where the inference that the mouse ate the cube is simple to explain). No objective reason is prescribed in such a choice. Philosophy of science needs to answer this. Also, we also come across several problems where philosophers of science are interested in probabilistic explanation apart from induction. Probability is used in many branches of science, especially in physics and biology. Kinetic theory of gas in physical science and transmission of genes from one generation to another in biological explanation may be referred among many. Probability also in some cases throws light on inductive inferences. Naturally, the question arises whether such inductive inference leads to truth of the conclusion. This also raises interesting questions about the structure of scientific reasoning, the nature of rationality, measure of confidence the society put on science and so on.

New Movement

Many philosophers of early twentieth century tried to establish a demarcation between metaphysics and science. Ernst Mach was one of the pioneers of this movement. By his influence, Moritz Schlick, Otto Neurath, Hans Hahn and many more formed a group called "Vienna Circle". The philosophy of the group was "Logical Positivism". Their positivism was nothing but continuation of the old philosophical tradition of David Hume. The starting point for this group was a general distrust of speculative metaphysics. The traditional metaphysical questions like – "what is reality's true nature?"; "what lies beyond observable things?" – were considered meaningless. They observed metaphysics as covering those philosophical enterprises which attempted to describe reality as a whole, or to find the purpose of the universe or to reach beyond the everyday world to some suprasensible spiritual order. Metaphysics was nonsensical to them. They suggested the existence of meaningful statement to describe science. According to them, the meaning of a statement is determined by the way in which it can be verified and where it is verified, it consists in its being tested by empirical observation. Naturally, the language for statements should impart factual statement. They termed it as "verification principle" to demarcate between metaphysics and science. In regard to value statement, they argued that one thing is excluded in their verification principle – the metaphysical views are descriptive in the realm of values and also it exists independently on its own in the natural world. This leads to another view of this group that it is not the business of the philosopher to make value judgments on metaphysical view. This led them to fix the domain of philosophy of science. According to them, science provides us the knowledge of world and there is no philosophical brand of knowledge which would compete with science. In a sense, philosophy is to be treated as logic of science or in other words, philosophy should merge into science. In the words of Moris Schlick, "Philosophy is to be regarded not as a body of doctrine but as an activity".

The entire issue is closely related to scientific explanation. Obviously, in the example this group that it of why the sky becomes red during sunrise or sunset may not be only verified by observation but also to be explained by a scientific generalisation through the phenomenon of scattering of light and the laws it follows. But, sometimes, we see more deepness in understanding the explanation of a phenomenon. If we try to explain the explanation of expansion of universe, it is understandable from the redshift indicating the movement of galaxies away from us, but this is not an explanation of why the universe is expanding.

In the same twentieth century, Karl Popper introduced – "Our science is not knowledge. It can never claim to have attained truth or even a substitute for it, such as probability". He treated scientific discoveries as a guesswork in sharp contrast to the theory of paradigm of Thomas Kuhn. So, the debate starts on explanation, verification and many more.

Debate

The debate starts with the problem of understanding how observations can confirm a scientific theory. This demands an answer to the question – what is the connection between an observation and a theory that makes the observation as an evidence to the theory? This was the central project of logical positivists and logical empiricists. Logical empiricists tried to develop a logical theory of evidence and confirmation. Here, the theory treated confirmation through an abstract relation between sentences. So, scientists and philosophers tried to develop a different kind of theory to analyse testing and evidence.

To address the issue of confirmation of theories, we need to understand the "Problem of Induction" commonly known as Hume's problem, named after David Hume, an eighteenth-century Scottish empiricist and philosopher. Hume was sceptical on induction, and according to him "what reason do we have for thinking the future will resemble past?" But, at the same time, he accepted that all are using induction to understand what is going around the world.

There are many examples we have mentioned and going to mention. In the example that all observed swans are white on the basis of multiple observations in the past lead one to conclude that all swans are white. Similar to a doctor's continuous observation helps him to diagnose that all colitis patients are anaemic. But in Copernicus's theory or in Darwin's theory of evolution, we do not have such observational data. In this background, Sir Karl Popper, a philosopher of science in the twentieth century, came forward to throw light on our ever-old question "what is science?". He was not interested on logical positivists' theory of science which contains general theory of language, meaning and knowledge.

He tried to understand science in a different and distinctive way. In 1919, Popper faced the problem of drawing a line of demarcation among those statements and systems of statements which could be properly described facts belonging to empirical science and others and which might be described as pseudoscience. In his opinion, the problem was lying unanswered since the time of Francis Bacon. In his time, the most accepted idea of science was characterised by its observational basis or by its inductive method, while pseudoscience or metaphysics were characterised by speculative method. Popper could not accept these views. He gave the example of the highly speculative general theory of relativity of Einstein in understanding his concept of demarcation. In this context, Popper felt the need for a different criterion of demarcation. He proposed his concept of "refutability" or "falsifiability" of a theory that should be taken as the criterion of demarcation. Moreover, according him, the testability is same as refutability and therefore might also be taken as a criterion of demarcation. His thought about "falsifiability" of scientific theory does not mean that theory is false. Rather, it means that the theory makes some definite predictions that are capable of being tested against experience.

In the face of his falsification theory, it seemed that progress of science might be difficult against refutation. Many scientists and philosophers raised questions on it. We are not going to discuss it in detail here.

But we want to discuss how Karl Popper expressed his view on scientific changes. Even in this view he maintained his concept of "falsification". According to him, science changes in a two-steps cycle, which repeats endlessly. In the first instance, it is conjecture – meaning, a scientist will offer a hypothesis that might describe and explain some part of the world, which must be bold and capable of taking risks by making exemplary prediction. In the second stage of the cycle, the scientist puts his hypothesis to critical testing, which Popper termed as attempted refutation. According to Popper, if the hypothesis is refuted, the scientist has to go back to the first stage to offer a new conjecture. Popper, in this argument, tries to describe a scientist as good if he was able to come up with imaginative, creative and risky ideas and at the same time had a strong willingness to stand against any imaginative ideas for critical testing. Here I find that he actually believed in brilliant inductive ideas.

Even with this discussion, we may say that Karl Popper's view was somewhat a replica of Hume's problem, which states that use of induction cannot be rationally justified. But it is our habit to use induction in achieving scientific goals.

Also, whenever we make inductive inferences, the presupposition is "Uniformity of Nature". Even Galileo insisted on the importance of abstraction and idealisation in physics, thereby extending the reach of inductive techniques. Galileo's anti-Aristotelian polemic was not directed against Aristotle's inductive–deductive method. He accepted Aristotle's view of scientific enquiry as a two-stage progression from observations to general principles and back to observations. Moreover, Galileo approved Aristotle's position that explanatory principles must be induced from the data of sense experience. In all his work, he made use of idealisations such as "free fall in a vacuum" and the "ideal pendulum". The idealisations used are not observed phenomena. Concept of falling body in vacuum (which is not observed in actual practice), concept of point mass, inextensible string and many more are examples of inductive approach. Though common perception is that the laws of gravity, which quantify the attraction between any two massive bodies in the universe, not only explain laws of free-falling body but also many more.

Similarly, observations of validity of Newton's law of gravity on certain planets persuade us to consider its validity for all planets. Also, all bodies obey the law of gravitation and all Down Syndrome sufferers have one extra chromosome (47 instead of 46) are the other examples. Accumulation of knowledge along with scientific explanation helped to establish them.

Hume's argument seems to show that induction cannot be rationally justified. Hume believed that it loosens the foundation of science, and he advocated it in his famous Hume's problem of induction. Hume's problem is the conflict between believer and doubter, and it also questions the advancement of science that is mostly invented on the basis of induction.

According to Karl Popper:

1   Scientific theories are never truly verified. Moreover, to be always verified is not a virtue in a scientific theory;
2   Verification and falsification are **asymmetrical**;
3   No accumulation of confirming instances is sufficient to verify a universal generalisation;
4   But only **one** disconfirming instance suffices to **refute** a universal generalisation;
5   Hypothesis is scientific if and only if it has the potential to be refuted by some possible observation. The theories are distinguished by the fact that they are **capable of being refuted.** They are **falsifiable;**
6   If the predictions turn out to be wrong, the theory is disproved;
7   Popper thought that some theories did not satisfy this condition and may be called pseudoscience instead of science.

To him Einstein's science was an example of genuine science while that of Freudian psychology and Marxist view of society and history were pseudoscience.

Now, the general concept is that a theory is built up with the empirical "trappings" of real science, including a system of theoretical concepts and a wealth of corroborating evidence. So, the so-called pseudoscience should have built-in "defense mechanisms" against possible refutation. The very idea of Popper would make the entire explanation of planetary motion falsified, if planet Neptune was not discovered. It was earlier observed that the orbit of Saturn indicates a departure from the prediction from Newton's theory of gravitation. This could have led to suggest Newton's theory a pseudoscience, but instead they continued to explain with the same theory and tried to explain the conflicting observations. The discovery of Neptune came to the rescue. Another example is Einstein's general relativity. If it had failed its famous test of 1919, during solar eclipse, where deflection of light was observed when the light from a star passed near the Sun, no one would have taken the theory seriously. Arthur Stanley Eddington carried out his observation during the solar eclipse of 1919. He observed the deflection of light at the Sun's edge during that solar eclipse where the light from stars that pass near the edge of the Sun deflected on its way to the Earth. Einstein's general theory of relativity predicted that the Sun would bend this light as it passed by the Sun. The results of Eddington's observations agreed with the relativity theory and conflicted with Newtonian classical mechanics. So, it passed the test with the evidence of the displacement of the star's apparent position. A new concept to Newton's theory of gravitation was established. It was clear that this episode verified the general relativity theory of Einstein and saved it from falsification.

Here we find the difference of Popper's idea from that of logical empiricists. While logical empiricists were of the opinion of the existence of theory of confirmation or inductive logic, Popper was a believer of deductive logic.

Imre Lakatos (1922–1974) tried to counter Logical Positivists of his time including Popper with the following questions:

1   How do scientists decide whether, or when, their theory is refuted?
2   How do we explain why scientists persist in working on theories in the face of counterexamples?

In fact, Lakatos emphasised that one or two unexplained falsifications – called anomalies – should not reject a theory. We discussed the same with examples earlier. Lakatos intended to develop a scheme, called "methodology of scientific research program" that would distinguish between theories which had a successful strategy for dealing with anomalies that arose, if any. They are "research programs". They consist of a "hard core" of fundamental principles that contain what the theory really says about the world and a "protective belt" of "auxiliary hypotheses" that explains how the fundamental principles apply to particular cases and how to deal with apparent discrepancies. Thus, contrary to Popper, *even good theories have "defense-mechanisms"*. While the research programme as a whole may change over time, its hard core remains the same. The role of auxiliary belt is to change according to observable phenomena. As for example taking the Maxwell's theory of distribution of velocity of gaseous molecules as hard-core theory, it helped us to explain specific heat, conductivity, viscosity and many more of the gases. Though Lakatos emphasised not to abandon the theory in the face of anomalies, he suggested the need to improve on approximations taken in the theory. In the same example of Maxwell's gaseous theory of molecules, we needed to rethink on approximations like point shape and interaction-free molecules. The same example may be cited for the application of Newton's law of motion and law of gravity on motion of ideal pendulum and free-falling bodies.

Lakatos introduced three conditions, which if followed, the programme would progress; otherwise, it would be degenerating. The programme consists of a series of theories superseding earlier ones, maintaining the same hardcore. The conditions are stated as:

(i) Later theories should have some content not proposed by earlier theories;
(ii) Later theories accept the success of earlier; and
(iii) *Later theories should have more information inputs than earlier.*

So, there is a possibility in Lakatos's idea that a theory may be degenerating. In that case, a competing programme may come up and allegiance to it may be inevitable. This, somehow, resembles the idea of Thomas Kuhn.

Paul Feyerabend questioned the rationality and irrationality of taking Lakatos's hard-core theory as a methodological tool, when the existing hard-core theory is degenerating. A response to this critique can be reconstructed from Lakatos's remarks and general positions may be put in stating that the theory about research programmes is not primarily intended as a methodological rulebook for ongoing research. Instead, it is to be seen as a methodology for rational reconstruction of the history of science. Lakatos tried to develop events as a rational process from history of science to fit his model. Whether a programme be abandoned or not depends on the degree of degeneracy. Here again, we have to rely on the subjective view of researchers.

On the other hand, Carl G. Hempel, the contemporary philosopher of the twentieth century, introduced covering law model. In the explanation of any event, he emphasised on "explanation seeking why questions". He suggested that for explanation of a fact or thing it might be required to show how it could be subsumed under a law or set of laws together with various relevant conditions. This approach of explanation was initially called deductive nomological (D-N) view, but predominance of induction in many scientific explanations also forced him to introduce the probabilistic-statistical model. Causal explanation also has some contribution in it. In a philosophical view of scientific explanation, we call a sentence in it which does the explaining as explanans and that which report the event to be explained is termed as explanandum.

In the D-N model, the philosophers look into the objective link between explanandum and explanans. This was considered from the belief that science is constituted by truth. When we ask for an explanation of an event, it means that already the event has happened. Now our task is to find those accumulated required information into our possession to explain even before the explanandum event occurred. This prior information is nothing but a law and a statement of boundary or initial conditions that together logically imply explanandum. This process must have two properties – (a) truth preserving and (b) to decide whether premises of an argument logically imply the conclusion as an objective matter of fact.

Let us consider examples like why sugar dissolves in water or when a lump of potassium is dropped in a beaker filled with water, it produces a gas and potassium disappears. The explanation is chemical – in the first case, it is the property of sugar molecules and water that causes sugar to dissolve while in the second case it is the chemical reaction which produces gas as per the reaction: $2K + 2H_2O = 2KOH + H_2$

In Hempel's own words, the requirements of the D-N model, or commonly called "Covering law model", are as follows.

(i) The explanation must be a valid deduction argument;
(ii) The Explanans must contain at least one general law actually needed in the deduction;
(iii) The explanans must be empirically testable;
(iv) The sentences in the explanans must be true.

The first condition guarantees the relevance of the explanans to the explanandum while the second condition excludes non-explanatory arguments such as the following.

Dew forms in winter.
Dew is found on a tree near my balcony on a Monday winter.
So, the dew will be observed on the same tree on next Monday.

The third condition stands for testability, as in the previous example, the testability may not be possible or has no relevance with explanans. But in the example of sugar dissolved in water, sugar will dissolve in water irrespective of space and time. The fourth condition indicates explanans to be true. Now we concentrate on another example: variation of pressure and volume ($PV = K$ at constant temperature) according to Boyle's law or variation of volume and temperature ($V/T = C$ when pressure is constant) according to Charles's law of ideal gas.

In the example, the very term "ideal" indicates that the aforementioned relations are approximate. So, there is lack of certainty. Interestingly, in the argument:

Law: at constant temperature $PV=K$ for ideal gas.
Conditions: Temperature is constant.
Volume decreased to one-third.
Entail
Explanundum: The pressure increased to threefold.

We see it follows all the conditions of Hempel, but there is uncertainty because of the condition "ideal". In fact, the empirical Boyle's law or Charles's law are actually the fruit of an entirely different logic – the kinetic theory of gases. This theory needs many empirical conditions like point-shaped molecules, interaction-free molecules, interacting elastically with each other and so on, where from the Boyle's law and Charles's law are deduced. That is why Hempel also accounted for probabilistic-statistical explanation.

An improved version of the D-N model is unification. In the D-N model, an explanandum is logically inferred from the explanans, but the explanatory force of an argument does not primarily lie in this particular inference. Whereas it is reality that many disparate phenomena can be similarly explained from the same explanans. This union is accomplished when the explanans not only explains a particular explanandum but also others simultaneously. As an illustration of this idea, once again we consider Newton's law of gravitation. Is it used to explain only the free fall acceleration of any object? In that case, we could not term it as universal law as termed by the scientists. However, we know that the law of gravitation can be used to explain many seemingly unrelated phenomena such as Kepler's three laws of planetary motion; the motion of pendulum; the tides; the orbits of comets; the Earth's flattening at the poles; the precession of the vernal equinox, and so on. This means that our reasons for believing the law of gravitation are not limited to the particular phenomenon we want to explain in the first place, but that there are other independent empirical observations that serve as evidence for the law of gravitation. This property that the law of gravitation as an explanatory force unifies the description of a number of phenomena into a coherent theory.

Scientific Reasons and Revolution in Science

In earlier sections we took the help of scientific facts, their explanation and philosophical thought patterns that are the subject of philosophy of science. In doing so, it becomes clear to us that scientific ideas change very fast in all branches of science. We know the journey of concept of light from Newton to modern quantum mechanics. Similarly, in case of constituent of elements, we saw the rapid change of ideas of Dalton's atomic theory, where hydrogen atom was the lightest atom, by the modern atomic theory of the twentieth century. After the discovery of electron, a particle lighter than hydrogen atom and negatively charged, modern atomic theory started its journey with Rutherford's idea of nucleus – then modified substantially with a new revolutionary concept of stationary quantised orbit of electron round the nucleus by Niels Bohr. Finally, the actual picture of atom was obtained through quantum mechanics. All this took place after the discovery of unobservable electron by J.J. Thomson in 1897, while explaining "Cathode Ray Tube Experiment". If we consider the position of science in any of its field – whether physical science or biological science, the prevalent theories are very different from those of 50 years ago. There is no doubt that science is a rapidly changing activity compared to any other field.

We are now going to discuss Thomas Kuhn, a prominent historian of science. In the process of explanation, we have discussed that if observational evidence undermines a theory, we need at least an explanation to understand the key factor(s) that determine the success of theory. In fact, the new idea on philosophy of science is stated by Kuhn in his famous book, *The Structure of Scientific Revolutions*. In this book, we get a unique philosophy which addresses the revolution of science from time to time. It is an entire world view, consists of "Metaphysical" views about the nature of the world and the things in it. He introduced the idea of a conception of what should constitute a legitimate scientific question and what should not and also a conception of what should constitute a scientific fact.

Kuhn discussed on scientific changes and scientific revolution with an emphasis on the need to know about history of science for addressing the sharp distinction between discovery and justification. It was particularly important in light of view of Logical Positivists. In fact, Logical Positivists paid very little attention to the history of science. As mentioned earlier, the main aim of Logical Positivists, who dominated for a short period immediately after revolutionary achievements of science in the early twentieth century, was to make philosophy itself more scientific. They emphasised on the "objectivity" in science. According to them, science must have rational activity and its goal is to find the surest path to reach the truth. Thomas Kuhn differed on it as the concept of positivists is to justify an existing theory. Kuhn addressed their drawback at this stage by pointing out that they had little concern on history of science. According to him, they failed to distinguish between "context of history" and "context of justification". They followed "context of justification" which means that the scientist justifies his theory once it is already there by way of testing or searching for evidences. The "context of history" is subjective, and here the positivists have no role in understanding science through it. An example may be given regarding the discovery of electric cell (commonly called battery) by a biologist's, Volta's, observation. He observed the vibration of a dead frog, soaked in acid solution, when it came into contact with metal. The entire explanation belongs to physical science. The theory of buoyancy of Archimedes is another example. We need to understand that in both the above examples, the hypothesises had to undergo scientific test, but simultaneously we can mention that both the cases are examples of the fact that they are not the product of careful, scientific thought.

Kuhn was especially interested in scientific revolution – the periods of great upheaval when existing thoughts and ideas of science were replaced by new ones. Kuhn termed those revolutionary changes in the idea of science as "paradigm". According to Kuhn "paradigm exemplars" of the right kind of problem is to solve and the right way to solve it. A paradigm, therefore, determines not only a set of beliefs about the world. It also defines what counts as good science and even determines what counts as a scientific fact. According to Kuhn, paradigms are more than just equations or laws or statements usually found in textbooks.

A number of examples of scientific revolutions may be given such as the revolution in astronomy by Copernicus refuting Ptolemy's geocentric view of universe, the revolution in physics by Einstein overcoming the long old idea of Newton where we find the changes of definition of mass as well as the changes in the concept of our world view which became four dimensional. Darwinian revolutions in biology are another example in biological science. The evolution of quantum mechanics dislodged the concept of deterministic science. Each of these revolutions led to fundamental changes in the understanding of science and its beliefs, and a completely different set of ideas emerged. To understand the role of paradigm, we can mention that the paradigm of Newtonian mechanics is not confined in its statements and equations, but it actually portrays the universe as a deterministic time evolution in which fundamental properties of things are position and momentum. They are capable to explain the rest of its behaviour. The paradigm also includes the set of equipment or apparatus, a methodology and many more, indeed the entire metaphysics. In support of his concept of "paradigm shift", Kuhn emphasised more on the exemplars than any statement or equation.

Now, let us summarise some philosophical claims arising from Kuhn's view:

1   *The conflict among paradigms cannot be settled on any rational methodological grounds, because each paradigm contains its own view of rational scientific methodology.*
2   *The conflict cannot be resolved by an appeal to the facts, since each paradigm contains a view of what counts as a fact and will determine how it adherents to view the facts.*
3   *Different and competing paradigms are in fact "incommensurable", not comparable by any neutral standard. Adherents of different paradigms "live in different worlds" and speak different languages that are not inter-translatable. Proponents of competing paradigms see certain types of phenomena in different ways. A change of paradigm involves changes in the meaning of basic theoretical terms. They reflect divergent conceptual orientations; for example where the Aristotelian "sees" the slow fall of a constrained body, the Newtonian "sees" it differently. A similar example of the isochronous motion of a pendulum by Newton may be mentioned here.*
4   *The replacement of one paradigm by another cannot be viewed as progression on any objective grounds. It is just different.*
5   *Since adherents of different paradigms define the questions differently, and accept different standards for a good answer, the conflict between them has no neutral resolution.*
6   *A scientific revolution has to be regarded as a social and psychological phenomenon rather than as a purely intellectual one. For an individual scientist, the change in point of view is more like a religious conversion than a rational process of comparing theories against facts.*

It is needless to mention that revolutions are not frequent events, but scientific explanation and theorisation are continuous processes. Kuhn introduced "normal science" to describe such day-to-day activities of scientists. But interestingly, scientists, in their activities, are helping to strengthen the existing paradigm or fine-tuning it on the basis of observations and explanation, without questioning the reliability of the paradigm. Thus, paradigm is a constellation of shared assumptions, beliefs and values that unites scientific community and allows normal science to proceed. Many questioned it by saying whether it led to a closed society.

During normal science, we deal with the following empirical enquiries.

(i) *It tries to re-determine relevant established observational claims, already existing, to affirm how precise the current paradigm is compared to its predecessor;*

(ii) *The role of normal science is to establish those facts that vindicate the paradigm;*

(iii) *It concentrates on experiments to solve those problems that the paradigm draws attention to.*

We can reiterate the example of deviation of the orbital path of Saturn which could not be solved from the then-available data. But scientists, keeping faith in the paradigm of Newtonian mechanics, continued to do normal science. They used sophisticated telescopes and found the presence of two new planets, Uranus and Neptune, which helped them to explain the anomaly. Now, we will try to understand the strength of Kuhn's idea. Kuhn turned down the common belief that when scientists try to find explanation to a new experiment/observation, they should do so on the basis of objective evidence. But as mentioned earlier, adoption of a new paradigm also involved some sort of acceptance of the paradigm and faith in it. A criticism between "the concept of falsifiability" and "idea of Growth of Knowledge in normal sciences" is the basic flashpoint for a well-known debate between Popper and Kuhn.

Like the falsifiability of Popper, there is dogmatism in the approach of Kuhn in proceeding normal science when no question can be raised on the paradigm by the scientists. In his writing, Popper also expressed the need of it. According to him "Dogmatism allows us to approach a good theory in stages, by way of approximations: if we accept defeat too easily, we may prevent ourselves from finding that we were very nearly right". However, the extent to which dogmatism is useful, according to this view, is only insofar as they are fallible. According to Kuhn, the research worker, so far as he is engaged in normal science, is a solver of puzzles, not a tester of paradigms.

The salient features of Kuhn's paradigm theory also raised a few questions which we will discuss now. In normal cases, it is imperative that when scientists transfer their allegiance from some existing theory to a new one, there should be objective evidence. But Kuhn wrote "the transfer of allegiance from paradigm to paradigm is a conversion of experience which cannot be forced". Or, in other words, it is the peer pressure of scientists. This idea caused an uproar among many as it questioned not only the objectivity of science but also whether we can rely on scientific truth.

According to Kuhn, in pre-paradigm state a few numbers of puzzles/problems and some unexpected phenomena might not find explanation with the prevailing paradigm. Normal science should take a role in this stage to explain them using existing paradigms and might get a partial solution. But revolution occurs when one or few of those solutions resists the very concept of paradigm. The concept of light wave composed of photon was used by Max Plank in 1895, to explain black body radiation, and the same photon, a particle having energy, was used by

Albert Einstein to explain photoelectric effect. During that pre-quantum era, these explanations were proposed without the knowledge of the dual character of photon. But the dual character of photon found theoretical explanation after quantum mechanics. The example of postulating the structure of atom which started from Rutherford to Niels Bohr is also a pre-paradigm explanation. These explanations were purely on inductive reasoning.

Also, Kuhn considered in his theory that "paradigm" is not cumulative, which was also disputed by many. There is no doubt that scientists and philosophers consider that the progress of science programmes is advancing linearly towards truth. Hence, progress of science is cumulative. But Kuhn emphasised that journey from Aristotelian mechanics to Newtonian mechanics and then to Einstein's relativistic mechanics is obviously not a linear journey as Einstein's relativity theory is closer to Aristotle's than to Newton's. To address the issue, he coined the language that a new paradigm is altogether a different world view. According to him, truth itself becomes relative to paradigm.

The two important aspects of Kuhn on paradigm are "incommensurability" and "theory ladenness". Kuhn argued that competing paradigms are "incommensurable". He used that "each paradigm is different world view" to establish that when an existing paradigm is replaced by a new one, scientists abandon the whole concept. The concept of "mass" in Newtonian mechanics (mass is a conserved quantity) is not comparable to the same entity "mass" in relativity theory (where it varies with its velocity and mass plus energy is constant). We need to take relativistic mass in synchrotron than Newtonian mass in calculating the energy. A similar change in the concept of space and time took place when we moved from Newton to Einstein. Both are not mere linear progressions as normally we believe. Kuhn's doctrine on paradigm states that when allegiance is transferred to a new paradigm, the process is more like a religious conversion than a rational shift of belief supported by relevant evidences. We cannot say the earlier paradigm is wrong and the new one is correct. To do so, there must be a common platform. But Kuhn insisted that they are just different.

Kuhn also expressed his argument on "theory ladenness" of data in establishing his theory of paradigm. To choose between two conflicting theories, it is a common practice by scientists to fit a particular piece of available data in the chosen theory. But this requires the data to be independent of theory. The existence of theory-neutral data was also the idea of Logical Positivists. Kuhn differed on it by saying that the idea of theory-neutral data is an illusion. According to him, a scientist cannot fix a set of pure data independent of his theoretical persuasion. As for example the fine structure of a spectral line cannot be explained from classical idea, it is purely a quantum mechanical effect.

According to Kuhn,

(i) If one is going to resolve between competing paradigms, it not only is possible by looking to the data or facts as what scientists count as data or facts but will also depend on his choice of paradigm.

(ii) Question may be raised on the idea of objective truth. As at one end the scientific theories and beliefs must satisfy the facts while on the other end these correspondences have no sense if the facts are themselves infected by theories. Thus, Kuhn's idea of truth is relative to paradigm.

Kuhn defended his statement that "all data or facts are theory laden" by arguing that perception is highly based on background beliefs. Psychological experiments acknowledge this. Also, scientists express their experimental and observational reports in a highly specialised language. In the previous example of Volta's invention of electric cell, observation during his experiment could not be answered if he had no understanding of electrical potential difference.

In fact, Kuhn gave an idea on how scientific training is pursued during a paradigm. The textbooks during this period contain normal science, demonstration, experiments and their lab manuals, as well as the chosen problems related to each chapter are depicted by the prevalent paradigm. The research problems are for fine-tuning the paradigm only.

The history of science observed that paradigm-testing occurs only after persistent failure to solve a noteworthy puzzle. In contrast to the view of Popper, Kuhn wrote "no theory ever solves all the puzzles with which it is confronted at a given time; nor are the solutions already achieved often perfect". On the contrary, it is just the incompleteness and imperfection of the existing data-theory. If it is found fit, at any time, it would define many of the puzzles that characterise normal science. If any and every failure to fit is the ground for theory rejection, all theories ought to be rejected at all times. The journey from Copernicus to Galileo to Newton in old classical physics and in modern physics Dalton to Niels Bohr to quantum mechanics may be cited as examples. Kuhn also commented on falsification of Popper by saying

> [F]alsification, though it surely occurs, does not happen with, or simply because of, the emergence of an anomaly or falsifying instance. Instead, it is a subsequent and separate process that might equally well be called verification since it consists in the triumph of a new paradigm over the old one.

Kuhn maintained that a logic of falsification is not applicable to the case of paradigm rejection. A paradigm cannot be rejected only on the basis of a comparison of its consequences and empirical evidence. On the contrary, paradigm rejection is a three-step process, which involves an established paradigm, a rival paradigm and the observational evidence.

In the debate about the scientific method and adherence to essential parts of Kuhn's view, Paul Feyerabend wholly accepted the incommensurability thesis. Though he went one step further than Kuhn in criticizing the popular philosophical position where science employs a single identifiable method and the success of that method explains scientific progress. He was partly a descriptive and partly a normative critique of those, like Popper, who maintain that there is only one general methodology that qualifies as scientific. His first point of concern was the history of science. Each proposal for a scientific method hitherto considered has, in practice, often been neglected or actively rejected by active researchers, and yet these researchers have managed to make progress. Feyerabend claims that if researchers were to accept any one of the philosophers' proposed methods, it would hinder scientific progress. Here, we give an alternative view to address two competing paradigms. According to Scheffler, Kuhn, by his appeal to the gestalt analogy, had promoted confusion between "seeing x" and "seeing x-as-something-other". Also, Scheffler noted that it does not follow that because the classification systems of two paradigms differ, they are about different objects. It is indeed that different paradigms introduce different ways of classifying one and the same set of objects. Consider the case of acceleration of electrons within a synchrotron. If we interpret the situation according to the conceptual scheme of Newtonian mechanics, then we attribute to the particles a "mass" that is independent of velocity. If we interpret the situation according to the conceptual scheme of special relativity theory, then we attribute to the particles a "mass" whose value varies with velocity. The two concepts of "mass" are not the same. Nevertheless, if the competing theories are referentially equivalent in such applications, and if the relativistic interpretation achieves superior predictive success, then replacement of Newtonian mechanics by special relativity theory counts as progress. A similar example may be given of seeing the electron moving round the nucleus according to Bohr's theory in specific Bohr orbits and its wave nature that indicates maximum probability of finding the electron in Bohr radii. Here, quantum mechanics may be counted as progress to classical mechanics in describing subatomic particles – a contradiction to Kuhn.

Scientific Realism – Debate Extended

From the ancient time, there are two thought patterns that exist in philosophy of science – realism and idealism. What does science try to describe? If the answer is that it tries to describe our world, then further questions may be raised – which world are we describing? These two are also queries from commoners which philosophers need to answer. We are aware about the presence of science well before the concept of invisible atom was proposed by Dalton. Today, we are in the world composed of invisible electron to explain different atomic phenomena in physical science and invisible quark to understand basic constituents of invisible subatomic particles.

Thus, the scientific understandings of the people who lived in the world of Aristotelian's age are not the same as that of the people of the world in the present age. The traditional issues on realism/idealism belong to the domain of metaphysics. But here we like to focus on the modern debate on scientific realism against some opposite view – known as anti-realism.

The common sense realism is conceptualised in the literature as the system of world that exists independently of what one thinks or states about it, except insofar as reality is consisted of, or is causally affected by thoughts, theories and other symbols. Apart from common sense realism, scientific realism in its modified version demands that the actual and reasonable aim of science should give us accurate description of what reality is like. This includes to give accurate representations of aspects of reality that are unobservable.

In short, realists hold that the aim of science is to provide a true description of the world. While to anti-realists, the aim of science is to provide a true description of a certain part of the world that is observable. The study of the branch of science that describes paleontology or study of fossils deals with the observable. Naturally, both realist and anti-realists agree with this branch of science. But when it comes to physics, we have to consider the unobservable to describe many physically observable phenomena. Even we use them to derive technology out of it. We may here take the example of kinetic theory of gas, which explains phenomena of gases like its pressure and temperature, their relationship and many more. Here, the entire theory is developed on the concept that gasses consists of randomly moving molecules which are, no doubt, unobservable. Similarly, the concept of electron in the outer part of atom and its excitation by energy leads to laser technology. Here, anti-realists disagree.

The anti-realists claim that these unobservable entities are merely convenient fictions introduced by physicists to predict observable phenomena. In the example of kinetic theory of gas, the understanding of anti-realists is that introduction of unobservable is a way of predicting observables – their presence does not matter. Here, we find the role of anti-realists as "instrumentalism". The main thrust of anti-realists on unobservable is their understanding that the unobservable cannot actually attain knowledge. So, according to them, power of observation puts limits on scientific knowledge while realists believe that unless they have sufficient knowledge of the existence of unobservable, say matter composed of atom, it is impossible to explain a wide range of phenomena/facts about the world.

Obviously, our discussion is not to establish that realists' thought pattern is right and that of anti-realists are wrong. Rather, we may conclude that realists' thought pattern is probably based on inference to best explanation. We may again cite the example of phlogiston in chemistry, which explained combustion and existed for long to explain many other facts, but later the theory was abandoned and replaced by combustion theory. The example of introduction of ether, a fictitious fluid that pervades the universe, by Christian Huygens in 1690, to explain wave phenomena of light and then mathematical explanations of some optical phenomena by Auguste Fresnel in 1816, can also be given here. Michelson Morley's experiment suggested the impossibility of existence of ether.

Anti-realists made these as issues to establish their views from the history of science. The American philosopher Larry Lauden narrated more than 30 such cases where the theories were very successful in explaining a number of facts and phenomena, but finally they were abandoned. In those cases the theories took the help of the presence of some unobservable like phlogiston and ether as mentioned earlier. So they argued why one should rely on the theories based on unobservable, despite their success over a reasonable time before they are replaced by some alternative explanation. Even they questioned the theories based on atom or electron which are still in existence with great success in explaining numerous phenomena and helped in deriving many fruitful technologies.

Another debate that cropped up on realism and anti-realism was to distinguish between entities that are observable and those that are not. A clear distinction in a principal way is absent. As we are not in a position of distinguishing observable and unobservable, the anti-realists demanded that such theories with unobservable are agnostics.

It was thus the responsibility of realists to solve the distinction between observable and unobservable. We are now aware of modern technology which helped us to detect the presence of, say, electron in a cloud chamber and Higgs boson, the main entity behind the explanation of Standard model, in Large Hadron Collider. Now, the problem of realists is to establish whether detection of unobservable is equivalent to observing the entities. Another American philosopher Grover Maxwell may be referred to here who came forward in defence of realism in 1960. According to him, many micro objects in both physical and biological sciences are now observable by the use of high-resolution microscopes, though they are not visible to the naked eye. Similarly, in cosmology, many events that took place long back or objects that are long distance away are now observed using high-power telescopes. He thus argued that when a sophisticated instrument allows us to observe some entities which were not observable earlier, should we call these entities as observable or unobservable. Or whether we are detecting them like we detect electrons in a cloud chamber. According to him, we are basically detecting.

Conclusion

So far, we have discussed about induction, explanation, realism and scientific changes which are within the purview of general philosophy of science. Naturalism is another important branch that requires to understand philosophy of science. In this small framework, we have skipped the discussion on naturalism. But we are always facing the question – whether human mind is modular or not. We may here refer to the idea of Francis Bacon regarding man's role on dominion over nature. He emphasised that men must control and redirect natural forces to improve the quality of life of their fellow human beings. Probably, scientists are keeping in mind this important concept of Francis Bacon in their research work. Scientific discoveries when translated to technology lead to better lifestyle. It gives us strength to fight against natural calamity and many more. No doubt, the development of science finally helped mankind to develop new inventions like electricity, safe drinking water, different life-saving drugs, smooth mode of transport, communication and so on. This twenty-first-century mankind is getting all the fruits because of revolution in technology. Most of the works are for the benefit of mankind, but they also observed and faced threat from destructive uses of technology using science. Uses of science in many cases also cause harm to mankind. That does not mean science is a curse. It is also evident that the words "science" and "scientific" have acquired a peculiar cachet in modern times. We have witnessed the failure of science at different stages not only in deriving theory but also in developing technology out of it. But according to Thomas Kuhn, we should not treat them as non-science.

Traditionally, philosophy is regarded as a humanities subject despite its close historical link with mathematics and science. The question arises whether science is the ultimate knowledge. Naturally, no branch of science tells us how we should lead our lives, what is knowledge, what involves human happiness. These are quintessentially philosophical questions.

Many philosophers of the late twentieth century tried to amalgamate empiricism, realism and naturalism. There is a belief that science is the only path of knowledge. They do not give importance to those questions which cannot be resolved scientifically. According to Willard Van Orman Quine, "naturalism" means that the human being is part and parcel of the natural world. The aim of science should be to study the whole of natural world to reveal the complete truth. Recent studies of cosmology, standard model, string theory, artificial intelligence, cognitive science are trying to understand the entire universal system and human cognition leaving nothing for philosophy. So, philosophers are facing the big question, whether the entire knowledge is scientific or not.

The conflict of science and religion is age-old history. The best-known example is Galileo's clash with the Catholic Church in 1633, on the Copernican theory. Interestingly, the theological opposition to Darwin's theory still persists in southern states of the United States. The conflict is such that even in the school curriculum, there are courses on Christian doctrine on evolution, which includes Asa Gray's view that evolution was God's method of creation along with the evolution theory of Darwin.

The great achievement in biological science in the middle of the twentieth century has broken the wall between the two different branches of science – physical science and biological science. Now, science allows us to consider that all living and non-living objects are created from the same source. Yet, we are facing the elementary question – what causes such diversity in creation of world that even the creation of life is from a chemical action? Bacteria to human and tree? At the same time, we are forced to believe from history of science and its progress that our knowledge is not absolute.

We still have the unsolved ideas of absolute space, absolute velocity in physical science and the problem of biological classification in biological science. The nature of mind is another unsolved issue. Philosophy always asks questions on justification to decide:

Is there any absolute Truth?
Will science be able to arrive at it?

Suggested Readings

Armstrong, D. (2016). *What Is a Law of Nature?* Cambridge University Press, Cambridge.
Ayer, A. J. et al. (1960). *The Revolution in Philosophy*. Macmillan & Co. Ltd., London.
Bird, A. (1998). *Philosophy of Science*. McGill-Queen's University Press, Montreal.
Godfrey-Smith, P. (2009). *Theory and Reality: An Introduction to the Philosophy of Science*. The University of Chicago Press, Chicago.

Johansson, L-G. (2015). *Philosophy of Science for Scientists*. Springer, Cham.

Kuhn, T. S. (1962). *The Structure of Scientific Revolutions*. University of Chicago Press, Chicago.

Losse, J. (2001). *A Historical Introduction to the Philosophy of Science*. Oxford University Press, Oxford.

Okasha, S. (2016). *Philosophy of Science: Very Short Introduction*. Oxford University Press, Oxford.

Popper, K. R. (1992). *The Logic of Scientific Discovery*. Routledge, London and New York. First English edition published 1959 by Hutchinson & Co.

Rosenberg, A. (2011). *Philosophy of Science: A Contemporary Introduction* (Routledge Contemporary Introductions to Philosophy). Routledge, London and New York.

Salmon, W. C. (1999). Scientific explanation. In Salmon, M. H., Earman, J., Glymour, C., Lennox, J. G., Machamer, P., McGuire, J. E. and Schaffner, K. F. (Eds.) *Introduction to the Philosophy of Science*. Hackett, Indianapolis, IN, 7–41.

8

WRITTEN ON THE BODY

Agency, Representation, Deviance

Samantak Das

> Know then thyself, presume not God to scan;
> The proper study of mankind is man.
> . . .
> He hangs between; in doubt to act, or rest,
> In doubt to deem himself a God, or Beast;
> In doubt his Mind or Body to prefer,
> Born but to die, and reas'ning but to err;
> (Alexander Pope, An Essay
on Man, Epistle II)

I

I begin with the perhaps banal observation that our bodies occupy space and undergo change over time. We experience the world through our bodies, interpret it through our bodies and change it through our bodies. Marx's famous eleventh thesis on Feuerbach, "Philosophers have hitherto only interpreted the world in various ways; the point is to change it", implicitly invokes the (human) body in the act of interpretation, the variety of such interpretations and the possibility (and the crying need) for fashioning change that is seen as an intrinsic part of what makes us human. In other words, the individual human body is or can be an *agent* of change – mental as well as physical. In a material sense, it is possible to assert, *contra* Descartes, that I am, therefore I can think.

To be an agent can mean two things – jointly or severally. In the first instance, an *agent* is a "free" being who – howsoever conditioned by the circumstances of her location in a particular place at a particular time – is nevertheless free to act for herself out of her own conscious choice. Such an agent is crucially free from external control and equally free to act effectively in the "real world". This, of course,

DOI. 10.4324/9781003033448-11

is part of the project of modernity, a project that sees agents who are less than truly autonomous as being somehow less than truly modern.

Or, to put it in another way, if I am truly modern then I am a free agent, responsible for my actions and even, if need arises, accountable to a court of law for what I have done or not done. If, for instance, I were to pull out a gun and shoot someone, I could not get away by saying that *I* did not shoot that individual, that someone or something else had done so or that "the Devil made me do it". That is, to be an agent in this sense *compels* me to be accountable for my actions, whether to a judge in a court of law, my family, my employers, my audience or other human beings at large.

But agency also has another meaning – that of *representation*. Think of the travel or insurance agent who acts, not for herself, but on *behalf of* someone else, who both *represents* and *re-presents* someone other than herself. Modern political theory has a longish debate on this notion of the agent and of agency as representation, articulated almost every day in the pages of newspapers. To what extent are our elected representatives responsible for their actions to themselves (as "free" agents in their own right) and to what extent are they acting for us, their constituents (whose representatives, or agents, they are)?

To go back to my earlier example, if the individual I shot happened to be wearing the uniform of an enemy power and if I happened to be in the uniform of the Indian army, then I would, in effect, have been representing, acting as the agent of, someone or something other than my own free, autonomous self. And then, of course, I could say, "My country made me do it" and not only not go unpunished but probably get a medal in the bargain!

Somewhat paradoxically, then, the agent acts on behalf of someone or something which is both absent and present at the same time. Competitive sport, where the sportswoman represents herself as well as her club/state/country, provides just such an example of an individual body which is an agent in both senses of the term – freely acting for herself as well as representing (and re-presenting) something that is absent. Theatre, or film, where the body of the actor makes present someone who is absent is another, somewhat different, instance of the same paradox of representation.

I started by speaking of agency – embodied in the individual human being – because this very embodiment has been the locus of debates concerning, among other things, morality and responsibility, freedom and constraint, free will and predeterminism, to name just a handful of issues, in the Western tradition. Let me try to illustrate this with an example taken from literature, in the figure of Oedipus.

One of the ways in which we are reminded, often inconveniently, of our bodies is through the enactment of pain and its twin, that is punishment. In his subtle and persuasive discussion of Sophocles' masterpiece, Talal Asad asserts,

> The tragedy of *Oedipus* depicts a story of suffering and disempowerment that is neither voluntary nor involuntary. For Oedipus is an agent who, not

knowing what he has done, makes a deep difference in the world. On gradually learning the secret of his past acts he inflicts terrible wounds on the body that performed them, on the self that can neither be recognised not repudiated.

(Asad, 2003)

Oedipus cannot recognise his self because he does not hold himself responsible for killing his father (as he will assert in *Oedipus at Colonus*), nor for marrying his mother. And yet, as the agent of his people he has no choice but to act to alleviate their suffering – by disempowering himself, by inflicting punishment for an act for which he was not really responsible. (Oedipus does accept responsibility for causing the death of a man at the crossroads but not for murdering his father, which he had tried specifically to avoid.)

II

It is in this dual sense of the body as agent that I now turn to representations of the body in nineteenth-century medicine and science.

Anyone who has seen a dissected body, whether human or otherwise, knows just how messy such an object is. Yet it is necessary for us to know the details and functioning of such a body/bodies, if we are to make sense of it/them. For a long time, this need to examine human bodies, to understand their mechanisms and thus to make effective interventions, was informed with a sense of sacrilege. For a dead body has, as it were, given up one of its agential functions – the ability to act autonomously, in howsoever circumscribed a manner – and is just a representative of something else, gender, perhaps, or species, or class, or race, or occupation.

Ernst Kantorowicz's notion of the monarch's two bodies (Kantorowicz, 1957), the body natural and the body politic, provides an example of just such a diminution of agency. While alive, the king retains agency in both senses of the term, but when no longer alive, the body of the king – the body politic – becomes wholly a symbol, a pure and unambiguous agent, a representation of kingship. Hence also the profound significance attached to the socially, morally, theologically, politically "correct" disposal of such a dead body. A notion that is still prevalent particularly, but not exclusively, in Christian societies (Verdery, 1999).

Part of the stink of sin, the unhallowed aura that clung to the medical profession in the West derived precisely from this notion. If the body is sacred, even if merely as a vessel for the immortal soul, it may, after death, lose its agential autonomy, but it still retains its sacramental value as representing (standing in for) something else. To interfere with this body, especially within the parameters of Christian theology, was thus "unholy", and doctors and surgeons had perforce to enter into dubious alliances with criminal elements to procure bodies on which they could sharpen their observation of what exactly was the mechanical arrangement of flesh, blood and bone that gives the human body its complex integrity.

One way of being properly respectful to the human bodies used for medical study was to represent them as accurately as possible, preserving all the individual idiosyncratic features that give each of us a body that is uniquely our own. Yet, paradoxically, such an accurate representation of the individual human body, whilst preserving (the vehicle of) one kind of agency (that of the unique individual self) reduced, or wholly removed, the other kind of agency standing in for the generalised (human body).

Sometime in late 1855, two young doctors from London's St. George's Hospital discussed the possibility of bringing out an illustrated textbook of anatomy to assist future surgeons. The result, *Anatomy Descriptive and Surgical*, with the text by Henry Gray and illustrations by Henry Vandyke Carter, arguably the best-known medical textbook of all time, came out in 1858, and has been continuously in print since. The fortieth edition of *Gray's Anatomy* was issued in the sesquicentennial year of the book's publication, 2008, under the editorship of Professor Susan Standring, Emeritus Professor of Anatomy at King's College, London.

As Ruth Richardson points out in her meticulously researched and wonderfully readable *The Making of Mr. Gray's Anatomy*,

> There is a silence at the centre of *Gray's*, as indeed there is in all anatomy books, which relates to the unutterable: a gap which no anatomist appears to address other than by turning away. It is the gap between the ostensible subject of the book and of the discipline, and the derivation of bodies from whom its knowledge is constituted, its illustrations made. In *Gray's*, the legally sanctioned bodies of people utterly alone in the metropolis were the raw material for dissections that served as the basis for illustrations, that were rendered in print as wood engravings. As mass-produced images, they have entered the brains of generations of the living – via the eyes, the minds, and the thoughts of those who have gazed at them.
>
> But nowhere in these books is the human predicament of those whose bodies constituted their basis addressed, or discussed. Nowhere is their native status as the defeated, dismembered, unconsidered, naked poor even mentioned.
>
> *(Richardson, 2008)*

Yet, I will argue, it is precisely *because* the bodies, as bodies, are made anonymous, their individualities effaced, that they can become the carriers (agents) of knowledge. Had this "unutterable" silence at the heart of *Gray's Anatomy* been sought to be articulated, the book itself, and the purpose it had been designed to serve, would have suffered. By making his illustrations both meticulous and anonymous at the same time, simultaneously real and abstract, Henry Vandyke Carter was able to transform the dead bodies he and Gray dissected into pure agents of knowledge whose lack of local habitations and names invested them with an authority far greater than they had possessed as living individuals.

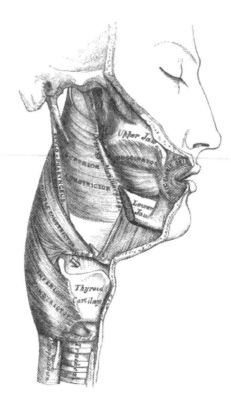

FIGURE 8.1 Muscles of the pharynx

Source: Gray's Anatomy, 1st edition, p. 211.

A quick look at a couple of illustrations from *Gray's* (Figures 8.1, 8.2 and 8.4) and one from an earlier textbook will, I hope, help us to see this better.

The next illustration (Figure 8.3) is from a textbook that preceded *Gray's Anatomy* by two years, Jones Quain's *Elements of Anatomy*, published in 1856.

Compare Quain's illustration with the same organ as depicted in *Gray's*.

Richardson's comment on these two images is instructive.

> Quain's version is in realistic mode, showing a real woman's womb separated from her body, the key parts enveloped in a ragged curtain of flesh. The entire specimen is nailed to a board in two places. The board has been propped up vertically, so gravity exerts its force on the entire specimen. It is not easy to look at, since it is, essentially, a crucifixion. Quain's version exemplifies the static sadism which anatomical images often represent, which is absent in *Gray's Anatomy*. Carter's image is a diagram of the life-giving womb, it does not – as in Quain's case – convey the impression that a woman has died for us to see it.

> *(Richardson, 2008)*

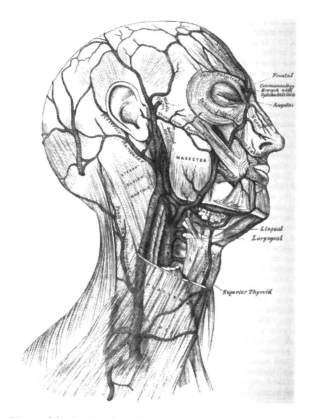

FIGURE 8.2   Veins of the head and neck

Source: Gray's Anatomy, 1st edition, p. 402.

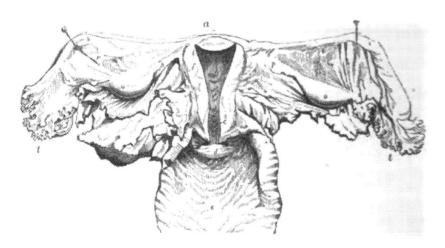

FIGURE 8.3   The uterus

Source: From Quain's *Elements of Anatomy*, Vol. II, 7th edition, p. 984.

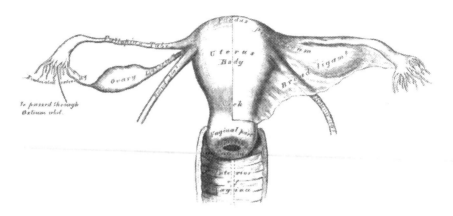

FIGURE 8.4   The uterus

Source: From *Gray's Anatomy*, 1st edition, p. 689)

The "sadistic" realism of Quain's woodcut illustration, even as it asserts the verisimilitude and accuracy of its representation, fails to transform its subject into an agent of useful anatomical knowledge. In contrast, the "unreal", abstract, map-like quality of Carter's illustration invests this (part of a) human body with agency – by removing its referents, Carter, again paradoxically, makes it a more real representation, one which, moreover, does not give us the sense that a woman died for us to see it (although a woman *did* have to die, and have her dead body dissected, for us to do so).

All these images are woodcuts, examples of an artist's rendering or representation/re-presentation of an object, allowing, as we have seen, a sometimes considerable latitude in how a body, or a part thereof, is shown. Such renderings were (and are) not, however, innocent, guided solely by the desire to impart useful knowledge. Nineteenth-century representations of the human body are rife with examples of artistic licence used to score ideological points, to turn such images into agents of a particular kind of mis-knowing or disinformation. I shall refer here to a few examples, taken from a book referred to in Stephen Jay Gould's path-breaking book, *The Mismeasure of Man* (Gould, 1992), to illustrate this.

The six illustrations in Figure 8.5 are taken from page 458 of a book published in 1854, that was, in Gould's words, "not a fringe document, but the leading American text on human racial differences" (Gould, 1992). This leading text had the formidable name of *Types of Mankind: or, Ethnological Researches, based upon the Ancient Monuments, Paintings, Sculptures, and Crania of Races, and upon their Natural Geographical, Philological, and Biblical History: Illustrated by selections from the inedited papers of Samuel George Morton, M.D., (Late President of the Academy of Natural Sciences of Philadelphia) and by additional contributions from Prof. L. Agassiz, LL.D.; W. Usher, M.D.; and Prof. H.S. Patterson, M.D.* This creation of Josiah Clark Nott and George Robins Gliddon (Nott and Gliddon, 1854) was some 780 pages long and had contributions from some of the leading naturalists of the time, including Louis Agassiz, arguably the best-known American biologist of the nineteenth

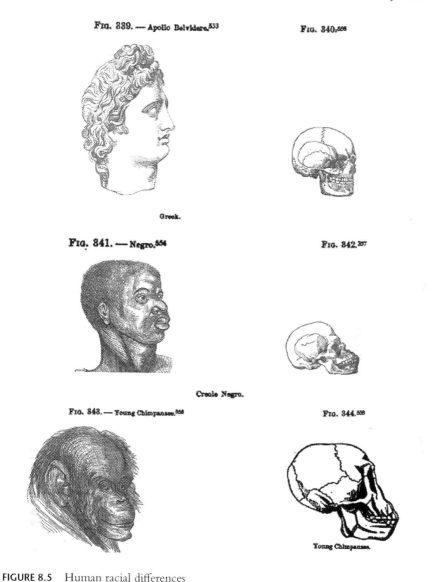

FIGURE 8.5   Human racial differences

Source: From page 458 of Nott and Gliddon's *Types of Mankind* (1854)

century. Agassiz's (1807–1873) scientific legacy is mixed. He was the first to propose the notion of Ice Age but held strongly racist views all his life, for which he sought to find scientific justification, and was a lifelong opponent of Darwin's theories of evolution.

Each illustration in *Types of Mankind* claims for itself complete verisimilitude, with the figures in superscript above the number of the picture itself (e.g. the number "554" for "Fig. 341. – Negro") referring to the source, given as part of a long list of "References and Notes" at the end of the book. Without spending too much time on *Types of Mankind*, suffice it to note for our purposes that the illustrations are neither accurate nor free from racial bias. For example in the earlier illustrations, the skull of the chimpanzee is inflated and the jaw of the Negro falsely extended to suggest that blacks may even be inferior to the "higher" apes.

Here, too, we find the bodies, or more accurately the heads and skulls, of individuals (human or otherwise), measured and noted according to the tenets of the "science" of craniometry, being used as agents to "prove" the inferiority of other races as compared to the white male of European descent.

Gray's Anatomy was published in August 1858. A little over a year later would appear Charles Darwin's *On the Origin of Species* (November 1859), a book in which bodies, their adaptations, modifications and mutability played a central role.

If the bodies in *Gray's Anatomy* are primarily *spatial* entities, in crucial ways immune to the changes wrought by time, Darwin's bodies are *temporal* things, bearing on their corporeal frame the marks wrought by the passage of time on their predecessors.

Such a temporal vision of the changing body is present in Darwin's *Descent of Man* (1871) and its companion volume, *The Expression of the Emotions in Man and Animals*, published a year later. In contrast to *Origin*, which had a single illustration, *Descent* had several, and *Expression* had many more, including several pages of photographs, in addition to drawn images.

What I have characterised as the temporality of bodies in Darwin's works had two primary functions, both central to Darwin's revolutionary reading of nature and natural processes. First, to show *change* – "descent with modification" was Darwin's preferred phrase – and second, to illustrate genealogical *affinity*. Or, to demonstrate how, in Darwin's own words, "not one living species will transmit its unaltered likeness to a distant futurity" (change) (Darwin, 1984) and how "all organic beings which have ever lived on this earth have descended from someone primordial form" (affinity) (Darwin, 1984).

Let us look at the first illustration of *Descent* to try and demonstrate this (Figure 8.6).

In this illustration, Darwin is, perhaps a bit provocatively, comparing the embryos of a dog and a human being with the intention of drawing his readers' attention to their common origin. Here, Darwin is using the notion of how ontogeny (the development of the individual) recapitulates phylogeny (the development of the species) to show genealogical affinity. This "recapitulation theory" is no longer in favour with biologists, but it is not wholly discredited either. A discussion of this fascinating aspect of evolutionary biology is obviously beyond the scope of this chapter. The bodies that are shown in this illustration are yet to become independent entities, they are still in the process of reaching that stage of agency. But even as process, rather than completed product, they are agents, representatives of two now separate, but once connected, lines of descent from one common, primordial, ancestor.

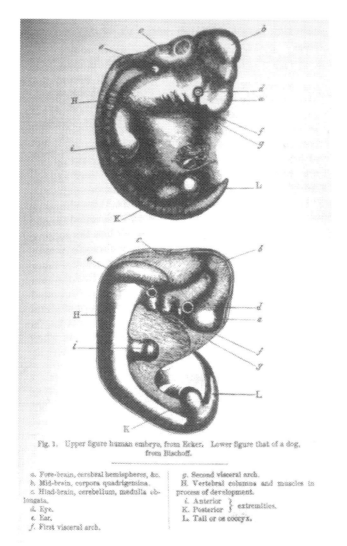

Fig. 1. Upper figure human embryo, from Ecker. Lower figure that of a dog, from Bischoff.

a. Fore-brain, cerebral hemispheres, &c.
b. Mid-brain, corpora quadrigemina.
c. Hind-brain, cerebellum, medulla oblongata.
d. Eye.
e. Ear.
f. First visceral arch.

g. Second visceral arch.
H. Vertebral columns and muscles in process of development.
i. Anterior }
K. Posterior } extremities.
L. Tail or os coccyx.

FIGURE 8.6   From *Descent of Man*

Source: Facsimile reprint of the first edition published in London: John Murray, 1871. Vol. I, Part I, the woodcuts appear as Fig. 1. on p. 15 (Darwin, 1871).

Expression of Emotions had originally been intended by Darwin to form part of *Descent*, but considerations of length forced him to abandon the idea. It was published as a separate volume in 1872, and contained, by Darwin's standards, a profusion of images. In trying to extract general rules about nervous and muscular movements in animals and humans, as a means to understanding their inner states (emotions), Darwin took help from the relatively new art of photography.

FIGURE 8.7 Plate I from *Expression* (1872)

Figure 8.7 shows Plate I from *Expression*, showing "weeping or crying, more especially in children" (Darwin, 1872).

Here, as in the other plates of *Expression*, Darwin is trying to analyse and "fix" for his readers, the dynamics of the human body as an agent of expression for emotions, whether voluntary or otherwise. Darwin was further interested in trying to show how, in the case of *involuntary* expression – especially as related to pain/fear and pleasure/joy – there are distinct physical/bodily affinities between human beings and so-called lower organisms. Once again, we find Darwin using bodies to show the affinities that exist between different kinds of animals (including human beings).

Nineteenth-century representations, and not just visual representations, of the body in the realms of medicine and science, especially evolutionary biology, thus showed the body, and especially the human body, in two linked but distinct ways. First, as an essentially spatial object, where mutability was not taken into consideration, and, second, as an essentially temporal entity, where the passage of time was fundamental to our understanding of the body – not just as the development of an individual or a species but as illustrative of genealogy and the descent that could be traced (however imperfectly) from a common ancestor.

III

These two ways of considering the body and its agency – in terms of time and in terms of space – come together in interesting and, to us, perhaps, comically horrifying, ways in the so-called science of criminology. Here, I will use a single text to make a few observations about how the body of the deviant, criminal human subject was sought to be scientifically analysed and anatomised.

The text in question is Henry Havelock Ellis's *The Criminal* (1890), a direct descendant of Cesare Lombroso's *L'uomo delinquente* ("Criminal Man", 1876), which, in turn, was a work directly inspired by Darwin's writings, particularly *Origin* and *Descent*.

Havelock Ellis's basic contention in *The Criminal* is that the criminal is a kind of brutish, underdeveloped cousin of the normal modern man (or woman). For Havelock Ellis, the true criminal is someone who "belongs as it were to a lower and older social state than in which he is actually living. It thus happens that our own criminals frequently resemble in physical and psychical characters the normal individuals of a lower race". Note the easy elision between "lower social state" and "lower race" in Havelock Ellis's formulation. This is reiterated a little later when he writes, "To admit, therefore, in the criminal, a certain psychical and even physical element belonging to a more primitive age is simple and perfectly reasonable". The chapter from which these quotations are taken is called "The Results of Criminal Anthropology". In an earlier section on the intelligence of criminals, Havelock Ellis had stated, "The stupidity and the cunning of the criminal are in reality closely related, and they approximate him to savages and to the lower animals" (p. 155). Statements of a like nature are scattered throughout the book (Ellis, 1890).

The agency of the criminal allows him or her to carry out acts that disrupt the social order. Since these acts are, by definition, abnormal, Havelock Ellis reads back from the act to the body that performed it and finds, to his satisfaction, that the abnormal/deviant act had, indeed, been performed by an abnormal/deviant body (which is also the vehicle of an abnormal/deviant mind). There is a neat dovetailing of both senses of the body as agent in Havelock Ellis's formulation. A criminal act of agency is performed by a criminal body, which then becomes the agent (representative) of all other bodies of its kind.

Part of the agenda of the science of criminology was therefore the identification of such criminal bodies *before* they could perform their criminal acts. And thus was inaugurated a long history of a form of biological determinism, centred on the body, one that has, alas, by no means disappeared. The "profiling" of potential terrorists post-9/11 being the latest manifestation of such a reading back from the act to the body that performed it.

Let us look at a couple of illustrations from *The Criminal* to understand this better.

Unless I am very mistaken, there is little that distinguishes the individuals in Havelock Ellis's Plate XVIII from those in Plate XIX in our eyes, except perhaps that those in the earlier plate appear to be somewhat younger, and neither group appears to be composed of individuals who appear to be obviously physically "abnormal". Yet, *The Criminal* clearly distinguishes between these two groups of men, in terms of their criminal natures. Plate XVIII is labelled "A group of sexual perverts (Elmira)" while Plate XIX reads "A group of the more manly and intelligent prisoners (Elmira)". Plate XVIII faces page 332 and Plate XIX faces page 334 of *The Criminal*. "Elmira" refers to the Elmira Reformatory of New York, founded in 1876, and the first prison to be so designated. It is now called the Elmira Correctional Facility. The Elmira Reformatory was widely lauded for its enlightened

FIGURE 8.8   Plates XVIII and XIX from *The Criminal* (1890)

FIGURE 8.9   Plate I, facing page 20, of *The Criminal*

view of criminals and crime, and many of its features were adopted by other prisons (Ellis, 1890). It is as though by studying these photographs closely, one will be able to spot the marks of criminality – especially those of sexual perversion – and be able to identify such deviant individuals by their physical characteristics.

The first numbered photographic plate (Plate I) in *The Criminal* is given in Figure 8.9.

This plate shows "Four youthful Russian minor criminals" (Ellis, 1890), not something that one would have readily guessed by simply looking at the countenances of the four boys shown. In fact, the individuals who are pictured in *The Criminal* do not appear (at least to our eyes) obviously abnormal, deviant or criminal. Yet, the book insists, as mentioned earlier, that there is something readily, scientifically, identifiable in the *body* of the criminal, a contention that it draws support for by showing its readers the apparatus whereby such criminals are measured, their criminal nature defined, refined and reduced to a set of figures.

Note, again, the strange backward logic used to identify criminality at work in *The Criminal*. X commits a crime. Since it *is* a crime, and X's body has committed it, then there must be something identifiably wrong with X's body. The criminologist's responsibility is to measure X's body (particularly X's head, since crimes are

FIGURE 8.10 Plate III, facing page 34 of *The Criminal*, showing the technique of mirror photography

hatched there), find the deviations and abnormalities and make scientific notes of them. Then the criminologist, assisted by all the awful majesty of the apparatus of the state, must go around, camera and measuring tape in hand, and find other bodies of X's kind. It is irrelevant whether these other X-like bodies have committed crimes or not, the very fact they are like X condemns them, for they carry, and display to the trained eye, the dangerous *possibility* of crime. In the concluding chapter of *The Criminal*, Havelock Ellis writes, "All education must include provision for the detection and special treatment of abnormal children. We cannot catch our criminals too young". It is instructive that Havelock Ellis was both a social reformer and a believer in eugenics, and he was not the only one of his kind in his time (Ellis, 1890).

IV

As we have seen, the materiality of the body and its agency (in all senses of the term), especially the human body, has been the locus of many kinds of investigation. Aristotle had it just right when he spoke of a particular kind of artistic representation as the imitation of human beings in action. If we substitute "beings" by "bodies", then we come closer to the truth of the representation of the human self in art, irrespective of the medium an art form uses.

In literature, the description, depiction, representation of a body, no matter how brief or indirect it may be, almost always carries with it, even if implicitly, the dual sense of agency that I have tried to indicate earlier. In the *Natyashastra*, Brahma instructs Bharata to include female bodies, in the forms of the *apsara*s, to make his *natya* (dramatic representation) more comprehensive. Bodies and their agency are central to epics – whether the *Iliad* or the *Odyssey* or the *Mahabharata* or the *Ramayana*. When Lakshmana kills the unarmed Meghanada in Michael Madhusu-dan Dutta's reworking of the *Ramayana*, what the reader's attention is drawn to is the unprepared, defenceless state of Meghanada's body. The body and its training (physical, intellectual, moral) form a significant part of Plato's *Republic*. It is difficult to understand either Renaissance art or literature without reference to the bodies that are exhibited, analysed, anatomised in the works that constitute, perhaps, the period's greatest triumphs (think of Michelangelo's *David*, thinks of the bodies scattered across John Donne's poetry, think of Othello, think of Gargantua or of Pantagruel, think of Montaigne's cannibals, the list can be extended almost indefinitely). In more modern times, it is impossible to ignore the bodies of some of the most influential figures in literature, whether of the West or of the East. Neither the protagonist of Rabindranath's *Gora*, nor that of Eliot's *The Love Song of J. Alfred Prufrock*, a poem begun the year Rabindranath's novel was published (1910), can be imagined without reference to their corporeality, and neither can be the protagonist of Woolf's *Orlando: A Biography* (1928), not to speak of the many heroines and heroes of popular genres like detective and science fiction.

In all of these instances, which can be multiplied manyfold, it may be worth our while to consider the *degree* of agency (of the autonomous self) as well as the *nature* of agency (as representing something or something that is absent) that an author invests her or his creations with. It would be even more interesting to see how such representations of the human body are related to contemporary notions of bodies and ideas relating to their agential status. As a student of literature who is also interested in the workings of science (especially the biological sciences) in society, I find it somewhat curious that there do not seem to be many studies of this sort. An honourable exception to this generalisation is Jonathan Sawday's *The Body Emblazoned: Dissection and the Human Body in Renaissance Culture*. My gratitude to Professor Supriya Chaudhuri for bringing this to my notice (Bakhtin, 1984; Sawday, 1995).

It may be worth our while to focus on the sheer material corporeality of the characters who continue to entertain and educate us long after the bodies which created them have ceased to exist in any material sense.

References

Agassiz's (1807–1873) scientific legacy is mixed. He was the first to propose the notion of an Ice Age but held strongly racist views all his life, for which he sought to find scientific justification, and was a lifelong opponent of Darwin's theories of evolution.

Asad, T. (2003). *Formations of the Secular: Christianity, Islam, Modernity*. Stanford University Press, Stanford, 92.

Bakhtin, M. (1984). *Rabelais and His World*. Iswolsky, H. Trans. Indiana University Press, Bloomington.

Darwin, C. (1872). *The Expression of the Emotions in Man and Animals*. John Murray, London. Reprinted, with an introduction by Konrad Lorenz, University of Chicago Press, Chicago, 1965). Plate I faces page 146 of *Expression*.

Darwin, C. (1981). *The Descent of Man, and Selection in Relation to Sex*. Princeton University Press, Princeton, NJ, facsimile reprint of the first edition published in London: John Murray, 1871 (I vol), Part I, the woodcuts appear as Fig 1. on p. 15.

Darwin, C. (1984). *On the Origin of Species by Means of Natural Selection, or the Preservation of Favoured Races in the Struggle for Life*. Penguin Books, London, Reprint of the first edition published in London: John Murray, 1859), 455, 459.

Ellis, H. H. (1890). *The Criminal*. The Walter Scott Publishing Co. Ltd., London (4th rev. ed.) 1910. 374, 251–252. Appendix A, Explanation of Plates, p. 377. In the concluding chapter of *The Criminal*, Havelock Ellis writes, "All education must include provision for the detection and special treatment of abnormal children. We cannot catch our criminals too young." It is instructive that Havelock Ellis was both a social reformer as well as a believer in eugenics and he was not the only one of his kind in his time.

Gould, S. J. (1992). *The Mismeasure of Man*. Penguin, Harmondsworth (1st ed. 1981), 36.

Gray, H. and Carter, H. V. (1858). *Anatomy Descriptive and Surgical*. John W. Parker and Son, London.

Kantorowicz, E. H. (1957). *The King's Two Bodies: A Study in Medieval Political Theology*. Princeton University Press, Princeton, NJ, Reprint 1997.

Nott, J. C. and Gliddon, G. R. (1854). *Types of mankind: Or, Ethnological researches based upon the ancient monuments, paintings, sculptures, and crania of races, and upon their natural, geographical, philological and biblical history: Illustrated by selections from the inedited papers of Samuel George Morton and by additional contributions from L. Agassiz, W. Usher and H. S. Patterson*, J. B. Lippincott, Grambo & Co., Philadelphia [Web.] The Library of Congress. https://lccn.loc.gov/49043133.

Quain, J. (1867). *Quain's Elements of Anatomy*, edited by William Sharpey, Allen Thomson, John Cleland, Seventh edition. Vol. II. James Walton, London.

Richardson, R. (2008). *The Making of Mr. Gray's Anatomy: Bodies, Books, Fortune, Fame*. Oxford University Press, Oxford, 227, 139.

Sawday, J. (1995). *The Body Emblazoned: Dissection and the Human Body in Renaissance Culture*. Routledge, London and New York.

Verdery, K. (1999). *The Political Lives of Dead Bodies: Reburial and Postsocialist Change*. Columbia University Press, New York.

9

A RATIONALE OF ĀRYABHATA I'S METHOD FOR SOLVING *AX+C=BY*

Pradip Kumar Majumdar

Introduction

Āryabhata (476 AD) gave a rule in his "Aryabhatiya" for obtaining the general solution of the linear equation of the type by $ax+c=by$. In this chapter we are going to deduce the formula $p_n q_{n-1} - q_n p_{n-1} = (-1)^n$ of the continued fraction from Āryabhata I's method of solution of indeterminate equation of the first degree.

A Few Lines About Continued Fraction

$$a/b = a_1 + \frac{1}{a_2} + \frac{1}{a_3} + T$$

Let $p_1/q_1, p_2/q_2, \ldots p_n/q_n$ be the successive convergents of a/b, then

$$p_1/q_1 = a_1(-i)\, p_2/q_2 = a_1 + \frac{1}{a_2} = \frac{a_1 a_2 + 1}{a_2} - \cdots$$

$$p_3/q_3 = a_1 + \frac{1}{a_2} + \frac{1}{a_3} = a_1 + \frac{1}{a_2 + \dfrac{1}{a_3}} = \frac{a_1(a_1 a_2 + 1)a_2}{a_2 a_3 + 1}$$

Aryabhata's Rule

Āryabhata I's Shaka (Verse) and Its English Translation

Āryabhata I gave the following rule in the *Ganitapada* of Āryabhata (Shukla, 1976).

DOI: 10.4324/9781003033448-12

Adhikāgrabhagaharain chindyadunagrabhegakarena

Sesa porasboraldaktarn matupunmagrantine kriptam

Alhauparugunitamantayugtingracatedalhantedesam

kepadedegunandi Lokedamadhikayayutar || 3 ||

Bibhuti Bhusan Datta and A.N. Singh gave the following translation of the afore-mentioned verses.

> Divide the divisor Corresponding to the smoother reminder the residue and the divine correspondancy to the smaller reminder being mutually divided, the last residue should be multiplied by such an optional integer that the product being added at even a substracted in case the number of quotients odd), by the different of the remainders will be exactly divisible he Id the last but one reminder (Datta and Singh, 1962). Place the quotient of the mutual division successively one below the other in a column, below them the optional multiplier and undermelt it the quatrent just obtained. Any number below it (i.e. the penultimate) is multiplied by one just above it and then added by that just below it. Divide the last number (obtained so doing repeatedly) by the divisor corresponding to the smaller number; then multiply the residue by the diviser corresponding to the greater reminder and add the greater reminder (the rarest will be). The result will be the number corresponding to the two divisions.

This gives us the following problems to find solution: (A) To find the number (N), which when divided by a given number a will leave a remainder $R1$ and when divided by another number b will leave reminder $R2$. That is,

$N = ax + R1 = by + R2$.
or, $ax + R1 - R2 = by$, if $R1 > R2$.
And take $R1 - R2 = c$. Then, we have $by = ax + c$.
If $R1 < R2$ and $R2 - R1 = c$, then we get
$by + c = ax$.
When $a = adhikaprabhagahanam$, that is, equal to the divisor corresponding to the greater remainder, and
$b = Unagrabhagahan$, that is, equal to the corresponding smaller remainder
$R1 =$ greater reminder
$R2 =$ lesser reminder
$c = R1 \sim R2$.

Also, for a general problem:

(B) To find a number ($N1$) which being divided several times by the given numbers $a1, a2 \ldots a_{n}$ leaves as reminders $R1, R2 \ldots R_{n}$ respectively, that is

$N1 = a1x1 + R1 = a2x2 + R2 = \ldots = anxn + Rn$.

It should be noted that Āryabhata I writes the equation in a form so as to keep c always positive.

Rationale of the Method

According to the translation, we have

$N=ax+R1=by+R2$
Let, $R1>R2$.
Then $ax+c=by$.

where c is positive and $c=R1-R2$

Now $y = \dfrac{ax + c}{b}$

b) $a(a_1$

$\qquad$ . . .

$\qquad\rule{2cm}{0.4pt}$

$r_1)$ $b(a_2$

$\qquad\qquad$ . . .

$\qquad\qquad\rule{1.5cm}{0.4pt}$

$r_2)$ $r1(a_3$

$\qquad\qquad\qquad$ . . .

$\qquad\qquad\qquad\rule{1.5cm}{0.4pt}$

$r_3)$ $r2(a_4$

$\qquad\qquad\qquad\qquad$ . . .

$\qquad\qquad\qquad\qquad\rule{1.5cm}{0.4pt}$

$r_4)$ $r3$ $(a_5$

$\qquad\qquad\qquad\qquad\qquad$ . . .

$\qquad\qquad\qquad\qquad\qquad\rule{1.5cm}{0.4pt}$

$r_5)$ $r4$ $(a_6$

$\qquad\qquad\qquad\qquad\qquad\qquad$ . . .

$\qquad\qquad\qquad\qquad\qquad\qquad\rule{1.5cm}{0.4pt}$

r_6 . . .

where

$a = ba_1 + r_1$ (i)

$b = r_1a_2 + r_2$ (ii)

$r_1 = r_2a_3 + r_3$ (iii)

$r_2 = r_3a_4 + r_4$ (iv)

$r_3 = r_4a_5 + r_5$ (v)

   (2)

. . . .

. . . .

Case I: When the number of (partial) quotients is even.

Let us consider when the number of (partial) quotients is four. Consider the optional number . Therefore, according to the rule we have

$$\frac{r_4 t_1 + c}{r_3} = K_1 \tag{3}$$

Now, consider the following table:

a_1	$a_1 L + s_2$	$= U(= y)$
a_2	$a_2 s_2 + s_1$	$= L(= x)$
a_3	$s_1 a_3 + t_1$	$= s_2$
a_4	$a_4 t_1 + T_1$	$= s1$
t_1	$t1$	
K_1		

Here,

$$s_1 = a_4 t_1 + K_1$$

Using $\dfrac{r_4 t_1 + c}{r_3} = K_1 \Rightarrow t_1 = \dfrac{r_3 K_1 - c}{r_4}$, we can rewrite s_1 as

$$s_1 = a_4 \left(\frac{r_3 K_1 - c}{r_4} \right) + K_1$$

$$= \frac{a_4 r_3 K_1 - a_{4c} + K_1 r_4}{r_4}$$

$$= \frac{K_1 \left(a_4 r_3 + r_4 \right) - a_{4c}}{r_4}$$

Hence, by equation (2iv),

$$s_1 \frac{K_1 r_2 - a_4 c}{r_4} \tag{4}$$

$$s_2 = a_3 s_1 + t_1$$

$$= a_3 \left(\frac{K_1 r_2 - a_4 c}{r_4} \right) + \frac{r_3 K_1 - c}{r_4}$$

$$= \frac{K_1 \left(a_3 r_2 + r_3 \right) - c \left(a_3 a_4 + 1 \right)}{r_4}$$

Hence by equation (2iii),

$$s_2 = \frac{K_1 r_1 - c(a_3 a_4 + 1)}{r_4} \tag{5}$$

$$L = a_2 s_2 + 1$$

$$= \frac{a_2 \left[K_1 r_1 - c(a_3 a_4 + 1) \right]}{r_4} + \frac{K_1 r_2 - a_4 c}{4}$$

$$= \frac{K_1 (a_2 r_1 + r_2) - c(a_2 a_3 a_4 + a_2 + a_4)}{r_4}$$

Hence by equation (2ii),

$$L = \frac{K_1 b - c(a_2 a_3 a_4 + a_2 + a_4)}{r_4} \tag{6}$$

Now,

$$U = a_1 L + s_2$$

which, using equations (5) and (6), can be written as

$$U = \frac{a_1 \left[K_1 b - c(a_2 a_3 a_4 + a_2 a_4) \right]}{r_4} + \frac{K_1 r_1 - c(a_3 a_4 + 1)}{r_4}$$

$$= \frac{K_1 (a_1 b + r_1) - c \left[a_1 (a_2 a_3 a_4 + a_2 + a_4) + (a_3 a_4 + 1) \right]}{r_4}$$

Hence by equation (2i)

$$U = \frac{a_1 \left[K_1 a - c[(a_2 a_3 a_4 + a_2 + a_4) + (a_3 a_4 + 1)] \right]}{r_4} \tag{7}$$

Therefore,

$$\frac{U}{L} = \frac{K_1 a - c \left[a_1 (a_2 a_3 a_4 + a_2 + a_4) + (a_3 a_4 + 1) \right]}{K_1 b - c(a_2 a_3 a_4 + a_2 a_4)}$$

Letting $p_4 = \left[a_1 (a_2 a_3 a_4 + a_2 + a_4) + (a_3 a_4 + 1) \right]$ and $q_4 = (a_2 a_3 a_4) + a_2 + a_4$ we can write

$$\frac{U}{L} = \frac{K_1 a - c p_4}{K_1 b - c q_4}$$

Here, $\dfrac{p_5}{q_5} = \dfrac{a}{b}, p_5 = a, q_5 = b$

Consider $p_5 L - q_5 u$

From the earlier expression we can write this as

$$p_5 L - q_5 U = P_5\left(K_1 b - cq_4\right) - q_5\left(K_1 a - cp_4\right)$$

$$= a\left(K_1 b - cq_4\right) - \left(K_1 a - cp_4\right)$$

$$= c\left(bp_4 - aq_4\right)$$

$$= c\left(q_5 p_4 - p_5 q_4\right) = -c\left(p_5 q_4 - q_5 p_4\right)$$

Now, since

$$\left(p_5 q_4 - q_5 p_4\right) = (-1),$$

So,

$$p_5 L - q_5 u \; c \tag{9}$$

We have taken L=x and U=y
So, from equation (9),

$$ax - by = c$$

or

$$ax - c = by \tag{10}$$

This is not the original form $ax + c = by$.

Case II: When the number of quotients is odd.

Let the number of quotients be five, and let the optional number be t_2. Then, according to the rule we have

$$\dfrac{r_5 t_2 - c}{r_4} = K_2\left(say\right) \tag{11}$$

Now, consider the following table:

a_1	$a_1 L + s_3$	$= U(= y)$
a_2	$s_3 a_2 + s_2$	$= L(= x)$
a_3	$s_2 a_3 + t_1$	$= s_3$
a_4	$s_1 a_4 + t_2$	$= s_2$
a_5	$a_5 t_2 + K_1$	$= s_1$
t_1	t_2	
K_2		

Now proceeding exactly as in Case I, we have

$$L = a_2 s_3 + s_2 = \frac{K_2 b + cq_5}{r_5}$$

and

$$U = a_1 L + s_3 = \frac{K_2 a + cp_5}{r_5}$$

Now,

$$\frac{U}{L} = \frac{K_2 a + cp_5}{K_2 b + cq_5} \tag{12}$$

Here, $\dfrac{p_6}{q_6} = \dfrac{a}{b}, p_6 = a, q_6 = b$

Consider, $p_6 L - q_6 U$. From the previous expressions we can write this as

$$p_6 L - q_6 U = p_6 \left(K_2 b + cq_5 \right) - q_6 \left(K_2 a + cp_5 \right)$$

$$= a \left(K_2 b + cq_5 \right) - b \left(K_2 a + cp_5 \right)$$

$$= c \left(aq_5 - bp_5 \right)$$

$$= c \left(p_6 q_5 - q_6 p_5 \right)$$

Now, since $\left(p_6 q_5 - q_6 p_5 \right) = (-1)^6$,
So,

$$p_6 L - q_6 U = c \tag{13}$$

We have taken L=*x* and U=*y*, so,

ax–by=*c*

or,

ax–c=by (14)

which is again not the original form *ax+c=by*.

Therefore, from equations (10) and (14) we have arrived at some mystery. What is that mystery? It might be that equations (3) and (11) are not of those forms. To see, let us take those in the following forms:

$$\frac{r_4 t_1 - c}{r_3} = K_1 \tag{15}$$

$$\frac{r_5 t_2 + c}{r_4} = K_2 \tag{16}$$

a_1	$a_1L + s_2$	$= U(= y)$
a_2	$a_2s_2 + s_1$	$= L(= x)$
a_3	$s_1a_3 + t_1$	$= s_2$
a_4	$a_4t_1 + K_1$	$= s_1$
t_1	t_1	
K_1		

Now proceed exactly as in Case I earlier to obtain

$$L = a_2s_2 + s_1$$
$$= \frac{K_1b + cq_4}{r_{45}}$$

(17i)

and

$$U = a_1L + s_2$$
$$= \frac{K_1a + cp_4}{r_4}$$

(17ii)

Here, $\dfrac{p_5}{q_5} = \dfrac{a}{b}, p_5 = a, q_5 = b$.

Again consider, $p_6L - q_6u$. From these expressions we can write this as

$$p_5L - q_5U = p_5\left(K_1b + cq_4\right) - q_5\left(K_1a + cp_4\right)$$

$$= a\left(K_1b + cq_4\right) - b\left(K_1a + cp_4\right)$$

$$= c\left(aq_4 - bp_4\right)$$

$$= c\left(p_5q_4 - q_5p_4\right)$$

Using $L=x$ and $U=y$, equation (18) now boils down to, $ax+c=by$, which is the original form of Aryabhata's equation.

Now consider Case II, when the number of quotients is odd, and let it be five. Then according to the rule we have

$$\frac{r_5t_2 + c}{r_3} = K_2$$

(15)

Proceed exactly as earlier to get

$$L = a_2s_3 + s_2 = \frac{K_2b + cq_5}{r_5}$$

and

$$U = a_1 L + s_3 = \frac{K_2 a - c p_5}{r_5}$$

Hence,

$$\frac{U}{L} = \frac{K_2 a - c p_5}{K_2 b - c q_5} \tag{12}$$

Here, $\dfrac{p_6}{q_6} = \dfrac{a}{b}, p_6 = a, q_6 = b$ so that

$$p_6 L - q_6 U = p_6 \left(K_2 b - c q_5 \right) - q_6 \left(K_2 a - c p_5 \right)$$

$$= a \left(K_2 b - c q_5 \right) - b \left(K_2 a - c p_5 \right)$$

$$= c \left(a q_5 - b p_5 \right)$$

$$= c \left(p_6 q_5 - q_6 p_5 \right)$$

Now, since $\left(p_6 q_5 - q_6 p_5 \right) = (-1)^6$, so

$$p_6 L - q_6 U = -c$$

We have taken *L=x* and *U=y*, so

$$ax + by = -c$$

or,

$$ax + c = by$$

or,

$$ax + c = by$$

which is again not the original form.

Thus, it appears that forms in equations (15) and (16) are the correct forms to arrive at the original form of the equation *ax+c=by*. To establish the previous Cases I and II under these forms, we must carefully analyse the Sanskrit verse "Matigu-namagrantare kspitam". Datta translates it as:

> Last residue should be multiplied by such and an optional integer that the product being added (in case of the number of quotients of mutual division is even), or subtracted (in case of the number of quotients is odd), by the difference of numbers.

> *(Datta, 1932)*

Āryabhata I did not explain when *ksepa* quantity c is to be added or subtracted. But Bhaskar I in his "Aryabhatiya bhasya" has written "Samesu ksiptain visamisu ansodhayan" (Shukla, 1976), that is add the *ksepa* quantity when n (the total number of quotients of mutual division) is even and subtract when n is odd. Datta and Singh [5] said "Neglect the first quotient of the mutual divison' and therefore when n (number of partial quotient) is even. Aryabhata I takes it one less, i.e., $n-1$ which is odd. Similarly when it is odd then it is actually even partial quotients".

From the discussion, we say that

$a_2, a_4, a_6 \ldots$ are all odd partial quotients.

$a_3, a_5, a_7 \ldots$ are all even partial quotients.

which establishes at once the Case (1) and Case (2). Thus, from the discussion and the equations (9), (13), (18) and (19), we see that the formula of the continued fraction is implicitly involved in Āryabhata I's method of solution of indeterminate equation of the first degree.

Suggested Readings

Aryabhatiya of Aryabhata I. Critically edited with introduction, English translation, notes, comment, and indexes by Kripa Sankar Shukla in collaboration with K. V. Sarma. Indian National Science Academy, New Delhi, 1976, 74.

Aryabhatiya of Āryabhata with Commentary of Bhaskara I and Somesvara, critically. Ed. and Intro. and Appendices by Kripa Sankar Shukla. (1976). Indian National Science Academy, New Delhi, 97, 132.

Datta, B. B. (1932). Elder Aryabhata's rule for the solution of indeterminate equation of the first degree. *Bulletin of the Calcutta Mathematical Society*, 24, 19–26.

Datta, B. B. and Singh, A. N. (1962). *History of Hindu Mathematics, Part II Algebra. A Source Book*. Asia Publishing House, Calcutta (2 vols).

10

THE "DEATH DRIVE" IN PSYCHOANALYSIS

Santanu Biswas

A Belated Discovery

The concept of "death drive" (*Todestrieb*) was introduced to the field of psychoanalysis somewhat belatedly by Sigmund Freud. This is evident from the fact that, although Freud had fathered psychoanalysis in the last decade of the nineteenth century, he was not able to identify the concept of the "death drive" properly before 1919, in spite of its being a fundamental concept of psychoanalysis in the final analysis of Freud himself. He first hinted at the concept of death drive in his 1919 essay "The Uncanny," but it was from his 1920 *Beyond the Pleasure Principle*, whose first draft was completed in 1919, that he started to give the concept its due importance as an unrelenting mental urge that is distinct from, and in fact opposed to, the pleasure principle.

Before identifying the "death drive," Freud used to explain the functioning of the human mind with the help of the framework of an opposition between the pleasure principle and the reality principle. Freud states in his short 1911 paper "Formulations on the Two Principles of Mental Functioning" that he first identified the "pleasure principle" – the short form of the "pleasure-unpleasure" principle – as that which governs the mind at its most primary level, where it is purely concerned with gaining pleasure and avoiding displeasure or pain with little or no regard for reality, and then identified the "reality principle" as a new principle that comes in the way of instant gratification and delays the satisfaction of the pleasure principle by compelling the mind, or the ego, to take "reality" into account while seeking gratification, even if it happens to be disagreeable in nature (Freud, 1911/1958, p. 219). Thus, Freud identified these two principles in the order of their advent in the mind, for the mind of the human infant that is innately governed by the pleasure principle has to develop a sufficiently matured ego to be able to apprehend and accommodate the principle of reality to its primary thrust

DOI: 10.4324/9781003033448-13

towards pleasure. After having partially foreshadowed some of these ideas as early as in his 1895 *Project for a Scientific Psychology*, published posthumously in 1950, Freud discusses the two principles in detail in this paper of 1911.[1] The introduction of the concept of the death drive to this framework of mental functioning altered the framework radically, because the death drive not only exceeds the existing binary framework by being situated beyond and independent of it, but it acts as a more fundamental governing principle of mental functioning than even the pleasure principle, insofar as the latter can be defied by the death drive.

Therefore, the first question we find ourselves asking is: why did Freud take so long to identify such an important concept of psychoanalysis? Freud explains that he was unable to identify the concept earlier because the death drive is in itself silent and never manifests itself directly in its pure form, as the death drive as such. He further clarifies that the death drive becomes discernible only when it gets mixed with its opposite, the life drives, also known as the erotic drives or the sexual drives. Freud mentions this in his article on "The Libido Theory" written in 1922, and published in 1923, thus:

> [T]he one set of drives, which work essentially in silence, . . . lead[s] the living creature to death and therefore deserve to be called the *"death drives"*. . . . The other set of drives would be those which are better known to us in analysis – the libidinal, sexual or life drives, which are best comprised under the name of *Eros*.
>
> *(Freud, 1923/1955, pp. 258–259)[2]*

The silence of the death drive being one of its key attributes, Freud continued to highlight it in some of his major writings from 1919, till the year before his death. Thus, he writes in the 1923 *The Ego and the Id*: "[W]e are driven to conclude that the death drives are by their nature mute and that the clamour of life proceeds for the most part from Eros" (Freud, 1923/1961, p. 46). He mentions in his 1929 work, *Civilisation and its Discontents*, denoting the death drive as "the desire for destruction": "(The desire for destruction when it is directed inwards mostly eludes our perception, of course, unless it is tinged with erotism)" (Freud, 1929/1961, p. 120). And he states in 1938, in *An Outline of Psycho-Analysis*: "So long as that drive operates internally, as a death drive, it remains silent; it only comes to our notice when it is diverted outwards as a drive of destruction" (Freud, 1940/1964, p. 150).

How does Freud describe the opposition between the life drives and the death drive?[3] To begin with, Freud states in *Beyond the Pleasure Principle* that the opposition between the life drives and the death drive is an ongoing one from the very beginning of life:

> Our speculations have suggested that Eros operates from the beginning of life and appears as a "life drive" in opposition to the "death drive" which was brought into being by the coming to life of inorganic substance. These

speculations seek to solve the riddle of life by supposing that these two drives were struggling with each other from the very first.

(Freud, 1920/1955, p. 61 fn1)

Following this, in *Group Psychology and the Analysis of the Ego*, Freud reiterates that the opposition between life drives and the death drive is related to the opposition between love and hate and clarifies that the sexual drives are the purest examples of the life drives:

> In a recently published study, *Beyond the Pleasure Principle*, I have attempted to connect the polarity of love and hatred with a hypothetical opposition between drives of life and death, and to establish the sexual drives as the purest examples of the former, the drives of life.
>
> *(Freud, 1921/1955, p. 102 fn1)*

Then, towards the end of his paper on "Negation," Freud equates "Eros" with "affirmation" and the destructive drive with "negation": "Affirmation – as a substitute for uniting – belongs to Eros; negation – the successor to expulsion – belongs to the drive of destruction" (Freud, 1925/1961, p. 239). Later, in *Civilisation and Its Discontents*, Freud regards the struggle between Eros and Death as the essence of life and as the basis of the evolution of human civilisation itself:

> [C]ivilisation is a process in the service of Eros, whose purpose is to combine single human individuals, and after that families, then races, peoples and nations, into one great unity, the unity of mankind. . . . But man's natural aggressive drive, the hostility of each against all and of all against each, opposes this programme of civilisation. This aggressive drive is the derivative and the main representative of the death drive which we have found alongside of Eros and which shares world-dominion with it. And now, I think, the meaning of the evolution of civilisation is no longer obscure to us. It must present the struggle between Eros and Death, between the drive of life and the drive of destruction, as it works itself out in the human species. This struggle is what all life essentially consists of, and the evolution of civilisation may therefore be simply described as the struggle for life of the human species. And it is this battle of the giants that our nurse-maids try to appease with their lullaby about Heaven.
>
> *(Freud, 1929/1961, p. 122)*

Finally, in the 1940, posthumously published, volume, *An Outline of Psycho-Analysis*, Freud further states that whereas the aim of the life drives is to unify and preserve, the aim of the death drive is to disunify, destroy and ultimately lead the living being into an inorganic state:

> The aim of [*Eros*] is to establish even greater unities and to preserve them thus – in short, to bind together; the aim of [the destructive drive] is, on the

contrary, to undo connections and so to destroy things. In the case of the destructive drive, we may suppose that its final aim is to lead what is living into an inorganic state.

(Freud, 1940/1964, p. 148)[4]

That the death drive was a belated discovery of extraordinary importance is evident from two simple facts: first, that although Freud was perfectly aware that the concept had failed to impress psychoanalysts and the general public alike, he insisted on the importance of the death drive for both the theory and the practice of psychoanalysis from the time of its discovery till the end of his life; and second, that whereas the concept as we know it, in its relation to repetition-compulsion, does not figure in Freud's writings prior to 1919, there is hardly any important work of Freud's written after 1919, in which it does not find direct mention.

Death Drive and Repetition-Compulsion in Freud

How did Freud come to know of the existence of the death drive? Well, the death drive became discernible to Freud thanks to its chief characteristic of "repetition-compulsion" (*Wiederholungszwang*), or "compulsion to repeat," or compulsive repetition, as Freud himself clarifies in *Beyond the Pleasure Principle*: "[T]he characteristic of a compulsion to repeat which first put us on the track of the death drives" (Freud, 1920/1955, p. 56).[5]

Freud was compelled to look for possible forces independent of, or indifferent to, or situated "beyond", the pleasure principle when he came across instances of psychopathology in his practice that could not be accounted for in any meaningful way in terms of the binary of the pleasure principle and the reality principle, especially, the self-harming tendency of some of his patients who would endlessly repeat acts that are distressful to them without ever noticing the element of repetition underlying their actions. Those who suffer from repetition-compulsion tend to justify their acts in terms of the circumstances around the acts, or the immediate causes motivating them, instead of recognising any pattern, or pattern of repetition, among a set of similar acts carried out by them over a period of time.

Freud clarifies in *Beyond the Pleasure Principle* that repetition-compulsion recalls past experiences that could not have been pleasurable at any point in time; that is to say, rather than becoming unpleasurable in course of time, they were unpleasurable right from the start and had simply continued to be so: "[T]he compulsion to repeat also recalls from the past experiences which include no possibility of pleasure, and which can never, even long ago, have brought satisfaction even to instinctual impulses which have since been repressed" (Freud, 1920/1955, p. 20). In the same work, Freud also mentions the conservatism or the tenacity of the drives. He states that despite repeatedly proving to be the source of un-pleasure, repetition-compulsion and the death drive can be extremely tenacious: "[B]ut no lesson has been learnt from the old experience of these activities having led only to unpleasure. In spite of that, they are repeated, under pressure of a compulsion" (p. 21).

Freud reiterates his point on the tenacity of death drive in his correspondence with Einstein "Why War?" wherein he writes, "there is no use in trying to get rid of men's aggressive inclinations" (Einstein and Freud, 1933/1960, p. 211).

In *Beyond the Pleasure Principle*, Freud further states that repetition-compulsion manifests itself not only in the neuroses, especially in traumatic neurosis, fate neurosis, the melancholic's masochistic superego, masochism, sadism, and negative therapeutic reaction but equally well in normative people, especially in terms of their acts that resemble fate neurosis, certain games played by very young children, and the destructive drive of the ego of individuals or of the ego of nations. The one element in common to all such expressions of the death drive through repetition-compulsion, be it neurotic or normative, is the repeated invitation of suffering, or the repeated staging of anguish or destruction, by an individual which explains why the compulsion is at once "repetitive" and related to the "death drive." How then does Freud explain these different expressions of the death drive via repetition-compulsion in his writings? Let us glance through his explanations.

Traumatic neurosis (*Traumatische Neurose*) usually occurs after severe mechanical concussions, excessive fright, or serious somatic shocks caused by accidents involving a risk to life, such as railway disasters, burials under earth, war, and so on. Freud rightly states that traumatic neurosis is a long-known condition. He adds that the dreams occurring in traumatic neuroses "have the characteristic of repeatedly bringing the patient back into the situation of his accident, a situation from which he wakes up in another fright" (Freud, 1920/1955, pp. 12–13). Such repetitive dreams made Freud classify traumatic neurosis as an expression of the death drive.

Speaking on "Fate neurosis" (*Schicksalsneurose*), Freud says that those suffering from it are not very different from the normative people whose human relationships always tend to have the same outcome at the end. Freud gives a number of examples:

> such as the benefactor who is abandoned in anger after a time by each of his *protégés*, however much they may otherwise differ from one another, and who thus seems doomed to taste all the bitterness of ingratitude; or the man whose friendships all end in betrayal by his friend; or the man who time after time in the course of his life raises someone else into a position of great private or public authority and then, after a certain interval, himself upsets that authority and replaces him by a new one; or, again, the lover each of whose love affairs with a woman passes through the same phases and reaches the same conclusion. This "perpetual recurrence of the same thing" causes us no astonishment.
>
> *(p. 22)*

Freud adds that rather than these cases, where the perpetrators had influenced their downfall, the psychoanalysts are more impressed by those cases where the perpetrator appears to have had no influence on the repetition, and, therefore, may be said to have repeated the act *unconsciously*; for example the repetition of the murder of his beloved, Clorinda, by the hero, Tancred, in Tasso's *Gerusalemme Liberata*, in which he first unwittingly kills her physically in a duel when she is disguised in the armour of an enemy knight, and then, following her burial, unwittingly wounds her soul contained in a tall tree in a strange enchanted forest when, deluded by voices, fire, and monsters, he slashes with his sword at the tree, only to see blood streaming from it and to hear her voice complaining that he has wounded her again (p. 22).

Freud further states that both normative people and neurotics give the impression "of being pursued by a malignant fate or possessed by some 'daemonic' power; but psychoanalysis has always taken the view that their fate is for the most part arranged by themselves and determined by early infantile influences" (p. 21), and describes it as "fate compulsion" (*Schicksalzwang*).

I have understood from my own practice that, although the patients of fate neurosis invariably complain against fate and attribute all mishaps or failures to fate, or to some divine or cosmic ill will, the truth is that, in quite an ironic way, they never ever allow fate to play any part in their lives at all! The fate-neurotics strongly insulate themselves from any possible influence of fate on their lives by always ultimately transforming whatever fate might offer them – good, bad or ugly – into material for compulsive repetition. Folklore captured this irony beautifully through the story of the poor, homeless, starving, destitute in rags who sat by the sea looking at the setting Sun, bitterly complaining against and cursing his luck, all the while unmindfully chucking into the sea one pebble after another, without ever looking at them, from a small heap that happened to lay next to his hand, and not realising until the last pebble was about to land in the water that those were pearls not pebbles.[6] The fate-neurotics have the extraordinary ability to latch on to any contingent factor in everyday life and deftly convert it into the basis of repetition. If you like, they convert pearls to pebbles and pebbles to nothing. Psychoanalysis seeks to help them break free from such compulsive cycles with the help of analysis and interpretation.

Freud then makes an extremely important clarification on the death drive in the context of his discussions on masochism and sadism in his 1924 essay on "The Economic Problem of Masochism" where he states that the death drive is first of all directed *inwards*, as a self-destructive impulse, in the form of an unconscious, erogenous, primary masochism of the superego that becomes evident from a very early stage of life and in which one can see the purest expression of death drive; but much of it is subsequently turned *outwards* in a conscious way towards the external world, in the form of the aggressive drive of the ego evident in sadism and in the ego's will to power and control over others, called the destructive drive of the ego or the ego-drive.

In addition to charting out many of the details of the psychopathological fall-outs of the journey of the death drive in the inward and outward directions in masochism and sadism respectively, Freud mentions a number of other things of importance regarding them in the same essay: that the primary masochism is a vestige of the union of the death drive and Eros; that the superego's masochism originates from the death drive and, instead of turning outward in the form of the ego's drive of destruction, continues to remain with the death drive from which it originated ("moral masochism becomes a classical piece of evidence for the existence of fusion of drive. Its danger lies in the fact that it originates from the death drive and corresponds to the part of that drive which has escaped being turned outwards as a drive of destruction" [Freud, 1924/1961, p. 170]); and that it is necessary to replace the expression "unconscious feeling of guilt" by the expression "need for punishment" (p. 166). The last point could be easily grasped with the help of the instance of Freud's unmarried female patient mentioned in *New Introductory Lectures on Psycho-Analysis*, who, whenever the people around her discouraged her in her attempt to cultivate her talent, met with an accident and injured her hand, or knee, or ankle and thus became physically unable to pursue her goals as before. When Freud alerted her to her own great share in these apparent accidents, she changed her technique: "Instead of accidents, indispositions appeared on the same provocations – catarrhs, sore throats, influenzal conditions, rheumatic swelling – till at last she made up her mind to resign her attempts and the whole agitation came to an end" (Freud, 1933, pp. 108–109). Such unconscious guilt expresses itself in the form of the need for punishment ultimately due to its relation to primary masochism.

Freud had already clarified in *The Ego and the Id* that the death drive governs the superego in melancholia in such a profound way that the ego can even be impelled towards death by it if it does not try to fend it off:

> [T]he destructive component had entrenched itself in the super-ego and turned itself against the ego. What is now holding sway in the superego is, as it were, a pure culture of the death drive, and in fact, it often enough succeeds in driving the ego into death, if the latter doesn't fend off its tyrant in time by the change round into mania.
>
> *(Freud, 1923/1961, p. 53)*

Simply put, the superego of melancholics can make them suffer from guilt, inadequacy, wrongdoing etc. to such an extreme degree that the ego may opt for the route of self-destruction to escape the tyranny of the superego. In *Civilisation and Its Discontents*, Freud further clarifies that it was possible for him to get the clearest insight into the nature of the death drive and its relation to Eros in the context of sadism, because in sadism alone the death drive twists the erotic aim in its own sense and yet fully satisfies the erotic urge (Freud, 1929/1961, p. 121).

The death drive also motivates "Negative therapeutic reaction" (*Negative therapeutische Reaktion*) in terms of which the analysands tend to protect their symptoms and thus refuse to be cured of their suffering, in spite of making strong demands of the psychoanalyst and others to the contrary; or, they paradoxically fall more seriously ill following a series of correct interpretations. Freud thinks that this phenomenon too derives from unconscious feelings of guilt, or primary maso-chism, and as such is linked to the death drive. Thus, in *The Ego and the Id* Freud writes:

> There are certain people who behave in a quite peculiar fashion during the work of analysis. When one speaks hopefully to them or expresses satisfac-tion with the progress of the treatment, they show signs of discontent and their condition invariably becomes worse. One begins by regarding this as defiance and as an attempt to prove their superiority to the physician, but later one comes to take a deeper and juster view. One becomes convinced, not only that such people cannot endure any praise or appreciation, but that they react inversely to the progress of the treatment. Every partial solution that ought to result, and in other people does result, in an improvement or a temporary suspension of symptoms produces in them for the time being an exacerbation of their illness; they get worse during the treatment instead of getting better. They exhibit what is known as a "negative therapeutic reaction.
>
> There is no doubt that there is something in these people that sets itself against their recovery. . . . We are accustomed to say that the need for illness has got the upper hand in them over the desire for recovery. . . . In the end we come to see that we are dealing with what may be called a "moral" factor, a sense of guilt, which is finding its satisfaction in the illness and refuses to give up the punishment of suffering.
>
> *(Freud, 1923/1961, p. 49)*

Freud thinks that here the unconscious feeling of guilt finds its satisfaction from the patient's falling ill and receiving punishment from suffering. This unconscious feel-ing of guilt is difficult to identify because the patient falls ill instead of feeling guilty, and it is difficult to treat because it takes an extremely obstinate form of resistance to analysis. Psychoanalysis addresses such stubborn unconscious guilt by first of all trying to make the analysand conscious of it. Freud reiterates much of this, relating negative therapeutic reaction to unconscious guilt, in a passage in the *New Introduc-tory Lectures on Psycho-Analysis*:

> People in whom this unconscious sense of guilt is excessively strong betray themselves in analytic treatment by the negative therapeutic reaction which is so disagreeable from the prognostic point of view. When one has given them the solution of a symptom, which should normally be followed by at least its temporary disappearance, what they produce instead is a momentary exacerbation of the symptom and of the illness. It is often enough to praise them for their behaviour in the treatment or to say a few hopeful words about the progress of the analysis in order to bring about an unmistakable worsening of their condition. A non-analyst would say that the "will to recovery" was absent. If you follow the analytic way of thinking, you will

see in this behaviour a manifestation of the unconscious sense of guilt, for which being ill, with its sufferings and impediments, is just what is wanted. The problems which the unconscious sense of guilt has opened up, its connections with morality, education, crime and delinquency, are at present the preferred field of work for psycho-analysts.

(Freud, 1933/1960, pp. 109–110)

Freud yet again links negative therapeutic reaction to the death drive for its incompatibility with the pleasure principle in *Analysis Terminable and Interminable*, regarding it as a form of resistance to cure.

Finally, in *Beyond the Pleasure Principle*, Freud describes the game invented and played by the one-and-a-half-year-old Ernst Wolfgang, the son of Freud's second daughter Sophie who would go on to become a psychoanalyst himself, with a reel and a piece of thread attached to it. The little boy played with it by swinging it under and out of his bed and uttering the sounds "o-o-o" and "a-a-a" respectively while doing so, in which both Freud and the baby's mother heard the German words *fort!* (gone!) and *da!* (there!). Freud interprets this self-invented game of the little boy as his way of representing his mother's departure and return so as to come to terms with her painful disappearance and absence that he could neither prevent nor control (Freud, 1920/1955, pp. 14–17). This is quite normative, for when babies are given injections, for instance, they cope with part of the suffering thereby caused to their egos by playing at giving injections to their toys or siblings or playmates or pets. Freud writes: "[C]hildren repeat everything that has made a great impression on them in real life, and that in doing so they abreact the strength of the impression and, as one might put it, make themselves master of the situation" (pp. 16–17). In the example of Freud's grandson, the mother's absence is the distressful act that the boy "constantly repeated" (p. 14) or "repeated untiringly" (p. 15). This is an instance of the compulsion to repeat what is distressful manifesting itself in a child's game, because the boy repeated only the "gone!" part of the game "as a game in itself and far more frequently than the episode in its entirety, with its pleasurable ending" (p. 16).

Although Freud does not directly make this point, the boy's act is both sadistic and masochistic. His act is sadistic because he rejects the abandoning mother by defiantly throwing away her toy replica himself, as if to say, "All right, then, go away! I don't need you. I am sending you away myself" (p. 16). The boy's sadism is also evident from the fact that a year later, whenever he was angry with a toy, he would throw it on the floor and exclaim "Go to the fwont!", which he did because he had learnt that his father was "at the front," and rather than regret his absence, he was enjoying his sole possession of his mother (p. 16). And the boy is masochistic because he untiringly repeats and thus endlessly suffers from the painful experience of his mother's withdrawal, exit, and absence. The boy's sadism and masochism in general are evident from the detail added by Freud in a footnote stating that when his mother died, that is "was really 'gone' ('o-o-o')," the boy, who was five and three-quarters, "showed no sign of grief" (p. 16 fn1).

In the following passage in *Analysis Terminable and Interminable*, Freud sums up his discussions on the death drive as a force incompatible with the pleasure principle, thus:

> If we take into consideration the total picture made up of the phenomena of masochism immanent in so many people, the negative therapeutic reaction and the sense of guilt found in so many neurotics, we shall no longer be able to adhere to the belief that mental events are exclusively governed by the desire for pleasure. These phenomena are unmistakable indications of the presence of a power in mental life which we call the drive of aggression or of destruction according to its aims, and which we trace back to the original death drive of living matter. It is not a question of an antithesis between an optimistic and a pessimistic theory of life. Only by the concurrent or mutually opposing action of the two primal drives – Eros and the death-drive –, never by one or the other alone, can we explain the rich multiplicity or the phenomena of life.
>
> *(Freud, 1937/1964, p. 243)*

As we have seen, Freud always found the death drive mixed with the life drives, and he separately upholds sadism and primary masochism as two indicators of the interplay of the death drive and the life drives. Another indicator of the same interplay is the binary concepts of "binding" (*Bindung*) and "unbinding" (*Ent-bindung*), which Freud consistently aligns with the pleasure principle and the death drive respectively. Freud himself states that the repetitive nightmares in traumatic neurosis are an attempt at "binding" (*Bindung*) that is essentially derived from the pleasure principle because it seeks to bind, bound, or contain the excitation caused by the trauma. In other words, the repeated staging of the trauma through recurrent dreams of the traumatic situation by the patients, suggestive of their fixation to the trauma, is really an attempt by the tendency of binding to come to grips with the trauma by bounding the latter through repetition, which is akin to how children symbolically bound their sense of loss in reality by repeatedly staging their painful loss through the games that they play.

That brings us to our last question: What does Freud attribute the two complementary concepts of the death drive and repetition-compulsion to? Well, Freud explains both the death drive and the compulsion to repeat as the biological urge of the living organism to return to an earlier inorganic state. Thus, Freud explains repetitive-compulsion in *Beyond the Pleasure Principle* as "*an urge inherent in organic life to restore an earlier state of things*" (Freud, 1920/1955, p. 36), which is the original inorganic condition of life, adding that "all living substance is bound to die from internal causes" (p. 44). He writes that he felt compelled to say that, "'*the aim of all life is death*', and, looking backwards, that '*inanimate things existed before living ones*'" (p. 38). In other words, the compulsion to repeat strives towards the complete reduction of excitation by trying to lead the living being back to its original inorganic state of complete rest once again. Freud repeats this argument in *An Outline of Psycho-Analysis* as follows:

> If we assume that living things came later than inanimate ones and arose from them, then the death drive fits in with the formula we have proposed to the effect that drives tend towards a return to an earlier state.
>
> *(Freud, 1940/1964, pp. 148–149)*

If living things came after or arose from inanimate ones and the aim of all life is death, then death may seem to be both the aim and origin of life, making life itself a detour from death that always ultimately returns to death. Although Freud believed that his ideas on the death drive were "left to future investigation" (Freud, 1933/1960, p. 107), as he says in the *New Introductory Lectures on Psycho-Analysis*, he never wavered on the biological explanation that he offered in *Beyond the Pleasure Principle* and in *An Outline of Psycho-Analysis*, namely that the living organism forever seeks to return to an earlier inorganic state.

To sum it up, the Freudian death drive is a silent, inexorable impulse towards an original inorganic state, whose presence becomes apparent only in its opposition to the life drives in the form of a powerful urge to overwhelm, dissolve, negate, unbind, or destroy and in terms of its characteristic of compulsive repetition. The death drive is first directed inwards, in the form of an unconscious primary masochism of the superego, from where it is directed outwards in the form of conscious sadism or destructivity of the ego. It is as much evident in normative people as in neurotics and as much evident in the behaviour of individuals as in the behaviour of nations.[7]

The death drive turned out to be one of the most controversial concepts put forward by Freud, for it generated huge resistances within the psychoanalytical community and was rejected by a large number of his disciples.[8] Melanie Klein was among the few psychoanalysts who took the concept seriously. Towards the end of his life, in his 1937 *Analysis Terminable and Interminable*, Freud states that he was well aware that his theory found little acceptance even among the psychoanalysts:

> I am well aware that the dualistic theory according to which a drive of death, destruction or aggression claims equal partnership with Eros as manifested in libido, has met with little general acceptance and has not really established itself even among psycho-analysts.
>
> *(Freud, 1937/1964, p. 244)*

Nevertheless, he continued to insist on the importance of the concept for the rest of his life. In fact, despite the huge controversy generated by the concept within the psychoanalytic community, Freud himself adhered to it more and more strongly as time went by. In *Civilisation and its Discontents*, Freud admits that the concept was advanced tentatively but stresses that it gradually imposed itself upon him:

> To begin with, it was only tentatively that I put forward the views I have developed here, but in the course of time they have gained such a hold upon me that I can no longer think in any other way.
>
> *(Freud, 1929/1961, p. 119)*

In a "Postscript" added in 1935, to *An Autobiographical Study*, Freud even regards the death drive as one of his last two decisive contributions to psychoanalysis, the other one being the discovery of the id, ego and superego:

> [I]t would be true to say that, since I put forward my hypothesis of the existence of two classes of drive (Eros and the death drive) and since I proposed a division of the mental personality into an ego, a superego, and an id [in 1923], I have made no further decisive contributions to psycho-analysis: what I have written on the subject since then has been either unessential or would soon have been supplied by someone else.
>
> *(Freud, 1925/1959, p. 72)*

Freud's Euthanasia

It is remarkable that the discoverer of the death drive consciously chose the route of euthanasia to end his own life. Dr Max Schur was a young medical intern who was introduced to Freud by Marie Bonaparte. He went on to become Freud's physician in 1929, treating Freud and the members of his family until Freud's death in 1939. When Freud interviewed Schur before appointing him as his new physician, he had just dismissed his previous physician for having lied to him about his health and was anxious that his new physician might similarly lie to him and not cooperate with him in the hour of need. Therefore, he categorically asked Schur for two promises: that he would always be told the truth and nothing but the truth about the state of his health, and that he would not be required to suffer unnecessarily when the time arrived, both of which were readily granted by Schur.

Schur ends his Freud-biography, *Freud: Living and Dying*, in which he also offers his precious opinion on Freud's ideas about death and the death drive, with a precise description of how he fulfilled his second promise to Freud by medically assisting his death:

> On . . . September 21, while I was sitting at his bedside, Freud took my hands and said to me: . . . "My dear Schur, you certainly remember our first talk. You promised me then not to forsake me when my time comes. Now it's nothing but torture and makes no sense any more."
>
> I indicated that I had not forgotten my promise. He sighed with relief, held my hand for a moment longer, and said: . . . "I thank you," and after

a moment of hesitation he added: . . . "Tell Anna about this." All this was said without a trace of emotionality or selfpity, and with full consciousness of reality.

I informed Anna of our conversation, as Freud had asked. When he was again in agony, I gave him a hypodermic of two centigrams of morphine. He soon felt relief and fell into a peaceful sleep. The expression of pain and suffering was gone. I repeated this dose after about twelve hours. Freud was obviously so close to the end of his reserves that he lapsed into a coma and did not wake up again. He died at 3.00 A.M. on September 23, 1939.

(Schur, 1972, p. 528)

Death Drive and Repetition-Compulsion in Tagore's "The Postmaster"

For an illustration of the twin Freudian concepts of death drive and repetition-compulsion through a widely known work of Indian literature, let us turn to one of Rabindranath Tagore's earliest short stories, "The Postmaster," first published in May 1891, in other words, almost three decades before Freud had discovered the concepts. The story deals with the somewhat abrupt end to the relationship, between a postmaster and his attendant, Ratan, that had developed over a brief period of time when they lived together in a "dark thatched shed" serving as the village post office, and the response of the two characters and the narrator to this end of the relationship.

The postmaster was a young man from Calcutta, who found it difficult to interact with the local people and missed his family, comprising his mother, elder sister, and younger brother. He felt himself aloof and stranded in a village of no consequence for an insignificant salary and secretly longed for the sight of tall buildings and metalled roads even as he indicated his happiness and love for nature in his poetry. Ratan, meanwhile, was a poor village orphan of 12 or 13, without much prospect of getting married, who did the postmaster's household work in exchange for food and shelter. The two characters start to come closer when one day the postmaster asks Ratan about her mother and about others in her family and then speaks at such length about his own family on subsequent days that Ratan is left viewing them through his eyes, and due to this identification with him, she begins to regard his family as her own:

> [T]he girl, in the course of the conversation, began to refer to the people in his family as "mother," "elder sister," "elder brother," as he did. She even drew, from imagination, their forms and features upon the small canvas of her heart.
>
> *(Tagore, 1891, p. 31)*

One day, during the seemingly endless monsoons, feeling idle and missing the company of a beloved, the postmaster decides to teach Ratan to read a little every day, which continues regularly until he falls ill one day, and longing for the touch of his mother or sister he asks Ratan to touch his forehead to check the temperature. This immediately transforms Ratan into a mother who calls in the local doctor, and for several days, cooks his sick meals, acts as his nurse, meticulously gives him the pills at the right time, and stays up by his bedside all night. Thus, while Ratan became the postmaster's attendant, cook, addressee of the more intimate discourse on his family that he could not share with anyone in office, surrogate mother in the form of his nurse, and a companion in general, the postmaster became the centre of her mental universe, as she hardly had anyone close to her to reflect on. However, his illness had made the postmaster decide to quit his job and return to Calcutta, if his application for a transfer to some other place was not granted by the authorities; and when the application is denied after a few days, he abruptly announces to Ratan one day that he is leaving for home the next day never to come back, leaving Ratan stunned, numbed, and speechless. But when in reply to her question "will you take me home with you?" the postmaster laughs and says, "How can I do that?", she is stung by the remark and the laughter accompanying it and is repeatedly reminded of them even in her sleep and dreams, as these had not only made her feel deeply insulted, abandoned, and derecognised but had also destroyed the entire surrogate family she had constructed in her mind in a flash. On the day of his parting, she is overwhelmed by both his offers and refuses both: she first refuses his offer to recommend her to the next postmaster, uncharacteristically crying out she would not stay there anymore, the unexpected nature of which declaration left the postmaster astonished; and, a little later, she refuses his offer of money, saying, as she falls to his feet in the dust with signs of suffering on her face, "no one" needs to worry about her, an expression which made the postmaster feel sad for her. Ratan's impersonal wording indicates that she felt the need to forcefully distance both him and her imaginary family, really his family, from her mind. It also indicates that the postmaster had become Ratan's "everyone." The postmaster leaves for the boat alone, nonetheless, and when the memory of her suffering face causes an intense ache in his heart, making him consider taking her with him, the wind in the sails and the monsoon current that carried the boat swiftly at this point were enough to dissuade him and replace any possible guilt ensuing in terms of thoughts of philosophical detachment, linking the separation to death in the process: "There are so many such separations, such deaths, in life, what will come of turning back? Who belongs to whom in this world?" (p. 34). Could he have declared in the same spirit, "There are so many such separations, such deaths, in life, *what will come of going home? Who belongs to whom in this world?*" Poor Ratan at the same time, bereft of any such philosophical insight, wept unstoppably, knowing he was gone, but stayed close to the premises nevertheless with the hope of his possible return, compelling the narrator to conclude with a sigh that the human heart prefers to remain eternally silly, as it promptly holds on to a pleasant delusion, at once ignoring reality and refusing to learn from all the heart-rending mishaps caused in the past by its weakness for such delusions.

By choosing to focus on the postmaster's separation from Ratan, or on the topic of human reaction to a loss, the story inadvertently concerns itself with a scenario in which the death drive and the compulsion to repeat tend to dominate. To begin with, the shock of the loss of dear ones was not a new experience to Ratan, as she must have experienced it repeatedly while losing her parents and her brother, presumably at different times. She experiences a semblance of the same shocking loss yet again when the postmaster says with a laugh that the idea of taking her home with him was unthinkable. She repeatedly recalls the painful experience despite being deeply distressed by it each time, owing to an attempt at *bindung* that the death drive hurries the life drives to set into motion in the wake of the psychical devastation caused by it.

But Ratan's real sense of loss is aroused when the postmaster is really gone (*fort!*), following which Ratan in a way physically enacts repetition-compulsion by going round and round the empty post-office building in which she used to live with him, feeling compelled to stay fixated to the very place that caused her inordinate sorrow:

> She [Ratan], weeping unstoppably, was only wandering again and again about the building of the post office. Perhaps there was a tenuous hope in her heart, to do with dadababu coming back – trapped, she found herself unable to go far from where she was roaming.
>
> *(p. 34)*

It is noteworthy that at the end, the narrator, instead of empathising with Ratan's heart-rending sorrow, speaks somewhat like a psychoanalyst, generalising Ratan's behaviour as a human weakness and largely holding her responsible for her own suffering: it is a sad truth that the forever-deluded human heart embraces false hopes tightly to the breast, and despite having its blood sucked out and its very connection with life destroyed by this mistake at the time of inevitable disillusionment, it recovers from its misery and returns to its right senses, only to crave to fall into the grip of a new self-destructive delusion:

> Alas, the mistaken human heart! Its delusions never end, the laws of reason enter the mind after much delay, disbelieving incontestable evidence it embraces false hope with both arms and all its might to its breast; in the end one day, severing the umbilical cord and sucking the heart empty of blood, it flees, there is then a return to one's right senses, and the mind grows restless again to embrace its next delusion.
>
> *(p. 34)*

The passage clearly foreshadows Freud's finding: "[B]ut no lesson has been learnt from the old experience of these activities having led only to unpleasure. In spite of that, they are repeated, under pressure of a compulsion." If the exclamatory tone of Tagore's slightly frustrated narrator is overlooked, his observation serves as fairly neat commentary, necessarily unintended, on how repetition-compulsion and death drive are but two sides of the same coin; on the extreme tenacity of the death drive and the forceful or compulsive character of repetition; and on human being's self-destructive impulse or eternal masochism as a form of expression of the death drive. By ending on this note, the story seems to elevate the idea of the insurmountability of the death drive to the status of its moral.

Death Drive and Repetition-Compulsion in Lacan

Arguably the most powerful criticism of Freud's concept of the death drive came from the French psychoanalyst and psychiatrist Jacques Lacan in the 1950s and 1960s. Unlike many of Freud's other followers, Lacan in fact agrees with Freud's view that the concept of the death drive is central to psychoanalysis. He states in "The Subversion of the Subject and the Dialectic of Desire in the Freudian Unconscious": "For to evade the death drive (*pulsion de mort*) in his [Freud's] doctrine is not to know his doctrine at all" (Lacan, 1960/2006a, p. 679). He also agrees with Freud's view that repetition-compulsion is the chief characteristic of the death drive and that they operate together beyond the pleasure principle, refining Freud's view slightly by pointing out that the death drive is the only form of transgression permitted by the pleasure principle. What is of much greater relevance, however, are the changes introduced to the concept by Lacan that ended in altering the concept radically.

The first of the two most prominent changes introduced by Lacan is the change of name of repetition-compulsion. Lacan renames it "insistence" of the signifier or significant insistence. He states in his Seminar of 1954–1955:

> This is where Freud realises that something doesn't satisfy the pleasure principle. He realises that what comes out of one of the systems – that of the unconscious – has a very particular insistence [*insistance*] – that is the word I wanted to bring in. I say insistence because it expresses rather well, in a familiar way, the meaning of what has been translated into French as *automatisme de répétition*, *Wiederholungszwang* (compulsion to repeat).
>
> *(Lacan, 1954–55/1991, p. 61)*

Lacan reiterates later in the same seminar: "I think I am giving you a better rendition with the notion of insistence, repetitive insistence, significant insistence. This function is at the very root of language in so far as a world is a universe subjected to language" (p. 206). At different moments in his early teaching, Lacan variously describes repetition-compulsion as the insistence of the signifier, the insistence of the signifying chain, the insistence of the letter, the insistence of speech, signifying insistence, the insistence of meaning, the insistence of the symbolic order itself, and so on.

Lacan introduced the other most prominent change by allowing the new term "insistence of the signifier" to subsume the Freudian concept of the "death drive" itself. Thus, Lacan concludes the Seminar of 1954–1955 by stressing that the death drive is non-being, dumb or silent, and thus the mask of the symbolic order, only until it is recognised, for the death drive is nothing but the insistence of the symbolic order on its recognition by consciousness:

> And the death drive is only the mask of the symbolic order, in so far – this is what Freud writes – as it is dumb, that is to say in so far as it hasn't been realised. As long as the symbolic recognition hasn't been instituted, by definition, the symbolic order is dumb. The symbolic order is simultaneously non-being and insisting to be, that is what Freud has in mind when he talks about the death drive as being what is most fundamental – a symbolic order in travail, in the process of coming, insisting on being realised.
>
> *(p. 326)*

By thus unambiguously defining the death drive as the insistence of the symbolic order, indicating that this very notion of insistence is what made Freud consider the death drive to be most fundamental, Lacan indicates that the death drive itself is reducible to insistence.

Why did Lacan feel the need to introduce these major changes to the two Freudian concepts? Well, Lacan introduced these changes so as to delink these two Freudian concepts from the hold of neurology and biology to which Freud had conclusively relegated them by mistake. Thus, Lacan states in his Seminar of 1954–1955 that the word "compulsion" denotes a false and therefore unacceptable ascendancy of neurology:

> The word *automatisme* has resonances for us of the complete ascendancy of neurology. That isn't how it should be understood. What it is is a compulsion to repeat [*compulsion à la répétition*], and that is why I think I am making it concrete by introducing the notion of insistence.
>
> *(p. 61)*

Lacan had categorically stated a couple of years earlier, in "The Function and Field of Speech and Language in Psychoanalysis," that if repetition-compulsion were a biological notion, it would have caused no difficulty to the psychoanalysts. Instead, it acts as an impediment to psychoanalysts precisely because it has nothing to do with biology: "the term 'automatism' . . . would not cause difficulty were it simply a question of a biological notion. But, as we all know, it is not, which is what makes the problem a stumbling block to so many of us" (Lacan, 1953/2006, p. 261). After all, what is "biological" about a mentor being serially betrayed by his *protégés*, or about a student failing again and again in examinations by being unable to study due to one reason or another, or about a businessman who makes loss-making his real business, as Atin jokingly mentions to Ela with reference to his housemate, who failed in all his business ventures, in Tagore's novel *Chaar Adhyaay* [Four Chapters]?

Lacan thinks that both the death drive and the repetition-compulsion are grounded in the symbolic order or the order of speech and language rather than in neurology or biology. According to Lacan, the drives are not instincts. Whereas instincts belong to the real body beyond language, drives are governed by the signifier. Additionally, whereas the instincts operate in the same way in most individuals, drives are extremely variable and develop in ways which are contingent on the life history of the individual, especially the demands of the big Other; for instance, in the case of the anal drive, the infant's decision to hold back or to release its faeces will be a response to the demands articulated by its toilet trainer as its big Other. Moreover, whereas instincts do not rest before attaining the object aimed at, the aim of the drive is always deflected as it procures satisfaction from a surrogate object. Above all, whereas the instincts are the "given" in the body as the archaic and primordial, the drives are a medley of four discontinuous elements: the pressure, the end, the object, and the source.

In the Seminar of 1954–1955, Lacan describes the death drive as a concept: "[t]he death drive isn't an admission of impotence, it isn't a coming to a halt before an irreducible, an ineffable last thing, it is a concept" (Lacan, 1954–55/1991, p. 70). He reiterates in the same seminar that the "insistence" of "meaning," or the insistence of the symbolic order, is connected to death – implying death as a signifier or death drive – in the Freudian dialectic:

> That is what life is – a detour, a dogged detour, in itself transitory and precarious, and deprived of any significance. Why, in that of its manifestations called man, does something happen, which insists throughout this life, which is called a meaning? We call it *human*, but are we so sure? Is this meaning as human as all that? A meaning is an order, that is to say, a sudden emergence. A meaning is an order which suddenly emerges. A life insists on entering into it, but it expresses something which is perhaps completely beyond this life, since when we get to the root of this life, behind the drama of the passage into existence, we find nothing besides life conjoined to death. That is where the Freudian dialectic leads us.
>
> *(p. 232)*

Again, in the Seminar of 1959–1960, Lacan relates the death drive to the signifying chain or a chain of signifiers:

> The death drive . . . is articulated at a level that can only be defined as a function of the signifying chain. . . . If everything that is immanent or implicit in the chain of natural events may be considered as subject to the so-called death drive, it is only because there is a signifying chain.
>
> *(Lacan, 1959–60/1992, pp. 211–212)*

Lacan moreover argues in this seminar that in its form of the destructive drive, the death drive must be *beyond* the urge to return to the state of rest rather than simply *be* that urge as Freud suggested:

> The drive as such, insofar as it is then a destruction drive, has to be beyond the drive to return to the state of equilibrium of the inanimate sphere. What can it be if it is not a direct will to destruction?
>
> *(p. 212)*

The answer is, it is the symbolic order's insistence through the signifying chain.

Thus, Lacan does not consider the death drive and repetition-compulsion to be the expressions of any archaic instinctual, biological, or neurological and thus "natural" urge as Freud did. Lacan considers them rather to constitute an insistence borne by the words of the speaking-being situated in the symbolic order. This is a radically path-breaking notion in psychoanalysis, wherein the drives have been always viewed as biological or organic impulses by all psychoanalysts beginning with Freud. By thus firmly situating the death drive and repetition-compulsion within the field of speech and language, Lacan distances both the Freudian concepts from neurology and biology and aligns them with the symbolic order.

Lacan not only dismisses Freud's biological explanations of the death drive and repetition-compulsion but also disagrees with Freud's view that the death drive and the life drives are two opposite drives despite all their overlaps. Departing from Freud, Lacan considered the death drive and the life drives to be two different aspects of the drive itself. He thinks that in the unconscious the life drives point to the death drive owing to this. Thus, he writes in his Seminar of 1964:

> The distinction between the life drive and the death drive is true in as much as it manifests two aspects of the drive. But this is so only on condition that one sees all the sexual drives as articulated at the level of significations in the unconscious, in as much as what they bring out is death – death as signifier and nothing but signifier.
>
> *(Lacan, 1964/1994, p. 257)*

Lacan had already indicated in the essay "Positions of the Unconscious" that the life drive is not any different from the death drive because "every drive," the life drives included, "is virtually a death drive" (Lacan, 1960/2006b, p. 719). There are several reasons why Lacan thinks that every drive – oral, anal, scopic, and invocatory – is a death drive. To begin with, the drives always extinguish themselves by completing the circuit. Drives ultimately bring down excitation to a state of rest. More importantly, owing to their repetitive nature, the drives insist on the recognition of something that is beyond this life and may be grasped only in relation to some signifier of death. Above all, drives are always partial, chaotic, and transgressive in nature and as such they tend to repeatedly urge the subject to transgress into the realm beyond the pleasure principle where the death drive rules, so as to be over-whelmed by an excess of *jouissance* there.

In this way, Lacan rescued Freud's death drive, life drives, and repetition-compulsion from the grip of neurology and biology and reinstated them in the symbolic order instead.

The Insistence of the Signifier in Poe's "The Purloined Letter"

For an illustration of the Lacanian notion of the insistence of the signifier, we need not look beyond Lacan's own "Seminar on 'The Purloined Letter'" in which Lacan had himself illustrated his complete argument, that the "insistence" of the signifier is correlated to the "ex-sistence" of subjects, with the help of Edgar Allan Poe's 1844 short story "The Purloined Letter" (Poe, 1844/1983, pp. 208–222).

Poe's story is about the theft and recovery of a private letter belonging to the Queen of France in the Restoration period. The letter, which the Queen had received from the Duke of S, is stolen from her by Minister D, who, taking advan-tage of the King's presence on the scene, picked up the letter from right under the Queen's nose. The Minister first kept a similar-looking letter belonging to him next to the Queen's letter lying on the table in the course of a conversation with the royal couple in the boudoir and then deliberately picked up the letter to which he had no claim in course of the same conversation. The Queen, who could see everything, felt compelled to keep quiet out of the fear of drawing the attention of the King to her private letter. After stealing the letter, the Minister distorted the external appearance of the letter by turning it inside out, getting his own name and address written on it in a feminine hand, putting a seal, crumpling it, et cetera, so as to make it look like a different and somewhat insignificant letter and then hid it in open view by casually thrusting it in a card-rack hanging from the mantelpiece where it was clearly visible to all. When the prefect of the Parisian Police fails to recover the letter in terms of several secret raids carried out on the Minister's premises in his absence and desperately seeks the assistance of the private detective Le Chevalier C. Auguste Dupin, the latter visually locates the letter during his first visit to the Minister's apartment, the Minister being one of Dupin's old acquaint-ances, and steals the letter in his next visit in the presence of the Minister in the same room – though not from under his nose – by replacing it with a facsimile let-ter that Dupin had prepared in the meantime and was armed with, doing so while the Minister was looking at the street through the window, his attention diverted by the sound of an explosion just below his window produced by an accomplice of Dupin, under the latter's instruction.

If we think of the letter here as a hidden or repressed signifier in the uncon-scious, then its "insistence" is clearly evident from the fact that the second theft is a repetition of the first one in many ways. According to Lacan, Poe's story is narrated with the help of two scenes, of which the second is a repetition of the first. In the first scene, although the Queen is able to prevent the King from noticing the letter by casually leaving it upside down on the table, in full view of everyone, when the King arrived, she is unable to prevent the cunning Minister D from stealing it from under her nose. The remainder or residue of the scene is the Minister's letter with which he had exchanged the letter belonging to the Queen. Similarly, in the second scene, although Minister D is able to prevent the Prefect of the Police from detecting the letter by hiding it in open view in his apartment, he is unable to prevent the clever detective Dupin from stealing the letter from there and that too when he was present close at hand. The remainder or residue in this scene is Dupin's facsimile letter with which he had exchanged the stolen letter belonging to the Queen. Both acts of theft, moreover, are carried out in course of inane conversations by the perpetrator.

The insistence of the signifier is correlated to the "ex-sistence" of subjects, according to Lacan. This is so insofar as sets of subjects – including esteemed and powerful ones, such as royal personages, ministers, and police commissioners – are compelled to occupy predetermined positions by a stolen letter, as well as to act in accordance with the precise dictates of that position, irrespective of their innate nature or personal wish. In the story, the purloined letter creates three interrelated positions, whereby the occupant of the first position shall be blind to and unable to act with the letter, the occupant of the second position shall be able to see the letter but unable to act with it, while the occupant of the third position shall be able to both see and act with the letter. Thus, in the first scene, the King sees nothing and is unable to act with the letter, the Queen sees a little but cannot act with the letter, and the Minister D sees the most, carries out a set of acts, and ends up possessing the letter. While in the second scene, the Prefect of the Police sees nothing and is unable to act with the letter, the Minister D sees a little but cannot act with the letter, and Dupin sees the most and ends up possessing the letter in terms of a set of acts. Lacan calls this an "intersubjective complex" involving three partners and describes it in terms of the technique legendarily attributed to the ostrich, wherein: "[T]he second believing himself invisible because the first has his head stuck in the sand, all the while letting the third calmly pluck his rear" (Lacan, 1955/2006, p. 10). Lacan ratifies that what confirms for us that this is repetition-compulsion or insistence of the signifier and nothing else is that the subjects "relay each other in course of the intersubjective repetition" owing precisely to their displacement determined by a pure signifier, the purloined letter, in their midst (p. 10).

Speaking on how sets of subjects are governed by the signifier, Lacan asserts:

> [I]t is the letter and its detour which governs their entrances and roles. While the letter may be *en souffrance*, they are the ones who shall suffer from it. By passing beneath its shadow, they become its reflection. By coming into the letter's possession . . . its meaning possesses them.
>
> *(p. 21)*

The case of Minister D, who moves from seeing the most and being able to act in the first scene to seeing a little and being unable to act in the second, best reveals how the subject's action, inaction, behaviour, role, et cetera are all determined by his or her relation to the repressed and insisting signifier. Lacan goes on to claim that in fact almost everything of importance about the subject is determined by the signifier:

> If what Freud discovered . . . has a meaning, it is that the signifier's displacement determines subjects' acts, destiny, refusals, blindnesses, success, and fate, regardless of their innate gifts and instruction, and irregardless of their character or sex; and that everything pertaining to the psychological pregiven follows willy-nilly the signifier's train, like weapon and baggage.
>
> *(p. 21)*

Lacan mentions that he singled out this story precisely because Poe had depicted the Freudian unconscious in it far more accurately than Freud himself and that too several decades before the advent of Freud. Lacan thinks that Poe had done so by depicting the unconscious in terms of intersubjectivity, which is how the Freudian unconscious ought to be depicted and viewed according to Lacan, instead of depicting it in terms of subjectivity, as Freud had done.

Lacan thus illustrates what he calls "the truth," namely "that it is the symbolic order which is constitutive for the subject," by demonstrating with the help of Poe's story "the major determination the subject receives from the itinerary of a signifier" (p. 7).

Notes

1 Freud borrowed the term "pleasure principle" (*Lustprinzip*) from the German philosopher, physician and psychologist Gustav Theodor Fechner, who, in an article titled "About the Principle of the Pleasure of Action" (*Über das Lustprinzip des Handelns*) dated 1848, discussed the principle of the pleasure of action, noting that the motives underlying such actions could well be unconscious, though the idea of greatest importance in psychoanalysis, namely the pleasure principle's struggle to deal with the reality principle, is Freud's own (See Fechner, 1848).

2 Since in all his works written in or after 1919, referred to in this chapter, Freud used the German word "trieb," not "instinkt," I have consistently altered James Strachey's English translation "instinct" to "drive." [Shouldn't "trieb" and "instinkt" be in italics, given that "*Lebenstrieb*" in end note 3 is in italics?]

3 Freud himself never used the Greek word "thanatos" to describe the death drive, though he often used its binary opposite, "eros" alongside the German word *Lebenstrieb* to describe the life drives. The expression "eros and thanatos" came from Freud's student Wilhelm Stekel, with whose understanding of psychoanalysis, let us keep in mind, Freud had often strongly disagreed. Freud himself preferred expressions like "Eros and death" or "eros and the death drive," as we shall see. "Eros and thanatos" is not an incorrect description; moreover, it has the advantage of being a balanced expression. However, since it is not a Freudian expression, it would be incorrect to attribute it to Freud.

4 Freud discusses the same opposition yet again, though without mentioning any new detail, in his 1932 correspondence with Albert Einstein published in 1933, under the title "Why War?" (Einstein and Freud, 1933/1960, p. 211), as well as in the 32nd lecture on

"Anxiety and Instinctual Life", of the *New Introductory Lectures on Psycho-Analysis*, written in 1932, and published in 1933 (Freud, 1933/1960, pp. 93–94).

5 Although Freud first used the term "compulsion to repeat" a little earlier, in 1914, in his paper on "Remembering, Repeating and Working-Through," he did not view it as a characteristic of the death drive there, nor did he do so until he wrote "The Uncanny," in which he regards it, for the first time, as the defining characteristic of the death drive and as the most significant component of the unconscious, which is the proper status of repetition-compulsion in psychoanalysis. Therefore, it is fair to say that Freud had not discovered the concept of repetition-compulsion before 1919, in spite of having identified the term in 1914.

6 Freud would have described the man's spontaneous, inadvertent gesture as a "symptomatic act," that is to say, an act that is carried out unmindfully while the conscious mind is actively focused on carrying out a completely different act of greater import, such as spontaneously taking to chewing nails while having anxious thoughts. Freud invokes the concept, for example, to explain Dora's act of unmindfully fiddling with the small reticule she had worn at her waist for the first time while she was consciously focused on answering Freud's question (Freud, 1901/1953, pp. 76–78).

7 Fritz Wittels speculated in the first biography of Freud, *Sigmund Freud*, published in German in 1923, that the death of Freud's daughter Sophie, in January 1920, had inspired him to identify the death drive:

What lives, wants to die again. Originating in dust, it wants to be dust again. Not only the life-drive is in them, but the death-drive as well. When Freud made this communication to an attentive world, he was under the impress of the death of a blooming daughter whom he lost after he had had to worry about the life of several of his nearest relatives, who had gone to war.(Wittels, 1923, p. 231)Although this view is factually incorrect because Freud's serious engagement with the death drive began in 1919, when Sophie was perfectly healthy, the speculation continues to be voiced (for instance, Grubrich-Simitis, 1993). Freud himself strongly dismissed many arguments and details in Wittels's biography in his stern letters to the latter dated 18 December 1923 and 15 August 1924 (Freud, 1960, pp. 345–347, 350–352). If it is at all necessary to speculate on the possible events beyond his clinical observations that might have moved Freud to turn his attention towards the death drive, the First World War seems to me to be a far more plausible conjecture than any personal tragedy or suffering of his own.

8 Among Freud's disciples who rejected the two concepts was Girindrasekhar Bose, the founding President of the Indian Psychoanalytical Society and the father of psychoanalysis in India. Bose thought that the pleasure principle was enough to account for the mental functioning of human beings, and he firmly believed that the incorporation of his own concept of the "opposite wish" into the psychoanalytic theory of the unconscious that existed prior to the discovery of the death drive and repetition-compulsion could simplify that theory enormously. Thus, Bose writes in a letter to Freud, dated 11 April 1929, that his own concept of the "opposite wish" can explain better and more simply most mechanisms pertaining to the Freudian unconscious, such as "repression" and "imitation, retaliation, conscience, projection, etc." Bose then singles out repetition-compulsion and states that it would be rendered a redundant concept in psychoanalysis if his concept of the opposite wish, which is a part of the pleasure principle itself, were to be accepted:

The facts that have led you to suppose the existence of the repetition compulsion in addition to the pleasure principle would be more easily explained on the basis of this theory [of opposite wishes]. . . . The repeated bringing up of the shock situation in dreams is an effort on the part of the unsatisfied opposite wish to get a satisfaction. This is determined by the pleasure principle. There is no need to suppose the functioning of the repetition compulsion.(Bose and Freud, 1921–37/1964, pp. 17–18)

References

Bose, G. and Freud, S. (1964). *The Beginnings of Psychoanalysis in India: Bose-Freud Correspondence.* Indian Psychoanalytical Society (Original work published 1921–37).

Einstein, A. and Freud, S. (1960). Why war? In Strachey, J. (Ed.) *The Standard Edition of the Complete Psychological Works of Sigmund Freud.* Vintage, Hogarth Press and the Institute of Psychoanalysis, 197–215 (22 vol) (Original work published 1933).

Fechner, G. T. (1848). *Über das lustprinzip des handelns* (About the principle of the pleasure of action). In *Zeitschrift für philosophie und philosophische kritik-neue* folge, 1–30 and 163–194 (19 vol).

Freud, S. (1953). Fragment of an analysis of a case of hysteria. In Strachey, J. (Ed.) *The Standard Edition of the Complete Psychological Works of Sigmund Freud.* Vintage, Hogarth Press and the Institute of Psychoanalysis, 7–122 (7 vol) (Original work published 1901).

Freud, S. (1955). The uncanny. In Strachey, J. (Ed.) *The Standard Edition of the Complete Psychological Works of Sigmund Freud.* Vintage, Hogarth Press and the Institute of Psychoanalysis (17 vol), 219–256 (Original work published 1919).

Freud, S. (1955). Beyond the pleasure principle. In Strachey, J. (Ed.) *The Standard Edition of the Complete Psychological Works of Sigmund Freud.* Vintage, Hogarth Press and the Institute of Psychoanalysis (18 vol), 7–64 (Original work published 1920).

Freud, S. (1955). Group psychology and the analysis of the Ego. In Strachey, J. (Ed.) *The Standard Edition of the Complete Psychological Works of Sigmund Freud.* Vintage, Hogarth Press and the Institute of Psychoanalysis (18 vol), 69–143 (Original work published 1921).

Freud, S. (1955). The libido theory. In Strachey, J. (Ed.) *The Standard Edition of the Complete Psychological Works of Sigmund Freud.* Vintage, Hogarth Press and the Institute of Psychoanalysis (18 vol), 255–259 (Original work published 1923).

Freud, S. (1958). Formulations on the two principles of mental functioning. In Strachey, J. (Ed.) *The Standard Edition of the Complete Psychological Works of Sigmund Freud.* Vintage, Hogarth Press and the Institute of Psychoanalysis (12 vol), 215–226 (Original work published 1911).

Freud, S. (1958). Remembering, repeating and working-through. In Strachey, J. (Ed.) *The Standard Edition of the Complete Psychological Works of Sigmund Freud.* Vintage, Hogarth Press and the Institute of Psychoanalysis (12 vol), 145–156 (Original work published 1914).

Freud, S. (1959). An autobiographical study. In Strachey, J. (Ed.) *The Standard Edition of the Complete Psychological Works of Sigmund Freud.* Vintage, Hogarth Press and the Institute of Psychoanalysis (20 vol), 7–74 (Original work published 1925).

Freud, S. (1960). *The Letters of Sigmund Freud.* Freud, E. L. Ed. and Stern, J. Trans. Basic Books Inc, New York.

Freud, S. (1960). New introductory lectures on psycho-analysis. In Strachey, J. (Ed.) *The Standard Edition of the Complete Psychological Works of Sigmund Freud.* Vintage, Hogarth Press and the Institute of Psychoanalysis (22 vol), 3–182 (Original work published 1933).

Freud, S. (1961). The ego and the id. In Strachey, J. (Ed.) *The Standard Edition of the Complete Psychological Works of Sigmund Freud.* Vintage, Hogarth Press and the Institute of Psychoanalysis (19 vol), 12–66 (Original work published 1923).

Freud, S. (1961). The economic problem of masochism. In Strachey, J. (Ed.) *The Standard Edition of the Complete Psychological Works of Sigmund Freud.* Vintage, Hogarth Press and the Institute of Psychoanalysis (19 vol), 159–170 (Original work published 1924).

Freud, S. (1961). Negation. In Strachey, J. (Ed.) *The Standard Edition of the Complete Psychological Works of Sigmund Freud.* Vintage, Hogarth Press and the Institute of Psychoanalysis (19 vol), 235–239 (Original work published 1925).

Freud, S. (1961). Civilisation and its discontents. In Strachey, J. (Ed.) *The Standard Edition of the Complete Psychological Works of Sigmund Freud*. Vintage, Hogarth Press and the Institute of Psychoanalysis (21 vol), 64–145 (Original work published 1929).

Freud, S. (1964). Analysis terminable and interminable. In Strachey, J. (Ed.) *The Standard Edition of the Complete Psychological Works of Sigmund Freud*. Vintage, Hogarth Press and the Institute of Psychoanalysis (23 vol), 216–253 (Original work published 1937).

Freud, S. (1964). An outline of psychoanalysis. In Strachey, J. (Ed.) *The Standard Edition of the Complete Psychological Works of Sigmund Freud*. Vintage, Hogarth Press and the Institute of Psychoanalysis (23 vol), 144–207 (Original work published 1940).

Freud, S. (1895 [1966]). Project for a scientific psychology. In Strachey, J. (Ed.) *The Standard Edition of the Complete Psychological Works of Sigmund Freud*. Vintage, Hogarth Press and the Institute of Psychoanalysis (19 vol), 295–397 (Original work published 1950).

Grubrich-Simitis, I. (1993). *Back to Freud's Texts: Making Silent Documents Speak*. Slotkin, P. Trans. Yale University Press, New Haven.

Lacan, J. (1991). *The Seminar of Jacques Lacan, Book II, the Ego in Freud's Theory and in the Technique of Psychoanalysis, 1954–1955*. Miller, J. A. Ed. and Tomaselli, S. Trans. W. W. Norton (Original work published 1954–55).

Lacan, J. (1992). *The Seminar of Jacques Lacan, Book VII, the Ethics of Psychoanalysis, 1959–1960*. Miller, J. A. Ed. and Porter, D. Trans. W. W. Norton (Original work published 1959–60).

Lacan, J. (1994). *The seminar of Jacques Lacan. Book XI, The four fundamental concepts of Psychoanalysis*. Miller, J. A. Ed. and Sheridan, A. Trans. Penguin Books (Original work published 1964).

Lacan, J. (2006). The function and field of speech and language in Psychoanalysis. In Fink, B. Trans. *Écrits*. W. W. Norton, 197–268 (Original work published 1953).

Lacan, J. (2006). Seminar on 'the purloined letter'. In Fink, B. Trans. *Écrits*. W. W. Norton, 6–48 (Original work published 1955).

Lacan, J. (2006a). The subversion of the subject and the dialectic of desire in the Freudian unconscious. In Fink, B. Trans. *Écrits*. W. W. Norton, 671–702 (Original work published 1960).

Lacan, J. (2006b). Positions of the unconscious. In Fink, B. Trans. *Écrits*. W. W. Norton, 703–721 (Original work published 1960).

Poe, E. A. (1983). The purloined latter. In *The Complete Tales and Poems of Edgar Allan Poe*. Penguin Books, 208–222 (Original work published 1844).

Schur, M. (1972). *Freud: Living and Dying*. International Universities Press, New York.

Tagore, R. (2001). The postmaster. In Chaudhuri, A. (Ed. and Trans.) *The Picador Book of Modern Indian Literature*. Picador, 29–34 (Original work published 1891).

Wittels, F. (1923). *Sigmund Freud, His Personality, His Teaching, His School*. Paul, E. and Paul, C. Trans. George Allen & Unwin, London.

PART III

Emerging Issues in Biomedical Sciences and Healthcare

11

ORIGIN OF LIFE ON EARTH

Bijan Das

Introduction

Today, our beautiful Earth is full of various forms of life. Living beings can be found almost ubiquitously on this planet, evolving their own ways for their survival. They have been found even in the strangest, apparently hostile, places on Earth and beyond. Microbial lives are found in the bubbling lakes of hot tar in the Caribbean island of Trinidad. Hot springs at the bottom of the Pacific Ocean are often swarmed with tubeworms and giant clams. The cold and dry valleys of Antarctica are found to be full of microbes. They are also found to flourish within the rocks up to several kilometres down the Earth's surface in gold and platinum mines in South Africa. Even in the open and harsh vacuum in the outer space, a region exposed to fatal radiation, are found tiny eight-legged creatures known colloquially as water bears or moss piglets. But this was not at all the case when the Earth was formed about four and a half billion years ago. There were no lives on Earth for the initial several hundreds of millions of years of its existence. How did life, then, on Earth, emerge? It is a question contemplated by humans since they developed cognition. It is a question that inspired a great deal of myth. It is a question that bewildered scientists and philosophers for millennia. It is a question that is yet to be answered satisfactorily.

Once the noted British astronomer Sir Fred Hoyle commented that the appearance of a living entity out of a non-living chemical species was almost as likely as the assemblage of a Boeing 747 aircraft by a tornado sweeping through a junkyard with all the components present therein. Sir Hoyle, instead, put forward the hypothesis that the first life evolved in space, which was then spread through the universe via celestial bodies such as comets, meteors and so on. Whereas the British evolutionary biologist Richard Dawkins commented otherwise: "My guess is that life probably isn't all that rare and the origin of life probably wasn't all that

DOI: 10.4324/9781003033448-15

improbable". This, of course, is a befitting debate as to the gravity and significance of the question on the emergence of life on Earth.

All living beings on Earth are now known to be made up of microscopic entities called cells. These are, in fact, the basic structural and functional units of all known living organisms. In other words, cells are the smallest possible units that manifest the characteristic properties of life. Although the cells were discovered back in the seventeenth century after the invention of modern microscopes (Lane, 2015; Nurse, 2000; Wollman et al., 2015), it took well over another century for people to realize that these were really the basis of all life forms. Now, such cells are known to arise only from a pre-existing cell. For this to happen, the cells must have the ability to self-replicate, that is to reproduce themselves on their own. The question of *how life on Earth began* thus reduces to the problem of *how cells first emerged*. To perform self-replication, a cell must have an in-built information store as to what to prepare, and it must also have a machinery to execute the process of self-replication.

In all living cells which now exist on Earth, self-replication is accomplished through the cooperative action of two key chemical species – deoxyribonucleic acid abbreviated as DNA and protein, which are confined within the cellular structure made up of lipid molecules. Here, DNA plays the role of an information store or a template while protein molecules help carry out the process of self-replication.

At present, there exists several competing theoretical approaches on how life on Earth could possibly have arisen. Some theories question if life began on Earth at all, asserting instead that it came from a distant place of the universe or from the core of a comet or an asteroid that happened to fall on Earth. Some even says life might have arisen here more than once. But, since it is indeed very hard to prove or disprove the theories put forward so far, a completely accepted theory is still lacking.

This chapter will attempt to provide a brief description of the plausible theories as to how life on Earth arose.

At first, however, we will introduce the reader to the molecules of life, that is the molecules which constitute the cells of all living beings on Earth.

Molecules of Life

As pointed out earlier, the three key molecules of cells and hence of life are protein, deoxyribonucleic acid (DNA) and lipid.

Of these three species, the former two are polymers. Polymers (also known as macromolecules) are giant chemical species formed by the combination of a large number of small molecules (commonly referred to as the monomers) through chemical bonds among themselves. Owing to their very wide spectrum of properties, both synthetic and natural polymers play vital and ubiquitous roles in our everyday life. These species range from the familiar synthetic plastics such as polystyrene to natural biopolymers such as proteins and DNA which are basic to the structures and functions of biological entities.

Proteins consist of amino acids as their monomeric units which are joined together by means of chemical linkages known as peptide bonds. Although about 500 naturally occurring amino acids are known, only 20 of them are found to occur in living organisms. These are responsible for a wide variety of jobs in the living cells. Among the very many roles of proteins in living cells, the best-known task is their enzymatic activity in which they speed up chemical reactions, which otherwise proceed very slowly in their absence. Enzymes are fantastic chemical species, and they can make the progress of a chemical reaction millions of times faster compared to what it would have been without them. The chemical reactions which keep us alive – the process of metabolism – depend on the activities which enzymes carry out.

DNA molecules are the key information carriers in all known life forms on Earth. They are made up of two polymeric strands, which coil around each other to form a structure referred to as a double helix. Each DNA strand, composed of simpler monomeric units called nucleotides, is also known as polynucleotide. Each nucleotide, in turn, consists of one of the four nitrogenous nucleobases [cytosine (C), guanine (G), adenine (A) and thymine (T)], a deoxyribose sugar and a phosphate group. These nucleotides are connected to one another through covalent chemical linkages or bonds between the sugar unit of one nucleotide and the phosphate unit of the next, thus forming a sugar–phosphate backbone. There is a special chemical affinity of A to T and G to C. A and T get chemically connected through hydrogen atoms, and in particular, there are two hydrogen bonds holding these two nitrogenous bases together. G and C, on the other hand, form three hydrogen bonds among themselves. These hydrogen bonds, thus, hold two DNA strands together and give them a helical structure. It should be pointed out here that the living organisms also rely on another polymeric species, ribonucleic acid (RNA) a close chemical cousin of DNA. Unlike DNA, RNA is a single-stranded molecule which contains uracil (U) instead of A and ribose sugar instead of deoxyribose sugar. In all modern living cells, self-replication is performed through the cooperative action of both DNA and RNA.

The membrane surrounding any modern cell serves as a barrier which separates the components of a cell from its external environment. Membranes of cells are made up of a double layer of lipid molecules which are chemically known as "phospholipids". These are responsible for controlling which substances are allowed to enter or leave a cell. A phospholipid molecule contains two water-hating (hydrophobic) fatty acid chains connected to a phosphate-containing water-loving (hydrophilic) part. Because of the poor water solubility of their fatty acid parts, phospholipids, in aqueous solutions, spontaneously form bilayer structures of the membrane in such a way that the hydrophobic tails are buried within the interior of the membrane (thus avoiding contact with water) and the hydrophilic parts are exposed on both sides and remain in contact with water.

Questions to Be Answered

To understand how life on Earth emerged from inanimate matters, the model/ hypothesis must, in principle, take care of the following questions:

1   How did the amino acids – the building blocks of proteins, DNAs and lipids – arise under primitive Earth conditions?
2   How did those building blocks join together to form the proteins, DNAs and lipids?
3   How did the proteins, DNAs and lipids combine and acquire self-replicating ability thus leading to the emergence of life on Earth?

Aristotle's Belief: Spontaneous Generation of Life

Spontaneous generation refers to the belief that complex living organisms arose instantaneously from decaying nonliving substances. In fact, the great Greek philosopher Aristotle (384–322 BCE) was one of the first who recorded his conclusions as to the possibility of transition from nonliving objects to living beings (Brack, 1998). He believed that living creatures could emerge from nonliving matters and that such transitions were very commonplace and could occur regularly. It was conjectured that certain forms of life, for example fleas, could arise from non-living matter such as dust, maggots could arise from rotten flesh, mice could arise within stored grain, aphids from the dew, crocodiles from rotting logs at the bottom of water bodies, so on and so forth. This belief persisted for over two millennia because people, in those days, did not test the validity or feasibility of these ideas. People thought that there was nothing special in the generation of life out of scratch. For example Egyptians noticed that when River Nile flooded every year, there were plenty of frogs around the river banks, and their conclusion was very simple and straightforward: it was the muddy soil that gave rise to the birth of frogs!

This idea of the spontaneous generation of life came under attack in the seventeenth century. In particular, Sir Thomas Browne, an English polymath and author, in 1646, published his encyclopedia, *Pseudodoxia Epidemica* (in English *Enquiries into Very Many Received Tenets, and Commonly Presumed Truths*), where he criticized vehemently these false beliefs which he referred to as "*vulgar errors*" (Breathnach, 2005). His ideas were not, however, widely accepted at that time. Franceso Redi, an Italian scientist, was the first to provide an impressive evidence against spontaneous generation in 1668, purely from a scientific viewpoint (Parke, 2014). Redi performed a very simple experiment. He placed fresh pieces of meat in open jars and observed accumulation of files on the rotting meat which soon swarmed with maggots that hatched into flies. In a separate experiment, the jars containing meat were covered to avoid the entry of the flies into them and observed no such development as observed in the previous experiment. He concluded that living beings, that is the maggots, could not evolve from the inanimate matter, that is meat.

However, some argued that the airtight cover could have cut off the entry of air necessary for the lives to appear in the second case. To rule out this possibility, Redi later used porous gauzes instead of an airtight lid to cover the jars in his experiments. Although the flies gathered onto the porous gauze which soon became full of maggots, the meat itself developed *no* maggots. It could thus be inferred that maggots did not appear on meat when flies were not allowed to enter the jar to lay eggs and that they actually came from the eggs of files when the meat was exposed to the flies. The obvious conclusion is that maggots did not arise spontaneously from decomposing meat.

In 1765, an Italian catholic priest, biologist and physiologist Lazzaro Spallanzani (1729–1799) demonstrated that microbes were present in the air, and any nonliving matter exposed to air could manifest the so-called spontaneous generation of life (Ariatti and Mandrioli, 1993). It was Louis Pasteur who put the final nails in the coffin. In 1861, Louis Pasteur carried out a series of experiments which confirmed that organisms like bacteria and fungi did not spontaneously appear in sterile, nutrient-rich media (Raulin-Cerceau, 2001). The failure of the hypothesis of the spontaneous generation of life, however, left a void in scientific thought on the basic question as to how life *had* emerged first.

The Alternative Theory: Biogenesis

The alternative approach to the spontaneous generation of life seemed to be biogenesis, which proposed that every living thing appeared from another preexisting living thing (*omne vivum ex ovo*, Latin for "every living thing from an egg"). Around the middle of the nineteenth century, the theory of biogenesis had received convincing evidential support, due, in particular, to the work of Pasteur. The basic question with regard to how the first life form appeared (which is the precondition of the theory of biogenesis), however, remained unanswered.

Charles Darwin and the Origin of Life

The great breakthrough of biology in the nineteenth century was, of course, the theory of evolution, as enunciated by Charles Darwin.

Darwin in his book *On the Origin of Species*, published in 1859, interpreted how the vast diverse life forms on Earth could all have appeared from an ancient single common ancestor rather than each of the different species being originated separately, that is all living beings on Earth descended from an ancient organism that existed millions of years ago. Darwin's theory of evolution provided no clue, however, to the problem as to how that first organism sprang up.

Darwin, nevertheless, was aware that it was a very big question, and he seemed to have discussed this issue only in his private notebooks and communications. The origin of life, to him, was an issue which could be elucidated from scientific point of view, and he also recognized that those times were not appropriate for such scientific exploration.

As is evident from his personal notebooks, written as early as 1837, Darwin argued that since the life and the universal laws of chemical combinations are intimately related with each other, spontaneous generation of life might not be improbable.

Now there is an intriguing question: if all the conditions for the first generation of a living being persist on Earth at the present time, can the life be evolved now from the inanimate matters? Darwin dealt with this issue in a letter written to his close friend Joseph Dalton Hooker on 1 February 1871. If we, according to Darwin, have a "warm, little pond" containing ammonia and phosphoric salts along with a sufficient supply of heat, light and electricity to produce a protein compound through chemical reactions, capable of readily undergoing further complex changes, the products so formed would be instantly decomposed or absorbed under the present environmental condition. This was, of course, not the case prior to the appearance of living beings on Earth. Thus, Darwin took it for granted that life on Earth originated naturally. This is also apparent from a letter which he wrote to D. Mackintosh on 28 February 1882 (De Beer, 1959), where he expressed his belief of the possibility of the evolution of living beings from inorganic substances even though there was no convincing evidence in favour of his opinion till that time. He, however, also believed that someday this possibility would find supporting proof in accordance with what he pointed out as the "law of continuity". Here, the word "continuity" is to be noted. Although he favoured the possibility that life could appear by natural processes from simple inorganic compounds, he was of the opinion that life forms could have first appeared from a simple chemical species gradually through a series of steps (i.e. chemical reactions) maintaining "continuity", *not* by a single magical step as proposed earlier in the hypothesis of the spontaneous generation of life. In fact, Darwin repeatedly asserted that the subject of spontaneous generation of life was not tractable by means of the knowledge of science of his time. That is why Darwin was reluctant to discuss the issue on how life could have appeared. This is directly evident from a letter which he wrote to George Charles Wallich (De Beer, 1959) on 28 March 1882, where he stated that Wallich quite correctly said that he had intentionally left the question of the origin of life unaddressed as being altogether beyond the state of knowledge of those days.

The Oparin–Haldane Hypothesis

In the early decades of the twentieth century, Russian biochemist Aleksandr Oparin (Oparin, 1924) and British scientist J.B.S. Haldane (Haldane, 1929), (who was unaware of the work of Oparin whose first book *The Origin of Life* was originally published in Russian) independently put forward a hypothesis proposing that life on Earth appeared as a result of *chemical evolution*. The ideas of Oparin and Haldane were essentially the same. Both independently assumed that the atmosphere of the Earth prior to the emergence of life was chemically reducing in nature without free oxygen (having methane, ammonia, hydrogen and water as the prevalent chemical species, among other gases) unlike the present oxidizing atmosphere (with free oxygen). Under these circumstances, according to this hypothesis, a variety of simple organic molecules could have been synthesized where lightning and/or ultraviolet light served as the source of energy. These organic compounds could have then undergone a series of chemical reactions to give rise to gradually more and more complex compounds.

According to Oparin, lipid molecules self-aggregate spontaneously in aqueous milieu to form spherical entities known as the "coacervates". The coacervates could have the ability to absorb and assimilate organic compounds from their environment in a way which is indicative of the process of metabolism in modern cells. These might have played a pivotal role toward the evolution of primitive cells and the emergence of life on Earth.

Haldane, unaware of Oparin's concept of the development of coacervates, proposed that simple organic compounds were formed initially in the primitive ocean (referred to as "prebiotic soup" by Haldane) and that those compounds became progressively more complex when subjected to ultraviolet radiation abundant in the prebiotic Earth. The ocean thereby became a "hot dilute soup" comprising a host of organic monomers and polymers, which then got encapsulated by membranes made up of lipid molecules. Further evolution finally led to the emergence of the first living cells.

The proposal of Oparin and Haldane was merely a hypothesis and there was no experimental evidence supporting this idea. Under these circumstances, the problem of the origin of life can be more precisely defined in the light of the Oparin–Haldane hypothesis in this way: a cell needs to be developed starting only with the materials and conditions which prevailed on the primitive Earth. Of course, the primary question is how the organic molecules – that is the building blocks of proteins, nucleic acids and lipids could appear on the prebiotic Earth.

Emergence of Organic Molecules on the Prebiotic Earth

Many scientists believe that small organic molecules including amino acids, nucleotides, fatty acids and so on could have been synthesized from inorganic molecules presumably available in the prebiotic Earth's atmosphere. While others hypothesized that these could have been synthesized at the hydrothermal vents (volcanic apertures at the bottom of the sea that emit chemicals and heat into the surrounding water) or from underwater volcanoes. Still another group of scientists is of the opinion that these could have been rained down on Earth from outer space.

Miller and Urey and the Synthesis of Organic Compounds in the Prebiotic Earth's Atmosphere

In 1951, Stanley Miller joined the PhD program of the University of Chicago, Illinois, USA, at the age of 21, under the supervision of an eminent theoretical physicist Professor Edward Teller and started his theoretical research on "The Synthesis of Elements in the Stars". He was, however, not so much interested in this project.

In September next year, Miller attended a chemistry seminar in which Nobel Laureate Professor Harold Urey (the discoverer of Deuterium) presented a lecture on "The Origin of Solar System and Possible Synthesis of Organic Molecules under the Primitive Earth's Atmosphere". According to Urey, free oxygen was probably absent in the atmosphere of the primitive Earth. This could probably provide the ideal conditions for the formation of the primordial soup (as described by Oparin and Haldane) where the fragile organic molecules would not have been destroyed by the atmospheric oxygen. Miller was greatly inspired. This event sparked Miller's enthusiasm for the topic. He decided to quit his PhD work and approached Urey for a new research with him. Urey was not initially enthusiastic on Miller's eagerness to synthesize organic molecules under prebiotic Earth condition, as no successful works had been done till then. Miller, however, persisted and succeeded in persuading Urey to take up a project aiming at synthesizing organic molecules by simulating the primitive Earth conditions.

Miller, under the supervision of Urey, conducted a simple experiment in 1952. In this pioneering endeavor, a mixture of methane, ammonia, hydrogen and water vapor (to mimic the assumed primitive Earth atmosphere) was subjected to a prolonged electrical discharge to simulate the lightning, believed to be prevalent on the primitive Earth. After one week of continuous operation, the compounds formed were accumulated after condensation. This mixture, upon analysis, was shown to contain a number of organic compounds (those in which one or more atoms of carbon are covalently linked to atoms of other elements, most commonly hydrogen, oxygen or nitrogen), including aldehydes, carboxylic acids and amino acids (amino acids are the building blocks of proteins in living cells) (Miller, 1953). Thereby, even though the Miller–Urey experiment produced some simple organic molecules and not a complete living biochemical system, this revolutionary experiment proved unequivocally that some important building blocks of life could be obtained from inanimate matter and thus supported the primordial soup hypothesis. In this context, the comment of Dr John Sutherland, of the Laboratory of Molecular Biology in Cambridge, UK, is noteworthy: "The strength of Miller-Urey experiment is to show that you can go from a simple atmosphere and produce lots of biological molecules".

Later, the Miller–Urey experiment has often been repeated by various groups of scientists around the globe, with similar set-ups but with different starting mixtures (Bada, 2013). These attempts have produced many organic compounds, including adenosine triphosphate, ATP (a complex organic chemical compound which supplies energy for driving many processes in living cells) when the initial reaction mixture contained phosphate. However, there are still various facets of the synthesis of organic compounds from inorganic substances which stimulate much debate and thus pave the way for further research.

Synthesis of Organic Compounds in the Hydrothermal Vents

In the year 1977, John B. Corliss of Oregon State University led a project team with a submersible 2.5 kilometers down into the eastern Pacific Ocean to search for the presumed hydrothermal vents near the Galápagos Islands. [This island group is a province of Equador in South America. These islands became internationally famous as a result of their being visited by Charles Darwin in 1835; their unusual fauna contributed to his revolutionary theories on natural selection presented in his *On the Origin of Species* (Corliss et al., 1979)]. The team was surveying the Galápagos hotspot, where tall ridges of rock rose from the bottom of the ocean. These ridges were also volcanically active. It was found that the ridges were essentially full of many hot springs. Hot, chemical-rich water was gushing up from below the seafloor and pumping out through holes in the rocks. These "hydrothermal vents" were heavily populated by various animals. Based on these observations, it was proposed that these hydrothermal vents could produce various chemicals. These vents, he believed, could have served as primordial soup dispensers.

Günter Wächtershäuser, a German chemist-turned patent lawyer, in the late 1980s, also held a similar view (Wächtershäuser, 1988). The key idea of his theory is that the early chemistry of life occurred *not* in bulk solution in the oceans as proposed by Oparin and Haldane *but* on the surfaces of minerals (e.g. iron pyrites, an ore of iron consisting of iron and sulfur) close to deep hydrothermal vents. According to Wächtershäuser, under an anaerobic (where free oxygen is absent), high-temperature, high-pressure environment one chemical species is converted into numerous chemical compounds through a series of chemical reactions, until eventually the original chemical species is recreated. In this process, the entire system takes up energy from the environment which can be used to initiate the cycle again – and to start synthesizing other chemical species. These cycles of chemical reactions do not sound much like life, rather they ultimately lead to the formation of the life-forming molecules.

Organic Compounds From Extraterrestrial Sources

From the foregoing discussion, it appears that organic molecules, which are the precursors of life forms, could have evolved on Earth through chemical pathways. By now, we know that many organic compounds, from methane to amino acids, exist in space, and scientists believe that organic molecules from space reached this planet aboard asteroids containing carbon compounds and created the building blocks for the first development of life.

On 28 September 1969, near the town of Murchison, Victoria, in Western Australia, a meteorite fell. Multiple studies have been successful in identifying over 15 amino acids, some of the basic constituents of life, in the meteorite (Lawless, 1973). This indicates that the Earth could have received the molecules of life from the outer space as well. A recent report on the chemical analysis of the pieces of two 4.5 billion-year-old meteorites Zag and Monahans (which landed on Earth in 1998) indicated that these meteorites did contain liquid water together with prebiotic complex organic molecules which might be the ingredients for life (Chan et al., 2018).

Very recently, in 2019, geologists of France and Italy carried out investigations on a region of the Makhonjwa Mountains in South Africa. This region contains a large deposit of 3.3-billion-year-old volcanic rock. The rock has been found to be formed in layers, and beneath the surface there are carbon-containing layers from which samples were collected by the researchers for their studies. The analyses indicated that some of the materials in these samples originated from sources out-side the Earth. This is, till date, the evidence of the oldest examples of these organic molecules of extraterrestrial origin on Earth (Gourier et al., 2019).

How Did Proteins and Nucleic Acids Evolve?

In the foregoing we have discussed some plausible mechanisms as to how the small chemical molecules which ultimately led to the emergence of life could have accu-mulated on Earth through one or more of the three pathways discussed in the pre-vious section. How did the proteins and nucleic acids – the fundamental molecules of life – then evolve in the primitive Earth which could have enough supply of their constituents?

The Chicken-and-the-Egg Dilemma

The mechanism for the appearance of protein and nucleic acid molecules is really very perplexing. Let me tell you why. For lives to start, there must have been some genetic molecules, something like DNA or RNA in modern cells, capable of pass-ing along templates for preparing proteins, the workhorse molecules of life. But, the synthesis of DNA or RNA in modern cells requires the active participation of enzymes (which are nothing but protein molecules). Thus, it appears that proteins could have evolved prior to the appearance of the nucleic acids. Synthesis of pro-teins, on the other hand, requires DNA which serves as the template in this process, and therefore nucleic acids should have emerged before the formation of the pro-tein molecules. This awkward situation in explaining the appearance of protein and nucleic acid molecules in the prebiotic earth is what is commonly known as "The Chicken-and-the-Egg Dilemma" over the origin of life on Earth.

Resolution of the Conundrum: the RNA World Hypothesis

The discovery of the existence of a particular class of RNA molecules, in 1982–1983, independently by two research groups helped resolve the Chicken-and-the Egg dilemma and showed a way out of the decades-long stalemate as to whether the first living beings on Earth had been based on nucleic acids or on proteins. It was established independently by two groups of researchers that some RNA molecules which could store information could also behave as enzymes. That is these molecules performed simultaneously the roles of both nucleic acids and pro-teins. These special RNA molecules are known as ribozymes (**Ribo**nucleic acid + **Enzyme**). Professor Thomas Robert Cech and his group at the University of Colorado, Boulder, USA, discovered that ribosomal RNAs were capable of excis-ing pieces of itself (Kruger et al., 1982). Around the same time, another group led by Professor Sidney Altman at Yale University, USA, had discovered that the catalytic part of an enzyme called ribonuclease P enzyme was in fact an RNA molecule and not a protein subunit (Guerrier-Takada et al., 1983). These two discoveries triggered Professor Gilbert to put forward his famous hypothesis, referred to as the RNA World Hypothesis in 1986 (Gilbert, 1986). According to this hypothesis, the earliest life forms might have based solely on an RNA molecule where it simultaneously played the roles of nucleic acid (as template) and protein (as catalyst). This means our earliest ancestors on Earth were self-replicating RNA systems. In particular, the discovery of the capability of the intron (a part of RNA) to catalyze the polymerization of RNA strands (Zaug and Cech, 1986) provided a support in favor of the RNA World Hypothesis. Although there are strong opponents to this hypothesis, many origin-of-life researchers agree that even though far from being complete, it still remains one of the best scientific theories we have to elucidate the origin of life on Earth. RNA molecules might not be as efficient as DNA for the purpose of storing information, being far less stable than the latter, nor as versatile as proteins, but these turned out to be a beautiful performer of dual roles. It is worth mentioning that whereas other researchers like Alexander Rich, Francis Crick, Leslie Orgel and Carl Woese had hinted, as early as in the 1960s (Orgel, 2004), at the possibilities that RNA might have preceded DNA in primitive life forms, no concrete suggestion on the possible role of RNA in the emergence of life on Earth had been made.

In the beginning of this millennium, a fascinating discovery provided a very strong supporting evidence in favor of the RNA World Hypothesis (Ban et al., 2000). Every living cell has an organelle called ribosome. This is a huge molecule that reads instructions from RNA and links amino acids to form protein chains. Ribosomes constitute most of our body, and they are known to contain RNA. In 2000, Steitz's group was successful to produce a detailed image of the structure of ribosome. This study discovered that RNA was the catalytic core of the ribosome. This was critical because the ribosome is so fundamental to all living cells and hence, ancient. This discovery made RNA World Hypothesis more plausible since ribosomes are based on RNA.

Emergence of Ribozyme on the Primitive Earth

Ribozymes (catalytic RNAs) were in the center of the presumed RNA World in the origin of life on Earth. However, direct evidence of these primitive organisms is unlikely to be found today. With a view to figure out how the first life might have looked, many laboratories around the globe have been attempting to recreate such an RNA species with catalytic activity in the laboratories. Of course, two types of RNAs are, therefore, possible – one with catalytic activity and the other which lacks such activity.

Now, an RNA nucleotide – the building block of RNA – could arise if a ribose sugar, a nucleobase and a phosphate could be assembled and connected chemically. If these nucleotides were then somehow activated chemically, they could get polymerized into a long RNA molecule. Each of these synthetic routes poses huge hurdles for the prebiotic Earth. Did nature in the prebiotic Earth then use some simpler routes to RNA? Further, arrangement of the nucleotides in an arbitrary manner could not lead to the development of their catalytic ability. How did nature evolve RNA molecules with the right sequence which was appropriate for their catalytic action?

In 2009, a group of chemists led by Professor Sutherland at the University of Cambridge in the United Kingdom, realized the feasibility for the synthesis of nucleotides through alternative pathways (Powner et al., 2009). It was established experimentally that other than conventional sugar–nucleobases–phosphate scheme, a few relatively simple precursor compounds assumed to be present on the prebiotic Earth could be combined to form an activated nucleotide species under relatively mild experimental conditions. In particular, they started with acetylene and formaldehyde, and then through a sequence of chemical reactions ended up with two out of RNA's four nucleotide building blocks. However, acetylene and formaldehyde being still somewhat complex molecules, their appearance on the primitive was questioned. Later, the Sutherland group showed that the nucleic acid precursors could also be synthesized with an initial mixture of just hydrogen cyanide and hydrogen sulfide under the action of ultraviolet light (Powner et al., 2009). Further, this experimental condition, according to Sutherland, could also lead to the formation of the starting materials required to produce natural amino acids and lipids. That is majority of the building blocks of life could have, on the primitive Earth, arisen from a single set of reactions. However, the issue is not yet completely solved. Sutherland has not, so far, been successful in producing the other two nucleotides of RNA in the laboratory. However, he says he is "closing in" on the other two ribonucleotides. If he comes out successful, it would show that the spontaneous formation of a self-replicating RNA molecule in the primitive Earth was not so improbable after all and that the first replicating species was most likely made up of RNA.

It was argued by the Sutherland group that primitive Earth could have provided favorable environment for those reactions to occur. Hydrogen cyanide is an abundant chemical species in comets, and evidences indicated that it rained down steadily for nearly the first several hundred million years of Earth's existence. The impacts of these comets with the Earth could also have generated sufficient energy to effect the synthesis of hydrogen cyanide from its elemental constituents, namely hydrogen, carbon and nitrogen. Similarly, according to Sutherland, hydrogen sulfide was also very common on the early Earth, as was the ultraviolet radiation, which could steer the chemical reactions with the metal-containing minerals acting as the catalyst.

Sutherland, however, pointed out that the chemical reactions which would have resulted in the different sets of building blocks might necessarily be sufficiently different from one another and that these would, likely, not have all taken place at the same site. Variations in chemistry and energy at different locations, according to him, could have favored the formation of one kind of building blocks over the other, such as amino acids, nucleotides or lipids. "Rainwater would then wash these compounds into a common pool", said Dave Deamer, another noted origin-of-life researcher at the University of California, Santa Cruz, USA.

How did these nucleotides then join to give rise to the earliest ribozyme molecules? Who played the role of the template for proper arrangement of the nucleotides in the ribozyme chains? Who played the role of a catalyst to join these nucleotides? Once formed, the ribozyme molecules powered by their catalytic and genetic properties could, in principle, produce their own copies. The problem, therefore, is how the ribozyme molecules could have first evolved with the assistance of other species (besides ribozyme) presumably present on the prebiotic Earth.

It was Professor James Ferris of the Department of Chemistry and Chemical Biology, Rensselaer Polytechnic Institute, USA, who contemplated that clay – yes clay – where the first self-replicating RNA could have appeared (Ferris, 2005). This theory proposes that life based on RNA preceded the current life, which is based on DNA and protein. Ferris and his group have been investigating the use of the mineral montmorillonite as a surface for ribonucleotide polymerization. Montmorillonite, a clay mineral, is formed as a result of the accumulation and breakdown of the volcanic ash and may have been present on the early Earth, thus making it a promising material for catalysis of prebiotic reactions. Because of the structures of their surfaces, these minerals are capable of holding the ribonucleotides by a process known as adsorption, and montmorillonite can catalyze the formation of longer molecules. Ferris demonstrated experimentally that, following adsorption of the nucleotides onto the mineral surface one after another (note that here the clay mineral serves as a template), the mineral can catalytically join them together. Ferris was successful to synthesize RNA chains with up to 50 nucleotides in length on the surfaces of the clay mineral. This discovery provides a great support to the RNA World Hypothesis.

It may be presumed that there might have been present innumerable kinds of surfaces of the montmorillonite clay mineral characterized by different structural features on the prebiotic Earth, and these surfaces could have led to the formation of innumerable RNA molecules with various lengths and a variety of nucleotide combinations. Now, some of these RNA molecules could have had the appropriate size and architecture to evolve catalytic or enzymatic activity. These catalytic RNA molecules (i.e. ribozymes) owing to their inherent genetic and catalytic properties could then have performed self-replication independent of the clay mineral surfaces. These could grow in number on their own without the assistance of the clay mineral surfaces any more, and, in no time, these could have far outnumbered the non-catalytic RNA molecules on the prebiotic Earth.

How Robust Were the Ribozymes on the Primitive Earth?

Now, could these self-replicating RNA molecules be considered as living species? Or, once formed, could they retain their structure and function for sufficient period of time so that they could continue self-replication? Since these were presumed to be formed in the so-called prebiotic or primordial soup, they were exposed to their environment with changing temperature, acidity, salinity etc. The variations in the environmental conditions could be harmful as far as their stability is concerned, and these might be broken apart. Further, since the process of replication was taking place in an open system, there might not be sufficient number of nucleotides to join in the vicinity of the ribozyme molecules as these monomers might have been diffused away to other regions. Therefore, the self-replication of ribozymes could be greatly impaired and could not continue for long. Thus, self-replication of these bare or "naked" ribozymes could not be a feasible process. Therefore, these ribozymes with self-replication potential could not be considered as living owing to their lack of sustenance.

Conferring Stability to Ribozymes: Development of Boundary Membranes

The limitation of such wasteful diffusion would bestow greater chance of synthesis and survival of the catalytic RNA molecules. This is possible if these RNA molecules are encapsulated within a vessel that protects them from their outer environment. Of course, the materials which made up the vessel must control the movement of all the substances in such a way that only the chemicals required for the synthesis of RNA molecules are allowed to enter the vessel while the RNA molecules are not permitted to leave the vessel. Now, let us consider a catalytic RNA molecule gets confined within such a vessel in a prebiotic water-body. Let us further consider that both the catalytic RNA molecule and the vessel perform concerted self-replication afterwards. Then, as time elapses, more entities consisting of RNA in the vessels will appear if the components of RNA and the vessel are available in the medium. These vessels containing self-replicating RNA can, therefore, be considered as living species. This is an assumed picture and was thought to be the way how independent self-replicating species (i.e. life forms) could have appeared on the prebiotic Earth by Professor Szostak and his group at Harvard Medical School of Harvard University (Hanczyc et al., 2003; Mansy et al., 2008; Szostak et al., 2001).

All present-day biological cells are membrane-bound compartments. Modern cell membranes are essentially composed of amphiphilic molecules such as phospholipids along with many other chemical entities that perform transport and enzymatic functions. The vessels in the first life forms on Earth can, therefore, be considered as the precursors of cell membranes.

Protocell: the First Life

According to Szostak, the first life forms must have been very simple and could have been made up of only two essential molecular components, namely a self-replicating RNA molecule and a fatty acid membrane the latter of which served as the vessel or vesicle. This entity is referred to as a protocell or a protobiont. These may be considered as the simplest of a modern cell.

Vesicles (small sac-like structures) formed by the fatty acid molecules have long been investigated as models of the membranes of protocells (Berclaz, 2001; Deamer et al., 2002; Gebicki and Hicks, 1973; Hargreaves and Deamer, 1978). Fatty acids have been considered to be the basic building blocks of protocell membranes because these are chemically much simpler than phospholipids, which constitute the membranes of modern cells. Spontaneous formation of bilayers of several fatty acids (e.g. oleic acid) in water led to an upsurge of interest in studies on the synthesis of membranes using fatty acids as model compounds (Markvoort et al., 2010). Theoretical and experimental studies further established that these vesicles grew in size when fatty acid molecules were available in the medium and these ultimately led to the formation new vesicles, that is self-reproduction of fatty acid vesicles indeed occurred (Markvoort et al., 2010). These fatty acid membranes are also reasonably permeable to smaller species including nucleotides (Mansy et al., 2008). As pointed out, ribozymes can also perform self-replication. Experiments by several researchers suggested that protocell-like structures could form spontaneously as new membranes self-assemble and encapsulate genetic polymer in solution (Ferris et al., 1996; Hanczyc et al., 2003). Making copies of a genetic polymer molecule confined within a membrane compartment is a very important step toward the realization of a self-replicating cell-like structure. Successful copying of encapsulated genetic molecules has already been achieved in the laboratory when nucleotides were added to the system outside the fatty acid vesicles (Mansy, 2010).

According to the origin of life researchers, these vesicles, during their formation, could have trapped some ribozymes – the early genetic polymers – if these were also available in the prebiotic environment. Then, these membrane-encapsulated ribozymes with a suitable environment could have led to the spontaneous development of new coded functions by the classical mechanism of evolution through the processes of variation and natural selection. Once such genetically encoded and, therefore, heritable functions have evolved, these coupled systems could be considered to be a complete, living biological cell, notwithstanding one much simpler than any modern cell (Szostak et al., 2001). These membrane-encapsulated ribozymes with self-replicating ability are referred to as the "Protocells". Although such protocells have not been realized so far by mimicking the assumed primitive Earth condition, results from various laboratories suggest that the assembly of protocell-like structures is not that difficult and that such structures could be achieved via multiple distinct mechanisms. We have already pointed out that the replication of the protocell membrane and the genetic material as separate entities is possible. To clarify the process of self-replication of the combined entity, scientists have been considering in more detail the chemical constituents and the nature of the protocell membrane and the encapsulated self-replicating material. Feasibility of constructing primitive cell-like compartments which allow the building blocks of the genetic material to enter has already been tested (Mansy, 2010; Mansy et al., 2008; Walde et al., 1994). The concerted act of replication of the genetic material and growth of the fatty acid compartment has been very encouraging. This, of course, is a very important step toward the realization of an entity capable of self-replication and Darwinian evolution. The appearance of such self-replicating protocells could be considered as the emergence of life on Earth.

There are, however, many issues which need to be resolved: how stable are the protocells under prebiotic Earth condition? How did the protocells become self-sufficient to make their own nucleotides and membrane materials from available nutrients instead of gathering the nucleotides and membrane materials as such from outside the compartments? Are they efficient enough to continue through many generations? How did they acquire adaptive innovations leading to the evolution of protein–DNA-based modern cells? Further, the RNA World Hypothesis emphasizes replication without paying attention to the sources of the driving forces needed to perform the synthesis. What was the energy source for the RNA World? Or, in other words, how was it possible to link a stable energy supply to a metabolic synthesis of RNA?

In spite of these unsolved questions, because of the tested feasibility of many of the chemical processes assumed to be responsible for the emergence of protocells under prebiotic conditions, the RNA World Hypothesis has gone from speculation to a prevailing idea during the last six decades.

When Did Life on Earth Begin?

Our Earth is about 4.54 billion years old. When did life on Earth appear first? To settle this, scientists have been trying to collect and analyze the fossilized living beings in very old rocks. Classically, the age of these fossilized species can be estimated by the well-known "radio carbon dating" method. Living beings prefer carbon-12, a variant of carbon (known as an isotope) with six protons and six neutrons. If the ratio of the amounts of carbon-12 to carbon-13 (another natural isotope of carbon, having six protons, but seven neutrons) in the fossil sample is much different from that found in minerals of nonbiological origin, it is considered as convincing evidence that the fossil found is of biological origin. In recent years, combinations of isotopes of other elements, for example lead-206/uranium-238, lead-206/lead-207, samarium-146/neodymium-142, neodymium-143/neodymium-144, have been used for determining the ages of old rocks and fossils of microorganisms in these rocks (Dodd et al., 2017; O'Neil et al., 2012).

Evidence of ancient microbes could be preserved in the form of fossils known as stromatolites. Thus, stromatolites could provide evidence of ancient life on Earth. A 2013 publication reported the discovery of fossilized microbial communities in 3.48-billion-year-old sandstones in Western Australia (Djokic et al., 2017; Noffke et al., 2013). Evidence of stromatolites was also discovered in 3.7-billion-year-old rocks in Greenland, and announced in 2016, in the famous science journal *Nature* (Allwood, 2016). Chemical signs of life were found in 4.1-billion-year-old rocks in Western Australia, and described in a 2015 study (Bell et al., 2015). The oldest evidence of life on Earth has been claimed to have been found in the precipitates of hydrothermal vents from an ancient seabed of the Nuvvuagittuq Belt in Canada. According to a 2017 report (Dodd et al., 2017), the fossilized microbes found in ancient rocks consisted of common assemblages of hematite (an iron-mineral) filaments and tubes. Such assemblages have been interpreted to represent Earth's oldest body fossils – Earth's oldest fossil fungi. These are similar in morphology and size to those produced today by bacteria which live within subsea hydrothermal vents. Several detailed microstructures, found in the seabed of the Nuvvuagittuq Belt, match modern structures. On the basis of these multiple observations the researchers concluded that such structures were produced by "biological activity" in submarine-hydrothermal environments at least 3.77 billion years and possibly 4.28 billion years ago. It was, however, reported in a 2019 paper that hematite tubes and filaments, similar to those found in the Nuvvuagittuq Belt, could also be produced abiotically by mixing appropriate inorganic chemicals, a process which may occur naturally in some hydrothermal settings (McMahon, 2019).

Conclusions

One of the central problems in natural science is how life on Earth appeared. We now know that all living beings on Earth rely on numerous chemical reactions. Chemistry, therefore, must have played a crucial role in the emergence of life. Majority of the origin-of-life researchers, based on the extensive research over the last six-to-seven decades, are now of the opinion that the first life possibly consisted of a chemical genetic material confined within a kind of vessel also made up of some other chemical species, and that this combined entity was capable of creating its own copies. It may, however, be noted that the feasibility of the chemical processes which ultimately led to the evolution of life could not be absolutely tested in the laboratories partly because of our inability to recreate the exact early Earth environmental conditions along with all necessary chemicals and partly because we cannot afford the long period of time of the order of many million years which nature could have provided after the origin of Earth for lives to emerge. Still, scientists have been trying to mimic various possible primitive Earth conditions and to "synthesize" life starting with various possible combinations of chemical species assumed to be present on the primitive Earth. Some results are really interesting and encouraging. However, the question remains, and it needs further scientific inquiry to shed more light on this issue.

References

Allwood, A. C. (2016). Evidence of life in Earth's oldest rocks. *Nature*, 537, 500–501.

Ariatti, A. and Mandrioli, P. (1993). Lazzaro Spallanzani: A blow against spontaneous generation. *Aerobiologia*, 9(1903), 101–107.

Bada, J. L. (2013). New insights into prebiotic chemistry from Stanley Miller's spark discharge experiments. *Chemical Society Reviews*, 42(5), 2186–2196.

Ban, N., Nissen, P., Hansen, J., Moore, P. B. and Steitz, T. A. (2000). The complete atomic structure of the large ribosomal subunit at 2.4 A resolution. *Science*, 289(5481), 905–920.

Beer, D. (1959). Some unpublished letters of Charles Darwin. *Notes and Records of the Royal Society*, 14(1), 12–66.

Bell, E., Boehnke, P., Harrison, T. M. and W.L Mao. (2015). Potentially biogenic carbon preserved in a 4.1 billion-year-old zircon. *Proceedings of the National Academy of Sciences of the United States of America*, 112(47), 14518–14521.

Berclaz, N., Muller, M., Walde, P. and Luisi, P. L. (2001). Growth and transformation of vesicles studied by ferritin labelling and cryotransmission electron microscopy. *Journal of Physical Chemistry B*, 105(5), 1056–1064.

Brack, A. Ed. (1998). *The Molecular Origins of Life*. Cambridge University Press, Cambridge, UK.

Breathnach, C. S. (2005). Sir Thomas Browne (1605–1682). *Journal of the Royal Society of Medicine*, 98(1), 33–36.

Chan, Q. H. S., Zolensky, M. E., Kebukawa, Y., Fries, M., Ito, M., Steele, A., Rahman, Z., Nakato, A., Kilcoyne, A. L. D., Suga, H., Takahashi, Y., Takeichi, Y. and Mase, K. (2018). Organic matter in extraterrestrial water-bearing salt crystals. *Science Advances*, 4(1), 1–10.

Corliss, J. B., Dymond, J., Gordon, L. I., Edmond, J. M., von Herzen, R. P., Ballard, R. D., Green, K., Williams, D., Bainbridge, A., Crane, K. and van Andel, T. H. (1979). Submarine thermal springs on the Galápagos rift. *Science*, 203(4385), 1073–1083.

Deamer, D., Dworkin, J. P., Sandford, S. A., Bernstein, M. P. and Allamandola, L. J. (2002). The first cell membranes. *Astrobiology*, 2(4), 371–381.

Djokic, T., Kranendonk, M. J. V., Campbell, K. A., Walter, M. R. and Ward, C. R. (2017). Earliest signs of life on land preserved in ca. 3.5 Ga hot spring deposits. *Nature Communications*, 8, 15263.

Dodd, M. S., Papineau, D., Grenne, T., Slack, J. F., Rittner, M., Pirajno, F., O'Neil, J. and Little, C. T. S. (2017). Evidence for early life in Earth's oldest hydrothermal vent precipitates. *Nature*, 543(7643), 60–64.

Ferris, J. P. (2005). Mineral catalysis and prebiotic synthesis: Montmorillonite-catalyzed formation of RNA. *Elements*, 1(3), 145–149.

Ferris, J. P., Hill Jr, A. R., Liu, R. and Orgel, L. E. (1996). Synthesis of long prebiotic oligomers on mineral surfaces. *Nature*, 381(6577), 59–61.

Gebicki, J. M. and Hicks, M. (1973). Ufasomes are stable particles surrounded by unsaturated fatty acid membranes. *Nature*, 243(5404), 232–234.

Gilbert, W. (1986). Origin of life: The RNA world. *Nature*, 319(6055), 618–618.

Gourier, D., Binet, L., Calligaro, T., Capelli, S., Vezin, H., Breheret, J., Hickman-Lweis, K., Gautret, P., Foucher, F., Campbell, K. and Westall, F. (2019). Extraterrestrial organic matter preserved in 3.33 Ga sediments from Barbetron, South Africa. *Geochimica et Cosmochimica Acta*, 258, 207–225.

Guerrier-Takada, C., Gardiner, K., Marsh, T., Pace, N. and Altman, S. (1983). The RNA moiety of ribonuclease P is the catalytic subunit of the enzyme. *Cell*, 35(3), 849–857.

Haldane, J. B. S. (1929). The origin of life. *Rationalist Annual*, 148, 3–10.

Hanczyc, M. M., Fujikawa, S. M. and Szostak, J. W. (2003). Experimental models of primitive cellular compartments: Encapsulation, growth, and division. *Science*, 302(5645), 618–622.

Hargreaves, W. R. and Deamer, D. W. (1978). Liposomes from ionic, single-chain amphiphiles. *Biochemistry*, 17(18), 3759–3768.

Kruger, K., Grabowski, P. J., Zaug, A. J., Sands, J., Gottschling, D. E. and Cech, T. R. (1982). Self-splicing RNA: Autoexcision and autocyclization of the ribosomal RNA intervening sequence of Tetrahymena. *Cell*, 31(1), 147–157.

Lane, N. (2015). The unseen world: Reflections on Leeuwenhoek (1677) "Concerning little animals." *Philosophical Transactions of the Royal Society B: Biological Sciences*, 370(1666), 20140344–20140344.

Lawless, J. G. (1973). Amino acids in the Murchison meteorite. *Geochimica et Cosmochimica Acta*, 37(9), 2207–2212.

Mansy, S. S. (2010). Membrane transport in primitive cells. *Cold Spring Harbor Perspectives in Biololy*, 2(8), a002188–a002188.

Mansy, S. S., Schrum, J. P., Krishnamurthy, M., Tobe´, S., Treco, D. A. and Szostak, J. W. (2008). Template-directed synthesis of a genetic polymer in a model protocell. *Nature*, 454(7200), 122–125.

Markvoort, A. J., Pfleger, N., Staffhorst, R., Hilbers, P. A. J., Rutger, A., Santen, V., Killian, J. A. and de Kruijff, B. (2010). Self-reproduction of fatty acid vesicles: A combined experimental and simulation study. *Biophysical Journal*, 99(5), 1520–1528.

McMahon, S. (2019). Earth's earliest and deepest purported fossils may be iron-mineralized chemical gardens. *Proceedings of the Royal Society B: Biological Sciences*, 286(1916), 20192410.

Miller, S. L. (1953). A production of amino acids under possible primitive earth conditions. *Science*, 117(3046), 528–529.

Noffke, N., Christian, D., Wacey, D. and Hazen, R. M. (2013). Microbially induced sedimentary structures recording an ancient ecosystem in the ca. 3.48 billion-year-old dresser formation, Pilbara, Western Australia. *Astrobiology*, 13(12), 1103–1124.

Nurse, P. (2000). The incredible life and times of biological cells. *Science*, 289(5485), 1711–1716.

O'Neil, J., Carlson, R. W., Paquette, J. L. and Francis, D. (2012). Formation age and metamorphic history of the Nuvvuagittuq Greenstone Belt. *Precambrian Research*, 220–221, 23–44.

Oparin, A. I. (1924). *Proiskhozhdenie zhizni*. Izd. Moskovskii Rabochii, Moscow (in Russian).

Orgel, L. E. (2004). Prebiotic chemistry and the origin of the RNA world. *Critical Reviews in Biochemistry and Molecular Biology*, 39(2), 99–23.

Parke, E. C. (2014). Flies from meat and wasps from trees: Reevaluating Francesco Redi's spontaneous generation experiments. *Studies in History and Philosophy of Biological and Biomedical Sciences*, 45, 34–42.

Powner, M. W., Gerland, B. and Sutherland, J. D. (2009). Synthesis of activated pyrimidine ribonucleotides in prebiotically plausible conditions. *Nature*, 459(7244), 239–242.

Raulin-Cerceau, F. (2001). Theories on origins of life between 1860 and 1900: The spontaneous generation controversy years post Darwin and Pasteur's works. In Chela-Flares, J. et al. (Eds.) *First Steps in the Origin of Life in the Universe*. Kluwer Academic Publishers, New York, 39–42.

Szostak, J. W., Bartel, D. P. and Luisi, P. L. (2001). Synthesizing life. *Nature*, 409(6818), 387–390.

Wächtershäuser, G. (1988). Pyrite formation, the first energy source for life: A hypothesis. *Systematic and Applied Microbiology*, 10(3), 207–210.

Walde, P., Wick, R., Fresta, M., Mangone, A. and Luisi, P. L. (1994). Autopoietic self-reproduction of fatty acid vesicles. *Journal of the American Chemical Society*, 116(26), 11649–11654.

Wollman, A. J. M., Nudd, R., Hedlund, E. G. and Leake, M. C. (2015). From animaculum to single molecules: 300 years of the light microscope. *Open Biology*, 5(4), 150019–150019.

Zaug, A. J. and Cech, T. R. (1986). The intervening sequence RNA of tetrahymena is an enzyme. *Science*, 231(4737), 470–475.

12

UNRAVELING THE FASCINATING WORLD OF RNA INTERFERENCE

Manika Pal Bhadra, Paromita Das,
Akash Mallick and Deepika Pamarthy

RNA interference (RNAi) is a revolutionary gene silencing mechanism that involves targeted suppression of messenger RNA (mRNA) transcription via post-transcriptional gene silencing (PTGS). It is mediated by double-stranded RNA (dsRNA) that directs the degradation of cognate mRNAs. Historically, several researchers reported the RNAi phenomenon which happened to be a chance experimental finding that eventually led to an overwhelming amount of information and a boom in the exploration of its therapeutic potential for agricultural and biomedical applications. Napoli and Jorgensen first reported RNA interference in 1990, while working on transgenic petunia plants to generate violet flowers through overexpression of the chalcone synthase (CHS) enzyme that is responsible for anthocyanin biosynthesis. Unexpectedly, this experiment led to white or variegated colored petunias, forming the foundation for their "cosuppression" hypothesis. In 1992, Romano and Macino observed "quelling" of the endogenous albino genes while working on *Neurospora crassa* transformants (Romano and Macino, 1992). In 1995, Guo and Kemphues documented silencing in *Caenorhabditis elegans* through the introduction of par-I sense or antisense RNA, resulting in degradation of the par-I message. In 1997, James Birchler reported for the first time in *Drosophila*, the phenomenon of "cosuppression" through the introduction of multiple copies of *white-Alcohol dehydrogenase (w-Adh)* transgenes. A progressive reduction in gene expression was observed when two to six copies of the *white* promoter of the *Alcohol dehydrogenase (Adh)* reporter fusion gene were introduced into the genome. In 1998, Andrew Fire and Craig Mello identified dsRNAs to be responsible for post-transcriptional gene silencing (PTGS) in *C. elegans* and termed the phenomenon RNA interference (RNAi). Over the years, RNA silencing has been used in functional genomics as a reverse genetic tool to understand the function of various genes. It has evolved as a defense mechanism to combat viral replication and mobile elements such as transposons. Several components of the RNAi machinery

DOI: 10,4324/9781003033448-16

have been identified and manipulated to elicit better therapeutic responses for the mitigation of harmful diseases such as cancer and viral infections. The discovery of the RNAi pathway has further opened opportunities for exploration of its multidimensional, precise mechanisms that can be tailored to develop RNA-based drugs. The recent 2018 US-FDA approval of the RNAi drug, Patisiran, a siRNA-based formulation useful for the treatment of hereditary transthyretin amyloidosis (hATTR) paves the way for breakthrough-health care innovations.

Discovery of RNA interference (RNAi)

Flower coloration in petunia plants

The history of RNAi dates to the early 1990s when scientists from different fields focused on understanding gene expression patterns in various biological organisms. The accidental discovery of color variation in petunia flowers by Napoli and Jorgensen resulted in their hypothesis of "cosuppression". Violet coloration in petunia is due to anthocyanin biosynthesis, which is regulated by a rate-limiting enzyme, called chalcone synthase (CHS). To generate deep violet-colored flowers, these scientists overexpressed CHS. Unexpectedly, the experiments produced white petunias or petunias with variegated colors. This bizarre phenomenon upon further examination revealed the phenomenon of "homology-dependent gene silencing" that was later termed "cosuppression", resulting in the reduction of CHS levels compared to wild-type petunias (Figure 12.1a).

The quelling phenomenon in Neurospora

A similar phenomenon was evident in *Neurospora crassa* and was reported by Romano and Macino in 1992 (Romano and Macino, 1992). During attempts to increase the levels of an orange pigment produced by the *al1* gene of the fungus, the "quelling" phenomenon came to light. A strain containing wild-type *al1*+ gene (orange phenotype) was transformed with a plasmid containing a 1,500-base pair fragment of the *al1* coding sequence. A few transformants got stably quelled and showed albino phenotype. It was confirmed that in the *al1*-quelled strain, the level of unspliced *al1* mRNA was found to be similar to that of the wild-type strain, whereas the native *al1* mRNA was highly silenced, indicating that quelling was responsible for the mature mRNA levels in a homology-dependent manner and not the rate of transcription.

Cosuppression in Drosophila

For the first time, Pal-Bhadra et al. (1997) (Pal-Bhadra et al., 1997) demonstrated the cosuppression phenomenon in *Drosophila*. A fusion construct containing the structural component of the *alcohol dehydrogenase* (*Adh*) gene under the control of white regulatory elements was introduced into different locations of the *Drosophila*

A.

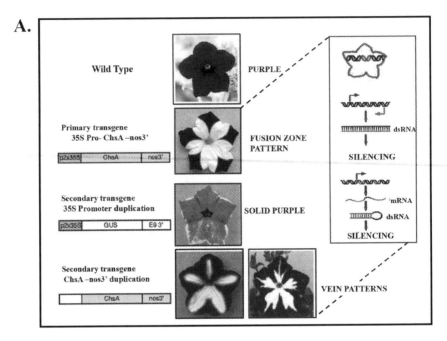

FIGURE 12.1A   The history of RNAi dates to the early 1990s when Napoli and Jorgensen serendipitously discovered the violet color variation in petunia flowers owing to "cosuppression" affecting the rate-limiting enzyme, chalcone synthase (CHS).

melanogaster genome in an *Adh*-null mutant background (Figure 12.1b). A reduction of the transgene, as well as endogenous gene expression upon increasing transgene dosage, was observed. This type of cosuppression was partially eliminated by heterozygous Polycomb-Group (PcG) mutations, and the cosuppressed insertion sites were found to be associated with Polycomb protein. PcG genes are required for the maintenance of transcriptionally repressed states in developmental gene expression. This study showed the involvement of the PcG complex in this form of cosuppression.

RNAi in nematodes

Guo and Kemphues first reported that when sense or antisense RNA was introduced to *par-1* mRNA, there was a degradation of the *par-1* mRNA in *C. elegans* (Guo and Kemphues, 1995) (Figure 12.1c). Until then, antisense was the preferred method for suppressing gene expression by hybridizing with endogenous mRNAs to form dsRNA, causing translational inhibition or ribonuclease degradation. Contradictorily, even when the sense *par-1* RNA did not hybridize with the endogenous *par-1* transcript, *par-1* still underwent degradation (Sen and Blau, 2006).

B.

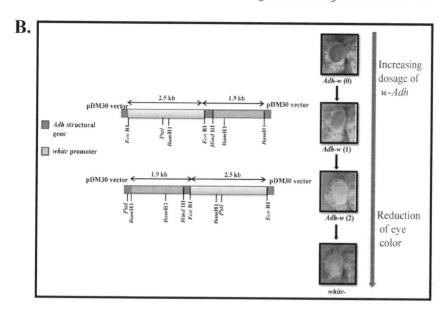

FIGURE 12.1B   In *Drosophila*, Pal-Bhadra et al. (1997) demonstrated the cosuppression in a fusion construct containing the *alcohol dehydrogenase (Adh)* structural construct under control of *white* regulatory elements that reduced the expression of the endogenous gene upon increasing transgene dosage.

C.

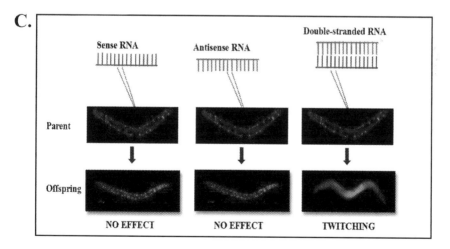

FIGURE 12.1C   In *Caenorhabditis elegans*, Guo and Kemphues reported that when sense or antisense RNA was introduced to *par-1* mRNA, a degradation of the *par-1* mRNA occurred, subsequent to which Andrew Fire and Craig Mello reported RNAi in *C. elegans* with dsRNA as a prerequisite for triggering the RNAi pathway.

Following this, in 1998, Andrew Fire and Craig Mello published their seminal paper on RNAi in *C. elegans*, identifying that dsRNA is a prerequisite for triggering the RNAi pathway (Fire et al., 1998). This discovery of RNAi led to a revolution that underscored the role of non-coding RNAs in the regulation of gene expression in multicellular organisms.

Role of RNAi in genetic studies and biomedical applications

It was in the late 1990s when gene silencing was found to be initiated across various organisms via targeted destruction of mRNA sequences based on sequence similarity by dsRNA formation. This led to the utilization of reverse genetics which employs dsRNA-mediated silencing to analyze gene function in organisms. Several biochemical and genetic studies were pursued to uncover the components of the RNA silencing machinery and in this way, the common core of proteins amplifying the interfering RNA signal and directing the endonucleolytic cleavage of target RNAs was discovered. RNA silencing is presumed to have evolved for the defense and suppression of transposon mobilization and viral replication. Over several years of intense research, RNAi machinery was found to be involved in the post-transcriptional regulation of endogenous genes and the structural and functional maintenance of heterochromatin. The research was carried out to understand the intrinsic biological functions of RNA silencing as well as for its application in antiviral, cancer therapies, and other biotechnological and biomedical areas.

Mechanism of RNAi

Gene silencing occurs through two processes, either through repression of transcription, which is known as transcriptional gene silencing (TGS), or through mRNA degradation, known as post-transcriptional gene silencing (PTGS). Both these have two alternative pathways to control the redundant and mobile nucleic acids.

Transcriptional gene silencing (TGS)

About three decades ago, Marjorie Matzke et al. identified that transgene overexpression led to DNA hypermethylation and transcriptional silencing in doubly transformed tobacco plants (Matzke et al., 1989). In human cells, small non-coding RNAs can modulate epigenetic regulation to achieve functional TGS. Mechanistically, this is distinct from the RNAi gene silencing pathway, resulting in stable, long-term epigenetic modifications that can be passed on to daughter cells, unlike RNAi which does not get transferred to daughter cells. In *Arabidopsis*, TGS was shown to involve Argonaute protein family members (Lippman et al., 2003), requiring the action of RNA-dependent DNA methylation (Mette et al., 2000; Wassenegger et al., 1994).

Mechanism of RNA-directed TGS

TGS is mechanistically distinct from the PTGS pathway of RNAi, which is more extensively studied. RNA-directed DNA methylation (RdDM) is the main small RNA pathway involved in TGS in plants. Earlier observations of siRNA-targeted TGS showed the involvement of epigenetic nuclear mechanisms (K. Morris, 2005). Studies showed that 5'-Azacytidine (5'-AzaC) and Trichostatin A (TSA) caused a reversion of siRNA-targeted TGS and not PTGS. TGS pathway is operative via RNA-directed methylation of histone 3 lysines, 9 and 27 (H3K9 and H3K27) and DNA methylation at the targeted promoter. Non-coding RNAs interact with target loci via Watson-Crick-based RNA: RNA hybridization and time-dependent studies showed that exogenously introduced siRNAs are targeted to a promoter region, first interacting with Argonautes 1 and 2 (AGO1 and AGO2) (Ahlenstiel et al., 2011; Janowski et al., 2006; D. H. Kim et al., 2006). siRNA and AGO interactions are observable within the first 24 hours at the siRNA targeted promoter and shortly followed by recruitment of H3K9me2 and H3K27me3 epigenetic markers, followed by DNA methyltransferase activation causing methylation of a few genes at 72–96 hours (Hawkins et al., 2009). This phenomenon may be governed by the duration of RNA targeting to the promoter, the occurrence of robust siRNA targeting, the presence of abundant promoter-occupied RNAs, and the dynamic interplay of proteins interacting with the promoter. A key consistent feature is the modulation of gene transcription by promoter-directed small RNAs causing epigenetic-based gene silencing. However, the role of DNA methylation is not as easily understood in TGS in human cells as in plants.

In *Arabidopsis*, TGS mainly depends on DNA methylation at cytosine residues by the RdDM pathway. This is the key pathway by which *de novo* DNA methylation occurs whereas other DNA methyltransferases such as MET1 or CMT3 are involved in maintaining the methylation during cell division (Law and Jacobsen, 2010; H. Zhang et al., 2018). The RdDM pathway is extremely important to methylate naïve DNA sequences such as transfer DNA (T-DNA), transposable elements (TEs), and even DNA viruses. The RdDM pathway, therefore, protects the genome stability during plant life and future generations (Heard and Martienssen, 2014). The canonical RdDM pathway involves two phases. The first phase involves the recruitment of RNA polymerase IV (Pol IV) to the target loci. This process is enhanced by the SSH1 interaction with CLSY1, and Pol IV transcribes a 25–45-nucleotide-long precursor RNA that gets processed by RNA-dependent-RNA polymerase 2 (RRD2) into a dsRNA. Further, this precursor is diced by DCL3 into 24-nucleotide (nt) siRNAs, which are stabilized by their 3'-end methylation by HEN1. Mutations of Pol IV, RDR2, and DCL3 result in the decrease of 24-nt siRNAs and DNA methylation at target loci. Phase two of the RdDM pathway involves transcription of the locus by a second RNA polymerase, RNA Pol V. The recruitment and activity of Pol V are not fully understood, though a few contributing proteins were identified. The chromatin remodeling complex

(DDR) is also involved, consisting of DMS3, RDM1, and DRD1 components, which were shown to be important for transcription of the scaffold RNA at specific loci. The siRNA that is generated in the first phase of the RdDM pathway is loaded onto the main effector, AGO4, which mostly may occur in the cytoplasm, and then the siRNA/AGO4 complex gets relocated to the nucleus. The siRNA/AGO4 complex then targets Pol V scaffold RNA, leading to recruitment of the de novo DNA methyltransferase, DRM2 via a direct protein interaction between DRM2 and AGO4 (Zhong et al., 2014). DRM2 recruitment causes local cytosine methylation; also, mutations in AGO4 cause a global decrease in DNA methylation. This decrease does not affect certain loci, most likely due to partial redundancy between AGO4 and AGO6. The RdDM loci in *Arabidopsis* depend on both AGO4 and AGO6, however, the process is not yet fully understood.

Post-transcriptional gene silencing (PTGS)

PTGS is a mechanism by which mRNAs get degraded, reducing gene expression. It is a varied process in different organisms and is known by different names: quelling in fungi, cosuppression in the plant kingdom, and RNA interference in animals. In all instances, mRNA degradation results in decreased gene expression. Plants and animals share common molecular components of the PTGS machinery. For example, the SGS2 gene in *Arabidopsis* and QDE1 in *Neurospora* encode gene products similar to an RNA-dependent RNA polymerase. Most studies of PTGS in plants involve silenced transgenes or endogenous genes, hence the scope of PTGS in plants is unclear. Small RNA molecules regulate gene expression in eukaryotes throughout development and respond to stress and viral infections. Specialized RNA digesting enzymes called ribonucleases and RNA-binding proteins govern the genesis and action of small regulatory RNAs. Once processed by Drosha in the nucleus, precursor microRNAs (pre-miRNAs) get transported into the cytoplasm where cleavage by Dicer causes the formation of mature miRNAs and short interfering RNAs (siRNAs). These products get assembled with AGO proteins in a way that one strand gets preferentially selected and used to guide sequence-specific silencing of cognate mRNAs via endonucleolytic cleavage or translational repression (Figure 12.4). Exciting insights into the molecular structures of Dicer, AGO proteins, and RNA-bound complexes offer details of the mechanisms of RNAi pathways.

miRNA- and siRNA-mediated PTGS

miRNAs and siRNAs are typical ~22 nucleotides-long single-stranded RNAs that cause RNA-mediated gene silencing by transcriptional degradation or repression of the target. They were initially found to have distinct pathways for biogenesis and action and were later shown to have a high degree of relatedness during biogenesis and even during gene silencing action. siRNA biogenesis was found to have an exogenous origin like transgenes or viral genome as a measure of genome defense. But studies showed that siRNA can be produced from other non-coding regions like transposons, centromeres, repeat sequences, and even from distinct genomic loci as found in the case of *trans*-acting siRNAs in plants. Recent research also showed that siRNAs can be endogenously produced from convergent mRNA transcripts, RNA duplexes having pseudogene-derived transcripts, and other hairpin RNAs. Unlike miRNAs, RNA duplexes for siRNA directly get transported to the cytoplasm and are subsequently processed by the Dicer-mediated pathway (Carthew and Sontheimer, 2009). On the other hand, miRNAs are chiefly transcribed by RNA Pol II from introns or lncRNA (long non-coding RNA) as primary miRNA (pri-miRNA) that undergoes capping and polyadenylation. miRNA biogenesis includes both mono-cistronic (single miRNA from the single gene) and polycistronic origin (single miRNA cluster coding for multiple miR-NAs) (Gebert and MacRae, 2019; Treiber et al., 2019) (Figure 12.2). miRNAs

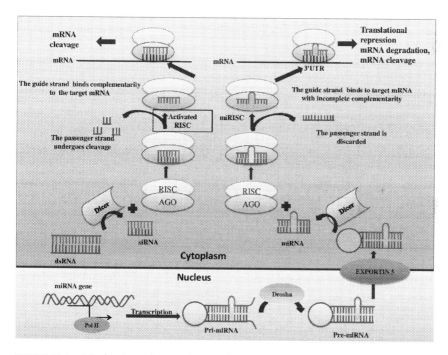

FIGURE 12.2   Mechanism of gene silencing by siRNA and miRNA.

In siRNA-mediated pathway, the dsRNA may be either transcribed or artificially introduced into the cell. It undergoes processing by Dicer to form siRNA, which undergoes loading into the RISC. RISC has a component called AGO2 which cleaves the passenger strand of siRNA, and the remaining guide strand then guides the active RISC to the target mRNA. siRNA guide strand completely binds to the target mRNA via complementarity of the sequences and leads to the cleavage of the mRNA.

In the miRNA-mediated pathway, the miRNA gene is transcribed by the RNA polymerase II in the nucleus to produce pri-miRNA, which is then cleaved by Drosha to form pre-miRNA. This pre-miRNA is transported by Exportin 5 to the cytoplasm where Dicer processes it into miRNA. The miRNA undergoes loading on the RISC where the passenger strand is discarded. The guide strand which remains guides the miRISC to the target mRNA via partial complementary binding. Hence in this way, the target mRNA undergoes inhibition via translational repression, degradation, or cleavage.

are typically endogenous in origin whereas siRNAs can have both exogenous and endogenous origins. miRNAs also differ in their mechanism of action. siRNAs undergo perfect pairing with the target sequence whereas miRNAs can tolerate imperfect pairing at the 3′ terminals (Carthew and Sontheimer, 2009).

The detailed mechanisms of miRNA- and siRNA-mediated RNAi

Both miRNA and siRNA are produced from a dsRNA duplex that undergoes trimming, processing, and finally loading onto AGO proteins to form RISC (RNA-induced silencing complex) and subsequently exert a silencing effect. miRNAs can be often structurally or functionally related and can be co-transcribed (Cullen, 2004). miRNA maturation occurs in two steps, mediated by the RNase III family members, Drosha and Dicer. Droshas are 130–160 kDa nuclear proteins containing two RNase III catalytic domains and a dsRNA-binding domain (dsRBD), along with other domains of unknown function in the N-terminal half (Y. Lee et al., 2003). Similar to mammals, in *Drosophila* and *Caenorhabditis*, Drosha works in a complex with a dsRBD protein called Pasha (in Drosophila) or DGCR8 (in mammals) (Denli et al., 2004; Gregory et al., 2004; J. Han et al., 2004; Landthaler et al., 2004). DGCR8 (DiGeorge critical region 8) or Pasha in *Drosophila* are necessary for processing primary miRNA transcripts (pri-miRNAs) to 70-nt hairpins, which are referred to as precursor miRNAs (pre-miRNAs). The Drosha–DGCR8 complex is a large complex of 650kDa due to the dimerization of its components and the presence of additional proteins (J. Han et al., 2004). In humans also, Drosha forms a much larger multicomponent protein complex, but its role in the biogenesis of miRNAs and other RNAs is unclear (Gregory et al., 2004). The genesis and processing steps of pri-miRNAs are tightly coordinated in the nucleus. Mammalian Drosha has a serine–arginine (SR)-rich domain like the protein–protein interaction domains of the SR family of splicing factors. This domain is absent in *Drosophila* protein. Plant genomes do not encode Drosha and in the case of *Arabidopsis*, miRNA biogenesis occurs through one of the four Dicer-like proteins called DCL-1, localized in the nucleus (Kurihara and Watanabe, 2004).

Pri-miRNAs form a hairpin loop because of sequence complementarity within the transcript, and the 20–25nt-containing mature miRNA sequence lies in the stem of the hairpin, in a double-stranded organization. Pri-miRNA undergoes an additional level of selection by double-stranded RNA-specific adenosine deaminase, ADAR, which can alter the sequence of pri-miRNA through "A to I" editing (adenosine to inosine via deamination), thereby determining its fate either for further processing or for degeneration (Treiber et al., 2019). During processing, pri-miRNAs first convert into a single hairpin by a nuclear protein complex called "micro-processor" to form pre-miRNA (precursor miRNA), which contains Drosha (RNAse-III enzyme) (Figure 12.2), DGCR8 (DiGeorge critical region 8, aka Pasha in *Drosophila*), dsRNA binding protein, and some additional factors like p68 and p72. Pre-miRNAs are of ~70-nt-long hairpin where the 3′ end contains a

2-nucleotide overhang and a 5′ phosphate with a 3′ hydroxyl. They are transported to the cytoplasm from the nucleus with the help of an exporter receptor called Exportin 5 and RanGTP recognizing the 3′ overhangs (Gebert and MacRae, 2019). Functional dimeric DGCR8 along with the heme cofactor binds to the apical loop of the pri-miRNA via recognition of the conserved UGU motif, whereas Drosha recognizes and binds to the conserved basal UG-enriched motif to ensure proper cleavage of the pri-miRNA. During this cleavage, the 11-base pair (bp) lower stem along with the 9-bp flanking region plays a crucial role in the recognition of the cleavage site by the microprocessor. Furthermore, the CNCC motif located at the 3′ flanking regions of the hairpin acts as a binding site of serine/arginine-rich splicing factor 3 (SRSF3) and helps to promote cleavage by the microprocessor. The crystal structure of Drosha showed that it contains a specialized *bump helix* which helps to cleave the pri-miRNA 11bp away from the basal site for accurate cleavage and thus acting as a "molecular ruler" (Gebert and MacRae, 2019; Treiber et al., 2019).

In the cytoplasm, dsRNA duplexes in both siRNA and miRNA pathway converge, and typically use the Dicer-mediated pathway for subsequent processing, then finally loaded to AGO protein to form the RISC complex. Dicer, an RNAse III enzyme (in *Drosophila*, Dicer 1), along with a dsRNA binding protein called TRBP (trans-activation-responsive RNA-binding protein) (Loquacious in *Drosophila*) and PACT (protein activator of the interferon-induced protein kinase) process the pre-miRNA into 20–25 dsRNA. In flies, two distinct Dicer proteins process miRNAs (Dicer-1) and siRNAs (Dicer-2) (Figure 12.2). The crystal structure of Dicer showed that it possesses the PAZ domain (a PIWI-AGO-Zwille) that binds to the 3′ overhangs and determines the distance of the cleavage site. The TRBP contains three distinct RBDs (RNA-binding domain), out of which two are used in direct interaction with the dsRNA and the rest is for binding with Dicer to make the catalytically active configuration along with two catalytic pockets made by PAZ and Platform domains. During the processing of pre-miRNA, Dicer forms a stable complex with TRBP and AGO called RISC loading complex and upon cleavage by Dicer, dsRNA is loaded onto AGO. AGO selects only one strand (guide strand) to produce mature miRNA and the 5′ ends of the guide strand bind to the MID domain of AGO whereas the 3′ end remains bound to the PAZ domain, which finally forms RISC; the opposite (passenger strand) is dissociated. An exonuclease called C3PO works in association with the AGO proteins of RISC to specifically remove the passenger strand. miR-451 is the only known Dicer-independent miRNA that is processed by AGO2 and trimmed by PRAN (poly(A)-specific ribonuclease). In the case of siRNAs, a similar RISC complex (siRISC) is formed to induce similar complexes like miRISC (miRNA containing RISC). In *Drosophila*, specifically, Dicer-2 interacts with dsRNA-binding protein R2D2 and other components of the RISC-loading complex to form active RISC (Cheloufi et al., 2010; Gebert and MacRae, 2019). Biochemical and electron microscopy-based studies showed that TRBP remains stably bound to the complex and helps in the transfer of the mature miRNAs to AGO proteins. AGO proteins are highly conserved and contain the PAZ domain, MID domain, and PIWI (P-element-induced wimpy testes) domain.

Types of regulatory RNAs

RNAi technology created a phenomenal revolution and broadened the scope for gaining a deeper understanding of non-coding and regulatory RNAs involved in the regulation of gene expression and a wide array of biological processes (Wilson and Doudna, 2013). Apart from classical RNAs like mRNA, tRNA, and rRNA, a wide array of non-coding RNAs (ncRNAs) are transcribed from the genome which is classified based on their biogenesis pathways and have overlapping functions (Bonnet et al., 2006). International Human Genome Sequencing Consortium (IHGSC) data showed that only 2% of the genome produces protein-coding genes, whereas primary transcription occurs from 75% of the genome and the transcripts undergo further processing, which covers 62.1% genome, clearly indicating diverse, unknown functions of such non-coding regions (Consortium, 2004; Djebali et al., 2012). Current annotations have shown that human long ncRNAs outstripped the number of protein-coding genes (Mattick et al., 2010). Non-coding RNAs (ncRNAs) are broadly classified into ~20–30 nt bearing small ncRNAs, which mainly include miRNA (micro-RNA), small-interfering RNA (siRNA), piRNA (PIWI-interacting RNA) and lncRNAs (long non-coding RNAs), which are longer than 200 nt (Borges and Martienssen, 2015; K. V. Morris and Mattick, 2014; Wilson and Doudna, 2013). Apart from this, several other specialized groups of ncRNAs have been found with diverse regulatory functions in recent years, which include snoRNAs (small nucleolar RNAs), circRNAs (circular RNAs), and circular intronic RNAs (ciRNAs) (Dieci et al., 2009; Kristensen et al., 2019; Q. Wang et al., 2016). miRNA, siRNA, and piRNAs are three major classes of small ncRNAs which undergo different biogenesis pathways and utilize AGO family proteins to regulate gene expression via targeting RNAs through complementary base pairing or via translational repression. miRNA and siRNA bind to AGO subfamily proteins and piRNA binds to PIWI subfamily proteins to exert their regulatory functions (Filipowicz et al., 2008; S. W. Kim et al., 2010; Malone and Hannon, 2009; Rana, 2007).

miRNA and siRNA

miRNAs and siRNAs are typical ~22-nt-long single-stranded RNAs that cause RNA-mediated gene silencing by transcriptional degradation or repression of the target. Though they were initially found to have distinct pathways for biogenesis and action, later they were shown to have a high degree of relatedness during biogenesis and even during gene silencing action. miRNAs were found to be involved in every cellular process including development, cell proliferation, differentiation, homeostasis, and even disease progression (Gebert and MacRae, 2019). They are quite widespread, and to date over 2,500 miRNAs have been discovered that can potentially target 60% of the human genes (Friedman et al., 2009; Kozomara and Griffiths-Jones, 2013). miRNAs are typically endogenous in origin whereas siRNAs can have both exogenous and endogenous origins. They also differ in their mechanism of action. siRNAs undergo perfect pairing with the target sequence whereas miRNAs can tolerate imperfect pairing at the 3' terminals (Carthew and Sontheimer, 2009). Both miRNA and siRNA are produced from a dsRNA duplex that undergoes trimming, processing, and finally loading to AGO proteins to form RISC and subsequently exert a silencing effect. Initially, siRNA biogenesis was found to have only exogenous origins like transgenes or viral genomes as a measure of genome defense. But later studies showed that siRNA can be produced from other non-coding regions like transposons, centromeres, repeat sequences, and even from distinct genomic loci as found in the case of *trans-acting siRNAs* in plants. Recent research also showed that siRNAs can be endogenously produced from convergent mRNA transcripts, RNA duplexes having pseudogene-derived transcripts, and other hairpin RNAs. Unlike miRNAs, RNA duplexes for siRNA directly get transported to the cytoplasm and are subsequently processed by the Dicer-mediated pathway (Carthew and Sontheimer, 2009). On the other hand, miRNAs are chiefly transcribed by RNA Pol II from introns or lncRNA (long non-coding RNA) as primary miRNA (pri-miRNA) that undergoes capping and polyadenylation. miRNA biogenesis includes both mono-cistronic (single miRNA from the single gene) and polycistronic origin (single miRNA cluster coding for multiple miRNAs) (Gebert and MacRae, 2019; Treiber et al., 2019).

piRNAs

piRNAs are quite diverse and form a large group of non-coding RNAs that are distinct from other classes of small RNAs in various dimensions including differences in the biogenesis pathways. They are comparatively longer (24–31 nt) in length as well as possess a site for 2'-O-methyl modification at the 3' termini and are especially found in germ cells (Gunawardane et al., 2007; Siomi et al., 2011; Vagin et al., 2006). piRNAs were initially investigated in *Drosophila melanogaster* while studying potential factors behind *Stellate* gene expression inhibition in male germlines (Aravin et al., 2001). piRNAs play a crucial role in the maintenance of genomic integrity by silencing transposable elements (TEs). They interact with PIWI proteins and form a piRNA-induced silencing complex (piRISC), which collectively recognizes and targets TEs. piRNAs exert silencing activity both at the transcriptional level and post-transcriptional level either by targeting the transcript or via chromatin directly (Kazazian, 2004; Siomi et al., 2011). piRNAs are produced from definite genomic locations termed *piRNA clusters*, cytologically located in heterochromatin and proximal heterochromatin–euchromatin boundary zone and surprisingly harbor abundant TEs. In *Drosophila*, 142 such clusters have been identified distinctly, coding for almost 90% of encoded piRNAs, where a majority of them are located in peri-centromeric and sub-telomeric heterochromatin regions and only seven of them in the euchromatin region (Figure 12.3). These

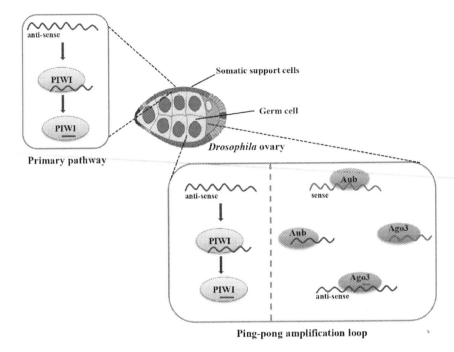

FIGURE 12.3 The PIWI-interacting RNA (piRNA) biogenesis pathway in the *Drosophila* ovary.

In the somatic support cells of the *Drosophila* ovary, the primary piRNA pathway is initiated by the transposon sequence in piRNA clusters that are oriented in an anti-sense fashion to the direction of transcription. The resultant transcripts formed undergo transportation to the cytoplasm where they are processed by factors like Zucchini, Armi, and Yb. The final products are then loaded onto the PIWI protein.

The ping-pong amplification loop exists in germ cells of the *Drosophila* ovary, where the transcripts from piRNA clusters and the active transposons undergo processing by Aub and AGO3 to form piR-NAs. Usually, the piRNAs from the sense transposon transcript are loaded onto AGO3, and those from anti-sense transposon transcript are loaded onto Aub.

clusters span hundreds of kilobases carrying TEs with inactive or truncated forms (Barckmann et al., 2015; Brennecke et al., 2007; Ishizu et al., 2012; Vagin et al., 2006). Reports showed that piRNAs can be derived from protein-coding genes and a majority of them are generated from the 3′-untranslated region (3′-UTR) of the main transcript like the *traffic jam* locus of *Drosophila* (Saito et al., 2009).

lncRNAs

lncRNAs include transcripts that are longer than 200 nucleotides and are not translated into proteins. They broadly cover different RNA transcripts including snoRNA, intergenic transcripts, enhancer RNA, and overlapping transcripts produced from "sense" or "anti-sense" strands. lncRNA shows higher enrichment in the nucleus compared to the cytoplasm, although much diversified and specific subcellular local-ization has been observed in well-defined lncRNAs like XIST (on the inactive X chromosome), GAS5 (exported to cytoplasm), and BORG (only nucleus) (Coccia et al., 1992; Djebali et al., 2012; Quinn and Chang, 2016; Ravasi et al., 2006; B. Zhang et al., 2014). Like mRNAs, lncRNA also shows cell and tissue developmental stage-specific expression, but with certain distinctive features which are not found in mRNAs, for example, cis-regulatory capacity and typical 3′-terminal process-ing (Batista and Chang, 2013; Flynn and Chang, 2014; Quinn and Chang, 2016). Highly annotated lncRNAs are similarly transcribed by RNA Pol II and undergo capping, polyadenylation, and splicing like mRNAs, but the process is weak and cryptic (Cabili et al., 2011; Guttman and Rinn, 2012). More robustly, lncRNAs are transcribed from intergenic regions (long intergenic noncoding RNA or lincRNA) or the opposite strands of the protein-coding genes while some others are transcribed from the long polyadenylated primary transcripts of protein-coding genes (Goff and Rinn, 2015). Like diversified distribution, lncRNAs are involved in similar diver-gent activities such as genetic imprinting (Igfr2r locus by Air) (Nagano et al., 2008), protein sequestration to regulate expression of *trans*-acting genes (sequestration of Fox2 to influence Fox2-mediated alternative splicing of genes *in trans*) (Yin et al., 2012), epigenetic regulation during development (HOTAIR-mediated regulation of HOX-D locus) (Rinn et al., 2007; Tsai et al., 2010), post-translational modifica-tions (lncRNA NKILA-mediated inhibition of I-κB) (Liu et al., 2015), miRNA-sponges (linc-MD1 act as a miR-133 sponge) (Cesana et al., 2011), translational regulation (lincRNA-p21-mediated targeting of JUNB and CTNNB1 mRNA for base pairing-mediated repression) (Yoon et al., 2012), and regulation of higher-order nuclear architecture (Batista and Chang, 2013; Quinn and Chang, 2016).

snoRNAs

snoRNAs were initially discovered as small ncRNAs and as part of ribonucleopro-tein (RNP) complexes which selectively localize at nucleolus, later on, emerged as crucial co-factor in RNA splicing (Butcher and Brow, 2005; Dreyfuss et al., 1988; K. V. Morris and Mattick, 2014). snoRNAs are non-polyadenylated ncR-NAs with highly conserved sequences (C/D box or H/ACA box) essentially found in all eukaryotes with varying lengths (60–300 nt long) (Dieci et al., 2009). They undergo various RNA–RNA and RNA–protein interactions and help in the assembly and function of canonical spliceosomes and are thus referred to as spliceosomal RNAs. Moreover, the loss of function of snoRNAs causes abnormal processing of core ribosomal RNAs (5.8S, 18S, 28S) emphasizing their funda-mental regulatory function (Butcher and Brow, 2005; Kufel and Grzechnik, 2018; Z. Wang and Burge, 2008). Specialized snoRNAs with C/D box, long UG repeats, and similar snoRNAs with H/ACA box, UGAG motif (CAB box) are called small Cajal body-associated RNA (scaRNA), typically localized in the subnuclear struc-ture called Cajal body, and may involve in the regulation of genome conformation (Figure 12.4) (Darzacq et al., 2002; Marnef et al., 2014; Q. Wang et al., 2016).

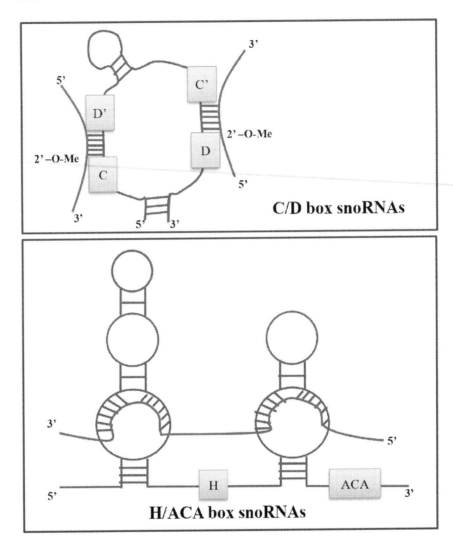

FIGURE 12.4 The structure of snoRNAs.

snoRNAs are non-polyadenylated ncRNAs with sequences like the C/D box or H/ACA box varying in lengths of 60–300 nt. Small Cajal-body associated RNA (scaRNA) is a specialized snoRNA with C/D box, long UG repeat and similar snoRNAs with H/ACA box, UGAG motif (CAB box). They typically localize in the subnuclear structure called the Cajal body and maintain genome conformation.

CircRNAs

Another less explored and large class of ncRNAs, called circRNA (circular RNA), are circular unlike other linear counterparts and have emerged as potential regulatory RNAs soon after their discovery (Kristensen et al., 2019). These are typically endogenous and eukaryotic RNAs where 5′ and 3′ ends are covalently closed.

In *Drosophila melanogaster*, it has been found that the biogenesis of such RNAs is mainly regulated by *trans*-acting and *cis*-acting elements that include "alternative splicing" and other specialized strategies (Kristensen et al., 2019). The majority of circRNAs are produced from protein-coding genes, predominantly by "alternative splicing" and contain single or multiple exons. Exons that are not included in the linear RNAs are found to be present in certain circRNAs (X.-O. Zhang et al., 2016). However, another form of "alternative splicing" called "back-splicing", where a downstream splice donor site gets covalently linked to the upstream splice acceptor site, results in the formation of both intron-containing and exon-intron circRNAs (Barrett et al., 2015; Schindewolf et al., 1996; Starke et al., 2015; Vicens and Westhof, 2014). On the other hand, abnormal debranching of intronic lariats during canonical splicing leads to the formation of circular intronic RNAs (ciR-NAs) (Z. Li et al., 2015; Y. Zhang et al., 2013). CircRNA shows differential distribution based on its structural organization, that is circRNAs purely with exons predominantly localized in cytoplasm might be associated with post-transcriptional gene regulation, whereas the intron-containing ones mainly accumulate in the nucleus and impart regulatory effects on transcription (Z. Li et al., 2015; Salzman et al., 2012; Wilusz, 2018). Surprisingly, recent reports have shown that circRNAs can directly regulate miRNAs via complementary base pairing as they might contain multiple miRNA binding sites and hence can act as miRNA sponges (Hansen et al., 2013; Memczak et al., 2013). Data showed that testis-specific circRNA produced from murine *sex-determining region Y (Sry)* and human circular RNA produced from the antisense strand of CDR1 genes can "sponge" miR-7 and miR-138 (Hansen et al., 2013; Memczak et al., 2013). Endogenous circRNA ZFN-609 contains an open reading frame and even gets translated to lower level indicating diversified functions of circRNAs (Legnini et al., 2017).

Applications of RNAi

The discovery of the RNAi pathway unlatched multidirectional yet efficient and precise mechanisms for fundamental research as well as new avenues for RNA-based drugs including distinct drug delivery. Fundamentally, it has provided an opportunity for spatial, selective silencing of genes and thus scope for a better understanding of gene function. Genome-wide understanding of RNAi for corresponding functional analysis in different model organisms including *Drosophila* and *C. elegans* deciphered a variety of unknown functions of several genes. Moreover, diverse interfaces of RNAi-associated proteins enabled researchers to understand the network of action of multiple pathways including new dimensions of RNA–protein interaction for fundamental biological processes. Mis-expression of miRNAs in disease conditions may help to understand the disease prognosis and modulate them accordingly to develop new RNAi-based drugs. RNAi-based strategies have effectively been used to combat fungal and viral infections in plants alongside strengthening the economic platforms (Martin and Caplen, 2007).

RNAi in functional genomics

RNAi technology can aid in identifying and functionally assessing thousands of genes that produce disease phenotypes. It effectively blocks the expression of a specific gene and helps in the evaluation of response to chemicals or changes in signalling pathways. RNAi altered the perspective of pursuing a genetic problem and understanding the underlying cellular mechanisms. Before the advent of RNAi, gene functional studies were done by DNA manipulation via different mutants. RNAi uses a reverse genetics approach that systematically selects genes with predetermined locations, reducing the cumbersome efforts otherwise involved in fishing for the genes.

RNAi in agriculture

RNA silencing mechanism in plants begins with the production of 20–26-nt small RNAs, via components like Dicer-like protein (DCL), AGO protein, and RNA-dependent RNA polymerase (RDRs) (Baulcombe, 2004; Chapman and Carrington, 2007; Hervé Vaucheret, 2006; Herve Vaucheret, 2008). The DCL proteins produce sRNAs (either siRNAs or miRNAs) from the dsRNA precursors which are then incorporated into the RISCs. AGO protein constitutes the larger part of the RISC-binding sRNAs and interacts with homologous RNAs that affect DNA methylation, endonuclease activity, or translational repression of mRNAs (Voinnet, 2009). The RDR enzymes synthesize dsRNAs through ssRNAs, which are processed by DCLs to initiate a new round of RNA silencing (Wassenegger and Krczal, 2006). RNAi has various applications in plants as follows.

RNAi in plant viral infections

RNAi was unknowingly used to combat viral infection in plants way before the discovery of the RNAi mechanism. Initial work with the Tobacco Mosaic Virus (TMV) by McKinney (1929) (McKinney, 1929) showed that tobacco plants infected with its mild forms provide resistance against the aggressive and virulent strains of the virus. Subsequent work with Tobacco Etch Virus (TEV) cDNA containing transgenic tobacco plants showed robust resistance against viruses having homologous sequence to that transgene, thereby consolidating the importance of RNAi for viral defense. Similar approaches were used in other plants like squash, tomato, and papaya and were commercially utilized in the United States during the mid-1990s, due to impressive responses. Further, mechanistic studies showed that plants also harbor a wide repertoire of ncRNAs and utilize the same defense mechanism as other eukaryotes, for siRNA and miRNA-mediated silencing during viral infections. Currently, a large number of transgenic plants are commercially available, based on RNAi technologies, to fight deadly viral infections mainly in bean golden mosaic virus, tomato yellow leaf curl virus, plum pox virus, cucumber mosaic virus, papaya ringspot virus, potato virus y, zucchini yellow mosaic virus, watermelon mosaic virus, etc. Besides these, RNAi has been explored for the recent outbreak of cassava brown streak disease caused by cassava brown streak virus (CBSV) or Ugandan cassava brown streak virus (UCBSV), which has affected millions of people in sub-Saharan Africa.

RNAi in plant fungal infections

RNAi techniques have been utilized to control fungal infections in plants. Nowara and colleagues showed a unique and most efficient approach to utilize RNAi, called host-induced gene silencing (HIGS), to control *Blumeria graminis*, which causes powdery mildew in barley and wheat. *B. graminis* remains in intimate association with the host plant and directly transports nutrients and other materials from the host. They utilized this free transport between the host and the pathogen for delivery of small RNAs to target multiple mRNAs of the fungal pathogen. This approach has been widely used against multiple fungal pathogens in a variety of crops like wheat, barley, maize, and other plants like banana, tobacco, cotton, and even *Arabidopsis*. A similar approach was utilized against cotton plant vascular fungal pathogen *Verticillium dahlias* and non-vascular plant *Botrytis cinereal* to transmit target miRNA against virulent genes of the pathogen. Disease suppression and reduced growth have also been observed in other phytogenic fungi such as *F. oxysporum*, *F. graminearum*, and *Puccinia triticin* using similar HIGS approaches in the lab (Hua et al., 2018). Most recently, another modified RNAi strategy called spray-induced gene silencing (SIGS) has been implicated to control pathogens simply by spraying dsRNA and small RNAs on the plant surface. Such RNAs are transported to the pathogen and target essential pathogenic genes (Hua et al., 2018). Plant fungal pathogens can penetrate the host through specialized hyphal structures into the natural opening or through wounds. Often, they also act as vectors for transmitting different viruses. Both plant and their fungal pathogen harbor similar RNAi machinery, which serves for defending the host on the one hand and for the pathogen to grow, develop, and establish pathogenesis. The DCLs in fungi synthesize sRNAs that anchor to AGO1 protein in plants to seize control over the RNAi machinery and dampen the host immune responses (Muhammad et al., 2019). To evade host immunity and cause pathogenesis, the fungus essentially needs to form conidia to let the fungal pathogen enter. MicroRNAs like miR160a, miR482, miR396a, miR398b, miR1444, miR2118, and miR7695 in plants are involved in the regulation of genes and providing immunity against fungal pathogens (Campo et al., 2013; L. Chen et al., 2015; M. Chen and Cao, 2015; Y. Li et al., 2014; Zhu et al., 2013).

RNAi in plant bacterial infections

Plants and bacteria may show positive or negative interactions, potentially causing the negative interactions to lead to the evolution of diseases in the host. Pathogenicity induced by bacteria spreads very rapidly and hence is difficult to regulate.

Usually, bacteria employ various means like phytohormone production, quorum sensing, siderophores, exopolysaccharides, and type III secretion system (T3SS), all of which contribute to virulence and finally, restrict host plant development (Aslam et al., 2008; Block et al., 2008; Fones and Preston, 2013; Kunkel and Harper, 2017; Quiñones et al., 2005; Ronald and Joe, 2017). Defense mechanisms in the host plant begin to occur only after it recognizes the components of bacterial translation or the flagellum. When the host initiates a pathogen-associated molecular pattern (PAMP)-triggered immunity (PTI) system (Pumplin and Voinnet, 2013), the bacteria retaliate by sending forth various effectors in the host cells and alter the transcriptome and proteome, all of which make the host cell susceptible to the pathogen. After this, the host triggers an effector-triggered immunity (ETI) against the pathogen, all fine-tuned by various miRNAs and siRNAs (Staiger et al., 2013). Both lines of defense initiated by the host plant target the iron-related sigma factor of the bacteria, affecting bacterial iron metabolism, which finally weakens the immunity of the bacteria and saves the host from pathogenesis (Nobori et al., 2018).

RNAi applications in health care

Macular degeneration

RNAi was first used to treat macular degeneration in 2004 since RNA could be directly injected into the diseased tissue. When the vascular endothelial growth factor (VEGF) is over-expressed in the eye, it leads to the accumulation of blood vessels behind the retina resulting in macular degeneration with blurred vision and blindness. When dsRNA binding to mRNAs encoding VEGF is injected into eye whites, it reduces the formation of the blood vessels and causes shrinkage of existing blood vessels. The first trial for RNAi-based drug for macular degeneration was administered, and it improved the vision of a quarter of its participants within a couple of months. Of late, a study involving siRNA called Cand5 is being conducted by Acuity Pharmaceuticals, Inc. for treating macular degeneration.

Cancer

RNAi is being used for developing future cancer therapeutics and is currently trending owing to the brilliant and promising results obtained from *in vitro* and *in vivo* studies. An increasing plethora of new gene targets is being discovered and sequenced and added to the new RNAi-based drug development. Specific siRNAs targeting telomerase are under development. Targeting telomerase brings about replicative control over cancer cells, which normally evade senescence to achieve immortality. In this way, cancer cells can be subjected to replicative senescence, and apoptosis is initiated.

HIV

RNAi can be utilized to inhibit human immunodeficiency virus (HIV) by targeting proteins critical for HIV manifestation. The critical genes for HIV's survival are the *nef* gene, producing the HIV-1 cellular receptor CD4, the *env* gene encoding the envelope-associated proteins, and the *gag* gene encoding the capsid proteins. The construction of siRNA libraries that can destroy complementary HIV mRNAs may successfully inhibit the replication of HIV and interfere with its ability to adhere to immune cells.

Cardiovascular and cerebrovascular diseases

Damage to vascular endothelial cells coupled with the local production of inflammatory cytokines and recruitment of macrophages to form foam cells occludes the arteries leading to atherosclerosis (Geng and Libby, 2002). Similarly, ischemia in the heart or brain cells during a myocardial infarction or stroke is detrimental to the cardiac muscle cells or the neurons. An RNAi intervention that prevents the formation of plaques by targeting the cell adhesion molecules can reduce the risk of atherosclerosis and cerebrovascular diseases.

Neurodegenerative disorders

Neurodegenerative diseases like Alzheimer's disease, Parkinson's disease, Huntington's disease, and amyotrophic lateral sclerosis are due to the dysfunction and death of specific populations of neurons. Huntington's disease occurs due to the polyglutamine expansion mutations in the Huntingtin protein (Rubinsztein, 2002). Animal and cell culture models for these diseases have disclosed various biochemical cascades that cause the death of the neurons due to an increase in oxidative stress, deregulated cellular calcium homeostasis, and apoptosis (Mattson, 2000). The enzymes, β- and γ-secretase, cleave the amyloid precursor protein to produce a neurotoxin. The amyloid β-peptide is responsible for the early progression of Alzheimer's disease. Hence, siRNAs targeted for these enzyme-coding genes can effectively check the progression of neurodegeneration.

RNAi-based therapeutics: advent and evolution

Ever since the advent of post-translational gene silencing in *C. elegans* termed RNA interference by Fire and Mello in 1998, non-coding RNA eventually was considered a central regulator of gene expression in multicellular organisms. This was followed by the prospect of harnessing the 21- and 22-nt dsRNAs (siRNA) to induce silencing in mammalian cells without evoking any interferon response compared to their classical small molecule counterpart. As a result, RNAi emerged as an excellent tool in biological research to induce gene inhibition by a single base.

The new potential and versatility to suppress the genes which code for undruggable targets and the capacity to repurpose and retarget these drugs without alteration of in vivo pharmacokinetics was the unique feature of this tool. As a result, by 2003, there was a booming increase in the development of such RNAi-based drugs (Figure 12.5).

The first clinical trial using unmodified siRNAs, unfortunately, led to toxic immune responses, which were corrected by systemic administration of siRNA nanoparticle formulations in the second wave of trials. However, along with the reduction of toxicity, the efficacy of the therapeutic was also reduced, which made major pharmaceutical companies opt out in the early 2010s, hampering the efforts made in this line (Haussecker, 2012). Averting these challenges, a few smaller RNAi companies were still persistent in constantly improving the trigger design, sequence selection, chemical formulation, and delivery mechanisms. Such measures along with judiciously selecting the indications and interventions of the disease have paved the way for a more mature development of therapeutics (Fambrough, 2012; Zuckerman and Davis, 2015). All such unified and consolidated successful attempts

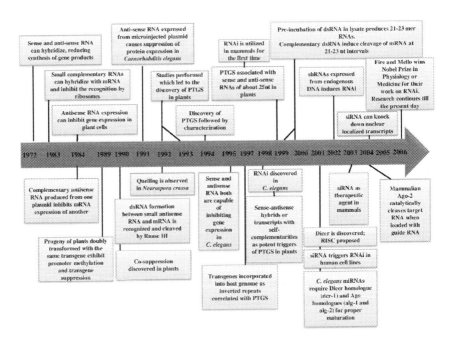

FIGURE 12.5 Chronological series of events in the discovery and further elucidation of the RNAi pathway. The timeline depicts all the pivotal developments that led to the discovery of RNA interference (RNAi) in animals and plants.

AGO, Argonaute; dsRNA, double-stranded RNA; miRNA, microRNA; nt, nucleotide; PTGS, post-transcriptional gene silencing; RISC, RNA-induced silencing complex; shRNA, short hairpin RNA; siRNA, small interfering RNA.

and efforts of Alnylam Pharmaceuticals have led to the evolution of the RNAi-based drug, Patisiran (Onpatro), approved by the US Food and Drug Administration (FDA) on 10 August 2018. It is a siRNA targeted to act on the liver for the treatment of transthyretin amyloidosis (hATTR) with polyneuropathy. After this, multiple drug candidates for liver, renal, and ocular applications have been forwarded for testing in phase I, II, and III clinical trials.

RNAi-based drugs for human diseases

Patisiran: Onpattro or Patisiran is a novel representative of new-generation RNAi therapeutics that ensures a safe and potent RNAi with safe delivery strategies. Other drug candidates in phases I, II, and III are being targeted to the liver and non-liver indications and are in the pipeline. Patisiran or ALN-TTR02 is a siRNA lipid nanoparticle (LNP) that is used for the treatment of a rare inherited life-threatening neurodegenerative disease called transthyretin (TTR) amyloidosis. The disease progresses via deposition of TTR amyloids in the peripheral nervous system, heart, and gastrointestinal tract which renders the patient with a lifespan of 5–15 years following diagnosis due to progressive neuropathy, cardiomyopathy, and other sorts of debilitating symptoms (Adams et al., 2018). The liver serves as the producer of the majority of TTR proteins via more than 120 mutations. Other earlier drugs that were developed before the evolution of Patisiran aimed at stabilizing the TTR tetramer in the native conformation, thereby slowing down disease progression (Adams et al., 2018; Benson et al., 2018). In the case of Patisiran siRNA (ALN-18328), both wild-type and mutant *TTR* mRNAs are silenced in the hepatocytes, such that there is a reduction in the serum levels of the TTR protein. To attain this far-fetched silencing activity, the guide strand which shows lesser variability targets the 3'-UTR of the mRNA (Adams et al., 2016; Adams et al., 2018; Butler et al., 2016). The delivery of ALN-18328 was achieved by siRNA encapsulation in an LNP that was formulated for uptake by the hepatocyte (Adams et al., 2018). ALN-TTR02 is the "second-generation" of pegylated LNP-containing cholesterol, a polar lipid (DSPC), a pegylated lipid (PEG2000-C-DMG), and an ionizable amino lipid (DLin-MC3-DMA) that normally has a pH 7 but may become cationic under an acidic pH (optimized pKa 6.44). The assembly of siRNA-LNP is achieved at an acidic pH under the influence of electrostatic interactions. This interaction is preserved until it enters the systemic circulation when serum proteins replace apolipoprotein E. In the liver, the apolipoprotein E-encapsulated LNPs are taken up and transferred to the endosomes where the pH causes disassembly due to reionization (Figure 12.6). The disassembled lipid globule then helps the siRNA escape into the cytosol via electrostatic and hydrophobic interactions. ALN-TTR02 is tenfold more potent *in vivo* and phase II clinical trials and achieved greater than 80% mean sustained reduction in circulation when administered intravenously once every three weeks (Coelho et al., 2013). Subsequently, a double-blind placebo-controlled clinical trial showed effective control over the progression of hATTR. The US-FDA has approved Patisiran for treating hATTR with polyneuropathy.

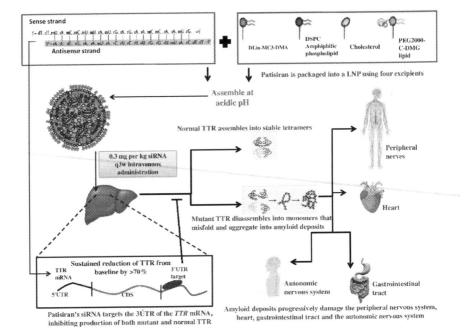

FIGURE 12.6 The therapeutic mechanism of Patisiran. Patisiran comprises a small interfering RNA (siRNA) encapsulated with lipid excipients. The lipid nanoparticles (LNPs) encapsulate these components under acidic pH. The drug is injected intravenously once every three weeks at 0.3 mg per kg dosage. The siRNA is targeted against the 3' untranslated region (UTR) of the *TTR* gene, which codes for transthyretin. In this way, it silences all possible mRNAs with coding region mutations. This RNA interference (RNAi) silencing results in sustained >70% reductions of circulating TTR proteins, preventing the deposition of TTR amyloids. For the siRNA, "m"=2'-O-methyl-modified bases, 'r'=RNA and 'd'=DNA.

(Adapted from Setten et al., 2019; *Nature Reviews Drug Discovery*)

Metabolically stabilized GalNAc-conjugated siRNAs

Nearly one-third of RNAi drugs currently in clinical trials include a single molecule that has been modified and conjugated to multivalent GalNAc ligands that target the asialoglycoprotein receptors (ASGPRs). GalNAc is a derivative of galactose that has a terminally lost sialic acid residue on its parent oligosaccharides. These proteins are normally cleared from the systemic circulation by the liver, which harbors the ASGPR receptors on the hepatocytes. At neutral pH, ASGPRs bind to GalNAcs for endocytosis and circulation, but at an acidic pH of 5–6, they release GalNAc to let go of the cargo and recycle back the ASGPRs to the cell surface for reuse (Spiess, 1990). The GalNac–siRNA conjugate approach turns out to be an ideal mode of systemic RNAi delivery to hepatocytes, owing to the suitable physiology of the liver, unique attributes of the ASGPRs, nontoxic nature of the ligands, nontoxic property of the conjugates (Spiess, 1990), and the ability to administer these drugs via the less cumbersome subcutaneous approach. This approach of delivering nucleic acids has been extensively studied for more than two decades, yet the caveat of developing RNAi triggers that are nontoxic yet equally stable and potent remains a challenge.

Revusiran

Revusiran is the first metabolically stabilized GalNAc–siRNA conjugate developed by Alnylam Pharmaceuticals to enter clinical trials. It is also used for the treatment of hATTR by targeting *TTR* mRNA (Zimmermann et al., 2017). The base positions were chemically modified such that the duplex regions bear an asymmetric, irregular pattern of 2′-O-methyl and 2′-F modifications in the duplex and DNA bases in the overhangs. Such a motif prevents degradation by serum nucleases and averts immunogenic reactions. Revusiran was administered subcutaneously in phase II clinical trials to achieve a 55–90% mean knockdown of serum TTR levels (Gillmore et al., 2015; Zimmermann et al., 2017) where it depicted mild side effects at the injection site with no evidence of systemic immune activation. The double-blind, placebo-controlled phase III ENDEAVOUR (NCT02319005) clinical trial of Revusiran for 18 months reported peripheral neuropathy and elevation in the blood lactate. However, the subjects who were treated with Revusiran showed drug-related effects which could not be explained, as a result of which the subsequent trials were withheld.

Advances in RNAi drug development

Alnylam Pharmaceuticals received a major setback with the failure of Revusiran, but it strived to persist in continuing trials with the development of GalNAc–siRNA conjugates, which led to the development of two generations of siRNA-enhanced stability chemistries (ESCs). The modification included the addition of phosphorothioate (PS) backbone to the two 5′ terminal nucleotides with 2′-O-methyl modifications on either strand of siRNA. Such modifications led to the enhanced potency of the siRNA–GalNAc conjugates and reduced the dosage by tenfold, thereby solving the issue of toxicity. An example of such ESC is Inclisiran, which is a PCSK9 inhibitor. Another candidate called Givosiran completed the phase III trial and complied with the FDA's new drug application. Thus, the recommendable potency and safety of the metabolically stabilized siRNAs abided by the chemical modifications and led to the evolution of simple yet less-toxic RNAi drugs. The development of chemically modified, metabolically stabilized RNAi triggers by altering the secondary structures was started by companies like Arrowhead Pharmaceuticals, Dicerna Pharmaceuticals, and Silence Therapeutics. Arrowhead's drugs ARO-HBV and ARO-AAT for hepatitis B infection and liver disease associated with α1-antitrypsin (AAT) deficiency showed a recommendable reduction in HBsAg (hepatitis B surface antigen) and serum AAT levels when administered subcutaneously. Dicerna's DCR-PHXC successfully treated primary hyperoxalurias in clinical trial I by silencing lactate dehydrogenase needed for oxalate production upon subcutaneous administration. In addition, Silence Therapeutics has developed SLN124, which is a GalNAc–siRNA targeting TMPRSS6, found beneficial for the treatment of disorders pertaining to iron regulation and is under preclinical development (Table 12.1).

RNAi drugs for non-liver targets

So far, all of the aforementioned milestones made in RNAi drug discovery were solely limited to targeting the liver, mainly through metabolically stabilized siR-NAs. Now the clinical RNAi development regimes have shifted their focus to targeting other tissues and organs with the stabilized siRNAs. Localized delivery has been used to achieve this, contrary to systemic drug distribution. Quark Pharmaceuticals has developed RNAi drugs for treating kidney injury (Demirjian et al., 2017) and eye diseases (Vigneswara and Ahmed, 2016) which have reached phase II and phase III clinical trials. One such siRNA is the QPI-1002, which targets the *TP53* gene upon intravenous administration to check acute kidney injury following cardiac surgery and delayed graft function following renal transplantation. Phases I and II of QPI-1002 have potency up to 10mg per kg if given during cardiac surgery (Demirjian et al., 2017). A chemically modified version of QPI-1002, known as QPI-1007, has been found to target Caspase 2 for treating non-arteritic anterior ischaemic optic neuropathy when administered up to doses of 6 mg (Antoszyk et al., 2013), and its III phase trial has already ensued. Alnylam Pharmaceuticals have recently concentrated its research and development on devising an agent to target amyloid precursor protein for treating cerebral amyloid angiopathy.

Current limitations and measures to meet the ongoing challenges

Although efforts have been made to develop clinically relevant RNAi drugs, many favorable changes made in pharmacokinetics, pharmacodynamics, and toxicity abetting strategies are yet to be met. The recent developments have witnessed persistent changes in already established technologies in the approaches involving polymer nanoparticles or LNPs, aptamers, molecular ligands and oligonucleotide base, and modifications (Rietwyk and Peer, 2017; Rosenblum et al., 2018; Springer and Dowdy, 2018; Zhou and Rossi, 2017). Apart from these approaches, novel ones have also been devised to modify the existing paradigms of delivery as follows:

For improvisation of endosomal escape

Endosomal escape poses to be a major obstacle to the expansion of RNAi-based therapeutics beyond the liver. siRNAs escape passively at the rate of <0.01% and

TABLE 12.1 Selected RNAi-based therapeutics currently in clinical trials

Sponsor: RNAi Therapy	Target	Route of Administration	Clinical Phase Trial Number; NCT Number	Comments
Phio Pharmaceuticals, Corp.: RXI-109 (sd-RxNA)	Age-related macular degeneration, retinal scarring: CTGF	Intravitreal	Phase I, II; NCT02599064	The estimated primary completion date is April 2018
Quark Pharmaceuticals: QPI-1002 (siRNA)	Cardiac surgery: kidney expression of p53	Intravenous	Phase III; NCT03510897	Phase II demonstrated protection against acute kidney injury
Quark Pharmaceuticals: QPI-1007 (siRNA)	Non-arteritic anterior ischaemic optic neuropathy: Caspase 2	Intravitreal	Phase II, III; NCT02341560	Single intra-vitreal injections well tolerated up to 6 mg, showed plausible vision protection
Alnylam Pharmaceuticals/ Genzyme (Sanofi): Fitusiran/ ALNAT3SC (GalNAc ESC siRNA)	Haemophilia A/haemophilia B: antithrombin	Subcutaneous	Phase III; NCT03417245, NCT03417102, NCT03549871, NCT03754790	One patient death in phase II open-label extension; FDA clinical hold lifted in November 2017; phase III trials recruited
Alnylam Pharmaceuticals/the Medicines Company: Inclisiran/ ALN-PCSSC (GalNAc ESC siRNA)	Hypercholesterolaemia, atherosclerotic cardiovascular disease, renal impairment: PCSK9	Subcutaneous	Phase I, II, III; NCT03060577, NCT03159416, NCT02963311, NCT03705234	Phase II ORION-1 trial achieved a reduction in low-density lipoprotein cholesterol up to 52.6% at 180 days
Alnylam Pharmaceuticals: Givosiran/ALN-AS1 (GalNac ESC siRNA)	Acute intermittent porphyria: ALAS1	Subcutaneous	Phase I, I/II, III; NCT02949830, NCT03338816, NCT02240784, NCT03547297	Positive interim results of phase III ENVISION trial, New Drug Application initiated
Alnylam Pharmaceuticals: Vutrisiran/ALN-TTRsc02 (GalNac ESC siRNA)	hATTR: transthyretin mRNA 3' untranslated region	Subcutaneous	Phase III; NCT03759379	Phase I was well tolerated, 83% mean knockdown of TTR

(*Continued*)

TABLE 12.1 (Continued)

Sponsor: RNAi Therapy	Target	Route of Administration	Clinical Phase Trial Number; NCT Number	Comments
Arrowhead Pharmaceuticals: ARO-AAT (GalNAc ligand siRNA)	α1-Antitrypsin deficiency liver disease: α1–antitrypsin	Subcutaneous	Phase I; NCT03362242	93% maximum AAT reduction at 6 weeks following a single dose, no severe AEs up to 300mg single dose
Arrowhead Pharmaceuticals: ARO-HBV (GalNAc ligand siRNA)	Hepatitis B: HBV mRNAs	Subcutaneous	Phase I, II; NCT03365947	100% of patients achieved >1 log10 reduction in HBsAg; well tolerated up to 400mg q4w
Dicerna Pharmaceuticals, Inc.: DCR-PHXC (GalNAc GalXC)	Primary hyperoxaluria: hepatic glycolate oxidase	Subcutaneous	Phase I; NCT03392896	Appears well tolerated, most patients reach normal circulating oxalate

Source: Adapted from Setten et al., 2019; *Nature Reviews Drug Discovery*.

require about 2,000–5,000 cytoplasmic siRNAs for complete knockdown of the target gene. Most of the surface receptors function in the range of 10,000–100,000, and the receptors recycle at an average rate of ~90 minutes. The ASGPR is an exception that expresses at levels exceeding ~500,000 and recycles at the rate of <20 minutes (D'souza and Devarajan, 2015). This ensures that enough conjugates of GalNAc–siRNA accumulate in the hepatocyte cytoplasm to reach the therapeutic threshold but fails to resolve the problem of escape for other cell types. Agents like chloroquine and pore-forming peptides like melittin, DPC, and/or NAG-MLP have been put into application to ensure endosomal escape without creating cytotoxicity but did not produce much success (Wadia et al., 2004; Yang et al., 2015). Efforts were made to probe for agents that can result in mild or localized destabilization of membranes with a lessened risk of endosmosis. An alternative approach was sought to exploit the retrograde transport in the cells from the AS5 toxin family (M.-S. Lee et al., 2016; Lord and Roberts, 1998). This strategy can target gene knockdown using siRNA or ASOs which can be also visualized by fluorescent microscopy. Alternatively, a strategy swapping conjugated 21-mer siRNA for a DSiRNA that can be later fed on signal is also sought (Pepin et al., 2012). All such strategies are in their infancy; however, if any of these strategies work out, they can guarantee a new nontoxic endosomal escape, serving the applications of RNAi therapy.

Usage of antibody conjugates with siRNA

The enhancement of potency and safety of RNAi therapeutics is necessary for improved systemic circulation and targeted delivery. Immunoglobulin G antibodies can remain in the systemic circulation for weeks and pervade evenly within tissues owing to the Fc–FcRn interactions that help in recycling and transcytosis (Roopenian and Akilesh, 2007). This property has been harnessed in a novel strategy involving the conjugation of antibodies with drug moieties that target specific tissue with enhanced pharmacokinetics (Beck et al., 2017). Avidity Biosciences recently developed an antibody–siRNA conjugate that by intravenous administration can knock down myostatin mRNA in unspecified muscle tissues by more than 90% efficiency (Geall et al., 2017). Such a strategy can be utilized for the delivery of siRNAs to non-liver tissues taking advantage of the cleavable linker structures with higher near-neutral stability and faster dissociation at endosomal pH 5.5 (Beck et al., 2017; Choy et al., 2016). Currently, Avidity Pharmaceuticals is involved in the discovery-stage development of Duchenne muscular dystrophy and myotonic dystrophy type 1.

Usage of hydrophobic siRNAs to improve potency

Since metabolically stabilized siRNAs are quite potent in their action, it has rekindled interest in initiating hydrophobic modifications, wherein motifs of cholesterol-conjugated PS-modified self-delivering siRNAs were improvised for increasing potency. An example of such an approach is utilizing FMS-like tyrosine kinase 1 siRNA with hydrophobic modifications which efficiently targeted silencing in pregnant mice upon systemic administration (Turanov et al., 2018).

Synthesis of stereo-selective phosphorothioate

Molecular heterogeneity impedes clinical development, so future RNAi agents may be more efficiently delivered if they harbor stereoselective synthesis of PS-modified.

Reduction of toxicity of LNPs

Metabolically stabilized RNAi are quite popular now after Patisiran, but the dosages of these drugs are very limited because such ionizable lipid excipients are toxic upon long-term use. To abrogate this issue, ester groups are being incorporated into the hydrophobic tails, so that the ionizable lipids are metabolically broken down. Such an ionizable lipid has been developed by Alnylam called L-319, which has symmetric enzyme-cleavable ester-linked alkyl tails and rapidly clears from tissues with lessened toxicity and sustained potency in the *in vivo* murine models (Borgheti-Cardoso et al., 2017; Nguyen et al., 2013). With the current development scenario, the biodegradable ionizable lipids may soon enter preclinical development in 2–5 years.

Systemic delivery of siRNA using exosomes

Exosomes have shown to be a promising vehicle for the systemic delivery of RNAi-based drugs. They are natural nanoparticle endogenous products that carry cargos such as microRNAs to distant tissues. Synthetic siRNAs can also be engulfed within the exosomes for targeted delivery. The circulation lifetime of an exosome in the system can be enhanced by the surface expression of CD47 and various endogenous ligands which ensures more time for retention and cellular uptake. Recently, M.D. Anderson Cancer Center has undertaken a phase I clinical trial for anti-KRAS siRNA against pancreatic cancer by exosome-based delivery.

Enhanced local delivery

System delivery of RNAi payloads is altogether fraught with difficulties of retention for sustained release; hence, localized delivery of RNAi-based drugs is preferable. The layer-by-layer electrostatic assemblies and injectable biodegradable hydrogels for localized therapeutic delivery seem to be potent in wound healing and tissue regeneration since they extend the time of local siRNA release while in the system (Borgheti-Cardoso et al., 2017; Nguyen et al., 2013). Very recently, nanoparticles with neutrally charged hydrophilic surface coatings have been found to pervade the mucus layer, which was hindered in the other modes of local delivery (Ensign et al., 2012; Lai et al., 2009; Mastorakos et al., 2015).

This has improved the delivery of RNAi to the gastrointestinal tract and lungs (Ball et al., 2018; Mastorakos et al., 2015).

Nanostructures comprising nucleic acids

Nanostructure nucleic acids face delivery obstacles owing to the intrinsic chemical and physical heterogeneity of the nanoparticles. Recently, DNA and RNA nanotechnology allowed siRNA nanoparticles to assemble and cargo payloads based on the number, type, shape, and size of the surface ligands (Khisamutdinov et al., 2016; Pi et al., 2018; Shu et al., 2014). However, the highly negative backbone charges of the nucleic acid aggravate the clearance from systemic circulation (He et al., 2010), and unmodified nucleic acids undergo rapid nuclease degradation and immunotoxicity (Surana et al., 2015). To abate these limitations, the thermodynamic stability of these nanostructure nucleic acids is enhanced using cross-linking and adding protecting adjuvants such as lipid and peptide-based coatings (Ponnuswamy et al., 2017). This can lead to well-defined nanostructures for RNAi delivery, but this area of research is still in its infancy.

Conditional RNAi activity

Antisense oligonucleotides anti-guide strand improves the duration of RNAi activity and thus restricts the activity to a specified population of cells. Chemically modified nucleic acids which can sense mRNAs in mammalian cells (riboswitches) have been proposed to trigger RNAi (Bindewald et al., 2016; S.-P. Han et al., 2015; Hochrein et al., 2013; Yin et al., 2012). Such switches may very specifically target disease-related cells and may manipulate the cellular functions.

Alternative preclinical models

The discovery and preclinical stages in RNAi therapeutic development are hindered because the non-primate model organisms have an insufficient overlap of genomic sequences with humans, so pharmacodynamics cannot be studied efficiently. This increases the cost, risk, and ethical concerns for the use of non-primate models. Alternatively, if human tissues could be grown and cultured *in vitro* in the form of organoids or organ-on-a-chip technologies, it can recapitulate the tissue organization, biochemical signals, and mechanical stimuli manifesting in human organs. Organoids are self-organized, pluripotent stem cell-derived, and can predict all the responses to drugs (Dutta et al., 2017). Specialized microfluidic chips help in providing spatial patterning cues and dynamic stimuli mimicking human organs. The current challenge with organoids and organs on chips involves the dearth of complete knowledge about the efficacy of drug response and the development of appropriate technologies. With proper research and further development, researchers can cut down the expenditure, risk, and complexity of preclinical studies in the future.

miRNA and small ds-RNA therapeutics

A careful study of miRNA-induced RNAi has induced the development of synthetic miRNA therapeutics and constructs that can inhibit the activity of specific miRNAs or silence a specific miRNA target. Synthetic constructs are called anti-mirs and blockers. These technologies can expand the disease treatment modality via therapeutics. Synthetic versions of endogenous miRNAs called miRNA mimics have the same guide strand sequence as an endogenous miRNA (Rupaimoole and Slack, 2017) such that when the guide strand is loaded into AGO1–AGO4, the resulting RISC mimics the corresponding miRNA. In this way, it may target genes like transcription factors, complementary to the guide strand via target sites in the 3'-UTR (Janssen et al., 2013; Van der Ree et al., 2016). Just like miRNAs, miRNA mimics can regulate developmental programs and pathways to preserve cellular identity. Small activating RNAs (saRNAs) causing RNA activation (RNAa) with sequences homologous to regions near or within gene promoters (Janowski et al., 2007; L.-C. Li et al., 2006) only target genes without loss-of-function mutation. RNA activation via saRNA depends on AGO2 and is limited to the nucleus where the AGO2–saRNA binds to sequences within chromatin-bound complementary to RNA and DNA transcripts (Core et al., 2008; Portnoy et al., 2016; Reebye et al., 2014; Schwartz et al., 2008; Seila et al., 2008; Voutila et al., 2017; Yue et al., 2010). To date, 14 genes have been activated by saRNAs (L.-C. Li, 2017). The first saRNA therapeutic, MTLCEBPA developed for the treatment of inoperable hepatocellular carcinoma entered clinical trials in 2016 (Reebye et al., 2014; Voutila et al., 2017). Thus, saRNAs can act as gene-expression-activating therapeutics complementing the siRNA-mediated gene-expression-suppressing therapeutics.

Conclusion

The discovery of RNAi serves as a cornerstone in the field of molecular biology. It has turned out to be a very potent tool for studying gene function in mammals as it enables researchers to silence virtually any gene with artificial triggers of RNAi and via appropriate cellular machinery for complementary-based targeting of transcripts. Studies involving the feasibility of the process *in vivo* demonstrated that delivery methods involving both viral and non-viral vectors can selectively and potently target gene suppression. RNAi has witnessed several breakthroughs in translational research via numerous human clinical trials. The RNAi-based drug evolution and delivery are fraught with challenges like overcoming off-target effects, prevention of type I interferon response trigger, competition with cellular RNAi components, and effective delivery *in vivo*. Like every other biological discovery, the success of RNAi involves properly understanding the mechanism so that it can be effectively harnessed in developing applications for human diseases. RNAi has so far revolutionized the area involving the treatment of human diseases like the way it revolutionized basic research. Despite the challenges which have been discussed and elaborated on earlier, RNAi has withstood its place for more than 20 years since its first advent. With numerous innovations and development in the technologies of payloads and excipients, more breakthroughs are yet to be witnessed.

References

Adams, D., Coelho, T., Conceicao, I., Waddington-Cruz, M., Schmidt, H., Buades, J. et al. (2016). Phase 2 open-label extension study (OLE) of Patisiran, an investigational RNAi therapeutic for familial amyloid polyneuropathy (FAP)(S38. 003): AAN Enterprises.

Adams, D., Gonzalez-Duarte, A., O'Riordan, W. D., Yang, C. C., Ueda, M., Kristen, A. V. et al. (2018). Patisiran, an RNAi therapeutic, for hereditary transthyretin amyloidosis. *New England Journal of Medicine*, 379(1), 11–21.

Ahlenstiel, C. L., Lim, H. G., Cooper, D. A., Ishida, T., Kelleher, A. D. and Suzuki, K. (2011). Direct evidence of nuclear Argonaute distribution during transcriptional silencing links the actin cytoskeleton to nuclear RNAi machinery in human cells. *Nucleic Acids Research*, 40(4), 1579–1595.

Antoszyk, A., Katz, B., Singh, R., Gurses-Ozden, R., Erlich, S., Rothenstein, D. et al. (2013). A phase I open-label, dose-escalation trial of QPI-1007 delivered by a single intravitreal (IVT) injection to subjects with low visual acuity and acute non-arteritic anterior ischemic optic neuropathy (NAION). *Investigative Ophthalmology & Visual Science*, 54(15), 4575–4575.

Aravin, A. A., Naumova, N. M., Tulin, A. V., Vagin, V. V., Rozovsky, Y. M. and Gvozdev, V. A. (2001). Double-stranded RNA-mediated silencing of genomic tandem repeats and transposable elements in the D. melanogaster germline. *Current Biology*, 11(13), 1017–1027.

Aslam, S. N., Newman, M.-A., Erbs, G., Morrissey, K. L., Chinchilla, D., Boller, T. et al. (2008). Bacterial polysaccharides suppress induced innate immunity by calcium chelation. *Current Biology*, 18(14), 1078–1083.

Ball, R. L., Bajaj, P. and Whitehead, K. A. (2018). Oral delivery of siRNA lipid nanoparticles: Fate in the GI tract. *Scientific Reports*, 8(1), 2178.

Barckmann, B., Pierson, S., Dufourt, J., Papin, C., Armenise, C., Port, F. et al. (2015). Aubergine iCLIP reveals piRNA-dependent decay of mRNAs involved in germ cell development in the early embryo. *Cell Reports*, 12(7), 1205–1216.

Barrett, S. P., Wang, P. L. and Salzman, J. (2015). Circular RNA biogenesis can proceed through an exon-containing lariat precursor. *Elife*, 4, e07540.

Batista, P. J. and Chang, H. Y. (2013). Long noncoding RNAs: Cellular address codes in development and disease. *Cell*, 152(6), 1298–1307.

Baulcombe, D. (2004). RNA silencing in plants. *Nature*, 431(7006), 356.

Beck, A., Goetsch, L., Dumontet, C. and Corvaïa, N. (2017). Strategies and challenges for the next generation of antibody-drug conjugates. *Nature Reviews Drug Discovery*, 16(5), 315.

Benson, M. D., Waddington-Cruz, M., Berk, J. L., Polydefkis, M., Dyck, P. J., Wang, A. K. et al. (2018). Inotersen treatment for patients with hereditary transthyretin amyloidosis. *New England Journal of Medicine*, 379(1), 22–31.

Bindewald, E., Afonin, K. A., Viard, M., Zakrevsky, P., Kim, T. and Shapiro, B. A. (2016). Multistrand structure prediction of nucleic acid assemblies and design of RNA switches. *Nano Letters*, 16(3), 1726–1735.

Block, A., Li, G., Fu, Z. Q. and Alfano, J. R. (2008). Phytopathogen type III effector weaponry and their plant targets. *Current Opinion in Plant Biology*, 11(4), 396–403.

Bonnet, E., Van de Peer, Y. and Rouzé, P. (2006). The small RNA world of plants. *New Phytologist*, 171(3), 451–468.

Borges, F. and Martienssen, R. A. (2015). The expanding world of small RNAs in plants. *Nature Reviews Molecular Cell Biology*, 16(12), 727–741.

Borgheti-Cardoso, L. N., Kooijmans, S. A., Fens, M. H., Van der Meel, R., Vicentini, F. T., Fantini, M. C. et al. (2017). In situ gelling liquid crystalline system as local siRNA delivery system. *Molecular Pharmaceutics*, 14(5), 1681–1690.

Brennecke, J., Aravin, A. A., Stark, A., Dus, M., Kellis, M., Sachidanandam, R. et al. (2007). Discrete small RNA-generating loci as master regulators of transposon activity in Drosophila. *Cell*, 128(6), 1089–1103.

Butcher, S. and Brow, D. (2005). Towards understanding the catalytic core structure of the spliceosome. *Biochemical Society Transactions*, 33(3), 447–449. https://doi.org/10.1042/BST0330447

Butler, J. S., Chan, A., Costelha, S., Fishman, S., Willoughby, J. L., Borland, T. D. et al. (2016). Preclinical evaluation of RNAi as a treatment for transthyretin-mediated amyloidosis. *Amyloid*, 23(2), 109–118.

Cabili, M. N., Trapnell, C., Goff, L., Koziol, M., Tazon-Vega, B., Regev, A. et al. (2011). Integrative annotation of human large intergenic noncoding RNAs reveals global properties and specific subclasses. *Genes & Development*, 25(18), 1915–1927.

Campo, S., Peris-Peris, C., Siré, C., Moreno, A. B., Donaire, L., Zytnicki, M. et al. (2013). Identification of a novel micro RNA (mi RNA) from rice that targets an alternatively spliced transcript of the N ramp6 (Natural resistance-associated macrophage protein 6) gene involved in pathogen resistance. *New Phytologist*, 199(1), 212–227.

Carthew, R. W. and Sontheimer, E. J. (2009). Origins and mechanisms of miRNAs and siRNAs. *Cell*, 136(4), 642–655.

Cesana, M., Cacchiarelli, D., Legnini, I., Santini, T., Sthandier, O., Chinappi, M. et al. (2011). A long noncoding RNA controls muscle differentiation by functioning as a competing endogenous RNA. *Cell*, 147(2), 358–369.

Chapman, E. J. and Carrington, J. C. (2007). Specialization and evolution of endogenous small RNA pathways. *Nature Reviews Genetics*, 8(11), 884.

Cheloufi, S., Dos Santos, C. O., Chong, M. M. and Hannon, G. J. (2010). A dicer-independent miRNA biogenesis pathway that requires Ago catalysis. *Nature*, 465 (7298), 584.

Chen, L., Luan, Y. and Zhai, J. (2015). Sp-miR396a-5p acts as a stress-responsive genes regulator by conferring tolerance to abiotic stresses and susceptibility to Phytophthora nicotianae infection in transgenic tobacco. *Plant Cell Reports*, 34(12), 2013–2025.

Chen, M. and Cao, Z. (2015). Genome-wide expression profiling of microRNAs in poplar upon infection with the foliar rust fungus Melampsora larici-populina. *BMC Genomics*, 16(1), 696.

Choy, C. J., Ley, C. R., Davis, A. L., Backer, B. S., Geruntho, J. J., Clowers, B. H. et al. (2016). Second-generation tunable pH-sensitive phosphoramidate-based linkers for controlled release. *Bioconjugate Chemistry*, 27(9), 2206–2213.

Coccia, E. M., Cicala, C., Charlesworth, A., Ciccarelli, C., Rossi, G., Philipson, L. et al. (1992). Regulation and expression of a growth arrest-specific gene (gas5) during growth, differentiation, and development. *Molecular and Cellular Biology*, 12(8), 3514–3521.

Coelho, T., Adams, D., Silva, A., Lozeron, P., Hawkins, P. N., Mant, T. et al. (2013). Safety and efficacy of RNAi therapy for transthyretin amyloidosis. *New England Journal of Medicine*, 369(9), 819–829.

Consortium, I. H. G. S. (2004). Finishing the euchromatic sequence of the human genome. *Nature*, 431(7011), 931.

Core, L. J., Waterfall, J. J. and Lis, J. T. (2008). Nascent RNA sequencing reveals widespread pausing and divergent initiation at human promoters. *Science*, 322(5909), 1845–1848.

Cullen, B. R. (2004). Transcription and processing of human microRNA precursors. *Molecular Cell*, 16(6), 861–865.

Darzacq, X., Jády, B. E., Verheggen, C., Kiss, A. M., Bertrand, E. and Kiss, T. (2002). Cajal body-specific small nuclear RNAs: A novel class of 2′-O-methylation and pseudouridylation guide RNAs. *The EMBO Journal*, 21(11), 2746–2756.

Demirjian, S., Ailawadi, G., Polinsky, M., Bitran, D., Silberman, S., Shernan, S. K. et al. (2017). Safety and tolerability study of an intravenously administered small interfering ribonucleic acid (siRNA) post-on-pump cardiothoracic surgery in patients at risk of acute kidney injury. *Kidney International Reports*, 2(5), 836–843.

Denli, A. M., Tops, B. B., Plasterk, R. H., Ketting, R. F. and Hannon, G. J. (2004). Processing of primary microRNAs by the Microprocessor complex. *Nature*, 432(7014), 231.

Dieci, G., Preti, M. and Montanini, B. (2009). Eukaryotic snoRNAs: A paradigm for gene expression flexibility. *Genomics*, 94(2), 83–88.

Djebali, S., Davis, C. A., Merkel, A., Dobin, A., Lassmann, T., Mortazavi, A. et al. (2012). Landscape of transcription in human cells. *Nature*, 489(7414), 101.

Dreyfuss, G., Philipson, L. and Mattaj, I. W. (1988). Ribonucleoprotein particles in cellular processes. *The Journal of Cell Biology*, 106(5), 1419–1425.

D'souza, A. A. and Devarajan, P. V. (2015). Asialoglycoprotein receptor-mediated hepatocyte targeting – strategies and applications. *Journal of Controlled Release*, 203, 126–139.

Dutta, D., Heo, I. and Clevers, H. (2017). Disease modeling in stem cell-derived 3D organoid systems. *Trends in Molecular Medicine*, 23(5), 393–410.

Ensign, L. M., Tang, B. C., Wang, Y.-Y., Terence, A. T., Hoen, T., Cone, R. et al. (2012). Mucus-penetrating nanoparticles for vaginal drug delivery protect against the herpes simplex virus. *Science Translational Medicine*, 4(138), 138ra179–138ra179.

Fambrough, D. (2012). Weathering a storm. *Nature Biotechnology*, 30(12), 1166.

Filipowicz, W., Bhattacharyya, S. N. and Sonenberg, N. (2008). Mechanisms of posttranscriptional regulation by microRNAs: Are the answers in sight? *Nature Reviews Genetics*, 9(2), 102.

Fire, A., Xu, S., Montgomery, M. K., Kostas, S. A., Driver, S. E. and Mello, C. C. (1998). Potent and specific genetic interference by double-stranded RNA in Caenorhabditis elegans. *Nature*, 391(6669), 806.

Flynn, R. A. and Chang, H. Y. (2014). Long noncoding RNAs in cell-fate programming and reprogramming. *Cell Stem Cell*, 14(6), 752–761.

Fones, H. and Preston, G. M. (2013). The impact of transition metals on bacterial plant disease. *FEMS Microbiology Reviews*, 37(4), 495–519.

Friedman, R. C., Farh, K. K.-H., Burge, C. B. and Bartel, D. P. (2009). Most mammalian mRNAs are conserved targets of microRNAs. *Genome Research*, 19(1), 92–105.

Geall, A. J., Doppalapudi, V. R., Chu, D. S. H., Cochran, M. C., Johns, R. E., Balu, P. et al. (2017). Nucleic acid-polypeptide compositions and uses thereof. Google Patents.

Gebert, L. F. and MacRae, I. J. (2019). Regulation of microRNA function in animals. *Nature Reviews Molecular Cell Biology*, 20(1), 21–37.

Geng, Y. J. and Libby, P. (2002). Progression of atheroma: A struggle between death and procreation. *Arteriosclerosis, Thrombosis, and Vascular Biology*, 22(9), 1370–1380.

Gillmore, J. D., Falk, R. H., Maurer, M. S., Hanna, M., Karsten, V., Vest, J. et al. (2015). Phase 2, open-label extension (OLE) study of revusiran, an investigational RNAi therapeutic for the treatment of patients with transthyretin cardiac amyloidosis. *Orphanet Journal of Rare Diseases*, 10(1), O21.

Goff, L. A. and Rinn, J. L. (2015). Linking RNA biology to lncRNAs. *Genome Research*, 25(10), 1456–1465.

Gregory, R. I., Yan, K. P., Amuthan, G., Chendrimada, T., Doratotaj, B., Cooch, N. et al. (2004). The Microprocessor complex mediates the genesis of microRNAs. *Nature*, 432(7014), 235.

Gunawardane, L. S., Saito, K., Nishida, K. M., Miyoshi, K., Kawamura, Y., Nagami, T. et al. (2007). A slicer-mediated mechanism for repeat-associated siRNA 5′ end formation in Drosophila. *Science*, 315(5818), 1587–1590.

Guo, S. and Kemphues, K. J. (1995). Part-1, a gene required for establishing polarity in C. elegans embryos, encodes a putative Ser/Thr kinase that is asymmetrically distributed. *Cell*, 81(4), 611–620.

Guttman, M. and Rinn, J. L. (2012). Modular regulatory principles of large non-coding RNAs. *Nature*, 482(7385), 339.

Han, J., Lee, Y., Yeom, K. H., Kim, Y. K., Jin, H. and Kim, V. N. (2004). The Drosha-DGCR8 complex in primary microRNA processing. *Genes & Development*, 18(24), 3016–3027.

Han, S. P., Barish, R. D. and Goddard III, W. A. (2015). Signal activated RNA interference. Google Patents.

Hansen, T. B., Jensen, T. I., Clausen, B. H., Bramsen, J. B., Finsen, B., Damgaard, C. K. et al. (2013). Natural RNA circles function as efficient microRNA sponges. *Nature*, 495(7441), 384.

Haussecker, D. (2012). The business of RNAi therapeutics in 2012. *Molecular Therapy-Nucleic Acids*, 1.

Hawkins, P. G., Santoso, S., Adams, C., Anest, V. and Morris, K. V. (2009). Promoter targeted small RNAs induce long-term transcriptional gene silencing in human cells. *Nucleic Acids Research*, 37(9), 2984–2995.

He, C., Hu, Y., Yin, L., Tang, C. and Yin, C. (2010). Effects of particle size and surface charge on cellular uptake and biodistribution of polymeric nanoparticles. *Biomaterials*, 31(13), 3657–3666.

Heard, E. and Martienssen, R. A. (2014). Transgenerational epigenetic inheritance: Myths and mechanisms. *Cell*, 157(1), 95–109.

Hochrein, L. M., Schwarzkopf, M., Shahgholi, M., Yin, P. and Pierce, N. A. (2013). Conditional Dicer substrate formation via shape and sequence transduction with small conditional RNAs. *Journal of the American Chemical Society*, 135(46), 17322–17330.

Hua, C., Zhao, J. H. and Guo, H. S. (2018). Trans-kingdom RNA silencing in plant – fungal pathogen interactions. *Molecular Plant*, 11(2), 235–244.

Ishizu, H., Siomi, H. and Siomi, M. C. (2012). Biology of PIWI-interacting RNAs: New insights into biogenesis and function inside and outside of germlines. *Genes & Development*, 26(21), 2361–2373.

Janowski, B. A., Huffman, K. E., Schwartz, J. C., Ram, R., Nordsell, R., Shames, D. S. et al. (2006). Involvement of AGO1 and AGO2 in mammalian transcriptional silencing. *Nature Structural & Molecular Biology*, 13(9), 787.

Janowski, B. A., Younger, S. T., Hardy, D. B., Ram, R., Huffman, K. E. and Corey, D. R. (2007). Activating gene expression in mammalian cells with promoter-targeted duplex RNAs. *Nature Chemical Biology*, 3(3), 166.

Janssen, H. L., Reesink, H. W., Lawitz, E. J., Zeuzem, S., Rodriguez-Torres, M., Patel, K. et al. (2013). Treatment of HCV infection by targeting microRNA. *New England Journal of Medicine*, 368(18), 1685–1694.

Kazazian, H. H. (2004). Mobile elements: Drivers of genome evolution. *Science*, 303(5664), 1626–1632.

Khisamutdinov, E. F., Jasinski, D. L., Li, H., Zhang, K., Chiu, W., and Guo, P. (2016). Fabrication of RNA 3D nanoprisms for loading and protection of small RNAs and model drugs. *Advanced Materials*, 28(45), 10079–10087.

Kim, D. H., Villeneuve, L. M., Morris, K. V. and Rossi, J. J. (2006). Argonaute-1 directs siRNA-mediated transcriptional gene silencing in human cells. *Nature Structural & Molecular Biology*, 13(9), 793.

Kim, S. W., Kim, N. Y., Choi, Y. B., Park, S. H., Yang, J. M. and Shin, S. (2010). RNA interference in vitro and in vivo using an arginine peptide/siRNA complex system. *Journal of Controlled Release*, 143(3), 335–343.

Kozomara, A. and Griffiths-Jones, S. (2013). miRBase: Annotating high confidence microRNAs using deep sequencing data. *Nucleic Acids Research*, 42(D1), D68–D73.

Kristensen, L. S., Andersen, M. S., Stagsted, L. V., Ebbesen, K. K., Hansen, T. B. and Kjems, J. (2019). The biogenesis, biology and characterization of circular RNAs. *Nature Reviews Genetics*, 20(11), 675–691.

Kufel, J. and Grzechnik, P. (2018). Small nucleolar RNAs tell a different tale. *Trends in Genetics*, 35(2), 104–117. doi: 10.1016/j.tig.2018.11.005.

Kunkel, B. N. and Harper, C. P. (2017). The roles of auxin during interactions between bacterial plant pathogens and their hosts. *Journal of Experimental Botany*, 69(2), 245–254.

Kurihara, Y. and Watanabe, Y. (2004). Arabidopsis micro-RNA biogenesis through Dicer-like 1 protein functions. *Proceedings of the National Academy of Sciences*, 101(34), 12753–12758.

Lai, S. K., Wang, Y. Y. and Hanes, J. (2009). Mucus-penetrating nanoparticles for drug and gene delivery to mucosal tissues. *Advanced Drug Delivery Reviews*, 61(2), 158–171.

Landthaler, M., Yalcin, A. and Tuschl, T. (2004). The human DiGeorge syndrome critical region gene 8 and its D. melanogaster homolog are required for miRNA biogenesis. *Current Biology*, 14(23), 2162–2167.

Law, J. A. and Jacobsen, S. E. (2010). Establishing, maintaining and modifying DNA methylation patterns in plants and animals. *Nature Reviews Genetics*, 11(3), 204.

Lee, M. S., Koo, S., Jeong, D. G. and Tesh, V. L. (2016). Shiga toxins as multi-functional proteins: Induction of host cellular stress responses, role in pathogenesis and therapeutic applications. *Toxins*, 8(3), 77.

Lee, Y., Ahn, C., Han, J., Choi, H., Kim, J., Yim, J. et al. (2003). The nuclear RNase III Drosha initiates microRNA processing. *Nature*, 425(6956), 415.

Legnini, I., Di Timoteo, G., Rossi, F., Morlando, M., Briganti, F., Sthandier, O. et al. (2017). Circ-ZNF609 is a circular RNA that can be translated and functions in myogenesis. *Molecular Cell*, 66(1), 22–37. e29.

Li, L. C. (2017). Small RNA-guided transcriptional gene activation (RNAa) in mammalian cells In *RNA Activation. Advances in Experimental Medicine and Biology*, 983, 1–20. doi: 10.1007/978-981-10-4310-9_1.

Li, L. C., Okino, S. T., Zhao, H., Pookot, D., Place, R. F., Urakami, S. et al. (2006). Small dsRNAs induce transcriptional activation in human cells. *Proceedings of the National Academy of Sciences*, 103(46), 17337–17342.

Li, Y., Lu, Y. G., Shi, Y., Wu, L., Xu, Y. J., Huang, F. et al. (2014). Multiple rice microRNAs are involved in immunity against the blast fungus Magnaporthe oryzae. *Plant Physiology*, 164(2), 1077–1092.

Li, Z., Huang, C., Bao, C., Chen, L., Lin, M., Wang, X. et al. (2015). Exon-intron circular RNAs regulate transcription in the nucleus. *Nature Structural & Molecular Biology*, 22(3), 256.

Lippman, Z., May, B., Yordan, C., Singer, T. and Martienssen, R. (2003). Distinct mechanisms determine transposon inheritance and methylation via small interfering RNA and histone modification. *PLoS Biology*, 1(3), e67.

Liu, B., Sun, L., Liu, Q., Gong, C., Yao, Y., Lv, X. et al. (2015). A cytoplasmic NF-κB interacting long noncoding RNA blocks IκB phosphorylation and suppresses breast cancer metastasis. *Cancer Cell*, 27(3), 370–381.

Lord, J. M. and Roberts, L. M. (1998). Toxin entry: Retrograde transport through the secretory pathway. *The Journal of Cell Biology*, 140(4), 733–736.

Malone, C. D. and Hannon, G. J. (2009). Small RNAs as guardians of the genome. *Cell*, 136(4), 656–668.

Marnef, A., Richard, P., Pinzón, N. and Kiss, T. (2014). Targeting vertebrate intron-encoded box C/D 2′-O-methylation guide RNAs into the Cajal body. *Nucleic Acids Research*, 42(10), 6616–6629.

Martin, S. E. and Caplen, N. J. (2007). Applications of RNA interference in mammalian systems. *Annual Review of Genomics and Human Genetics*, 8, 81–108.

Mastorakos, P., Da Silva, A. L., Chisholm, J., Song, E., Choi, W. K., Boyle, M. P. et al. (2015). Highly compacted biodegradable DNA nanoparticles capable of overcoming the mucus barrier for inhaled lung gene therapy. *Proceedings of the National Academy of Sciences*, 112(28), 8720–8725.

Mattick, J. S., Taft, R. J. and Faulkner, G. J. (2010). A global view of genomic information – moving beyond the gene and the master regulator. *Trends in Genetics*, 26(1), 21–28.

Mattson, M. P. (2000). Apoptosis in neurodegenerative disorders. *Nature Reviews Molecular Cell Biology*, 1(2), 120.

Matzke, M., Primig, M., Trnovsky, J. and Matzke, A. (1989). Reversible methylation and inactivation of marker genes in sequentially transformed tobacco plants. *The EMBO Journal*, 8(3), 643–649.

McKinney, H. (1929). Mosaic diseases in the Canary Islands, West Africa and Gibraltar. *Journal of Agricultural Research*, 39, 577–578.

Memczak, S., Jens, M., Elefsinioti, A., Torti, F., Krueger, J., Rybak, A. et al. (2013). Circular RNAs are a large class of animal RNAs with regulatory potency. *Nature*, 495(7441), 333.

Mette, M., Aufsatz, W., Van der Winden, J., Matzke, M. and Matzke, A. (2000). Transcriptional silencing and promoter methylation triggered by double-stranded RNA. *The EMBO Journal*, 19(19), 5194–5201.

Morris, K. V. (2005). siRNA-mediated transcriptional gene silencing: The potential mechanism and a possible role in the histone code. *Cellular and Molecular Life Sciences CMLS*, 62(24), 3057–3066.

Morris, K. V. and Mattick, J. S. (2014). The rise of regulatory RNA. *Nature Reviews Genetics*, 15(6), 423–437.

Muhammad, T., Zhang, F., Zhang, Y. and Liang, Y. (2019). RNA interference: A natural immune system of plants to counteract biotic stressors. *Cells*, 8(1), 38.

Nagano, T., Mitchell, J. A., Sanz, L. A., Pauler, F. M., Ferguson-Smith, A. C., Feil, R. et al. (2008). The Air noncoding RNA epigenetically silences transcription by targeting G9a to chromatin. *Science*, 322(5908), 1717–1720.

Nguyen, K., Dang, P. N. and Alsberg, E. (2013). Functionalized, biodegradable hydrogels for control over sustained and localized siRNA delivery to incorporated and surrounding cells. *Acta Biomaterialia*, 9(1), 4487–4495.

Nobori, T., Velásquez, A. C., Wu, J., Kvitko, B. H., Kremer, J. M., Wang, Y. et al. (2018). Transcriptome landscape of a bacterial pathogen under plant immunity. *Proceedings of the National Academy of Sciences*, 115(13), E3055–E3064.

Pal-Bhadra, M., Bhadra, U. and Birchler, J. A. (1997). Cosuppression in Drosophila: Gene silencing of Alcohol dehydrogenase by white-Adh transgenes is Polycomb dependent. *Cell*, 90(3), 479–490.

Pepin, G., Perron, M. P. and Provost, P. (2012). Regulation of human Dicer by the resident ER membrane protein CLIMP-63. *Nucleic Acids Research*, 40(22), 11603–11617.

Pi, F., Binzel, D. W., Lee, T. J., Li, Z., Sun, M., Rychahou, P. et al. (2018). Nanoparticle orientation to control RNA loading and ligand display on extracellular vesicles for cancer regression. *Nature Nanotechnology*, 13(1), 82.

Ponnuswamy, N., Bastings, M. M., Nathwani, B., Ryu, J. H., Chou, L. Y., Vinther, M. et al. (2017). Oligolysine-based coating protects DNA nanostructures from low-salt denaturation and nuclease degradation. *Nature Communications*, 8, 15654.

Portnoy, V., Lin, S. H. S., Li, K. H., Burlingame, A., Hu, Z. H., Li, H. et al. (2016). saRNA-guided Ago2 targets the RITA complex to promoters to stimulate transcription. *Cell Research*, 26(3), 320.

Pumplin, N. and Voinnet, O. (2013). RNA silencing suppression by plant pathogens: Defence, counter-defence and counter-counter-defence. *Nature Reviews Microbiology*, 11(11), 745–760.

Quinn, J. J. and Chang, H. Y. (2016). Unique features of long non-coding RNA biogenesis and function. *Nature Reviews Genetics*, 17(1), 47.

Quiñones, B., Dulla, G. and Lindow, S. E. (2005). Quorum sensing regulates exopolysaccharide production, motility, and virulence in Pseudomonas syringae. *Molecular Plant-Microbe Interactions*, 18(7), 682–693.

Rana, T. M. (2007). Illuminating the silence: Understanding the structure and function of small RNAs. *Nature Reviews Molecular Cell Biology*, 8(1), 23.

Ravasi, T., Suzuki, H., Pang, K. C., Katayama, S., Furuno, M., Okunishi, R. et al. (2006). Experimental validation of the regulated expression of large numbers of non-coding RNAs from the mouse genome. *Genome Research*, 16(1), 11–19.

Reebye, V., Sætrom, P., Mintz, P. J., Huang, K. W., Swiderski, P., Peng, L. et al. (2014). Novel RNA oligonucleotide improves liver function and inhibits liver carcinogenesis in vivo. *Hepatology*, 59(1), 216–227.

Rietwyk, S. and Peer, D. (2017). Next-generation lipids in RNA interference therapeutics. *ACS Nano*, 11(8), 7572–7586.

Rinn, J. L., Kertesz, M., Wang, J. K., Squazzo, S. L., Xu, X., Brugmann, S. A. et al. (2007). Functional demarcation of active and silent chromatin domains in human HOX loci by noncoding RNAs. *Cell*, 129(7), 1311–1323.

Romano, N. and Macino, G. (1992). Quelling: Transient inactivation of gene expression in Neurospora crassa by transformation with homologous sequences. *Molecular Microbiology*, 6(22), 3343–3353.

Ronald, P. and Joe, A. (2017). Molecular mimicry modulates plant host responses to pathogens. *Annals of Botany*, 121(1), 17–23.

Roopenian, D. C. and Akilesh, S. (2007). FcRn: The neonatal Fc receptor comes of age. *Nature Reviews Immunology*, 7(9), 715.

Rosenblum, D., Joshi, N., Tao, W., Karp, J. M. and Peer, D. (2018). Progress and challenges towards targeted delivery of cancer therapeutics. *Nature Communications*, 9(1), 1–12.

Rubinsztein, D. C. (2002). Lessons from animal models of Huntington's disease. *TRENDS in Genetics*, 18(4), 202–209.

Rupaimoole, R. and Slack, F. J. (2017). MicroRNA therapeutics: Towards a new era for the management of cancer and other diseases. *Nature Reviews Drug Discovery*, 16(3), 203.

Saito, K., Inagaki, S., Mituyama, T., Kawamura, Y., Ono, Y., Sakota, E. et al. (2009). A regulatory circuit for piwi by the large Maf gene traffic jam in Drosophila. *Nature*, 461(7268), 1296.

Salzman, J., Gawad, C., Wang, P. L., Lacayo, N. and Brown, P. O. (2012). Circular RNAs are the predominant transcript isoform from hundreds of human genes in diverse cell types. *PloS One*, 7(2), e30733.

Schindewolf, C., Braun, S. and Domdey, H. (1996). In vitro generation of a circular exon from a linear pre-mRNA transcript. *Nucleic Acids Research*, 24(7), 1260–1266.

Schwartz, J. C., Younger, S. T., Nguyen, N.-B., Hardy, D. B., Monia, B. P., Corey, D. R. et al. (2008). Antisense transcripts are targets for activating small RNAs. *Nature Structural & Molecular Biology*, 15(8), 842.

Seila, A. C., Calabrese, J. M., Levine, S. S., Yeo, G. W., Rahl, P. B., Flynn, R. A. et al. (2008). Divergent transcription from active promoters. *Science*, 322(5909), 1849–1851.

Sen, G. L. and Blau, H. M. (2006). A brief history of RNAi: The silence of the genes. *The FASEB Journal*, 20(9), 1293–1299.

Setten, S. P. (2019). The current state and future directions of RNAi-based therapeutics. *Nature Reviews Drug Discovery*, 18(6), 421–446. doi: 10.1038/s41573-019-0017-4.

Shu, Y., Pi, F., Sharma, A., Rajabi, M., Haque, F., Shu, D. et al. (2014). Stable RNA nanoparticles as potential new generation drugs for cancer therapy. *Advanced Drug Delivery Reviews*, 66, 74–89.

Siomi, M. C., Sato, K., Pezic, D. and Aravin, A. A. (2011). PIWI-interacting small RNAs: The vanguard of genome defence. *Nature Reviews Molecular Cell Biology*, 12(4), 246.

Spiess, M. (1990). The asialoglycoprotein receptor: A model for endocytic transport receptors. *Biochemistry*, 29(43), 10009–10018.

Springer, A. D. and Dowdy, S. F. (2018). GalNAc-siRNA conjugates: Leading the way for delivery of RNAi therapeutics. *Nucleic Acid Therapeutics*, 28(3), 109–118.

Staiger, D., Korneli, C., Lummer, M. and Navarro, L. (2013). Emerging role for RNA-based regulation in plant immunity. *New Phytologist*, 197(2), 394–404.

Starke, S., Jost, I., Rossbach, O., Schneider, T., Schreiner, S., Hung, L. H. et al. (2015). Exon circularization requires canonical splice signals. *Cell Reports*, 10(1), 103–111.

Surana, S., Shenoy, A. R. and Krishnan, Y. (2015). Designing DNA nanodevices for compatibility with the immune system of higher organisms. *Nature Nanotechnology*, 10(9), 741.

Treiber, T., Treiber, N. and Meister, G. (2019). Regulation of microRNA biogenesis and its crosstalk with other cellular pathways. *Nature Reviews Molecular Cell Biology*, 20(1), 5–20.

Tsai, M. C., Manor, O., Wan, Y., Mosammaparast, N., Wang, J. K., Lan, F. et al. (2010). Long noncoding RNA as modular scaffold of histone modification complexes. *Science*, 329(5992), 689–693.

Turanov, A. A., Lo, A., Hassler, M. R., Makris, A., Ashar-Patel, A., Alterman, J. F. et al. (2018). RNAi modulation of placental sFLT1 for the treatment of preeclampsia. *Nature Biotechnology*, November 19. doi: 10.1038/nbt.4297.

Vagin, V. V., Sigova, A., Li, C., Seitz, H., Gvozdev, V. and Zamore, P. D. (2006). A distinct small RNA pathway silences selfish genetic elements in the germline. *Science*, 313(5785), 320–324.

Van der Ree, M., Van Der Meer, A., Van Nuenen, A., De Bruijne, J., Ottosen, S., Janssen, H. et al. (2016). Miravirsen dosing in chronic hepatitis C patients results in decreased micro RNA-122 levels without affecting other micro RNA s in plasma. *Alimentary Pharmacology & Therapeutics*, 43(1), 102–113.

Vaucheret, H. (2006). Post-transcriptional small RNA pathways in plants: Mechanisms and regulations. *Genes & Development*, 20(7), 759–771.

Vaucheret, H. (2008). Plant argonautes. *Trends in Plant Science*, 13(7), 350–358.

Vicens, Q. and Westhof, E. (2014). Biogenesis of circular RNAs. *Cell*, 159(1), 13–14.

Vigneswara, V. and Ahmed, Z. (2016). Long-term neuroprotection of retinal ganglion cells by inhibiting caspase-2. *Cell Death Discovery*, 2, 16044.

Voinnet, O. (2009). Origin, biogenesis, and activity of plant microRNAs. *Cell*, 136(4), 669–687.

Voutila, J., Reebye, V., Roberts, T. C., Protopapa, P., Andrikakou, P., Blakey, D. C. et al. (2017). Development and mechanism of small activating RNA targeting CEBPA, a novel therapeutic in clinical trials for liver cancer. *Molecular Therapy*, 25(12), 2705–2714.

Wadia, J. S., Stan, R. V. and Dowdy, S. F. (2004). Transducible TAT-HA fusogenic peptide enhances the escape of TAT-fusion proteins after lipid raft macropinocytosis. *Nature Medicine*, 10(3), 310.

Wang, Q., Sawyer, I. A., Sung, M. H., Sturgill, D., Shevtsov, S. P., Pegoraro, G. et al. (2016). Cajal bodies are linked to genome conformation. *Nature Communications*, 7, 10966.

Wang, Z. and Burge, C. B. (2008). Splicing regulation: From a parts list of regulatory elements to an integrated splicing code. *RNA*, 14(5), 802–813.

Wassenegger, M., Heimes, S., Riedel, L. and Sänger, H. L. (1994). RNA-directed de novo methylation of genomic sequences in plants. *Cell*, 76(3), 567–576.

Wassenegger, M. and Krczal, G. (2006). Nomenclature and functions of RNA-directed RNA polymerases. *Trends in Plant Science*, 11(3), 142–151.

Wilson, R. C. and Doudna, J. A. (2013). Molecular mechanisms of RNA interference. *Annual Review of Biophysics*, 42, 217–239.

Wilusz, J. E. (2018). A 360 view of circular RNAs: From biogenesis to functions. *Wiley Interdisciplinary Reviews: RNA*, 9(4), e1478.

Yang, B., Ming, X., Cao, C., Laing, B., Yuan, A., Porter, M. et al. (2015). High-throughput screening identifies small molecules that enhance the pharmacological effects of oligonucleotides. *Nucleic Acids Research*, 43(4), 1987–1996.

Yin, Q. F., Yang, L., Zhang, Y., Xiang, J. F., Wu, Y. W., Carmichael, G. G. et al. (2012). Long noncoding RNAs with snoRNA ends. *Molecular Cell*, 48(2), 219–230.

Yoon, J. H., Abdelmohsen, K., Srikantan, S., Yang, X., Martindale, J. L., De, S. et al. (2012). LincRNA-p21 suppresses target mRNA translation. *Molecular Cell*, 47(4), 648–655.

Yue, X., Schwartz, J. C., Chu, Y., Younger, S. T., Gagnon, K. T., Elbashir, S. et al. (2010). Transcriptional regulation by small RNAs at sequences downstream from 3' gene termini. *Nature Chemical Biology*, 6(8), 621.

Zhang, B., Gunawardane, L., Niazi, F., Jahanbani, F., Chen, X. and Valadkhan, S. (2014). A novel RNA motif mediates the strict nuclear localization of a long noncoding RNA. *Molecular and Cellular Biology*, 34(12), 2318–2329.

Zhang, H., Lang, Z. and Zhu, J. K. (2018). Dynamics and function of DNA methylation in plants. *Nature Reviews Molecular Cell Biology*, 19(8), 489.

Zhang, X. O., Dong, R., Zhang, Y., Zhang, J. L., Luo, Z., Zhang, J. et al. (2016). Diverse alternative back-splicing and alternative splicing landscape of circular RNAs. *Genome Research*, 26(9), 1277–1287.

Zhang, Y., Zhang, X. O., Chen, T., Xiang, J. F., Yin, Q. F., Xing, Y. H. et al. (2013). Circular intronic long noncoding RNAs. *Molecular Cell*, 51(6), 792–806.

Zhong, X., Du, J., Hale, C. J., Gallego-Bartolome, J., Feng, S., Vashisht, A. A. et al. (2014). Molecular mechanism of action of plant DRM de novo DNA methyltransferases. *Cell*, 157(5), 1050–1060.

Zhou, J. and Rossi, J. (2017). Aptamers as targeted therapeutics: Current potential and challenges. *Nature Reviews Drug Discovery*, 16(3), 181.

Zhu, Q. H., Fan, L., Liu, Y., Xu, H., Llewellyn, D. and Wilson, I. (2013). miR482 regulation of NBS-LRR defense genes during fungal pathogen infection in cotton. *PLoS One*, 8(12), e84390.

Zimmermann, T. S., Karsten, V., Chan, A., Chiesa, J., Boyce, M., Bettencourt, B. R. et al. (2017). Clinical proof of concept for a novel hepatocyte-targeting GalNAc-siRNA conjugate. *Molecular Therapy*, 25(1), 71–78.

Zuckerman, J. E. and Davis, M. E. (2015). Clinical experiences with systemically administered siRNA-based therapeutics in cancer. *Nature Reviews Drug Discovery*, 14(12), 843–856.

13

ROLE OF ADDITIVES AND NUTRIENT SUPPLEMENTATION FOR ENHANCEMENT OF SOMATIC EMBRYOGENESIS IN *MOMORDICA CHARANTIA* L.

Subhasree Das, Anwesh Roy, Puja Chakraborty and Sarmistha Sen Raychaudhuri

Introduction

The genus *Momordica* consists of about 19 species of herbaceous plants that are mainly climbers and belong to the family *Cucurbitaceae*. Most of the plants of this family are popularly used as vegetable and are rich in nutrients. *Momordica charantia* L. (*M. charantia*) is a monoecious climber found widely in India, and the fruits are consumed in all the states either as juice or after cooking. In this country, the ethnobotanical uses of *M. charantia* are mainly for lowering blood glucose level in diabetic patients. It is generally thought that the more bitter the plant is, the more medicinal value it has (Sethi, 2012). The fruits of bitter gourd contain very high amounts of vitamins A and C, iron and minerals (Sultana and Bari Miah, 2003; Paul et al., 2009).

M. charantia is a fast-growing vine and seeds germinate readily in moist warm soil even if covered with pasture or shaded by crops. Seedling development and growth is very rapid. Flowering starts about 30 days after germination and young fruits can be harvested 10–14 days after anthesis. Continuous harvesting of all young fruits prolongs crop duration (Holm et al., 1991).

In vitro tissue culture is a technique by which totipotent plant cells can be exploited to regenerate into a whole plant (George et al., 2008). Several authors have attempted tissue culture of *M. charantia* to obtain unique plants with novel phytochemicals. Several additives like coconut water, casein hydrolysate and polyamines have been supplemented in the culture media to enhance somatic embryogenesis. In our laboratory, *M. charantia* has been cultured and simultaneously studied to observe the expression of *SERK* gene as well as effects of polyamines like Putrescine, Spermidine and Spermine to enhance embryogenesis. In the present investigation. Studies on *M. charantia* will be correlated with stress and trace elemental profile as well as *SERK* gene expression. HPLC method has been utilized to determine the content of antidiabetic factor charantin in *M. charantia* var charantia and *M. charantia* var muricata varieties.

DOI: 10.4324/9781003033448-17

Habitat and Traditional Uses

Numerous studies have revealed that, *M. charantia*, a member of the *Cucurbitaceae* family, renders broad-ranging health benefits such as anti-cancer, anti-viral, anti-inflammatory, analgesic, hypolipidemic and hypocholesterolemic effects (Tan et al., 2016). *M. charantia* fruits can reduce blood sugar level in diabetic rats as the fruit possesses phytochemicals such as momordicin and charantin, along with insulin-like peptides and a few galactose-binding lectins (Patel et al., 2012). It was also demonstrated that an aqueous solution of unripe *M. charantia* fruits can fractionally stimulate insulin release from isolated beta cells in obese hypoglycemic mice (Grover and Yadav, 2004). Different plant parts of *M. charantia* such as leaf, vine, root and seed have anti-helminthic, emmenagogue, antidiabetic, and anti-pneumonial properties as well. A wide array of recent studies has highlighted the hypoglycemic activity of *M. charantia*. Its use as an alternative treatment for diabetes mellitus has been proposed since it does not have any major side effects unlike the current methods of diabetes treatment. Phytochemical screening of this plant revealed the presence of some chemical compounds possessing antidiabetic property. Among them charantin has drawn considerable attention from researchers (Paul et al., 2009).

The mechanism of the antidiabetic activity of charantin *is* being explored but has not been very well established. The most plausible mechanisms for the hypoglycemic effects of extracts of *M. charantia* may be due to some physiological, pharmacological and biochemical means (Akhtar et al., 1981; Ahmed et al., 2004; Hlaing and Kyaw, 2005). A study proposed *M. charantia* extract to increase insulin sensitivity by causing reduction in PTP 1B activity, which is a physiological antagonist in the insulin-signaling pathway (Klomann et al., 2010). Extracts of *M. charantia* are also known to have lipid-lowering effect (Senanayake et al., 2007). Moreover, *M. charantia* has been shown to have an effective role in non-insulin-dependent diabetes mellitus (NIDDM) (Leung et al., 2009). Bitter melon was reported to increase the mass of beta cells and insulin production in the pancreas (Shetty et al., 2005; Chao and Huang, 2003). An amelioration of about 30% in fasting blood glucose was found when streptozotocin-induced diabetic rats have been provided with an edible portion of bitter melon at 10% level in the diet (Shetty et al., 2005). It has been observed in biochemical studies that bitter melon plays a role in the regulation of cell-signaling pathways in pancreatic beta cells, adipocytes and muscles (Chao and Huang, 2003; Chuang et al., 2006). Moreover, the momordicosides (Q, R, S and T) are known to stimulate GLUT4 (Glucose transporter type 4) translocation of the cell membrane and increases the activity of AMP-activated protein kinase (AMPK) in both L6 myotubes and 3T3-L1 adipocytes. This causes an enhancement in fatty acid oxidation and glucose disposal during glucose tolerance tests in both insulin-sensitive and insulin-insensitive mice (Tan et al., 2008).

Phytochemistry

Momordica charantia contains bioactive chemical compounds such as glycosides, saponins, alkaloids, fixed oils, triterpenes, proteins and steroids. Among them, the compound that is responsible for the antidiabetic action is a non-nitrogenous substance charantin, which is a mixture of two compounds, namely, sitosteryl glucoside and stigmasteryl glucoside. Though there are other hypoglycemic agents as well, we have focused our studies exclusively on charantin. Charantin can potentially reduce blood sugar level in both diabetic and non-diabetic rabbits (Raman and Lau, 1996). These chemicals are concentrated in fruits of *M. charantia* and has shown more pronounced hypoglycemic/antihyperglycemic activity (Mahmoud et al., 2017). Studies have also reported that the compound is more effective than the oral hypoglycemic agent, tolbutamide (Cousens, 2008).

In a current study carried out in our laboratory, charantin was estimated using reverse phase high performance liquid chromatography (RP-HPLC) from two varieties of *M. charantia*, namely *M. charantia* var *charantia* and *M. charantia* var *muricata* collected from two different districts of West Bengal, India. The result showed higher charantin content in var *charantia* than var *muricata* from fruits of both the areas. However, seeds contain less amount of or no charantin in both varieties of fruits (Figures 13.1 and 13.6).

In a current investigation, antimicrobial activity of fruit extracts of *M. charantia* against Gram-positive (*Staphylococcus aureus*) and Gram-negative bacteria (*Escherichia coli*) has been determined. For this study, two varieties of *M. charantia*, namely *M. charantia* var *charantia* and *M. charantia* var *muricata* were used as test systems. The antimicrobial activity of *M. charantia* var *charantia* was found to be more effective than that of the *charantia* var *muricata* collected from two different districts of West Bengal, India. The seeds in both varieties were found to possess lesser antimicrobial activity (Figures 13.2, 13.3 and 13.6).

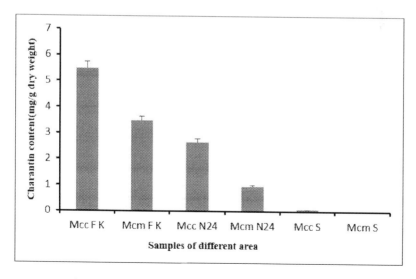

FIGURE 13.1   Charantin content in *M. charantia*

Source: (Unpublished Inhouse Data).

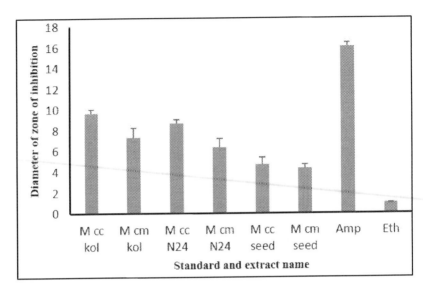

FIGURE 13.2 Zone of inhibition for *E.coli*

Source: (Unpublished Inhouse Data).

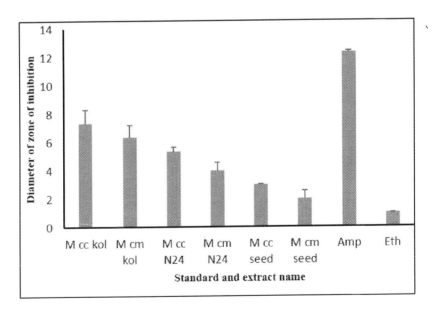

FIGURE 13.3 Zone of inhibition for *S. aureus*

Source: (Unpublished Inhouse Data).

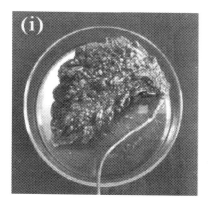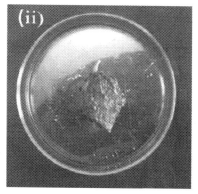

FIGURE 13.4 Fruits of *M. charantia* (i) variety charantia; (ii) variety muricata

Source: (Unpublished Inhouse Data).

Trace Elements in *M. charantia*

Medicinal plants are frequently used for prevention, diagnosis and treatment of diseases, and they are referred to as herbal medicines. These plants possess some important factors in small amounts having both therapeutic and prophylactic properties (IARC, 2002). Around 17 elements in the periodic table are found to be required by higher plants. Of these essential elements, nine are recognized as macronutrients (carbon, C; hydrogen, H; oxygen, O; nitrogen, N; potassium, K; calcium, Ca; magnesium, Mg; phosphorus, P, and sulphur, S), which are are normally present in plant tissues at concentrations greater than 0.1% (dry weight). Micronutrients are defined as essential elements that are required in plant tissues at concentrations less than 100 μg/g dry weight. Eight micronutrients essential for higher plants- boron(B), chlorine (Cl), copper(Cu), iron(Fe), manganese (Mn), molybdenum (Mo), nickel(Ni), and zinc(Zn) are referred to as trace elements also (Asher, 1991). They are required by plants and animals fundamentally for the formation of pigments and enzymes respectively. Their function is mainly to facilitate certain important metabolic processes. Many of the trace elements conjugate with vitamins in the metabolism of carbohydrates, fats and proteins. Metabolic disorders may arise due to the absence of trace elements (Ogurinola et al., 2004). The fruits of *M. charantia* contain about 7% ash. The major elements present in *M. charantia* are silicon (Si), P, Fe, sodium(Na), Zn, Cu, Ca and strontium (Sr). The group (authors) screened plants of Congolese origin, and it showed that the plants possess trace amounts of alkaloids and saponins but no flavonoids, tannins, steroids and terpenes. They also found Zn) to be the major trace element followed by chromium (cr) (Ayoola and Adeyeye, 2010). Some trace elements have been thought to be essential for glucose tolerance and utilization. Vanadium-containing compounds have been evaluated clinically for the treatment of human diabetic patients (Kosanovic et al., 2009).

The spectral study of plant products using laser-induced breakdown spectroscopy (LIBS) found several atomic lines such as Na, K, Mg, Ca, Fe, aluminium (Al) and so on. The concentrations of these minerals were determined and the correlation between the concentration of these elements/minerals and their defined role in diabetes management was studied in normal as well as diabetic animal models (Rai et al., 2009). From the Energy Dispersive X-Ray Florescence (EDXRF) study of *M. charantia,* Obiajunwa et al., 2002 revealed that aerial part of *M. charantia* contains Fe, Mn, Cu, Zn, Ni, titanium(Ti), rubidium (Ru), Sr, bromine(Br) and vanadium (V). The different parts of the plants such as the stem, root, unripe fruit flesh, ripe fruit flesh, leaf and seed parts were taken analyzed by induced coupled plasma optical emission spectroscopy (ICP-OES). The levels of cadmium (Cd), lead (Pb), Ni, Fe, Zn, Cu, Al, Cr and Mn were determined. All the parts were found to contain higher amounts of Al, Fe, Mn and Zn; except Zn and Mn, the root was found to contain high concentrations of all the other elements. Mn was found highest in leaves and branches. The trace elemental content studied in all parts of the bitter melon showed high accumulation of Fe and Al in the root whereas in other parts trace elements level was below the maximum permissible limits (Savsatli et al., 2016). According to Sofowora 1982, the major constituents in *M. charantia* root are Si, Ca, P, Sr, Cu, Pb, Zn, Na, and Fe. In an experiment the plants were treated with organic and non-organic fertilizers and pesticides, and an inductively coupled plasma atomic emission spectroscopy (ICP-AES) analysis of unripe fruit was performed. Higher values for total bitters, vitamin C, and mineral contents (K, Ca, Mg, Fe, Na, Zn, Cu, and Mn) were found in organic *M. charantia* (OMC). In contrast, non-organic fruits of *M. charantia* (NMC) contained a higher amount of toxic heavy metals such as Pd and cadmium (Cd) (Itankar et al., 2016).

Induced diabetes mellitus in rats resulted in an increase in lipid peroxide levels in blood. Reduced activity of red blood cell (RBC) antioxidant enzymes such as superoxide dismutase, catalase, glutathione reductase, and glutathione peroxidase was found to be associated with depletion of plasma reduced glutathione (GSH) and Cu, Zn, Fe, Mg and selenium (Se) levels. Oral treatment of diabetic rats with *M. charantia* and other three plants (500 mg/kg of body weight) lowered the blood glucose level as well as inhibited the formation of lipid peroxides, reactivated the antioxidant enzymes, and restored the levels of GSH and metals such as Cu, Zn, Fe, Mg and Se in the model (Chandra et al., 2008). A study to evaluate and compare the scavenging efficiency of *M. charantia* for Cu, cobalt (Co), Cd and Fe uptake in *in vitro* plants cultured using a mixture of 2,4-dichlorophenoxyacetic acid (2,4-D) (2.5 mg/L) and Napthaleneacetic acid (NAA) (2.0 mg/L) in *Murashige and Skoog basal medium* (MS basal medium). Atomic absorption spectrophotometric data showed lesser absorption of the metals by *in vitro* plants as compared to field-grown plants (Niamat et al., 2012).

In a current study (data unpublished) by our group, eight varieties of *M. charantia* were collected from different districts of West Bengal, India, and trace elemental

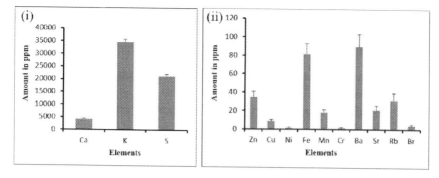

FIGURE 13.5   Trace elemental profiling of *M. charantia* fruit pulp from North 24 Parganas, West Bengal, India:(i) Ca, K, S (ii) Zn, Cu, Ni, Fe, Mn, Cr, Ba, Sr, Rb, Br

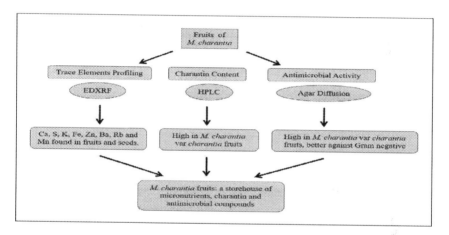

FIGURE 13.6   Schematic diagram showing medicinal properties of fruits of *M. charantia*

content of the fruit pulp was determined by EDXRF technique. Macronutrients like Ca, S and K were found to be higher in concentration (ppm level) and also high amounts of micronutrients (ppm level) such as Fe, Zn, barium (Ba), Rb and Mn have been accumulated in fruits. Cu and S have been found in greater amount in the seeds within the fruits than the fruit pulp (Figure 13.5 (i) and 13.5 (ii)).

Organogenesis in *M. charantia*

In comparison with animals, plants possess a high level of developmental flexibility and exhibit various types of tissue or organ regeneration. Plant regeneration through *de novo* shoot organogenesis in tissue culture is the determining step in plant transformation and micropropagation procedures (Ikeuchi et al., 2016; Motte et al., 2014). However, this plan of action is required by the factors that are particularly able to persuade developmental programs that lead to the formation of entire

TABLE 13.1 Organogenesis in *M. charantia*

Type of Explant	Media, Hormone, Additives	Reference
Cotyledon explant	MS medium, high concentration of auxin, low concentration of cytokinin, shoot regeneration from callus, regenerated shoot, developed on MS medium with 0.5 mg/L of kinetin and gibberellic acid (GA_3) Root initiation in 0.5 mg/L NAA supplemented half strength MS	(Islam et al., 1994)
Seedling explant	Shoot differentiation on MS medium supplemented with 6-benzylaminopurine (BAP) Root callus formed on indole-3-butyric acid (IBA) and 2, 4-D. Multiple shoots and roots were formed on MS media without hormones.	(Agarwal et al., 2004)
Nodal segment and shoot tip	MS medium supplemented with different concentrations and combinations of cytokinins (BAP, kinetin) and auxins (NAA, IAA). Direct shoot regeneration occurs.	(Sultana and Bari Miah, 2003)
Cotyledonary node and shoot tip explant	Poor differentiation	(Malik et al., 2007)
Leaf explant	Media supplemented with 2, 4-D (2mg/L) resulted in callogenesis.	(Saglam S, 2017)

organs from virtually differentiated cells (Pernisová et al., 2009). The interaction between auxin and cytokinin during organogenesis is a long-known phenomenon. Skoog and Miller (1957) in their study identified auxin-to-cytokinin concentration ratios as an important factor in regulating the developmental fate of plant tissue explants. Since then, the role of both growth factors in plant development has been extensively studied (Table 13.1).

Somatic Embryogenesis in *M. charantia*

In vitro somatic embryogenesis is a type of vegetative propagation, in which somatic cells, differentiate into somatic embryos and later into regenerated plantlets. The developmental stages of somatic embryo resembles the zygotic embryo as exhibited by morphological characteristics of the embryos (Santacruz-Ruvalcaba et al., 1998; Liu et al., 2015). Somatic embryogenesis (SE) is an essential pathway for the regeneration of plant, biomass production, and genetic transformation (Elhiti et al., 2013; Feher A, 2015). Molecular biology techniques have provided new methods for studying the morphology of SE, embryo induction and development mechanism. Many genes and proteins related to SE have been identified in various species

TABLE 13.2 Somatic embryogenesis in *M. charantia*

Type of Explant	Media, Hormone, Additives	Reference
Leaf explant	Globular embryos produced in liquid MS medium supplemented with 1.5 mg/L 2, 4-D. Complete removal of 2, 4-D at later stages of the culture stimulated their further development.	(Thiruvengadam et al., 2006)
Leaf explant	MS medium supplemented with 0.5 mg/L NAA and 5 mg/L BAP. Somatic embryo developed after 21 days of callus culture. Media supplemented by polyamines viz putrescine, spermidine and Spermine, which were found to promote somatic embryogenesis.	(Paul et al., 2009)
Leaf explant	0.5 mg/L NAA and 5 mg/L BAP in MS medium. Formation of globular embryo confirmed by histology analysis and scanning electron microscopy (SEM). Casein hydrolysate and coconut water were found to enhance somatic embryo formation.	(Talapatra et al., 2014)
Petiole explant	For callus induction MS media was supplemented with NAA ($3\mu M$) and thiadiazuron (TDZ) ($1\mu M$) along with polyamines (Putrescine (Put), spermidine (spd), and Spermine (0.1, 0.5, 1.0 and $1.5\mu M$). Maximum percentage (95%) of compact greenish callus induced with $3\mu M$ NAA, $1\mu M$ TDZ and 1.0 Put. Maximum increase (74%) in fresh weight of organogenic calli was observed.	(Thiruvengadam et al., 2012)
Stem explant genotype Silifke	Media supplemented with 2, 4-D (8mg/L) resulted in callogenesis and plantlets were obtained by indirect somatic embryogenesis.	(Saglam S, 2017)

of plants (Liu et al., 2015). In various studies, it has been observed that both auxin and cytokinin are required for obtaining competent cells (Table 13.2).

Enhancement of Somatic Embryogenesis by Elicitors

Proteins play a crucial role in plant metabolism. Various studies reported protein accumulation during maturation phase of SE and changes in their profile or their function as somatic embryogenic receptors (Misra et al., 1993; Roja Rani et al., 2005). *In vitro* SE is a direct result of the impact of developmental and environmental conditions as well as culture media (Williams and Maheswaran, 1986). Nitrogen is known as a major component for *in vitro* morphogenesis and balance of nitrogen in culture media induces SE in some plant species. By observing the contents of polyamines, proline and proteins difference between embryogenic and

TABLE 13.3 Enhancement of somatic embryogenesis by elicitors in *M. charantia*

Elicitors	Media, PGRs	Reference
Coconut water (CW)	Embryogenic callus culture was set up from leaf disc explants in MS medium containing 0.5 mg/L NAA and 5mg/L BAP. Coconut water, an organic additive, was added in three different concentrations. A 2.3-fold increase in the number of embryos was observed in 5% CW-treated callus. But in 10% and 15% CW-treated callus, the results were not commendable.	(Talapatra et al., 2016)
Casein hydrolysate (CH)	SE was induced in MS media with 0.5 mg/L NAA and 5mg/L BAP. CH was added to enhance the number of somatic embryos in the culture. In the case of 1g/L CH, embryo count increased slightly (1.8-fold) than the control set without CH. However, in 2 g/L CH, 1.8-fold increase in somatic embryo formation was observed.	(Talapatra et al., 2016)
Polyamines		
Put	Crystal form of putrescine dihydrochloride was used in MS media supplemented with 0.5 mg/L NAA and 5mg/L BAP and 1mM Put resulted in 2.5-fold increase in the number of somatic embryos per 0.2 g of callus.	(Paul et al., 2009)
Spd	Crystal form of spd was added exogenously with 0.5 mg/L NAA, 5 mg/L BAP and 0.1μM spd. 1.8-fold increase in the number of somatic embryos per 0.2 g of callus.	(Paul et al., 2009)
Spm	Powdered form of spermine dehydrate was used to make the stock solution. MS media was supplemented with plant growth regulators (PGRs) (0.5 mg/L NAA, 5mg/L BAP and 0.1 μM Spm was added to the media). 2.3-fold increase in the number of somatic embryos was observed.	(Paul et al., 2009)

non-embryogenic tissues can be determined (Nieves et al., 2003). Various studies support the role of polyamines in the modulation of various physiological processes which range from cell growth and differentiation to stress responses (Table 13.3.) (Bais and Ravishankar, 2002); (Aziz A, 2003); (Gemperlova et al., 2005). The type and concentration of amino acid have been found to play pivotal roles in different stages of the SE process (Robichauda et al., 2004).

Stress-Induced Somatic Embryogenesis

Plants possess the special property called cellular totipotency. It is used as a model system for studying the mechanisms of dedifferentiation and redifferentiation of plant cells. SE is a reliable and useful tool for *in vitro* propagation of plants by exploitation of competent somatic cells in the presence of endogenous or exogenous signals. Ikeda-Iwai et al. (2003) developed the idea that stress treatment could induce formation of somatic embryo from shoot-apical-tip and floral bud explants. According to these authors, the somatic embryos grew into complete plantlets with normal morphology and some embryo-specific genes, for example ABI3 and FUS3 were expressed during embryogenesis. Stress induced by heavy metal ions and osmotic and dehydration stress resulted in induction of SE in *Arabidopsis*. The authors conjectured that at least five factors that is tissue used, developmental phase of the source plant, stress source, stress chemical concentration and duration of stress treatment are important for induction of somatic embryos of *A. thaliana*.

Effect of sodium arsenate on *M. charantia* L. seeds was studied *in vitro* by Ray and Raychaudhuri (2017). A comparative analysis on fruit yield and *in vitro* efficiency of *M. charantia* was conducted to establish callus culture from seeds collected from geographically arsenic-contaminated and arsenic-free areas of West Bengal. AAS analysis showed that content of eight metals (Ca, Cu, As, Zn, Fe, Mn, Pb and Cd) under excess arsenic treatment *in vitro* was determined. The level of endogenous As was also determined. Under As treatment the percentage of seed germination, fresh weight and dry weight of the seedlings grown *in vitro* were found to decrease in dose-dependent manner. The content of Ca both in root and shoot was decreased by As treatment. Mn content in roots was also increased, but no significant difference in root and shoot was found in Fe concentration. The concentration of Cu and Zn increased in a dose-dependent manner. Cd and Pb content decreased in both root and shoot. Plants require balance of inorganic nutrients for maximum growth and development under optimal and stressful conditions. Mineral deficiencies cause depression of plant growth and development. In plants there might be some metal-metal interactions or relation among ions which maintains the balance. Micronutrients are essential when present in lower concentrations for plant growth and development, but it can be toxic when present in higher concentrations. As is non-essential and toxic for plants.

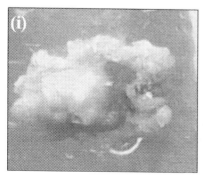

FIGURE 13.7   Somatic embryogenesis in *M. charantia* (i) 21-day-old first-passage callus culture; (ii) prolonged second-passage callus culture (Das et al., 2021).

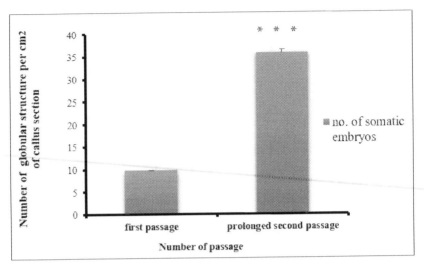

FIGURE 13.8   The graph represents the number of globular structures of somatic embryos per cm^2 of callus sections of first passage and prolonged second passage of *M. charantia* (Das et al., 2021)

In a study of our group (unpublished results), it was observed that when leaf explants of *M. charantia* were cultured in different MS mediums supplemented with and without auxin and cytokinin concentrations and combinations resulted in enhanced formation of somatic embryo count (Figure 13.7). It was observed that when cultures were maintained in the same culture medium without subculturing for a prolonged period of time, increase in number of somatic embryos occurred due to nutrition depletion (Figure 13.8). However, the molecular mechanism involved in the SE is not understood. Many authors reported the active involvement of the genes in regulation of the later stages of SE (Talapatra et al., 2016). Ectopic expression of a number of different genes in *Arabidopsis* has been shown to induce somatic cells to become embryogenic. *SERK* gene, a leucine-rich receptor-like kinase, has been shown to be a marker of embryogenesis in many plants. Our study was next focused on SE and *SERK* expression in *M. charantia* (Talapatra et al., 2014).

Expression of *SERK* Induced by Abiotic Stress

Plants face different types of environmental cues in the form of biotic and abiotic stress. Stress is an adapted physiological condition caused by several factors which lead to regulation of gene expression, signal transduction, accumulation of stress-related genes and activation of various defence mechanisms in plants (Figure 13.10) (Li et al., 2017). Recent studies indicated a cross talk between plant signaling pathways and extracellular stress (Fujita et al., 2006). Receptor-like-kinases (RLKs) are a group of transmembrane proteins pivotal for communication between external stimuli and internal cell signaling. RLKs possess three domains: extracellular domain for receiving extracellular signals, a single transmembrane domain located on plasma membrane and an intracellular cytoplasmic kinase domain for transducing signals to intracellular processes (Li J, 2010). The *somatic embryogenesis receptor kinase* also known as *SERK* belongs to leucine-rich-repeat like kinase II group. With the presence of proline-rich SPP motif in between the LRRs and transmembrane region of the protein structure makes the sequence distinguishable from other RLKs (Hecht et al., 2001). Some studies reported that *SERKs* are basically involved in SE in monocotyledons and dicotyledons and expresses in proembryogenic cells and declines after the globular stage (Somleva et al., 2000; Nolan et al., 2003; Singla et al., 2008). *SERK* gene expresses both in embryogenic and non-embryogenic callus cultures in *in vitro* conditions, associates with embryonic competence and acts as a molecular marker for SE (Sharma, Millam, Hedley et al., 2008; Sharma, Millam, Hein et al., 2008). *SERK* genes are involved in plant responses against biotic and abiotic environmental stresses (Santos and Arago, 2009). The SE process is so complicated that it gets manipulated by alterations in the amounts of micronutrients supplemented in the culture media. Several non-hormonal, stress-inducing factors help in the formation of competent cells (Pandey et al., 2012; Feher et al., 2003).

Talapatra et al. (2014) reported the isolation and characterization of an *SERK* gene ortholog designated as McSERK in *M. charantia*. Morphological and histological studies carried out by the authors revealed the presence of globular somatic embryo. According to these authors, the prerequisite for molecular regulation of SE is the expression of *SERK* gene playing a critical role in embryo formation.

Though the data is unpublished, a study conducted in our laboratory to find the effect of nutrition depletion, leaf explants of germinated seedlings of *M. charantia* were cultured on various strengths of MS medium and calcium chloride ($CaCl_2$) (full strength and half strength) in the presence and absence of different concentrations of auxin (NAA) and cytokinin (BAP) as plant hormones for first-passage subculture. Cultures from MS with hormone of first passage were further cultured on full strength (MS with hormone) and half strength (½ MS without hormone and ½ MS with hormone) medium for second-passage subculture. The same process was continued till fourth-passage subculture. From semi-quantitative expression study data, it was observed that *SERK* gene expresses in all passage cultures. In first-passage callus culture maximum band intensity was found in MS with hormone and decreases in ½ MS with hormone. In second-passage callus culture, maximum band intensity was observed in ½ MS without hormone in comparison with MS with hormone and ½ MS with hormone. Similar results were obtained from the third- and fourth-passage subcultures. From these results, it can be assumed that half strength of MS media and no hormone supplementation act as nutritional stress on growing somatic embryos, there by having a positive correlation with *SERK* expression. *SERK* protein was localized in the tissue sections of embryogenic cultures without subculturing for a prolonged period of time, treated with *SERK*-specific primary antibody and fluorescein isothiocyanate (FITC) conjugated

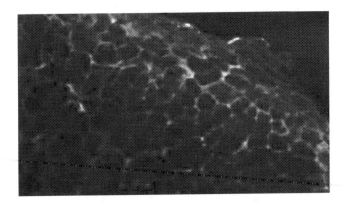

FIGURE 13.9   Transverse sections of callus derived from prolonged second passage culture of *M. charantia* showing localization of *SERK* protein (Das et al., 2021)

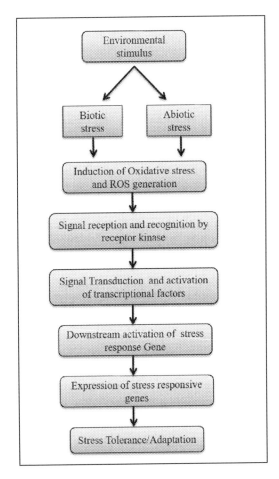

FIGURE 13.10   Schematic diagram representing plant cellular response against biotic and abiotic stress

secondary antibody. It was found that *SERK* protein localized on the peripheral region of the somatic embryo (Figure 13.9).

Concluding Remarks

From the discussion, it can be concluded that *M. charantia* has huge medicinal values, and it can be used as a remedy for several diseases. Moreover, SE has been a useful strategy to propagate the plant *in vitro*. Therefore, regeneration of plants using somatic embryogenesis with the help of tissue culture technique can be exploited to open new gates for researchers (Figure 13.11). Along with additives and hormones, abiotic stresses are found to be a potential inducer of SE. Even nutrient depletion can influence the initiation of embryogenesis that has been shown in this present investigation. Here, it has also been shown that *M. charantia* has antimicrobial activity against both Gram-positive and Gram-negative bacteria up to an extent and also possesses phytochemicals such as charantin, which hypoglycemic action. These properties can further be investigated to explain mechanisms behind

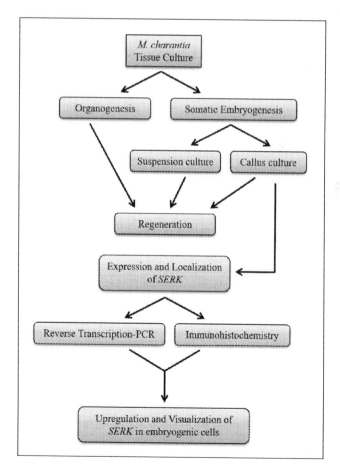

FIGURE 13.11   Schematic diagram representing tissue culture of *M. charantia*

the actions. It has also been discussed that trace elements such as Ca, K, S, Fe, and Mn and so on are found in *M. charantia* that can serve as a good source of micronutrients. Hence, in a nutshell, trace elements, different additives and nutrient supplements can be considered as few pivotal streams in plant research that may lead to betterment of crop production, agricultural development.

References

Agarwal, M and Kamal, R. (2004). *In vitro* clonal propagation of *Momordica charantia* L. *Indian Journal of Biotechnology*, 3, 426–430.

Ahmed, I., Cummings, E., Sharma, A. K., Adeghate, E. and Singh, J. (2004). Beneficial effects and mechanism of action of *Momordica charantia* juice in the treatment of streptozotocin-induced diabetes mellitus in rat. *Molecular and Cellular Biochemistry*, 261, 63–70.

Akhtar, M. S., Athar, M. A., and Yaqub, M. (1981). Effect of *Momordica charantia* on blood glucose level of normal and alloxan-diabetic rabbits. *Planta Medica*, 42, 205–212.

Asher, C.J. (1991). Beneficial Elements, Functional Nutrients, and Possible New Essential Elements. In Micronutrients in Agriculture, J.J. Mortvedt (Ed.).

Ayoola, P. B. and Adeyeye, A. (2010). Phytochemical and nutrient evaluation of *Carica papaya* (pawpaw) leaves. *International Journal Research and Review in Science*, 5, 325–328.

Aziz, A. (2003). Spermidine and related-metabolic inhibitors modulate sugar and amino acid levels in *Vitis vinifera* L: Possible relationships with initial fruitlet abscission. *Journal of Experimental Botany*, 54, 355–363.

Bais, H. P. and Ravishankar, G. A. (2002). Role of polyamines in the ontogeny of plants and their biotechnological applications. *Plant Cell Tissue Organ Culture*, 69, 1–34.

Chao, C. Y. and Huang, C. J. (2003). Bitter gourd (*Momordica charantia*) extract activates peroxisome proliferators-activated receptors and upregulates the expression of the acyl CoA oxidase gene in H4IIEC3 gepatoma cells. *Journal of Biomedical Science*, 10, 782–791.

Chandra, A., Mahdi, A. A., Singh, R. K., Mahdi, F. and Chander, R. (2008). Effect of Indian herbal hypoglycemic agents on antioxidant capacity and trace elements content in diabetic Rats. *Journal of Medicinal Food*, 11(3), 506–512.

Chuang, C. Y., Hsu, C., Chao, C. Y., Wein, Y. S., Kuo, Y. S. and Huang, C. J. (2006). Fractionation and identification of 9c, 11t, 13t-conjugated linolenic acid as an activator of PPAR in bitter gourd (*Momordica charantia* L.). *Journal of Biomedical Science*, 13, 763–772.

Cousens, G. (2008). *There is a Cure for Diabetes: The Tree of Life 21day Program.* California: North Atlantic Books, 191–192.

Das, S., Talapatra, S., & Raychaudhuri, S. S. (2021). Studies on the Effect of Starvation on Prolonged Callus Cultures and Alterations in SERK Gene Expression during Somatic Embryogenesis in Momordica charantia Linn. *Plant Tissue Culture and Biotechnology*, *31*(1), 109–114. DOI: 10.3329/ptcb.v31i1.54116

Elhiti, M., Stasolla, C. and Wang, A. M. (2013). Molecular regulation of plant somatic embryogenesis. *In Vitro Cellular & Developmental Biology – Plant*, 49, 631–642.

Feher, A. (2015). Somatic embryogenesis – Stress-induced remodeling of plant cell fate. *BBA Gene Regulatory Mechanisms*, 1849, 385–402.

Feher, A., Pasternak, T. and Dudits, D. (2003). Transition of somatic plant cells to an embryogenic state. *Plant Cell, Tissue and Organ Culture*, 74, 201–228.

Fujita, M., Fujita, Y., Noutoshi, Y., Takahashi, F., Narusaka, Y., Yamaguchi-Shinozaki, K. and Shinozaki, K. (2006). Crosstalk between abiotic and biotic stress responses: A current view from the points of convergence in the stress signaling networks. *Current Opinion in Plant Biology*, 9, 436–442.

Gemperlova, L., Eder, J. and Cvikrova, M. (2005). Polyamine metabolism during the growth cycle of tobacco BY-2 cells. *Plant Physiology and Biochemistry*, 43, 375–381.

George, E. F., Hall, M. A. and Klerk, G. J. D. (2008). Plant tissue culture procedure-background. In *Plant Propagation by Tissue Culture*. Springer, Dordrecht, 1–28.

Grover, J. K. and Yadav, S. P. (2004). Pharmacological actions and potential uses of *Momordica charantia*: A review. *Journal of Ethnopharmacology*, 93, 123–132.

Hecht, V., Vielle-Calzada, J. P., Hartog, M. V., Schmidt, E. D., Boutilier, K., Grossniklaus, U. and de Vries, S. C. (2001). The Arabidopsis somatic embryogenesis receptor kinase1 gene is expressed in developing ovules and embryos and enhances embryogenic competence in culture. *Plant Physiology*, 127, 803–816.

Hlaing, S. and Kyaw, H. A. (2005). Phytochemical Studies on *Momordica* spp. Linn. And Extraction and Isolation of Charantin from the fruit of *M. Charantia* L. *Journal of the Myanmar Academy of Arts and Science*, 3, 225–236.

Holm, L. G.; Pancho, J. V. Herberger, J. P. Plucknett, D. L. (1991). *A geographical atlas of world weeds*. Krieger Publisher Company, Malabar, Florida, USA.

IARC. (2002). *IARC Monographs on the Evaluation of Carcinogenic Risks to Humans, Volume 82, Some Traditional Herbal Medicines, Some Mycotoxins, Naphthalene and Styrene*. IARC Press, Lyon, France.

Ikeda-Iwai, M., Umehara, M., Satoh, S. and Kamada, H. (2003). Stress-induced somatic embryogenesis in vegetative tissues of *Arabidopsis thaliana*. *The Plant Journal*, 34, 107–114.

Ikeuchi, M., Ogawa, Y., Iwase, A. and Sugimoto, K. (2016). Plant regeneration: Cellular origins and molecular mechanisms. *Development*, 143, 1442–1451.

Islam, M. A., Hossain, M. D., Balbul, S. M. and Howlider, M. A. R. (1994). Unconventional feeds for broilers. *Indian Veterinary Journal*, 71, 775–780.

Klomann, S. D., Mueller, A. S., Pallauf, J. and Krawinkel, M. B. (2010). Antidiabetic effects of bitter gourd extracts in insulin-resistant db/db mice. *British Journal of Nutrtion*, 104, 1613–1620.

Kosanovic, M., Hasan, M. Y., Petrianu, G., Marzouqi, A., Abdulrahman, O. and Adem, A. (2009). Assesment of essential and toxic mineral elements in bitter gourd (*Momordica charantia*) fruit. *International Journal of Food properties*, 12, 766–773.

Leung, L., Birtwhistle, R., Kotecha, J. and Hannah, S. (2009). Anti-diabetic and hypo-glycaemic effects of *Momordica charantia* (bitter melon): A mini review. *British Journal of Nutrition*, 102, 1703–1708.

Li, J. (2010). Multi-tasking of somatic embryogenesis receptor like-protein kinases. *Current Opinion in Plant Biology*, 13, 509–514.

Li, Y., Liu, C., Guo, G., He, T., Chen, Z., Gao, R., Xu, H., Faheem, M., Lu, R. and Huang, J. (2017). Expression analysis of three *SERK*-like genes in barley under abiotic and biotic stresses. *Journal of Plant Interactions*, 12, 279–285.

Liu, C. P., Yang, L. and Long, S. H. (2015). Proteomic analysis of immature fraxinus man-dshurica cotyledon tissues during somatic embryogenesis: Effects of explant browning on somatic embryogenesis. *International Journal of Molecular Sciences*, 16, 13692–13713.

Mahmoud, M. F., El Ashry, F. Z., El Maraghy, N. N. and Fahmy, A. (2017). Studies on the antidiabetic activities of *Momordica charantia* fruit juice in streptozotocin-induced diabetic rats. *Pharmaceutical Biology*, 55, 758–765.

Malik, M. R., Wang, F., Dirpaul, J. M., Zhou, N., Polowick, P. L., Ferrie, A. M. R. and Krochko, J. E. (2007). Transcript profiling and identification of molecular markers for early microspore embryogenesis in *Brassica napus*. *Plant Physiology*, 144, 134–154.

Misra, S., Attree, S. M., Leal, I. and Fowke, L. C. (1993). Effect of Abscisic acid, osmoticum and dessication on synthesis of storage proteins during the development of white spruce somatic embryos. *Annals of Botany*, 71, 11–22.

Motte, H., Vereecke, D., Geelen, D. and Werbrouck, S. (2014). The molecular path to in vitro shoot regeneration. *Biotechnology Advances*, 32, 107–121.

Niamat, Rabia, Khan, Mir, Ali, Barkat and Khan, kiran Yasmin. (2012). Element content of some ethnomedicinal Ziziphus Linn. Species using atomic absorption spectroscopy technique. *Journal of Applied Pharmaceutical Sciences*, 02, 96–100.

Nieves, N., Segura-Nieto, M., Blanco, M. A., Sa´nchez, M., Gonza´lez, A. and Gonza´lez, J. L. (2003). Biochemical characterization of embryogenic and non-embryogenic calluses of sugarcane. *In Vitro Cellular & Developmental Biology – Plant*, 39, 343–345.

Nolan, K. E., Irwanto, R. R. and Rose, R. J. (2003). Auxin up-regulates MtSERK1 expression in both *Medicago truncatula* root-forming and embryogenic cultures. *Plant Physiology*, 133, 218–230.

Obiajunwa, Eusebius, Pelemo, D. A., Owolabi, Sandra, Fasasi, M. K. and Johnson-Fatokun, F. O. (2002). Characterisation of heavy metal pollutants of soils and sediments around a crude-oil production terminal using EDXRF. *Nuclear Instruments and Methods in Physics Research Section B: Beam Interactions with Materials and Atoms*, 194, 61–64. 10.1016/S0168-583X(02)00499-8.

Ogurinola, O. O., Odulae, J. E. and Elemo, B. O. (2004). Proximate analysis and pharmacognostical investigation of some medicinal plants: *Naudea latifolia*, *Morinda lucida*, *Alstonea congesis* and *Anchornea cordifolia*. *Nigerian Journal Research and Review in Science*, 3, 190–193.

Pandey, D. K., Singh, A. and Chaudhary, B. (2012). Boron-mediated plant somatic embryogenesis: A provocative model. *Journal of Botany*, 9.

Patel, D. K., Kumar, R., Laloo, D. and Hemalatha, S. (2012). Diabetes mellitus: An overview on its pharmacological aspects and reported medicinal plants having antidiabetic activity. *Asian Pacific Journal of Tropical Biomedicine*, 2, 411–420.

Paul, A., Mitter, K. and Raychaudhuri, S. S. (2009). Effect of polyamines on in vitro somatic embryogenesis in *Momordica charantia* L. *Plant Cell Tissue Organ Culture*, 97, 303–311.

Pernisová, M., Klíma, P., Horák, J., Válková, M., Malbeck, J., Soucek, P., Reichman, P., Hoyerová, K., Dubová, J., Friml, J., Zazímalová, E. and Hejátko, J. (2009). Cytokinins modulate auxin-induced organogenesis in plants via regulation of the auxin efflux. *Proceedings of the National Academy of Sciences of the United States of America*, 106, 3609–3614.

Rai, N. K., Rai, P. K., Pandhija, S., Watal, G., Rai, A. K and Bicanic, D. (2009). Application of LIBS in detection of antihyperglycemic trace elements in *Momordica charantia*. *Food Biophysics*, 4, 167–171.

Raman, A. and Lau, C. (1996). Anti-diabetic properties and phytochemistry of *Momordica charantia* L. (Cucurbitaceae). *Phytomedicine*, 2, 349–362.

Ray, S. K. and Raychaudhuri, S. S. (2017). Effect of Sodium Arsenate on *Momordica charantia* L. Seeds *in vitro*. *International Journal of Current Research in Biosciences and Plant Biology*, 4, 51–61.

Robichauda, R. L., Lessard, V. C. and Merkle, S. A. (2004). Treatments affecting maturation and germination of American chestnut somatic embryos. *Journal of Plant Physiology*, 161, 957–969.

Roja Rani, A., Reddy, V. D., Prakash Babu, P. and Padmaja, G. (2005). Changes in protein profiles associated with somatic embryogenesis in peanut. *Biologia Plantarum*, 49, 347–354.

Saglam, S. (2017). *In vitro* propagation of Bitter Gourd (*Momordica charantia* L.). *Scientific Bulletin Series F. Biotechnologies*, 21, 46–50.

Santacruz-Ruvalcaba, F., Gutiérrez-Mora, A. and Rodriguez-Garay, B. (1998). Somatic embryogenesis in some cactus and agave species. *Journal of the Professional Association for Cactus Development*, 3, 15–26.

Santos, M. O. and Arago, F. J. L. (2009). Role of SERK genes in plant environmental response. *Plant Signaling & Behavior*, 4, 1111–1113.

Savsatli, Y., Ozcan, A., Catal, M. İ., Seyis, F., Akbulut, M. and Akyuz Turumtay, E. (2016). Trace elements in bitter melon (*Momordica charantia*L.) and theirdistribution in different plant parts. *ARPN Journal of Agriculture and Biological Sciences*, 11, 437–443.

Senanayake, G.V., Maruyama, M., Sakono, M., Fukuda, N., Morishita, T., Yukizaki, C., Kawano, M. and Ohta, H. (2007). The effects of bitter melon (*Momordica charantia*) extracts on serum and liver lipid parameters in hamsters fed cholesterol-free and cholesterol-enriched diets. *Journal of Nutritional Science and Vitaminology*, 50, 253–257.

Sethi, P. (2012). *Momordica charantia* L-An Ethnobotanical Drug. *International Journal of Pharma and Bio Sciences*, 3, 1–5.

Sharma, S. K., Millam, S., Hedley, P. E., McNicol, J. and Bryan, G. J. (2008). Molecular regulation of somatic embryogenesis in potato: An auxin led perspective. *Plant Molecular Biology*, 68, 185–201.

Sharma, S. K., Millam, S., Hein, I. and Bryan, G. J. (2008b). Cloning and molecular characterisation of a potato *SERK* gene transcriptionally induced during initiation of somatic embryogenesis. *Planta*, 228, 319–330.

Shetty, A. K., Suresh, G., Sambaiah, K. K. and Salimath, P. V. (2005). Effect of bitter gourd (*Momordica charantia*) on glycaemic status in streptozotocin induced diabetic rats. *Plant Foods for Human Nutrition*, 60, 109–112.

Singla, B., Khurana, J. P. and Khurana, P. (2008). Characterization of three somatic embryogenesis receptor kinase genes from wheat, *Triticum aestivum*. *Plant Cell Reports*, 27, 833–843.

Skoog, F. and Miller, C. O. (1957). Chemical regulation of growth and organ formation in plant tissue cultures *in vitro*. *Symposia of the Society of Experimetal Biology*, 11, 118–131.

Sofowora, A. (1982). *Medicinal Plants and Traditional Medicine in Africa*. John Wiley and Sons, Chinchester, and New York (1ˢᵗ ed.).

Somleva, M., Kapchina-Toteva, V., Alexieva, V., Sergiev, I. and Karanov, E. (2000). Novel physiological properties of two cytokinin antagonists. *Journal of Plant Physiology*, 156, 623–627.

Sultana, R. S. and Bari Miah, M. A. (2003). *In vitro* Propagation of Karalla (*Momordica charantia* Linn.) from nodal segment and shoot tip. *Journal of Biological Sciences*, 3, 1134–1139.

Talapatra, S., Ghoshal, N. and Raychaudhuri, S. S. (2014). Molecular characterization, modeling and expression analysis of a somatic embryogenesis receptor kinase (*SERK*) gene in *Momordica charantia* L. during somatic embryogenesis. *Plant Cell, Tissue and Organ Culture*, 116, 271–283.

Talapatra, S., Goswami, P., Das, S., Raychaudhuri, S.S. (2016). Role of SERK During Somatic Embryogenesis and Its Interaction with Brassinosteroids. In Mujib, A. (Ed.), *Somatic Embryogenesis in Ornamentals and Its Applications*. Springer, New Delhi.

Tan, M. J., Ye, J. M., Turner, N., Hohnen-Behrens, Ke, C. Q., Tang, C. P., Chen, T., Weiss, H. C., Gesing, E. R., Rowland, A., James, D. E. and Ye, Y. (2008). Antidiabetic activities of triterpenoids isolated from bitter melon associated with activation of the AMPK pathway. *Chemistry & Biology*, 15, 263–273.

Tan, S. P., Kha, T. C., Parks, S. E. and Roach, P. D. (2016). Bitter melon (*Momordica charantia* L.) bioactive composition and health benefits: A review. *Food Reviews International*, 15, 181–202.

Thiruvengadam, M., Praveen, N. and Chung, I. M. (2012). An efficient *Agrobacterium tumefaciens*-mediated genetic transformation of bitter melon (*Momordica charantia* L.). *Australian Journal of Crop Science*, 6, 1094–1100.

Thiruvengadam, M., Varisai Mohamed, S., Yang, C. H. and Jayabalan, N. (2006). Development of an embryogenic suspension culture of bitter melon (*Momordica charantia* L.). *Scientia Horticulturae*, 109, 123–129.

Williams, E. G. and Maheswaran, G. (1986). Somatic embryogenesis: Factors influencing coordinated behaviour of cells as an embryogenic group. *Annals of Botany*, 57, 443–462.

Annexure

Bitter gourd: – Common name in India is *Karela* (scientific name – *Momordica charantia* L.) and belongs to the family *Cucurbitaceae*.

Somatic embryogenesis: – It is a process by which a plant has the ability to regenerate an embryo-like structure from its somatic (other than germinal) cells. These embryos are capable of producing a whole plant.

***In vitro*:** – *Performed* or taking place in a test tube, culture dish, or elsewhere outside a living organism.

Totipotency: – It is the ability of a single cell to divide and produce all of the differentiated cells in an organism.

Additive: – A substance added to culture media in small quantities to elicit the secondary metabolite contents of a plant.

Embryogenic culture: – A culture medium is a matrix where plants can grow in laboratory environment as necessary nutrients are provided within it. It contains all the important factors for growth such as sugar (carbon source), water, and salts, and in some cases, hormones etc. Therefore, an embryogenic culture is a technique where scientists use specifically designed culture media containing necessary ingredients for SE. It results in the quick and successful generation of somatic embryos.

Macronutrients and micronutrients: – Macronutrients are nutrients that are required in larger amounts by plants (N, K, Ca, Mg, P, and S) whereas micronutrients are required in trace amounts (Cl, Fe, B, Mn, Zn, Cu, Mo, and Ni) but both are essential for the growth of plants.

Stress tolerance: As a result of the inability to move, plants can adapt various strategies to combat extreme variations in environmental conditions or hazards such as temperature, draught, high salt content in the soil, heavy metal contamination (altogether called abiotic stress) and even pathogenic infections (biotic stress). This proficiency of withstanding stress is referred to as stress tolerance.

SERK: Behind every biological function, there is one or more genes responsible. Gene is a part of DNA which makes proteins and the proteins perform assigned functions to run the biological systems. SERK or *somatic embryogenesis receptor kinase* is a gene, giving rise to a protein called SERK as well, which has a key role in SE (explained earlier) and also in stress tolerance.

Explants: It is the part of a plant or a piece of tissue (generally leaves, shoot, root etc.), which can be transferred to a culture media for plant regeneration.

Subculture: A subculture is a new cell culture made by transferring some or all cells from a previous culture to a fresh growth medium.

Prolonged culture: It is a culture treated for a long passage of time, without transferring it to a fresh growth medium.

Immunohistochemistry: It is a common technique to stain biological samples using antibodies which can bind specific proteins selectively (antigens). As antigen-antibody interaction is involved, the term 'immune' appears; while "histo" means tissue. Generally, the antibodies are tagged with special substance/compounds and upon selective binding with the antigens present in the tissue; they give different colours that indicate the presence and abundance of different proteins in the tissue.

Herbaceous:–Plants which have the characteristic of herbs; generally with soft stem.

Cucurbitaceae:–It is the gourd family of flowering plants. According to Carolus Linnaeus, family is one of the eight major hierarchical taxonomic ranks, classified between order and genus. *Cucurbitaceae* family contains almost 98 genera and around 975 species; among which *M. charantia* L., our plant of interest is included.

Monoecious: Having both male and female reproductive organs in the same plant.

Ethnobotany: It is the scientific study of the traditional knowledge and customs of a people concerning plants and their medical, religious and other uses.

Anthesis: The flowering period of a plant, from the opening of the flower bud.

Regeneration: It is the capacity of a plant to renew or repair its cells physiologically.

HPLC: Chromatography is a technique to separate molecules/compounds present in a mixture on the basis of molecular properties such as molecular weight, polarity, charge, affinity to specific compounds and so on. The principle of HPLC or high-performance liquid chromatography exploits the polarity of compounds to separate by retaining them in a matrix of comparatively opposite polarity. When the matrix or stationary phase is non-polar and the mobile phase is polar, it is referred to as reverse phase HPLC (RP-HPLC).

Anticancer: Compounds which have the ability to partially or fully cure cancer.

Antiviral: Compounds which have the ability to partially or fully cure viral infections.

Anti-inflammatory: Compounds which have the ability to partially or fully reduce inflammation.

Hypolipidemic: Compounds which have the ability to lower lipid (fat) content in blood.

Hypocholesterolemic: Compounds which have the ability to lower cholesterol content in blood.

Hypoglycemic: Compounds which have the ability to lower glucose content in blood.

Anti-helmintic: Compounds which have the ability to partially or fully cure parasitic worm infection.

Emmenagogue: A substance that stimulates or increases menstrual flow.

PTP1B: Protein tyrosine phosphatase 1B or PTP 1B is a protein involved in insulin signaling pathway. It is a therapeutic target for type-2 diabetes.

Antagonist: It is a molecule which interferes with or inhibits the physiological action of another molecule.

Insulin signaling pathway: Insulin is a hormone secreted from the pancreatic beta cells in response to elevated levels of glucose in blood and helps to store glucose in muscle, liver and adipose tissues. Failure to uptake and store glucose results in diabetes. There is an insulin receptor on the cell membrane where insulin binds and induces a series of protein-protein interactions, resulting in the expression of different proteins involved in glucose storage and uptake. The cascade of processes is known as insulin signaling pathway.

Prophylactic: Having a property of preventing a disease.

ICP-OES and ICP-AES: ICP stands for inductively coupled plasma whereas OES and AES stand for optical emission spectrometry and atomic emission spectrometry, respectively. These two techniques are used to analyze the elemental content in a biological sample. Plasma of a gas is used to excite the atoms of elements present in the sample, leading the technique toward better sensitivity, multi-elemental analysis and high-throughput properties.

Molecular biology: It is a field of science to study the chemical structures and processes of biological phenomena that involve the basic units of life and including the interactions between DNA, RNA, proteins and their biosynthesis.

Elicitor: It is a molecule that triggers the physiological and morphological response in plants against microbial, physical or chemical factors. Elicitation is a process of induction or enhancement of secondary metabolite synthesis by plants to ensure their survival.

Dedifferentiation: A biological phenomenon in which a differentiated cell regains its capacity of cell division under certain conditions.

Redifferentiation: A biological phenomenon in which a dedifferentiated cell loses its capacity to cell division and mature.

14

APPLICATION OF COGNITIVE ERGONOMICS IN COMMUNICATION

A Social Perspective

Somnath Gangopadhyay

Communication

Communication may be described as the transferring of information from one person to another. Every communication deals with a sender, a message and a recipient. The communication is incomplete without a recipient. In a very simple way, it may be described as the interaction between the transmitting and the receiving part of a system. If a message is simple, and the transmission is complicated or done wrongly, then for the receiving part it is very difficult to understand the message. The result of which is no response from the recipient part or getting a wrong response from recipient part. This "no" or "wrong" will create problems in a system. If we do not consider this action or wrong action properly, then this wrong action will generate a condition which may be dangerous to humans and may cause harm to a system.

This wrong action due to wrong interpretation of message or information will generate system disturbances or failure. In a regular circumstance, this will be the accident. This accident may be without physical injury, there may be no bloodshed or no factures of bones.

An accident happened in communication (wrong understanding of information) is known as poor communication. The opposite of poor communication is good communication.

Good communication is about understanding of instructions. It is a skill, perhaps the most basic skill, that one can possess for enhancement of system performance. These include the medium used for communication. Medium of communication may be visual, auditory, tactile, olfactory or gustatory.

Visual Communication

Visual communication is the mode or form to convey ideas and information that can be seen. In other words, visual communication is the delivery of messages

DOI: 10.4324/9781003033448-18

Medium of Communication		
Auditory	**Visual**	
Describes what we hear	Describes what we see	
- Music - Noise - Silence	- Colors - Size - Patterns - Shapes	
Olfactory	**Gustatory**	**Tactile**
Describes what we smell	Describes what we Taste	Describes what we Touch or Feel
- Nice Fragrances - Bad Odors	- Bitter - Acidic - Sour - Sweet - Salty	- Texture - Movement - Temperatue

FIGURE 14.1   Medium of communication.

through visual elements, as charts, graphs or electronic images. Visual communication plays an important role in daily life. But it has no use for a visually challenged person. Perception is the key end part of communication. We have to give more importance to the perception of recipient end – whether the recipient will understand or will not be able to understand.

There are some rules of visual communication, and we have to obey these rules for good communication. The rules are as follows.

- Colors
- Typography
- Shapes
- Hierarchy
- Lines
- Iconography
- Contrast
- Order

All these rules depend on the objective related to visual communication. Two foremost questions should be asked before extending the communication visually: for whom and where.

If it is for children, then all the aforementioned rules or more precisely characters of factors will be changed differently from if it is for adults. Among the children and adults, the gender will play a reason for acceptability of this communication.

Placement or position (where) of visual communication will change the characters of factors. Here, visual communication depends on education and culture of the recipients.

Sometimes, this "where" also depends on some physical factors like level of illumination and sound of "where" it is placed.

Auditory Communication

Auditory communication, in other words, is the medium of sound to send as well as to receive information. It is the simplest way of interaction in the whole planet. Some rules are linked with this communication and they should be kept in mind during auditory communication.

The most important rule is the nature of auditory signal. The nature of auditory signal for a specific condition should be unique and same so the recipient will understand and recognise the condition easily. When it is verbal, then information must be very precise and very clear and simple, so for recipient end it will be very easy to understand. If the communication is through signal, then it may be one-way communication and that needs the recipient's prompt action. When it is verbal, it may be one way or both ways. All the ways of communication (signal, one way or both ways verbal) will entirely depend on the level of the understanding of the recipient.

In humans, the sound of our voice, including the tone, range, volume and speed affects how our messages are received and interpreted by others. We have to control these factors or change these factors depending on what we want to communicate and of course to whom we want to communicate. For example fast talkers will find it beneficial to slow down their speech when speaking to a thoughtful, introverted person or risk being unheard. That means the auditory communication as visual is a skill of the sender.

Auditory communication helps senders to express their ideas and feelings, and it, at the same time, helps recipients to understand emotion and thoughts of the senders. As a result, positive or negative relationships will be created between senders and recipients.

Tactile, Olfactory and Gustatory Communication

Tactile communication may be defined as what we communicate through the sense of touch. This communication may be or may not be mixed with verbal and auditory. By touching, a person can feel the texture of a surface and by feeling the pattern the recipient can identify an object. Through this way, a sender can transmit information to a recipient and can count his/her action. Through touch one can feel the temperature and pattern of a product and use of this feeling is important for recognition of a product especially by visually challenged persons.

Olfactory communication is the process by which organisms are able to communicate with each other through different scents and odors. It may be represented as information passing to recipient from sender side through scents and odors or vice versa. This way of communication may involve emotions of both the ends. Information or message through odors and scents will be equally applicable to visually, auditory challenged and normal persons.

It is a little bit difficult to consider the good communication through taste. Sometimes, to a recipient, a single taste may elicit, at the same time, some good (positive) and bad (negative) feelings. These feelings may be considered as related to emotions and past experiences.

Communication and Cognitive Science, Ergonomics

International Ergonomics Association (IEA) defines

> Ergonomics (or human factors) is the scientific discipline concerned with the understanding of interactions among humans and other elements of a system, and the profession that applies theory, principles, data and methods to design in order to optimize human well-being and overall system performance.

Cognitive ergonomics is concerned with mental processes, such as perception, memory, reasoning and motor response, as they affect interactions among humans and other elements of a system. Relevant topics include mental workload, decision-making, skilled performance, human–computer interaction, human reliability, work stress and training, as these may relate to human-system design.

All the different types of communications, discussed earlier, are concerned with human perception, recognition and finally the decision-making power and the aim of this relation toward development of artificial intelligence (AI). The systemic approach of ergonomics has an application in the building up of relationship between communication and cognition. Cognitive ergonomics is more focused on information receiving, processing and action of recipient end. This recipient end, in product design, is considered as the user of the product. The quality of a product towards usability depends on the understanding of a product by user through perfect form and function of the product.

Need of Cognitive Ergonomics

The way of human perception on received information and their action after processing of information is applied directly to the design of a product. It is the way of application of cognitive ergonomics in product design or in the design of interventions. By the application of cognitive ergonomics, the product will become user-friendly. This will decrease the chances of errors and at the same time the user performance and productivity will be increased.

The product will be designed in such a way that it will transfer the information to users (recipients) properly by considering the users' capabilities, limitations and needs.

The cognitive processing starts at the user part by receiving of information and ends in the motor system of human by action. The action, actually, is the result of user's decision in information processing.

In design or redesign of a product, by changing the communication part the usability of the product may be improved. It is true both in the development of website and AI. The ultimate destination is society. Society will be benefited.

Stress-Free Condition

If the design of a product in a system becomes user-friendly, then it will create a stress-free condition. The interaction between user and product will become more efficient. Moreover, stress-free condition will give comfort to the users. The prime objective of evaluation of a product is to find out whether the product is easily usable or not.

Cognitive Task Analysis (CTA): a Method for Product Evaluation

Cognitive ergonomics evaluates the operational tasks of user while using a particular product. The method identifies bottlenecks and critical paths to find out opportunities for improvement of a product. Improvement means to minimize the risks (such as human error) and to maximize the user understanding with the product. Misunderstanding or improper understanding is considered to be the key point for creation of social unrest. Its applications through improper way of communications among users in a society may cause disorders. Disorders in other words create social unrest.

Bibliography

Gangopadhyay, S. (2012). Guest editorial: Humanizing work and work environment: A challenge for developing countries. *Work*, 43(4), 399–401.

Gangopadhyay, S. (2017). A human factors perspective from India. *The Ergonomist* (560), July–August, 24–25.

Gangopadhyay, S. (2019). Editorial: Effects of interactive environment on occupational health and safety. *International Journal of Occupational Safety and Health*, 9(1), 1–2.

15

EVOLUTIONARY TREND OF ECOLOGICAL CONCEPTS, HYPOTHESIS AND THEORIES: PERSPECTIVES ON BIODIVERSITY

Susanta Kumar Chakraborty

Human beings have entered the *Age of Ecology* as over the previous one century, tremendous momentum has been geared up in the realm of ecological studies and research, centering on the relationships between humans and their environment. The very concept of ecology being the interrelationships among the organisms is used to unravel the mysteries behind the functioning of the natural worlds, which have been under threat during the last couple of centuries on sustaining the continuous onslaughts from the human civilization. Different environmental perturbations resulting from developmental activities of human beings in tune with the demand of the time such as agricultural activities (impacts by pesticides, nutrients, habitat alteration, changes in land quality, soil fertility, drainage, etc.), industrial activities (releasing of pollutants from the point sources like industrial sewage, gases, acidification, biodiversity loss, deforestation, desertification, ozone depletion in the stratosphere, climate change, and so on) and domestic activities (demography, economy and culture in the whole population, dumping of garbage, discharge of domestic sewages, surface water degradation, deterioration of water quality, and so on) can be tackled only by rigidly adhering to ecological principles in the process of undertaking strategies for the conservation of depleting biodiversity and ecorestoration of ecodegraded ecosystems (Odum, 1981; MEA, 2005; Miller and Spoolman, 2010; Urban, 2015).

The subject ecology has emerged as an interdisciplinary discipline involving most of the subjects of science for effective observations, generation of research information and analytical synthesis of the newly generated research data pertaining to nature in general and living organisms in particular. Newton once remarked that he had been fortunate enough to stand on the shoulders of some great thinkers of the world like Aristotle, Descartes, Galileo, Kepler and others, all giants of physics, as well as father figures of mathematics and philosophy in some cases. The subject mostly enunciated by the biologists has been very generous since its very origin in

DOI: 10.4324/9781003033448-19

receiving inputs from the giants of other sister disciplines like Haeckel, Darwin, Dobszansky, Elton, Lotka, Volterra, Lack and Mac-Arthur. Human societies, and their well-being, depending on the state of their surrounding ecosystems are likely to become prone to the impact of environmental changes and the best ways to manage them is predictive systems ecology, which explicitly tries to understand the dynamics of ecological systems by an integrated analysis of interactions and relationships with their abiotic and biotic environments, which in turn help understand and establish the ways and means of ecological interactive changes. In such a context, this chapter tries to record the historical pathways and evolutionary trends of development of ecological sciences along with highlighting basic, traditional and modern subject components of the ecology by citing several relevant models, hypothesis and theories.

Concept and development of the subject ecology

Alongside many other phases of learning, ecology has had a gradual but abrupt mode of development during recorded history. The term ecology (derived from the Greek words, *Oikos*, meaning household and *logos* meaning the study) was first coined in the year1869 by the German biologist, Ernst Haeckel, who defined ecology as the study of the natural environment including the relations of organisms to one another and to their natural surroundings. The subject ecology, to analyze and understand nature, raises fascinating questions in the different stages of the onward march of human civilization during the last couple of centuries, especially after the Industrial Revolution in Europe. The relation between nature and human beings has been dealt with in many ways by intermingling hard-core science subjects with the subjects of social sciences and philosophy. In such a context, instead of considering ecology just as a subject under biological science, it should be treated as a human science to address from the simplest to the complex slopes of biological organization in a holistic and integrative manner. Human beings, being a species in an ecosystem, exactly follow the same principles of ecology as followed by all other species of this planet.

History of ecology

The root of ecology embedded in natural history has almost the same age as the human civilization because the tribes of that primitive period, living on hunting, fishing and food gathering, required detailed knowledge of the occurrences, distribution and modes of interactions of plants and animals obeying the ecological harmony and the guiding principles of balance of nature. The practical relevance of the subject ecology in the human history mainly relies on the close and intimate association of all living organisms with human beings since the very initial phase of human civilization. The initiation and expansion of the human civilization coincided with the discovery of fire, followed by the invention of several implements and tools for hunting, fishing, agriculture etc., the steady applications of which incited to bring about a series of alterations to that erstwhile environmental condition. Further pace of technological development had compelled the human beings to depend less on the natural environment for their daily needs disobeying the realization of the continued dependences of human beings on nature for procuring the necessary ecological services in the form of fresh air, clean water, healthy foods, recreation etc.

Besides, simultaneous development of economic systems, irrespective of political ideology, tended to afford value for those commodities made by human beings to extend benefit to the individuals but applying inappropriate monetary values on the goods and services derived from nature. Although the recognition of the subject ecology as a distinct field of science dates from about 1900, but only the past few decades have experienced a steady momentum of this subject maintaining sharp dichotomy, one along taxonomic lines, (diversity and ecology of plants and animals) and the other emphasizing on ideas and underlying scientific principles pertaining to biotic community advocated by Frederick E. Clements and Victor E. Shelford and the food chain and material cycling elaborated by Raymond Lindeman and G. Evelyn Hutchinson, among others, and thereby enabled to establish the subject ecology as an interdisciplinary science subject endowed with so many scientific concepts, principles, hypothesis and theories. The studies on the development of ecology during the last century have been viewed from three points of views, which are descriptive, functional and evolutionary (Clements, 1904, 1905; Hutchinson, 1957; Whittaker, 1962; Odum, 1971; Smith, 1996).

The *descriptive point of view*, emphasizing more on natural history, proceeded by highlighting the structural excellence of the living organisms whereas the *functional point of view* focused on the uniqueness of the dynamics of the interrelationships to identify and analyze general problems. Functional ecological studies dealing with populations and communities can be measured by analyzing the proximate causes and the dynamic responses of populations and communities to immediate factors of the environment. The *point of view with evolutionary ecology* is that it tries to trace the historical perspectives of the impact of natural selection in favoring and facilitating adaptation of particular organisms and their relationships as historical products of evolution. The environment of an organism embodies all the selective forces that not only design the process of evolution but sharpen the viewpoints of treating both ecology and evolution as two of the same reality.

This has necessitated for the evolutionary ecologists to undertake studies with functional ecologists to understand ecological systems. Ecology being a recently developed scientific discipline within the subject of biology helps interpreting different environmental issues starting from energy flow through trophic interactions, biodiversity development and loss, eco-toxicological assessment of the impacts of pollution, sustainable management of environmental resource etc. The last few decades have witnessed a wide range of ramifications in the developmental phases of this subject in different dimensions with manifold applications of this subject from almost from its nascent state to fully matured state. The subject ecology embraces the unfolding of the relationships among organisms with their environment, as an interdisciplinary subject of natural sciences, especially by emphasizing on some specified fields such as evolution, zoogeography, biosystematics, biomathematics and molecular biology.

Concept of life, nature and ecology

The concept of life revolves on the idea that living organisms have the ability to make their own replica by possessing and utilizing the wonder molecule DNA with some necessary enzymes. Besides the reproductive ability, all living organisms possess the power of mutations to be transmitted to their progeny and contribute as one of the determining factors for evolution. But all living organisms should have a source of energy to undertake different activities with the help of so many biochemical reactions which drive the life processes. Plants and other autotrophic organisms (self-energy-producing organisms) obtain their energy primarily from the sunlight whereas animals derive energy from the oxidation of compounds by molecular energy.

The two widely discussed old views of the origin of life that attracted the attention of human beings are first, the origin of life by a supernatural or omnipotent power, commonly believed as "God" and second, the spontaneous generation of life, which advocated that generation and decay of life which was possible because of the activities of microorganisms. This presumption was continued till the middle of the nineteenth century and was then contradicted by the discovery of Louis Pasteur (1862) and J. Tyndall (1861), who experimentally proved that decomposition of organic matters could not take place in microbes-free environment (Schwartz, 2018). However, the path-breaking theories put forward by Charles Darwin (1809–1882) supported by A.R. Wallace (1823–1913) had the proper scientific explanation about the origin of life which occur because of the chain-wise effects of mutation followed by genetic drift, migration, reproductive isolation and natural selection (Darwin, 1859).

All eukaryotic (developed form) living organisms from the simplest to the complicated ones are constituted by two categories of cells – germ cells and somatic cells. Genes, the smallest structural and functional unit of life, pass from one generation to the next while somatic cells are mainly responsible for the growth and development of body. The DNA in the germ cells are encoded with the instruction necessary for the synthesis of different other biochemical compounds such as proteins, fats, carbohydrates and so on. Their structural arrangements and interplay among them make an array of metabolic processes within the living organisms which ensure the biological development possible. The development of modern science and technology since the seventeenth century and the emergence of evolutionary debates during the late nineteenth century started re-examining the roles of human beings which resulted in the replacement of the earlier perception of human beings on the roles of only physical environment in determining the characteristics of environmental set-ups with the enhanced emphasis of the organic and integrated approaches putting more importance on the functional contribution of living organisms. A modern approach involving and elevating the position of humans above the rest of nature relies mostly on realizing the potential of human beings for underlying and governing the rest of the natural world. The steady expansion of human beings' relationship with nature, by harvesting resources from forests and mining activities and entering into industrial production systems, led to a shift of perceptions where the Mother Earth with her natural wealth was disorderly threatened and defamed. The interaction between man and nature in many ways have contributed to shape human history and several geonatural settings and forces such as flows of rivers and winds, biological fixation of solar energy, floods and earthquakes and so on, all of which have not only structured the geological formation of the Earth but also driven the evolution of life on Earth. Besides, so many human activities during the last 15–20 million years have caused drastic changes in the land use patterns (agricultural activities, deforestation, mining, urbanization etc.) and imposed a lot of pressure on the ecology of the Earth resulting in the loss of an array of environmental wealth. The intimate approximation between ecology and natural history is central to one's conception of ecology as a science and therefore to its practice.

Peters (1991) in his attempt to make ecology more predictive tried to drive a huge wedge between the study of natural history and the underlying concepts of the subject ecology, pointing out that the former as more of an art and the latter as a science and thereby providing little scope to do for each other. In fact, the art of natural history is more advanced than the science of ecology, and natural historians make more testable predictions than do theoreticians which in contrast to the ecological science. The goals of which is to transform the intuitive knowledge into scientific knowledge involving analytical quantitative exercises to help the researchers to derive more focused and pinpoint research information on the complex relationships among living and nonliving structural components of the ecosystem. Using the craft of natural history, ecologists can create a wetland similar in most measurable ways to naturally occurring wetlands. There is a wealth of ecological knowledge, but most of it today acts as the craft of natural history rather than the science of ecology (Chapman and Reiss, 1999).

Noted ecologists and their contributions

The idea and related concepts of ecology were enunciated during the early 1930s by some noted naturalists like August Thienemann from Germany and Charles Elton and Alfred George Tansley from England (Tansley, 1935). Since the 1950s, after the Second World War, the subject ecology had emerged as a potential discipline and contributed profusely toward environmental management processes on getting out societal support and control for describing and remedying the ongoing environmental perturbations. At that point of time, a number of naturalists started their meticulous research followed by analytical interpretations in explaining the changing environmental conditions through integrative and interdisciplinary ecological research.

Two great ecologists of the world, Odum brothers (late Eugene Odum and Howard Odum) imparted the initial leadership for projecting ecological research in more popular, acceptable and effective approaches by analyzing the structure (organisms, communities) and functioning of the ecosystems of the environment in an integrative and holistic manner. Their first textbook *Fundamentals of Ecology*, published in the year 1953, has opened up new vistas on ecological research throughout the world by imposing greatest influence on the mindsets and research orientations of biologists and ecologists in dealing with ecological problems in pragmatic ways. The concepts pertaining to ecosystem have become central to the discipline of ecology during the last several decades, and the underlying principles of ecosystem ecology mostly include cycles of chemical matters, energy fluxes and food chains, population and community ecology, ecological guilds, niches and habitats, ecological succession and so on, the knowledge of which have appeared to be the prerequisite for the conservation of natural environment.

The relevance of this subject in the sphere of several ecosystems and landscapes, such as forests, rivers, estuaries, deserts and mountains across the globe, has appeared to be immense for developing an integrated and interdisciplinary challenge in the field of eco-management. Application of all these ecological ideas renders valuable aids not only to have an understanding toward conflicts between man and nature but also to resolve the problems of undertaking a multidisciplinary research appeal by involving ecology, economics and sociology for solving the environmental problems.

Chronological pathway of ecological research during the last century

Ernst Heinrich Philipp August Haeckel (1834–1919), who wanted to be a botanist, turned into one of the world's best-known and most-read zoologists and one of the founder ecologists after projecting a new science "Oecologie"(Haeckel, 1866). However, many people presumed that the driving force behind Haeckel's ecological thoughts was enunciated from Darwin's concept of competition as elaborated in his world-famous book on evolution, *On the Origin of Species*, but Alexander von Humboldt's ecological perspectives were read and absorbed by Haeckel long before the published documents of Charles Darwin (Uschmann, 1972; Krausse, 1987; Hopwood, 2006; Di Gregorio, 2005; Richards, 2008). While studying medicine at universities in Berlin and Würzburg, a number of his teachers, especially Johannes Müller, having sound knowledge base of zoology, tempted him to pursue studies in zoology, and subsequently, he became interested in the galaxy of species under invertebrates after participating in a field trip to Helgoland Island, North Sea, in August1854 (Bulnheim, 1990; Lohff, 1990). After obtaining his degree (MD) in medicine, he came to his home in Potsdam in 1858, but instead of practicing as a doctor, he started spending his time studying marine life in Italy, during 1859–1860, and came into close association with Charles Darwin and the paleontologist–zoologist Heinrich Georg Bronn (1800–1862), who was authorized by Darwin to translate his works in German.

In 1861, Haeckel joined as a faculty of Jena University, based on his publication on invertebrate diversity, relationships and genealogy on reorganizing all research facts of zoology in tune with Darwinian lines, and was subsequently promoted as associate professor and director of the zoological museum. His impressive performance through the publication of a monograph, *Die Radiolarien*, in the year 1862, based on collected faunal materials in Italy, drew the attention of several giants in the sphere of natural sciences like Huxley, Lamarck and Darwin (Wilson and Doner, 1937; Allee, 1938; Smit, 1967; Breidbach, 2006). In addition, his hypothesis on biogenetic law (ontogeny recapitulates phylogeny), as a Haeckelian pronouncement, went too far with scientific elegance and elicited far more disagreement than agreement (Churchill, 1980; Rinard, 1981).

The subject ecology contemplates science dealing with the relationships of the organisms with respect to the environment which in a broad sense encompasses all the "conditions of existence" and includes both organic and inorganic entities in nature as being the constituents of living organisms. The structural elements of the living organisms are modified in tune with their adaptability to sustain and survive in the changing environmental conditions. The adaptability of every organism in respect of their inorganic conditions of existence includes the physical and chemical properties of its habitat, the climatic factors such as rainfall, sunlight, temperature, atmospheric density, moisture and humidity, nutrients of inorganic nature in water and soils and so on. As per organic conditions of existence are concerned, the relationships of one organism with others involve intimate contact mostly because of prey–predator relationships and thereby promoting energy flows and movement of matters for contributing either to their advantage or harm. Ecological significance of all these relations is that the continuous interspecies and intraspecies interactions lead to form biotic assemblages where organic conditions of existence in course of time exert profound transforming effect on organisms and their assemblages in comparison to inorganic ones. The conserving functions of organisms with preservation of the individuals, population, interaction and exchange of materials within biotic community mainly for nutrition and reproduction are possible because of the biotransformation of materials from organic to inorganic and vice versa.

The Darwinian concept of struggle for existence, along with the concept of balance of nature as proposed by Haeckel, had revealed the tendency of an average for the absolute number of organic individuals populating the mother world to remain constant and only the relative numbers of the individual species undergoing alterations continually in relation to each other (Haeckel, 1866; Egerton, 2011). However, the broad views of Haeckel, instead of restricting only to the paradigm of Darwinian theory of *Struggle for Existence*, coupled with the concept of *Natural selection* enabled the subject ecology to flourish as the body of knowledge concerning the ecological evolution of nature, which includes the investigation of the total relations of the animals both to the inorganic and to its organic environment through the process of complementary interactions among animals and plants and were referred to by Darwin as the conditions of the struggle for existence (Egerton, 2013).

After having its emergence during the period from 1860 to the 1920s, population ecology flourished in three major dimensions mostly involving field studies, laboratory studies and theoretical studies based on mathematical interpretations (Cole, 1954a, Kingsland, 1985; Egerton, 2014). Several researchers in dealing with population ecology emphasized on invasive species, rare and extinct species, the history of population ecology and also on theories of biological control and the interactions of populations, history and scope of population ecology, social organization in animals, history of human and animal demography (Allee, 1938; Thompson, 1939; Cole, 1954a).

David Lack's natural regulation of animal numbers based on the study of population of birds (Lack, 1954, 1966)

Use of mathematics in population ecology was popularized by Kenneth (Watt, 1962). The population regulation by Hutchinson, 1978, and the natural causes of mortality in insect populations involving two major categories: "catastrophic" (factors that destroy a constant percentage irrespective of the abundance of form) and "facultative" (refers to factors that destroy a percentage increasing as the density increases) (Allee et al., 1949). The density-dependent factors had appeared to play more important roles in the population regulation and thereby to maintain the balance of nature (Tamarin, 1977, 1978). During the early 1920s, animal ecologists did not possess any competence to pursue the ecological problems quantitatively because they were not highly trained in mathematics-oriented ecology problems. But two noted ecologists, Alfred Lotka (1880–1949) and Vito Volterra (1860–1940) started publishing their research papers explaining the applicability of mathematics to calculate animal population dynamics (Whittaker, 1941; Scudo, 1971, 1984; Gridgeman, 1973; Volterra, 1976; Scudo and Ziegler, 1978; Kingsland, 1982, 1985; Fuchsman, 1999).

However, Volterra did not have that much knowledge on biological principles but had an understanding of the essence of Darwin's theory of evolution by natural selection. Therefore, Volterra had to collaborate with a number of researchers to undertake the problems of biological mathematics such as Vladimir Kostitzin (1882/1883; to about 1963), who was impressed by the lecture of Volterra on the topic on animals struggling for existence.

Italian mathematician Giorgio Israel (1993) analyzed Lotka's and Volterra's contributions and put forward his views making comments that the approach of Volterra strictly adhering to the classical physico-mathematical paradigm whereas the point of view of Lotka was with more wider perspectives of new developments of physics. Volterra was more inclined on the "mechanical analogy" whereas Lotka emphasized on the "thermodynamic analogy" putting more interest for the energetic problems in population dynamics.

An important paper based on the survey of grasshoppers pertaining to "Ecology of Populations" could help develop a mathematical formula to study the relationship between species abundance and environmental factors, which was published in the journal *Ecology* (Gause, 1934a), and that publication opened up new vistas on the relationships of the biological and nonbiological components of nature. Afterward, Gause conducted experiments on two basic phenomena concerning species relations: competition and predation mainly based on the ecological interactions of microorganisms. Gause had confirmed the results of competition between two similar species for the same resource, leading to the extinction of one species (Gause, 1934a, 1934b), now called Gause's axiom, "the competitive exclusion principle."

An informal "biotic school of population dynamics," was conceptualized by Howard and Fisk (1911) with an aim to corroborate the observations of Nicholson and Bailey (1935) on "Balance of Animal Populations" highlighting multidimensional facets of population regulation (Nicholson and Bailey, 1935; Tamarin, 1978; Kimler, 1986). This piece of research work enabled Nicholson to explore a new science of population dynamics with quantification but should not be considered as mathematical (Nicholson and Bailey, 1935). Coincidentally, another great ecologist Charles Sutherland Elton wrote a textbook *Animal Ecology* elaborating the phenomenon of animal population cycles with their determining attributes responsible for causes and effects. The significance of Elton's contribution lies on formulating basic questions of ecology relating to animal ecology and evolution focusing on the regulation of numbers and thereby toward maintaining the balance of nature (Elton, 1927; Egerton, 1973; Leibold and Wootton, 2001). Another great naturalist, David Lack (1910–1973), started contributing in the field of natural sciences on nesting, foraging and reproductive behaviors of birds with the publication of a book *Darwin's Finches* published in the year 1947 after making an expedition to Galapagos Islands in the year1938 (Lack, 1973; Anderson, 2013). The ecological thinking and scientific contributions of both Elton and Lack had paved the way for the emergence of another important field of ecology, "Evolutionary ecology with the use of natural selection in ecological theory," and such developments were thought to have been influenced by Darwin's book *On the Origin of Species* (Darwin, 1859).

Another book published by Elton, *The Ecology of Invasions by Animals and Plants*, brought about a new dimension in ecological research establishing the relevance of population ecology where the local increase in numbers enabled species to invade a new territory in search of a suitable ecological niche (Elton, 1958; Chew, 2006). During the same period, another leader in the field of ecology from the United States, Robert H. MacArthur (1930–1972), emphasized on the hypothetico-deductive method to derive research information of population dynamics: "Fluctuations of Animal Populations and a Measure of Community Stability" mostly emphasizing the resource sharing and partitioning where several species enjoy coexistence within the same habitat not disobeying the ecological principles as put forward by Gause from his experimental evidences of competitive exclusion principle

(MacArthur, 1955; Cody and Diamond, 1975; Fretwell, 1975; Kingsland, 1985; Wilson and Hutchinson, 1989; Pianka and Horn, 2005; Kaspari, 2008; Birkhead et al., 2014). Two other new dimensions in the field of ecology emerged during the last couple of decades with the publications of *Complex Population Dynamics* (an advanced-level synthesis of population ecology) by Peter Turchin and *Macroevolutionary Theory on Macroecological Patterns* (a complete and holistic interpretation of distribution, abundance and population variability of animals in an evolutionary framework) by Peter Price (Price, 2003; Turchin, 2003).

Progress of ecology and its analytical approaches

The integrity and acceptability of a subject tend to depend on the perceptions and the dependence of the researchers and practitioners of the concerned subject as being an emerging field of study. Ecologists have always been skeptical and critical of the utility of their methods in on-living the mysteries of intricate relationships among different structural components of nature which causes this subject to suffer from steady and rapid progress in contrast to other scientific disciplines because that progress can be measured only by scientific standards based on the advancement and evolution of testable theories (Allen and Starr, 1982).

In such a context, the subject ecology, initially not being treated just as science, underwent steady development as an application-based scientific discipline accommodating a variety of concepts and approaches substantiated by an array of theories and hypotheses, which provided a strong scientific platform for the judicious analysis and interpretation of nature. The classic dichotomy prevailing in ecology has been initiated at the earlier phases of the development of this subject which mostly emphasized on the structural and functional association of life forms with nature. This had led to the transformation of the subject from the descriptive treatise of ecology during the periods of the 1950s and 1960s into the causal–analytic studies of the present era. The prime objective of utilizing the knowledge bases derived from the applications of some modern research fields of emerging subjects like molecular biology, population biology, systems ecology and other related specialized subject components dealing with the natural world are for developing the concept of "biodiversity," which popped up in the **year 1992,** based on the resolutions taken in the Conference of United Nations on Environment and Development held at Rio, Brazil, where considerable emphasis was laid on the diversity of plants and animals. Weiner (1995) advocated for the ecologists who intended to replace the concepts of truth and reality with those of taste and aesthetics whereas Fagerstrom (1987) postulated that the studies on ecology have been advanced not only by exploring testable theories but also by the cultivation and appreciation of beauty in theories.

Instead of ensuring accumulation of definitive answers from testing falsifiable theories, progress in ecology can be assessed by way of developing inspiration, finding out possible answers and generating new intriguing questions. To accommodate the subject ecology in the domain of science, Weiner (1995) put forward the idea of "centrifugal force" that separates the theory from data, which are counterbalanced by pulling theory which "fight against these centrifugal forces and empirical work together and directing them to answer the questions in ecology." The "centrifugal force" in ecology that keeps theory and data apart is largely a consequence of the human nature of some to be more preoccupied with ideas than with facts and vice versa. However, the progress of science takes place by a series of small steps contributed by both theoreticians and empiricists, who often work in isolation.

The blending of theory and data certainly contributes to the progress by integrating them to cause the change. The progress of the subject ecology, mostly dealing with patterns and effective processes in respect of the abundance, distribution, trophic interactions, energy flows, biomass and productivity, diversity of taxa in nature by merging and blending with other disciplines such as different branches of life sciences (botany, zoology, anthropology, microbiology, molecular biology, physiology etc.) and physical sciences (physics, chemistry, mathematics, statistics etc.) or being distracted by them, can be measured only by developing some standards which are practically achievable. Despite having inspiration and an unwavering belief on the subject ecology considering its importance, ecologists often endure self-doubt regarding the major advances in the understanding of fundamental ecological processes and progress of the subject, especially in utilizing the inputs from other sister disciplines such as molecular biology, biochemistry, biostatistics and so on. The criticisms pertaining to the applicability and thereby all-round acceptability of ecology have emerged primarily from within the field, often from the contributions of established and successful ecologists, who attribute the lacunae in the progress of the ecological science mainly to the deficiency in the interpretation of the extent and principles behind the controlling of many ecological phenomena with proper prediction of the outcome of several ecological interactions (Chakraborty, 2013, 2017, 2018, 2021a, 2021b).

Organizational ecology

Recent research on organizational ecology has recommended five levels of thrust areas and approaches in the evolution of ecosystem with ecological analysis which include ecosystem ecology, population ecology, community ecology, habitat ecology and evolutionary ecology. **The first level**, the ecosystem ecology, is organized with the cybernetics of ecosystem functioning with trophic relationships coupled with flow of nature. **The second level,** the population ecology, embodies the ups and downs of population by two pronounced population parameters such as natality (birth rate) and mortality (death rate) and highlights the interactions between multiple population levels, using a selection approach and a shift from deterministic models to probabilistic models. **The third level**, analytical studies, includes community ecology relying on a macroevolutionary approach that is primarily concerned with the emergence and disappearance of organizational forms. **The fourth** category, habitat ecology, takes care of the distribution of organisms in temporal and spatial scales after being determined by the ecological gradients. **The fifth one**, evolutionary ecology, being an important focus for problems of adaptation and studies of natural selection in population, integrates evolution with ecology in accordance of selection approach and with the presumption that structural changes over time are regulated by structural pressures and constraints (Pimm, 1984; Picket et al., 1994; Qian and White, 2004).

Applied ecology and implications

The application of basic principles of ecology is needed to address the problems of environmental change and its continued roles in monitoring and detecting ecological problems so that proper environmental management strategies can be devised. This approach in dealing with the environmental problems has necessitated the usage of another term, "bio-ecology" used by Shelford (1913) and Clements (1905) to render justification of the community concept involving the combination of animal and plant ecology. F.E. Clements (1904, 1905, 1916) was the champion of the super-organism concept of the plant community in dealing with the process of succession to climax as a physiological development to a self-regulating and mature entity after being determined by the regional climate integrating homeostasis to develop the concept of the "balance of nature" concept. Applied ecologists, after being equipped with the baseline ecological information, can render effective leadership in tackling the ongoing environmental challenges at spatiotemporal scales by devising and applying innovative and advantageous experimental tools and methods including several statistical analytical formulations like correlation, regression, ANOVA, canonical analysis, principal component analysis, and so on.

The acceptable conceptual framework of applied ecology, which is bound to be elusive, encompasses a wide array of issues falling within the purview of this subject, such as food chain–food web dynamics, energy flows, biogeochemical cycling and biological productivity, different factors regulating population and community habitat fragmentation resulting to develop different biogeographic eco-zones and similar other attributes as applied ecological problems which provide scope for testing as well as developing ecological theory to enable the ecological managers to successfully manage ecosystems (Odum, 1971; MacArthur, 1972).

Environmental stabilization versus fluctuation: key for eco-assessment

Seasonal, annual and decadal changes of environment hardly provide scope for coexistence of the structural components of the environment in the absence of any explicitly stabilizing process, and thereby one out of several co-occurring species must have the greatest long-term propagation, eliminating its associates over events of fluctuations of environmental parameters and also in finding no mechanisms of coexistence. The relative non-linearity and the storage effect have been found to result in stable coexistence via environmental fluctuation mainly because two species tend to exhibit different responses to a resource. The effect of environmental fluctuation on the balance between the two species necessarily develops favorable environmental conditions because of least interspecies competition. Four conditions can be suggested to depict these phenomena, which are:

(a) the species are competing for a resource;
(b) different species respond differently to an environmental factor (non-resource);
(c) favorable environmental conditions promote more competition on a species with higher bio mass and
(d) persistence of the population in the face of environmental fluctuations (buffering effect), which tend to impose controlling effects on competition on the population of a species.

Applicability of ecology for environmental accounting

Different environmental perturbations resulting from different developmental activities of human beings in tune with the demand on time such as agriculture activities (impacts by pesticides, nutrients, habitat alteration, changes in land quality, soil fertility, drainage, etc.), industrial activities (releasing of pollutants from the point sources like industrial sewage, gases, acidification, biodiversity loss, deforestation, desertification and ozone depletion in the stratosphere climate change), domestic activities (demography, economy and culture in the whole population, dumping of garbage, discharge of domestic sewages, surface water degradation, deterioration of water quality, etc.) may not appear to be inimical to nature conservation because proper understanding and adhering to basic ecological principles help monitoring of ecological systems and thereby help overcoming the environmental problems. Applied ecology tends to justify the classical, novel, robust, but tried-and-tested ecological approaches to address environmental problems by using at experimental scales and offers innovative eco-friendly options and methods for working where experimentation seldom the purpose. Besides, it can also justify the value of ecological goods and services, with proper identification of their contribution to the quality of life (Naveh and Bailey, 1935; Whittaker, 1975; MEA, 2005; Miller and Spoolman, 2010).

New paradigm in ecological study in respect of its roles in eco-assessment

Rachel Carson (1962), through the publication of her world-famous scientific novel, *Silent Spring*, elaborately and analytically pointed out the significance of ecosystem ecology and evolutionary ecology. The name Rachel Carson has been emitted and surfaced onto the society during middle of the **1960s** with her adopted science, as a sequel of publishing of the book, *Silent Spring* and perhaps few biologists could match the influence of her to the scientific world dealing with the environment of mother earth with the obvious exception of Charles Darwin.

The Ecological Society of America (ESA) credited this novel written based on scientific interpretation of the deteriorating ecological quality of nature due to the pervasive human roles toward environment and that never allows professional ecologists to shake of their moral responsibility to understand the ongoing ecological perturbations with the formulating of combating strategies. Although ecological histories have begun to incorporate the facts of the pro-environmental movement with that of the science, Carson's works demand full integration into the history of ecology (Carson, 1962). The impact of multidimensional and changing states of the subject ecology during the post-Second World War period on the life of Rachel Carson enabled her to realize and identify target indicators for the right evaluation of ongoing environmental perturbations.

Carson was able to expose the flavors to ecology, but with different tilts from the mainstream of traditional ecology that was burst out with all the evil ecological consequences of the so-called scientific achievements during that period (discovery and application of persistent pesticides, chemical fertilizers etc.), which helped proclaiming the science of the environment essentially with the publication of the book, *Silent Spring*. In the book, the name of Charles Elton was mentioned, who being the founder of modern ecology, put forward his views in developing the ecosystem concept which was fervently promoted by E.P. Odum (Carson, 1962).

The ecological explanation for drastic decline of the population of raptors, Bald Eagles, because of bioaccumulation of the nondegradable pesticides, dichloro-diphenyl-trichloro-ethane (DDT) and also scientific narration of energy and nutrient dynamics in the system approach as postulated by Raymond Lindeman along with mentioning the outcomes of radioactive tracer studies of the Odum brothers have been dealt in this scientifically loaded and literature-flavored novel. The literary device used by Carson in *Silent Spring* along with relying heavily on wildlife biologists such as Clarence Cottam, F. Raymond Fosburg and Frank E. Egler emphasize more on the relationship between DDT and the decline of population of raptors. However, noted ecologists like E.O. Wilson, Paul Errington and C.S. Holling and Robert Rudd urged her to present "good ecology" to the public, integrating biological, chemical and sociological ingredients, alongside focusing more on to "balance of nature" with its supposed homeostatic mechanisms through equating ecology with "interrelationships" and "interdependence."

The indirect poisoning of robins by insecticides reflects "the web of life or death, that is familiar to scientists as ecology." Noted ecologists like Cole and Ehrlich and Eugene Odum alongside taking a lenient attitude toward the hidden messages of the book, *Silent Spring*, proclaimed new ecology to relying chiefly on the ecosystem concept, which was subsequently substantiated by Pierre Dansereau, who projected "ecosystem ecology" as to be the ecology of the future. Frank Blair, besides clearly pointing out the demerits of the descriptive knowledge about ecosystem interactions, stressed the need to refine and elevate the standard of the subject so that understanding of the basic ecological principles and knowledge of the ecological interactions and interdependencies at the levels of organization can enable both the ecologists and the formulators of public policy to deal and solve ongoing environmental problems for man's present and future welfare by seeking and procuring financial support from the pro-environmental national and international bodies for their research.

Although mathematical analysis has all through claimed as legitimate path to unravel the underlying scientific principles behind energy flows and nutrient cycling, ecologists tend to regard mathematics and the physical sciences not as their cup of tea, as they feel comfortable with their naturalistic studies into the framework being created around the work of Robert MacArthur. Besides, having some concrete lacunae with regard to the methodology, the subject ecology was to undergo distorted controversies over the research outcomes and their applicability. The book, *Silent Spring*, triggered an exacerbated conflict that had already been solidifying between ecosystem and evolutionary ecology. In general, the influence of Rachel Carson's book had made it possible for a transition of a mystical academic science of natural environments to one as applied science, loaded with so many theoretical exercises. Since that crucial juncture, ecological research has assumed the importance of multidimensional global issues (Carson, 1962).

The concept of ecosystem: backbone of the subject ecology

The ecosystem concept being the central perception of the subject ecology since its origin in 1935 (Tansley, 1935), the term "ecosystem" proved to be a strong, convincing and holistic ecological concept integrating scientific contribution from several disciplines of science that combined both living and non-living environmental components into a system. Nowadays, ecosystem integrity and health are both defined as referring to the state or condition of an ecosystem in which its dynamic attributes are expressed in relation to its ecological stage of development in different spheres of landscapes such as rivers and estuaries (MEA, 2005; Miller and Spoolman, 2010; Whittaker, 1962). The definition of the term ecosystem was first coined by A.G. Tansley (1935), extracting the idea for a system from physics which encompasses a biotic community or assemblage and its associated physical environment in a specific place. This implicates that the concept of an ecosystem requires a biotic complex, an abiotic complex, interaction between them and a physical space. Summing up most of these definitions, the term ecosystem can be defined as an open and self-sustaining ecological unit or system within an environmental set-up constituted by unique and specific structural components (biotic and abiotic), the interactions of which result in the flow of energy and cyclical movement of matters.

The very definition of ecosystem aims at understanding the controlling power of physical environmental processes and the extent of the transformation of energy and materials in ecosystems. Over the years, manifold distinctions to the basic concept of ecosystem have emerged, using different foci like energy, nutrients, organisms and the inclusion of human sciences. Odum (1969), in explaining the process of ecological succession, considered ecosystem as a unit where flow of energy determines the trophic structure and material cycles within the system. Other contemporary ecologists highlighted cybernetic functioning of the ecosystem to achieve ecological stability resulting from the feedback controls as well as functions of redundancy of components such living and resilience stabilities which act as the physical templates of the functioning of ecosystems. More recent perspectives have widened the ecosystem concept from "natural" to "human-inclusive," thereby acknowledging that humans may be regarded as an integral part of ecosystems. This has resulted in developing ecosystem models that account for economic flows in respect of goods and services (Costanza et al., 1997) and also in the development of models based on the interlinkages and interdependences of several ecotoxicological factors that incorporate several human institutions (Pickett et al., 1994; Naveh, 2000).

Stability of ecosystem: homeostasis

Environmental parameters display diurnal, monthly, seasonal and annual variations in a cyclic, regular or irregular manner, which impose lot of impacts on occurrences, distributions, diversity, population dynamics, community interactions, etc. in the changing ecological conditions by virtue of the morphological adaptabilities and ecophysiological adjustments. In achieving the adaptive success, the living organisms always endeavor to keep the fluctuation of internal environment either in a steady state condition or sometimes experiencing very narrow range of variations in withstanding any changes of the external environment. The mode of adaptation required to maintain the stability of internal environment, known as homeostasis, at the organism level can be achieved by gearing up all the physiological activities in tune with the biological needs of the species. But, at the ecosystem level, such stability is ensured by the independent or combined activities of physiological, molecular, behavioral and ecological adaptations. Stability of ecosystem is maintained by the following ecological processes (Hairston et al., 1989; Molles, 2008).

Through feedback control: [controlling of one group of organisms (herbivores) by others (carnivores) and vice versa]

Through redundancy of components

This includes resilience stability, the ability of a perturbed ecosystem to come back to its normal state after being functionally displaced and deviated from the normal condition, and resistance stability, the inherent power of a community to avoid displacement by resisting any perturbation and maintenance of its own structure and function (Harte et al., 2008; Harte, 2011).

Energy flows in the ecosystem

The chief source of energy for ecosystems is the Sun. Solar energy is received by the green plants as radiant energy and subsequently transformed into chemical (static) energy by the photosynthetic process and follows the pathways as energy flows. In any ecosystem, energy always flows in a unidirectional pathway, which abides the following two important laws of thermodynamics (Morowitz, 1968; Molles, 2008).

The first law of thermodynamics

This being the law of conservation of energy affirms that the total amount of energy in the universe is fixed, transformed and transferred from one form to another, but it is neither created nor destroyed. As example, light energy can neither be created nor destroyed but can be transformed into other forms of energy, such as chemical energy or heat energy.

The second law of thermodynamics

This states that non-random energy (mechanical, chemical, radiant energy) cannot be changed without some degradation into heat energy. The processes of energy transformation do not happen spontaneously unless experiencing decrease in the capacity of performing work, and this flow of energy takes place from higher to lower trophic level. In the second law of thermodynamics, the flow of energy decreases at each step due to the heat loss occurring with each transfer of energy from one form to another and such mode of reduction of energy, designated as entropy, tends to increase at the time of its transfer because of its dispersion or absorption in the surroundings.

Ecosystem health – an assessment tool of environmental relevance

Although divergent meanings are assigned to "ecosystem health," the evolution of the concept of ecosystem health is decided by ecological criteria as well as human values enunciated with the close interactions of human beings with nature. In the context of recognizing health as freedom and ability to cope with distress and maintaining essential functions, ecosystem health being an environmental state developed in response to the human-induced perturbations and dysfunctioning of ecosystems, where an ecosystem is considered like an organism, which is built up from the behavior of its parts (Costanza et al., 1997, 1999).

In the early definitions of ecosystem health, more focus was placed on a number of functional attributes of ecosystem, such as primary productivity and nutrient cycling being the prime manifestation of healthy system substantiated further by the activity, stability, resistance and resilience of the ecosystem (Odum, 1969; Holling, 1973; May, 1973).

Ecosystems and predictive approach in ecology

The structure and function of ecosystems profusely influence the well-being of human societies that surround them by way of providing a lot of ecosystem goods and services (Chakraborty, 2018). Devising of suitable environmental management measures to combat and control the ongoing environmental perturbations, systems ecology based on predictive approach explicitly tries to understand the dynamics and behavior of ecological systems by analyzing the interactions among abiotic and biotic components, relationships and feedbacks across organization and scale, in an integrative and holistic manner (Proctor and Brendon, 2005). The most positive aspects of predictive systems ecology, after experiencing the bonding of a range of an array of ecosystem components, suggest that ecology would benefit and increase its impact in society after being projected more on to quantitative measures than qualitative ones.

Bottom-up and top-down control in ecosystem: theory of trophic cascades

Trophic networks in an ecosystem are considered as linear chains in which nutritive elements flow from lower trophic level (primary producers) toward higher trophic levels (carnivores/omnivores). In such a context, it can be affirmed with acceptable logic that the competition among primary producers for sharing and utilizing nutritive elements can play a decisive role in population regulation. The hypothesis proposed by Hairston et al. (1960) on the "balance of nature" rests upon the ecological facts that primary consumers are limited by secondary consumers and primary producers as being their foods and thereby making them resource limited rather than of grazers limited. These trophic relationships ultimately lead to develop "bottom-up" versus "top-down" hypothesis in the understanding of food chain dynamics which holds that biological production is mainly regulated by nutrient availability with an active functional role of predators or grazers. Odum (1971) pointed out that in an ecosystem having low nutrient availability, an increase in biodiversity tends to enhance productivity, which in contrast to the ecosystem loaded with high-nutrient contents, where an increase in productivity augments higher dominance and lesser diversity. In a freshwater aquatic system, nutrient inputs through bottom-up control regulate the rate of production whereas both the piscivorous and planktivorous fish can cause significant devastations in the rate of primary production which propagates through the food webs or trophic levels, and such effects in the ecosystem dynamics are termed as trophic cascades (Carpenter et al., 1985, 2001; Pim et al., 1991). The trophic cascades hypothesis proposes that feeding by piscivorous and planktivorous consumers affects the rate of primary production in the water by top-down influence. On the other hand, an increase in predation by piscivores result in reduction of the biomass of zooplanktophagous fish and thereby also a decrease of predation pressure upon zooplankton causing an enhancement of the biomass of zooplankton, which in turn reduces the biomass of phytoplankton in the face of higher grazing pressure (Caswell, 1978).

Although there always exists a coexistence of both the bottom–up and top–down controls within ecosystems, their relative importance depends on the prevailing environmental conditions as bottom–up control exhibits direct relationship with the level of biological production, whereas top-down control has more impact upon the structure of communities. Based on this theory, the biomanipulation of aquatic environments by adjusting the biomass of the predators, it is possible to control the cascade of trophic interactions that regulate algal dynamics by increasing or decreasing the number of consumers and thereby establishing the functional roles of the consumers in determining the primary productivity in an aquatic ecosystem.

Origin and establishment of the concept of evolutionary ecology

The concept of a sub-discipline "evolutionary ecology" has been conceived by deriving the merits of the subject ecology on integrating some components of the subject population genetics, against physically stressful environments which include so many eco-evolutionary components such as evolution of life histories, mating systems and sex, the adaptability for territoriality, foraging, reproductive and social behaviors, the theory of co-evolution and its application to adaptive radiation, the species diversity of communities, the role of environmental heterogeneity in maintaining genetic variation. In such a context, ecology as a self-conscious discipline assumed tremendous momentum in its development, enjoying considerable autonomy throughout the first half of the twentieth century, which afterward (in the 1960s) experienced its conjunction with evolutionary biology, leading to develop another specialized discipline like evolutionary ecology.

This striking event was given much emphasis by the evolutionary ecologists, especially in view of the fresh interpretation of Darwinian theory in light of traditional taxonomy, paleontology, molecular biology and population genetics enjoying a separate line of evolutionary synthesis, which was termed as the Neo-Darwinian synthesis during the 1930s and 1940s. The impression of the newly emerged subject, the evolutionary ecology was marked vividly with works and messages of G.E. Hutchinson and theoretical formulations of Robert MacArthur, Richard Levins and G.C. Williams, who put more emphasis on the contributions on-livingogy (ecology of individuals in a population) and genetic selection to straighten out mysteries in the realms of ecology. The concepts put forward by James Collins, and afterwards substantiated by Allee et al. (1949), strengthened the close bonding between ecology and evolution instead of dealing either of the subjects separately. The late 1950s and 1960s had also witnessed a redirection in the fields of evolutionary ecology with its close ally of population biology to unravel the mystery of so many behavioral manifestations of the animal kingdom (Maynard, 1972).

Darwin's pioneering evolutionary synthesis based on theorizing ecological facts had constituted integral structural elements to the evolutionary theory in interpreting the biogeography and its influence on flora and fauna. Much of the early ecological research was dependent on the physiological interpretations of the organisms' adaptations in the oscillating ecological set-ups, but those ecologists were not much concerned of the root causes of different interacting mechanisms, remaining skeptical of natural selection. Those ecologists were more inclined to claim themselves as naturalists, often more specifically ornithologists, entomologists, botanists or ichthyologists, with little interest on the central concept of evolutionary biology. In such a context, some ecologists emphasized rigidity with their preferences toward the experimental sciences to achieve respectability, rejecting the speculation, descriptive narration and imprecision with which the traditional subjects like taxonomy, phylogenetic analysis, natural history, biogeography and so on were handicapped.

Four major propositions have been assigned with regard to the assessment of the roles of evolutionary ecology:

First, the emergence of evolutionary ecology was facilitated by natural selection, granting its distinctions in all levels of bioecological organization and applied the concepts of individual selection and adaptation to properties of species, such as life history patterns.

Second, the new evolutionary ecology, having several historical roots, mostly relied on the legacy of the evolutionary synthesis of natural selection which plays powerful and dynamic roles in bringing ecological changes.

Third, adaptation and natural selection had launched an era of individual-selectionist interpretation of life histories and behavioral aspects that had been central in the arguments of Lack and Wynne-Edwards. The appeals of Williams were on genetic framework in contrast to the breadth of vision and search for coherence in polyhistorical perspectives of the ecology of diversity as put forward by Hutchinson. Robert MacArthur, to ensure living of the targets, attempted to use simple models that abstract the essence from the variety of the ecological world, recapturing Volterra's theory and pressing it into the service of new questions about the nature of communities. Although much of MacArthur's theory is an abstraction from pure population dynamics, questions were raised about resource utilization and the coexistence of species which rapidly and inevitably acquired an evolutionary dimension.

Fourth, as Collins in 1978 has pointed out, ecological and evolutionary processes could be commensurate in time and space. This assessment came largely from the work of Dobzhansky and his collaborators and from the British ecological geneticists. It enabled ecologists to imagine and undertake experiments on genetic changes with regard to the ecological relations of species, which consequently led Levins and others to argue that ecology could not ignore genetic processes as to be the facilitator of the evolutionary changes and thereby results to constitute the present form of biological world (Dobzhansky, 1950; Fischer, 1930; Levins, 1966, 1968, 1985).

The present and future of evolutionary ecology

A synthesis of ecology and evolutionary theory encompasses both phenotypic and explicitly genetic models of coevolution, demographic properties, migration, niche breadth and other population attributes such as fecundity, natality, mortality and so on. However, an evolutionary theory fails to justify the structure and function of community as doubt persists on the success of predictability in the community structure. However, ecosystems ecology including energy flow and nitrogen cycles remains by and large uninfluenced by evolution. This has made it difficult to understand the reasons behind the difference in respect of primary productivity of a coevolved community of plants, the assemblage of species taken from around the world. It is primarily the theory of evolutionary mechanisms which become integrated with ecology to analysis of evolutionary mechanisms and the inference of the history of evolution (Ricklefs and Miller, 1999).

Ecological models and their relevance to explain ecological complexities

A model being a formulation mimics a real-world phenomenon to predict future consequences and predictions. Besides, models are designed and developed not only for the prediction of the trend and mode of responses to environmental changes but also to forecast with perfection of the possible future state of a system meeting the need of the potential environmental management options, as for example throwing light on evaluation of the ecological impacts of climate change, changes in land use patterns and nutrient flows. Therefore, ecological models, alongside serving for such prediction and generation of research ideas, can also be used to devise strategies for the mitigation or adaptation of the impacts of change (Holling, 1966; Allen and Starr, 1982; Israel, 1993; Chesson, 1998).

In simplest forms, models can become verbal or graphical as representatives of informal models whereas actual models are developed using statistical and mathematical formulations to make quantitative predictions to be reasonably good. In computer-simulated models, required tuning or refinement of mathematical formulations are made by computer operations by adding a new parameter or removing an existing one to ensure more perfection in the probable and predicted outcomes. Understanding the importance of ecosystems for the effective protection of natural resources and their services with regard to a range of contemporary pressures, ecological models are being devised and projected for the solution of future environmental problems in view of realistic future scenarios which have made decision-making more challenging and far from complete due to the inherently complex, nonlinear and variable ecological system.

The unusually rich and complete research attempts are being taken to look to the future for describing the natural world with very different outlook from today's, by meticulously observing the ecosystem responses, which help develop credible response models dealing with empirical relationships that allow drivers for the quantification of ecosystem services. In addition to predicting the trend and mode of responses to environmental changes, models are designed and developed to meet the need of evaluating the potential environmental management options and also to forecast accurately and successfully the ecological consequences, especially in respect of global warming-associated climate change, continuous changes in land use patterns, nutrient flow, devising of strategies for the mitigation, the mode of adaptability against the impacts of all such environmental changes. In the sphere of the subject ecology, while dealing with complicated bioecological relationships and interactions, special emphasis has to be made in devising suitable models to unravel complexity pertaining to both living aon-livinging environmental realms.

Development of two major types of mathematical models has received wide acceptance for fruitful interpretation and prediction of the burning issues on ecology and conservation biology, giving thrust to the relationship between mathematical models and the target system. The first one designated as "descriptive model" has become very familiar and popular too in depicting of single-species population growth, such as the logistic equation and the second one as the "multi-species model" such as the Lotka–Volterra predator–prey equations, which attempt to depict some ecological issues involving so many parameters. Descriptive models consider a number of idealizations about the target biological system as evident from the model developed to predict population dynamics through the logistic equation, which assumes a constant carrying capacity coupled with a constant growth rate, ignoring the complications of age structure. The Lotka–Volterra equation on the other hand is based on the presumption that the predator acts as a specialist form of animal that captures the preys experiencing constant conversion efficiencies (Lotka, 1925; Volterra, 1926).

Basic components required for devising ecological theories

Generating theories make claims about the prediction of world, and different predictions lead to scientific progress associated with the generation of better theories. Ecologists in the process of developing explanatory theories depend more on mechanistic explanation to arrive at much broader and stronger predictions. The construction of deductive mathematical models substantiating the explanatory theories is often used as logical instruments for demonstrating the mathematical consequences of clearly stated assumptions and help make verbal models evolve into predictive theories (Caswell, 1978; Murdoch et al., 1992). However, deductive models can contribute least to the ecological problems, which rely more on theoretical models producing testable predictions as evident from the Lotka–Volterra predator–prey model, which predicts oscillations (either neutral stability, limit cycles, damped oscillations converging on an equilibrium point) in which the predator and prey cycle (oscillations in the prey population drive oscillations in the predator populations and viceversa). Two approaches alongside distinct imaginary expectation and speculation are being pointed out to establish important roles in the generation of explanatory theories:

(1) Searching, recording, processing and analyzing of the patterns in nature
(2) The framing of deductive mathematical models

Pluralism in ecology: different dimensions

Ecology needs new ideas, approaches and theories to address the diversity and pluralism in ecological research by adopting bold and open views to new ideas, as the general theories of population dynamics, species diversity etc. have not been very successful in generating testable hypotheses because of so many prevailing debates and conflicts limiting population size by density-independent or density-dependent factors and assuming the facts that population size may not be controlled by the same factors in all species in all communities. In such a context, the following factors represent different options to deal with the different dimensions of ecological studies.

(1) **Ecological theory**: Theoretical work should eventually contribute to the development of testable theories. Totally abstract theoretical development without paying attention to immediate predictions is desirable because it may eventually contribute to the development of testable theories, but such theoretical exercises seldom yield predictions after several years or decades or series of publications.

(2) **Empirical work**: Data are used to serve some purposes such as

   (a) Look for patterns that can be the basis for generating hypotheses and theories. Case studies act as a prerequisite to develop patterns, especially in the exploration of previously little-studied systems, but one can ask how long this phase should be pursued if it does not yield compelling patterns;

   (b) Develop and calibrate empirical calculation tools which can be used for making theoretical prediction; and

   (c) Test calibrated calculation tools and explanatory theories.

(3) **The organization, politics and funding of ecological research**:

   The general argument outlined earlier also leads to some recommendations for how ecological research is organized. The need for pluralism argues strongly against concentration of power embedded within different ecological researches which are not supposed to serve well by the presence of dominant "schools of thought."

(4) **The teaching of ecology**: Ecology should be taught with a relatively high degree of skepticism and criticism rather than as a body of accepted theory. Ecology being a unique subject may require special approaches, methodologies and skills, which to some degrees have to be defined in its own terms. For example MacFadyen (1975) argued that unlike other scientists, ecologists should remain broad and resist the urge to specialize. Continuous exchanges of dialogs along with undertaking debates are needed to bridge the gap between theoreticians and empiricists in ecology instead of restricting the newly emerged ideas and thoughts within the individual ecologists, theoreticians and empiricists. Modelers should learn as much as

possible about the natural history of the systems they are trying to model, and empiricists should learn as much as possible about any model that may be relevant to their research. An interdisciplinary approach has to be devised involving mathematics, statistics, physiology etc. to address the problems of ecology which as a subject seems to be "cannibalized," as it forms a source of interesting questions for other research fields but questions that often do not advance ecology itself.

Population dynamics and the controlling factors

Population dynamics represents defined patterns of continuous change due to birth, death and movement of individuals along with changing time scales and exhibits variations among different species. Growth among populations and their competitive interactions for available resources are fundamental to nearly all aspects of biological limnology. Analyses of population growth have been the subject of intensive quantitative and theoretical study. Two parametric models, viz. the logistic model and the linear partial adjustment model dominating the ecological research on populations of organizations, consider population growth as being curvilinear and stress on the phenomenon carrying capacity, which specifies a ceiling on population size.

Sometimes, populations are small with very restricted distribution while in others, populations constituted by a large number of species enjoying vast range of distributions. Moreover, different living and nonliving factors determining the population dynamics govern the expansion, decline and maintenance of populations. This very important aspect of ecology holds a great promise in explaining the ways and means for preventing the decline and extinction of threatened (endangered) species, the control of noxious species of pests, parasites and pathogens causing harm to human beings and also protection and conservation of ecologically and economically important populations. A population is a spatially defined assemblage of individuals of one species where all individuals live, interact and migrate through the same niche and habitat or populate a more localized area, such as a particular lake or a section of flowing water. Population density, expressed as the number of individuals per unit area or volume of water, is an index of population size at any given time (Israel, 1993).

Growth among populations and their competitive interactions for available resources are fundamental to nearly all aspects of quantitative and theoretical study, which emphasizes several fundamental relationships among the constituent individuals and ecological parameters. The Malthusian growth model still being considered as the primary law of population ecology advocates that "the exponential growth and decline of population will take place as long as all individuals in the population inhabiting in the surrounding environment remains constant. Simplified population models usually start with four variables such as death, birth, immigration and emigration.

Population regulation and environmental factors

The fluctuations of populations are governed by a multitude of environmental factors, such as living components (parasitism, diseases, predation, sizes, shapeson-livingliving (temperature, pH, oxygen), climatic (water currents, atmospheric density, rainfall, wind), socio-eco-political (urbanization, demography, crowding, economic condition), which independently or in combination regulate biological processes. Population growth and the sizes of populations are often regulated by environmental factors (Cole, 1951; Leigh, 1975; Smith, 1996; Kingsland, 1985; Koromondy, 2002; Krebs, 2008). Environmental factors which are responsible for regulating populations are often the ones that affect the growth of the individual. As populations are made up of individuals, population increase depends on the reproductive fitness and life span of these individuals. Factors such as energy and nutrient availability, flood, drought, predators and disease tend to control the population size. Constantly limiting factors are always in short supply, maintaining the relative constancy so that a population is limited to a certain fairly constant size by those limiting factors. Individuals may have to compete for the resource. It has become an established fact that ecosystems having low biological diversities because of less perturbations are controllon-livingliving environmental factors whereas non-stressed ecosystems with higher biological diversity are regulated by living environmental factors (Cole, 1954b; Odum, 1971; Cohen et al., 1980). All these determining factors of ecosystems are divided into two categories.

(1) **Density-dependent factors:** Environmental factors impacting on a population as the function of the size of or density of the population are termed as density-dependent factors (population interactions, diseases etc.).

(2) **Density-independent factors:** The actions of those factors not relating to population density and driving the ecosystem processes independent of the size of population are designated as density-independent factors such as wind flow, intensity of sunlight, temperature, rainfall and other natural disasters (fire, flood, drought etc.).

Explanation of life-history evolution: r and K strategies

An increase of these environmental factors exceeding the tolerance limits of an organism results in deleterious effects on the growth, propagation, reproduction and other behavioral activities of the organism, including continuous higher rates of mortality even leading to extinction of local populations. However, ecologists are mostly reluctant in attaching more importance on the processes of natural selection operating on different individuals within populations but rather emphasize more on the distribution, abundance and interactions among individuals in a population. Therefore, the main concern of ecologists rests on the phenomenon of higher levels of organization ranging from the ecosystems to the whole biosphere, ignoring individual variation and the evolution of populations.

This reductionist approach begins with the manner in which natural selection generates the properties of populations. The best-known example of this style of theorizing is MacArthur and Wilson's (1967) discussion of "r" and "K" selection, where r and K are the conventional symbols for the reproductive capacity or Malthusian parameter (r) and the carrying capacity parameter (K) in the logistic growth equation $dN=rN (K/N)/dt (K)$ is constant and N is population numbers. MacArthur (1957, 1972) argued that certain habitats (old islands) favor organisms with a high stable situation, for many species are endowed with high reproductive rates and competitive ability (r selected) in comparison to other forms (K selected) with low reproductive rates. As the properties of populations are explained by natural selection operating on individual genotypes to produce adaptations, the development of ecological theory must take into account the processes by which populations interact to produce the behavior of higher units of organization. Natural selection also induces specialization of populations in respect of population attributes which occur in natural biotic communities where specialized populations undertake interactions among themselves and outcompete a single generalized one. This process has resulted in the division of the world's biota into several million species and their associated ecological niches (MacArthur and Levins, 1967; Leigh, 1975; Krebs, 1994; Koromondy, 2002).

As competition between species involves costly investment in respect of energy, resources and time, natural selection tends to favor individuals within populations which avoid it. Special evolutionary processes of speciation allow specialization by protecting the isolated gene pools which in turn result in patterns and magnify the population interaction by the process of competitive exclusion where the requirements of two species in a community are sufficiently similar. This mechanism is responsible for a kind of community evolution, called succession, which means the replacement of one group of organisms by others in time and space. The life history of organisms is determined by several attributes such as pattern of growth, morphological differentiation, building up of biomass, different practices and rate of reproduction, the variability in fecundity and mortality (MacArthur and Wilson, 1967).

To assess life history strategies, the following three aspects are given priority:

(1) To identify individual life history traits;
(2) To establish the links among all those traits;
(3) To detect the links between traits and habitats.

Considering all those facts stated, it is being hypothesized that one life history trait may limit the possible range of other traits as the morphology and physiology are observed to limit most of the traits of life history.

Variability and influence of competition in life processes

Since Darwin (1859), ecologists have emphasized the significance of competition in shaping the community structure including the patterns of species composition and distribution, resource availabilities and mode of reallocations, niche segregation and resource partitioning and so on. Competition within the local community structure mainly aimed at procuring food and space is of exploitative type, which is influenced by the nature of niche of each species composing the community and is usually evident at the level of ecological guild. The ecological guild is defined as a group of species that similarly exploit the same class of environmental resources (Root, 1967; Tilman, 1994). Competition involving interference and interactions among individuals for the exploitation of similar and mostly scarce resources limit the growth and development. A high population density is inversely proportional to survivability of individuals constituting the said population whereas mortality enhances resource availability to result in increased growth for the alive individuals.

Predation: Lotka–Volterra model of predation

Predation is the act of feeding on a living organism (prey) by another living organism (predator) to obtain all those nutrients and energy needed to live, grow and reproduce from the prey's tissues. In more simplistic words, in predation one animal species eats all or part of a second species (Krebs, 1994). It is a special case of the consumer versus resource (or trophic) interaction, which includes processes that cannot be classified as predation such as detritivory (the consumption of dead organic matter). Predation and the network of predatory interactions represent the basis for other biological interactions such as competition, an important category of species interaction in the ecological processes, which ultimately determines developmental changes of an ecosystem (from an "ecological succession" and "food web," point of view). (However, such status is shaped by multiple ecological processes instead of not only being limited to trophic interactions (Ulanowicz, 1997). Predation involves the death of the prey, which is being eaten, but this is not always true (grazing).

The Lotka–Volterra model has been deduced involving several mathematical formulations and deductions out of the interactions between two species in an ecosystem, a predator and a prey, which describes how the prey population changes and the second one describes how the predator population changes. Such thinking has opened up new possibilities that, in some cases, could not even be otherwise entertained. For example exponential growth of both predator and prey is a possibility in the ratio-dependent view but not on the standard Lotka–Volterra model. Also, it is interesting to note that there are "balanced growth" models in economics that allow joint coordinated exponential expansion across several sectors (Cooley et al., 1995). The core of the ratio-dependent predation debate is whether "Malthusian growth" is truly fundamental in ecology or whether it disappears as species interact.

Community ecology, biodiversity and hypothesis

Although dealing of communities of living organisms in the study of nature is very old, the study of their interrelationships and quantification of community interaction is a relatively recent concept. The interactions of each organism with the environment and with other associated organisms generate a set of genetically based physical, physiological and behavioral features that shape life processes of each individual (Shelford, 1913; Strong et al., 1984; Smith, 1996; Roughgarden, 2009; Stileng, 2002). Noted ecologist F.E. Clements (1916) defined community as discrete units having own biological organizations with sharp boundaries (closed community), whereas another legendary naturalist H.A. Gleason (1926) considered the community (open community) as an intimate association of organisms possessing the adaptability to live together in a specific site endowed with unique physical and biological conditions where each species co-occur within a particular association and enjoys geographic and ecological distributions of their component species, even extending their ranges independently into other associations overcoming the limits of boundaries (Elton, 1942, 1966; Enquist et al., 1998).

The pattern of evolutionary relationships among different species, designated as phylogeny, demands more attention to strengthen the understanding of its ecological relationships. The ecological studies focusing on the causes and adaptability of ecological interaction with the environment is referred to as eco-physiology, which explains the physiological adjustments of the organisms with the changing environment (Clements et al., 1929; Clements and Shelford, 1939; Ricklefs, 1987, 2008). Different individuals under the same species inhabiting the same habitat and time are said to constitute an ecological population. These suits of interacting populations are called ecological communities, which control the structure and functions of the respective ecosystems by such interacting processes rather to delineate a single community process or an attribute. The species richness, the number of species, types of species present and their relative abundances, the physical characteristics of the species assemblages, the trophic relationships among the interacting populations in the community represent important attributes of community structure.

Rates of energy flow, properties of community resiliencies to perturbations and productivity are examples of community function. Community structure and function are manifested by a complex array of interactions directly or indirectly involving all members of the community together into the food web. The influence of a population extends to ecologically distinct parts of the community through its competitors, predators and preys. Community ecology, being the study of patterns in the diversity, abundance and composition of species in communities and of the processes underlying these patterns, involves only four distinct kinds of processes: selection, drift, speciation and dispersal, which are in sharp contrast to four other eco-biological attributes applicable to population genetics such as selection, drift, mutation and gene flow. Population genetics, being the study of the composition and diversity of alleles in populations, gets involved in the complex interactions between species and their environments which are ultimately screened and processed by the evolutionary agents of natural selection.

Expanding branches of ecology and forces behind it

Looking back over the last few decades, it has been observed that studies on processes and functional aspects of ecological systems and all kinds of experimental works have expanded in ecology, partly at the expense of more descriptive studies and inventories. Further, the new methods and the experimental approaches have above all facilitated a reductionist development in the gamut of science as is the case in all branches of biology with a major emphasis on holistic approaches on the ecological studies of whole ecosystems. Forces behind progress in ecology operate in two widely different but equally important dimensions to drive the scientific progress in ecology (Molles, 2008). The first one involves the construction and access to instruments providing scopes for the rapid use and reliable analytical methods as practiced in other subjects of physical sciences. The second one deals with the development of new theories and scientific ideas created by ecologists introducing new paths for research to be followed. In contrast, in the social sciences domain, excessive efforts are made to study about changes in paradigms than to strive for an understanding of the effects of the implementation of new technical tools and analytical instruments to make many measurements of variables.

Throughout the existence of ecology as a science, there have been numerous examples of the process of implementation of new ideas and concepts, including the concepts pertaining to energy flow and trophic interactions. Since 1935, when Tansley, in the year 1935, developed the concept of ecosystem, which with the passage of time through Lindeman (1942), the Odum brothers (Odum, 1971, 1981) etc. not only was able to gain rational and strong scientific foundation and develop a strong impression on a whole generation of ecologists but had a great influence also outside the community of ecologists. Based on all of these developments, it could be hypothesized that the rate of innovations of new ideas and the extent of new thinking should grow in proportion to the increase in the number of active scientists. No such growth in innovation seems to have taken place during the last few decades when the number of active ecologists and the number of published articles have increased considerably, resulting in a condition for developing so many hypotheses explaining the trend of progress in several fields of ecology along with predicting the actual possibilities for the progress of research in ecology in the near future.

Molecular genetics and molecular biology in general have revolutionized much of the research conducted in biology during the last couple of decades or so. Chemistry has provided biology very powerful tools to investigate various processes on cellular and organismal levels. For instance researchers have been trying to combine studies on various ecological processes of evolutionary importance with insights from population genetics and at the same time use analytical methods from molecular biology to study the genome level and also to link up the findings with the ecological processes under investigation.

Diversity in ecology is at present combined with the speciation process, but in an ecological context, it ought to be approached also on a lower taxonomic rank. During the last couple of decades, there has been an increasing interest in the ecological aspects of evolution which led to merging of population genetics, systematics and ecology to explain the different pros and cons of various evolutionary processes. These expanding branches in ecology will certainly in the future be working close to those parts of genetics and systematics which share an interest in evolutionary biology. The urgent need for developing and standardizing relevant methods of molecular biology to study and unravel the intricacy of living organisms at molecular levels will certainly favor in bringing a new dimension in molecular phylogeny and based on which evolutionary significance of diversity of organisms in respect of changing ecological perspectives can be clearly explained.

Paradigms in ecology: past, present and future

Ecologists tend to emphasize certain fundamental principles, or "paradigms," that enable to conceptualize patterns and processes operating in biological functioning of organisms and also to promote the advancement of ecology toward making more generalizations about nature, which are expected to contribute to scientific interpretation of ecological concepts. The importance of paradigms for studying, analyzing and interpreting the evolution of ecological concepts and theories after being tested, and accepted, enables ecologists to examine and explain various ecological processes leading to ecological progress. Putting more stress on the increased appreciation of historical contributions in ecology has become a prerequisite to sustain scientific momentum by way of impeding the resynthesis and recycling of ideas. It has been substantiated by the facts that the unchecked growth of the natural populations triggers population regulation, which was a major area of research during the past century. The fundamental principles of the population regulation paradigm have been developed by exploring current empirical and theoretical issues, as population regulation is dependent on demographic density and occurs solely due to competitive interactions (Hairston, 1989; Pimm, 1991; Harte, 2011).

However, the inability of undertaking proper fieldwork coupled with the application of appropriate theory generate constrains to understand the concepts pertaining to the advances of population regulation in demographically open systems after being stalled at different scales over which density dependence can act. The expression of density dependence over broad scales from individuals to metapopulations has been considered to be the key to further advances in understanding population regulation. Evolution of the life-history traits of organisms takes place in response to variable environmental conditions which led to the origination of theory of r- and K-selection, which failed initially to incorporate important aspects of selection and such paradigm's original concepts appeared to be crucial for establishing the roles of density dependence, resource availability and environmental fluctuations as selective agents in the evolution of life-history patterns (May, 1973; Graham et al., 2002).

Different models, hypothesis and theories in ecology

In interpreting research data and information of ecology, ecologists have been using theory and hypothesis. A theory after being defined as a hierarchical framework contains clearly formulated postulates, based on a minimal set of assumptions, from which a set of predictions logically follows as most of the theories are inherently deductive because of advances and refinement of baseline research data on ecology. Data undergo different forms of processing (mathematical, statistical, computational etc.) and in course of time expands, and replaces old theory, by correcting flaws with proper explanation and prediction in the domain. The subject ecology is very rich with theories and several of which are actually specific hypotheses or models. Ecologists and other scientists often apply the terms model and theory indistinguishably, but both of these terms bear different meanings (Pielou, 1981; Pickett et al., 1994; Chesson, 1998). Models being the simplified, partial statements of theories are developed to enhance the ideas of a specific subject alongside attempts to solve a particular problem in a particular domain. Out of so many of the theories, some theories have appeared to be more efficient than others because they exhibit better explanations and predictions on the research data of almost similar implications (Caswell, 1978).

Some examples of efficient theories

The repetitive processes of induction, deduction, prediction and testing result in advances in science which play positive roles interplaying with each other in achieving significantly enhanced scientific progress in biology in general and in ecology, in particular. Directly linking of research information makes it possible toward acquisition of well-posed theories and hypotheses. Several deductive frameworks for becoming efficient theory in ecology and evolutionary ecology include some key characteristics which are simple, parsimonious, quantitative and mathematical, enjoying little inputs but resulting in many predictions (Odum, 1971; May, 1973, 1981, 2004; Krebs, 1994; Smith, 1996; Ricklefs and Miller, 1999; Begon et al., 2006).

The Gaia hypothesis to explain the origin of the Earth system

Gaia hypothesis highlighted first by Lovelock embodies a structure for understanding the Earth's geophysical and biological systems which advocated the organically regulated origin of the Earth's atmosphere, temperature, hydrosphere etc. This hypothesis holds that the erstwhile microorganisms since their origin through evolution provide an intricate, self-regulatory control system that keeps conditions favorable for life on Earth (Lovelock, 1979, 1995). A strongly systems-oriented approach to the Earth, with a major emphasis on negative feedback loops heavily influenced by the biota, was emphasized in this hypothesis. This theory considers the Earth to be a cybernetic system where organisms have evolved within the physical environment to provide an integrated control system called Gaia, which keeps the Earth's condition favorable for the existence of life.

It was concluded that the atmosphere of the present Earth, with its unique high-oxygen-to-low-carbon dioxide content, moderate temperature and permissible pH in air–water interface, resulted because of the effective buffering activities of early forms of anaerobic microbial organisms, the coordinated activities of which also contributed in the evolution of aerobic microbes and plants. The web of life of microorganisms tended to control ecosystems to maintain a pulsing and home-orhetic balance and thereby making the Earth a complex but unified cybernetic system, establishing the biological influence over the nonliving components. Some topics of great importance in Earth System science are noticeably absent, the idea of nutrient cycling being a striking example.

Fisher's sex ratio theory

This theory proposed by Fischer (1930) was conceived with the proposition that the relative reproductive value to parents of sons instead of daughters exhibited equality to the relative selection pressure favoring the production of sons. Also, this theory postulated that parents determine the sex of their offsprings where a reproductive value has been defined in the context of populations with varied age structures.

Optimal Foraging Theory (OFT)

This theory was put forward based on the understanding of the foraging activities of a population in heterogeneous environments and explains the foraging behavior of animals by means of a quantitative theory following the first principles of energy and mass balance and natural selection (MacArthur and Pianka, 1966; Charnov, 1976). It stressed upon the roles played by the natural selection in molding the biological potentialities of organisms so as to maximize fitness, and thereby it yielded more scopes for predicting on a variety of eco-biological phenomena, including optimal diets, patch choice, duration to ensure optimal foraging in a patch and also the frequencies and rates of movement and visiting different ecozones (Pyke, 1984). Studies on optimal foraging support point out that animals are adapted in their search for food in such a way that ensures achieving maximum relative benefit after being favored by natural selection on efficient foraging traits. The **OFT** theory interprets behavioral strategies pertaining to decisions for maximizing the net rate of food intake for enhancing foraging efficiency. This theory simultaneously considers the benefit of fitness for perfecting the search for reproductive advantages that might have driven the evolution of behavioral traits that on appearing initially are responsible to make individuals more vulnerable to predation.

Metabolic theory of ecology (MTE)

The prime antecedent of this theory revolves on the fundamental roles of metabolic rate to the world of ecology because organisms can adapt with their environments through metabolism. This theory focuses on the roles individual metabolic rate plays in controlling the interplay among physiological, ecological and evolutionary processes which are found to have been affected by each other (Brown et al., 2004; West and Brown, 2005; Sibly et al., 2012; Kearney and White, 2012). The metabolic theory of ecology tends to predict the qualitative set of relationships of an organism's body size with the fluctuating temperature and metabolic processes. In general, smaller organisms inhabiting tropical warmer climate are usually characterized by sizes having higher metabolic, individual somatic and population growth rates, prolific power of reproduction, larger population size and greater resource uptake rates. The different traits of these organisms tend to vary temporally and spatially through acclimatization, development and evolution. All those points have focused to conclude the significance of biological attributes of individuals toward developing concept and knowledge in the subject ecology, in general and evolutionary ecology, in particular (Kearney and White, 2012). MTE has brought about two types of models.

(1) **The first type** of this model focuses on the prediction of the roles of two variables – body size and temperature, both being the primary determinant of metabolic rate in diversified forms of life (Arrhenius, 1889; Kleiber, 1961; Robinson et al., 1983), which affect the adaptability of the organisms (Spatz, 1991; West et al., 1997; Gillooly et al., 2001).

(2) **The second type** of this model highlights the consequences of metabolic rate at different levels of biological organization, from genes to ecosystems, and imposes constraints on varied forms of life processes, including the origin and evolution of DNA (Gillooly et al., 2005), growth and dynamics of population (Savage et al., 2004) and carbon flux within an ecosystem (Enquist et al., 1998, 2009; Allen et al., 2005; López-Urrutia et al., 2006), with the predictions of the effects of MTE on size and temperature for developing an efficient theory in ecology.

Maximum entropy theory of ecology (METE)

METE predicts realistic functions describing different patterns as prevailed in the field of macro-ecology which include the species abundance distribution, the spatial distribution of individuals within species, the species–area and endemics–area relationships, the distribution of metabolic rates within and among individuals and species populations (Jaynes, 1982; Harte et al., 2008, 2009).

The neutral theory of biodiversity: the unified neutral theory of biodiversity and biogeography

The neutral theory of biodiversity (NTB) is developed based on the understanding of the role of stochastic demographic processes in regulating the formation and community interactions from ecological to macroevolutionary time scales

(Hubbell, 2001; Ricklefs and Schluter, 1993). The theory also helps predicting diverse phenomena, including the frequency of distribution and abundance of species, species–area relationships, characteristics of phylogenetic tree and the relationship of species richness to the macroevolutionary rates of speciation and extinction (Rosenzweig, 1995; Hubbell, 2001; Price, 2003). The NTB being an efficient theory explains the origin of variation among species leading to different relative abundance following stochastic rules that apply to all the species constituting a biotic community and thereby provides a useful baseline information against which empirical data can be compared (Hubbell, 2001; Leigh, 1975). In ecology, this theory, first proposed by Stephen P. Hubbel (2001), is also considered as a generalization and extension of the theory of island biogeography by MacArthur and Wilson, 1967, who first published this theory to state that the species abundance on an island is determined by the equilibrium between the immigration and extinction depending on the size of the island as well as its distance from the mainland.

This theory, adopting the regional and historical perspectives, states that the number of species on islands balances regional processes governing immigration against local processes, governing extinction, assuming the facts that immigration and extinction rates probably do not vary in strict proportion to the number of potential colonists and the number of species established on the island. The theory of MacArthur–Wilson also predicts the steady-state patterns for species commonness and rarity (relative species abundance on islands or in local communities) but avoids incorporating the process of speciation in the original theory of Island biogeography.

The very term neutral theory stems from the fact that all species are treated as having identical vital rates on a per capita basis (the same birth and death rates, the same rate of dispersal and the same rate of speciation). This theory moreover attempts to give a better explanation for many landscape-level ecological patterns. It applies to those biotic communities where the organisms enjoy the same trophic level competing for the similar limiting resources by largely substitutable in their use of limiting resources, which is evident when the absence or disappearance of one species from a community is utilized by other species by comfortably using the resources in the absence of the former species.

Intermediate disturbance hypothesis

The intermediate disturbance hypothesis, as proposed by Connell (1978), unfolds the prospective ecological consequences of several disturbances resulted due to the alterations of physical environmental conditions, roles of predators or several disturbances-related factors prohibiting colonization and growth of biota and also disruption of the process of succession by species adapted to colonize disturbed sites. Many ecological investigations have substantiated and corroborated the main flavors of this theory on the ground that disturbances favor the flourishing of biodiversity by lessening the action of stronger species on the weaker ones promoting the latter to grow and increase in their density. It also states that high diversity is a consequence of continually changing conditions, not of competitive accommo-dation at equilibrium and also predicts an increasing trend of species richness in communities experiencing moderate levels of perturbation than in communities without any disturbances or in the communities sustaining very high and frequent disturbances.

This hypothesis subsequently paved the way for the development of a relevant model, named as dynamic equilibrium model, which was proposed by Huston (1979, 1994) to focus on the contributory roles of interactions between the extent of disturbance in the community and the rates of population growth of the species in the community. Huston (1979, 1994) advocated that the existence of highly diverse biotic communities composed of several species but rendering similar eco-logical functions might be understood in terms of interactions between the extent of disturbance in the community and the rates of population growth of the species in the community.

Some examples of inefficient theories

Continuous impact of variable environmental conditions facilitate the evolution of life-history traits of organisms and the knowledge of which enabled to develop the theory of r- and K-selection, which at the initial state could not incorporate important aspects of selection, and such paradigm's original concepts appeared to be crucial for establishing the roles of density dependence, resource availability and environmental fluctuations as selective agents in the evolution of life-history patterns. It is also valuable for the sake of clarity to highlight some more theories that appear to be not as effective as others as they do not fit with some of the characteristics used to define efficient theories. The R* or resource-ratio theory, first proposed by MacArthur and Levins (1964), was afterward expanded by Tilman (1982), which had stimulated a series of research for predicting compe-tition among consumer species and also for limiting resources, especially for a single homogenously distributed limiting nutrient. In this respect, the R* theory tends to predict the roles of superior (the winner) species which are able to maintain a positive population growth rate at the lowest concentration of the limiting nutrient. Prediction can also be made with this theory pertaining to the coexistence of two species, where the growth rate of each one is limited by a different nutrient.

However, in the presence of heterogeneously distributed resources, the number of species can become larger than the availability of limiting resources. R* theory is considered as a conceptual advance over the other competition theories, such as the Lotka–Volterra predator–prey model, which theoretically predicts the outcome of competition even prior to facing the same as such theory faces the difficulty in measuring and testing a large number of free parameters (a minimum of three parameters per species – resource combination, mortality rates and resource supply rates) to yield predictions.

Evolutionary stable strategy (ESS)

ESS advocates that inheritable traits within a specified population oppose the intrusion of any such traits or a mutant variety of other populations to retain the existing genotypes avoiding the replacement of the existing variety. ESSis an important approach for understanding and explaining the behavioral manifestation of animals, especially valuable in the discrete phenotypes which interact with one another (Smith and Price, 1973; Parker, 1984). Maynard Smith (1964) and Maynard Smith and Slatkin (1973) explain ESS as such a strategy that resist the invasion of a mutant strategy by the combined strengths of all the individuals of a population. Dispersal is said to be an evolutionary stable strategy as a population in the process of dispersal. Therefore, dispersers facing no selective pressure can achieve that tendency (**ESS**) (Maynard Smith, 1972).

Game theory and its relevance in ecology

This theory depicts the ecological relationships within a community (assemblages of species or of traits under the command of those organisms) and can be regarded as a contest, that is a game in which each biotic component solicits to have some advantages. Numerical values are used to evaluate the losses and gains mathematically on devising proper formulations to be used in ecological modelings. The application of game theory has produced many insights into ecological relationships and the significance of particular aspects of animal behavior. The game theory explains the behavioral evolution by considering both the costs and the benefits of several behavioral decisions of individuals who unconsciously endeavor to maximize their reproductive success.

The proponents of this theory had focused on cases where competing individuals tended to display fitness consequences of a given behavioral option, depending on the actions of the other competitors. In such a context, decision-making is treated as a game to understand the choices made by people as they compete with one another for their benefit in respect of resources. One of the noted evolutionary biologists, W.D. Hamilton, was a pioneer in thinking about evolution as a game between competing phenotypes, where he argued that best-suited ecological conditions enable an individual to live alone by adopting its own behavioral strategy. The end result, according to Hamilton, could be a selfish herd in which all individuals try to hide behind others to reduce the probability of being selected by a predator (Krebs, 1994; Smith, 1996; Begon et al., 2006).

The macroevolutionary approach

The theoretical logic of macroevolutionary approach seems to differ from the developmental approach of developmental theorists who tend to focus on change over time in individual organizations, whereas macroevolutionists examine communities of organizations (Price, 1997, 2003; Ricklefs, 1987). Macroevolutionary research has resulted in dichotomous interpretations of the ecological findings: **the first** involves analysis of whole societies where the researchers use this approach with an objective to identify the structural characteristics of societies and to analyze societal changes over long historical periods (Duncan, 1964). **The second** line of macro-evolutionary research revolves within urban sociology examining the changes in cities over time and more recently, in whole systems of cities over time utilizing much of the logic inherent in the developmental approach to derive understand-ing from the deterministic evolutionary sequences for the transformation of social units over time.

Hypothesis pertaining to species diversity

Evolutionary time hypothesis

This hypothesis, proposed first by Fischer in 1960 and substantiated by Simpson (1964), highlights the relationship of the age of the community with the struc-tural intensity of diversity. Old biotic communities developed long back support a greater diversity than the recently grown-up biotic communities. Older communi-ties of tropical environment display more diversity propagated in faster pace than the biotic community of temperate ecological conditions.

Spatial heterogeneity hypothesis

This hypothesis postulated first by Simpson (1964) adheres to the opinion that the development of more complex and heterogenous physical environment makes the biotic community more complex in respect of the complex interactions among the constituent floral and faunal components. The varied types of habitats having own communities are formed with the higher variation in topographic reliefs and the more occurrence of complexities in the vertical structure of vegetation help flourishing of diversified forms of species.

Predation hypothesis

This hypothesis, proposed first by Paine, in 1966, has also accounted for species diver-sity on a local and regional basis. The hypothesis states that a higher species diversity prevails in those biotic communities in which prey species are numerically controlled by predators. Such biotic communities experiencing reduced interspecific competition among them facilitate developing fruitful coexistence among the prey species.

Dynamic equilibrium hypothesis

This hypothesis, first advocated by Huston (1979), highlights the differences in the rates at which populations of competitive species reach competitive equilibrium. The population growth rate of the competitors within the biotic community acts as the major determinant of diversity in nonequilibrium ecological conditions. Inability to reach and achieve equilibrium states by most biotic communities is attributed to the fluctuating environmental conditions and periodic decline of populations caused by several disturbances, the least occurrences of which help in an increase of the abundances of major competitors resulting in low diversity.

Productivity–stability hypothesis

This theory proposed by Tilman and Pacala (1993) states that species diversity within a biotic community exhibits positive correlation to the productivity pointing out the fact that diversity does not follow the monotonical form of increase with productivity for any species assemblages; instead, the species richness of that community undergoes changes depending on the roles of some specified environmental factors which impart influences on some definite species. Differential nutrients availability decides varied forms of relationships between biodiversity and productivity as revealed; an increase in biodiversity enhances productivity in the low-nutrient natural environments (Tilman, 1988) whereas an increase in productivity causes higher dominance and reduces diversity in high-nutrient environments (Carson and Barrett, 1988).

The inter taxon competition hypothesis

As proposed by Rosenzweig and Abramsky (1993), this hypothesis advocates that peaks of species diversity for multispecies taxa (orders/classes etc.) occur in areas having different productivity levels whereas another hypothesis put forward by Tilman (1982) has suggested that habitat heterogeneity increases with productivity to a certain point after which it decreases.

The random niche model

This model, proposed by MacArthur in 1960, considers that the abundance of different species within a biotic community is determined by random partitioning of resources distributed along a continuum. The model also implies that different species in the biota do not undertake any overlapping between species in search of and for the use of the critical resource bases.

The niche preemption hypothesis

This hypothesis states that the most successful or dominant species within the biotic community tends to preempt most of the habitable space. The next most successful species then claims the next largest share of space, and the least successful occupies what little space is left.

The log-normal hypothesis This hypothesis first mentioned by Preston (1962) highlights that the niche space occupied by a species is determined by a number of ecological attributes such as food, space, biotic association, microclimate and other related parameters that affect the growth and propagation of one species in the face of competition from another.

The log-normal distribution most closely resembles the distribution of importance values (density, diversity, mode of interactions etc.) obtained from communities rich in species.

Hypothesis pertaining to climate

The climate stability hypothesis

This hypothesis, proposed by Fischer in 1960 and supported by Connel and Orias (1964), asserts that a stable climate seldom varies in accordance with the variability of seasonal factors and thereby offer a more favorable environment for the biological adjustment of the constituent species, leading to higher species richness. Organisms living in a favorable climate having stability such as in tropical regions do not need to have the broad ecological and biological tolerance limits needed by species inhabiting in those eco-regions with a more variable climate. Besides, constancy in the ecological conditions also triggers to achieve more specialization in respect of feeding niches and microhabitats which in turn promote for an increase in species diversity.

The climatic stability hypothesis was restructured by Sanders (1968), pointing out the diversity patterns in physically controlled and biologically controlled communities. The organisms are subjected to more physiological stress leading to less reproductive success and survival and thereby leading to diversity. The biologically controlled communities are not critical in controlling species because of creating relatively uniform physical conditions over long periods of time. However, no community has been found to be completely physically controlled or biologically controlled. In addition, another hypothesis, designated as productivity hypothesis in relation to climate stability (Connel and Orias, 1964), states that the energy flowing through the food web determines not only the diversity but also the productivity of the community. This hypothesis also states that the greater productivity and diversity of the community are positively related to the availability of nutrients in the habitat.

The competition hypothesis

Another hypothesis named as competition hypothesis, proposed by Dobzhansky (1951) and subsequently corroborated by Williams (1964), is considered as a derivative of climate stability hypothesis because both the hypotheses have some common elements within themselves. In the benign, favorable and stable climatic conditions of tropical regions, populations of species reach near maximal size due to high interspecific and intraspecific competitions under selection pressures favoring strong specialization in foods and microhabitats. Species occupying narrow niches result in high diversity. In temperate and polar regions, where selection after being controlled largely by physical habitats makes the species least specialized which prefer to enjoy a broad niche and thereby result in low diversity of species.

The climate predictability hypothesis

This hypothesis attempts to draw relationships between species diversity with the ecological set-ups unique for the temperate and polar regions, which are subjected to a fluctuating but predictable climate. In such ecological conditions, organisms have to evolve some mechanisms to cope with regularly occurring changes and also to develop specialization to adjust with all-annual ecological events. Migration of birds occurs in response to seasonal climate changes which enable them to arrive at their favorable habitats, which are endowed to offer them feeding and nesting opportunities.

The energy hypothesis This hypothesis, first advanced by J. Brown in 1981, advocates that in habitats having roughly equal areas, energy flux per unit area is considered as the major determinant of species diversity. Primary production by the green plants represents the realized capture of solar energy, which is indirectly indicated by the quantified information of actual evapotranspiration. The regulation of body temperature in vertebrates is closely linked to atmospheric energy, the availability of which in turn is dependent on the biogeography determined by latitudes and longitudes influencing the variability in solar radiation.

Dynamic energy budget (DEB) theory

The theory of DEB, based on the first principle of thermodynamics of energy and material fluxes, has attempted to mathematically interpret the life history of organisms which grow up in an environment provided with necessary resource bases for their survival, emphasizing mostly on finding out the rates at which individuals assimilate and use energy and other life-supporting ingredients for their growth, reproduction, development and sustenance.

Theory of complexity and sustainability

The increase in the size and complexity of an ecosystem necessitates a proportional increase of the energy cost of maintenance. A doubling in size requires even more than double the amount of energy, which is also utilized to pump out the increased entropy associated with the maintaining of the increased structural and functional complexity.

There are increasing returns to several category of scales (economies of scale) as increased quality and stability in the face of disturbances and also there exist diminishing returns to scale (diseconomies of scale) involved in the cost of pumping out the disorder. As an ecosystem becomes larger and more complex, the proportion of gross primary production that must be respired by the community to sustain itself increases, and the proportion that can go onto further growth in size declines. At that certain point of time of distinct balance between the inputs and outputs, size of the ecosystem fails to increase, further overshooting maintenance capacity and thereafter result in a pulsing "bottom and bust" sequence.

Concepts of carrying capacity and sustainability

The carrying capacity, being a direct reflection of the concept of sustainability of an ecosystem through maintaining of natural capital and resources, denotes energetic involvement for the utilization of all available incoming energy that are required to sustain all the basic structures and functions of that ecosystem, when production (P) equals respiratory (R) maintenance. The amount of biomass that can be supported under these conditions is known as maximum carrying capacity. The optimum carrying capacity that is sustainable over long periods in the face of environmental uncertainties tends to be lower than the maximum carrying capacity (Barrett and Odum, 2000). To tackle the problems enunciated from the ongoing environmental imbalance, a conference on human environment was held in Stockholm, in June 1972, where a decision was taken that all the countries of the world have to put their efforts to control the degrading environmental conditions of the globe. This was followed by the formation of United Nations Environment Programme (UNEP), under whose auspices another international conference was held at Brazil, popularly named as Rio Conference in 1982, where the resolution was adopted as the world chapter for the sustainability of nature followed by the publication of a report, named as "The Brundtland Report" with the title "Our Common Future," which put forward the most acceptable definition of "Sustainable Development," the extracts of which can be summed up as the development that meets the needs of the present generation in supplying the natural resources without disrupting and thereby compromising the carrying capacity of the resources for the future generations. Afterwards, a lot of debates and discourses had taken place on this newly emerged subject, which resulted in the development of general acceptable concepts of sustainable development as the combination of ecological, economical and social sustainability that necessitated to undertake environmental management strategies toward ensuring sustainability in an integrated and holistic manner (Grime, 1993; Goodland, 1995).

Ecology versus biodiversity

Environmental factors determining biological productivity

Different environmental factors and processes influencing the biological production in an ecosystem include intensity of solar radiation, temperature, moisture in air and soil, chlorophyll pigments of leaves, availability of water, precipitation, minerals, nutrients and several biotic activities such as grazing, herbivory, preda-tion, parasitism, diseases and so on. In addition, the impacts of human population, pollution of different forms, changes in the natural ecosystem functioning due to the inputs of exotic or alien species, habitat destruction, and so on also determine the rate of biological productivity. The biological productivity takes into consid-eration three different aspects such as standing crops, biomass and ecophysiological processes regulating the biological productivity. Standing crop refers to the total amount of living materials in a particular population in a specified time, expressed as biomass (standing biomass) or its equivalent in terms of energy. Biomass is meas-ured in terms of the living weight, dry weight (gm/m^2) and even by means of energy contents ($calories/m^2$). Biomass differs from the productivity, which refers to the rate at which organic matter is produced by photosynthesis.

Different eco physiological processes involved for secondary production are consumption, ingestion, assimilation, respiration and production. In all ecosystems, the sequential relationships and interactions result in the development of trophic structures, which include producers, herbivores, carnivores and decomposers as the representatives of different trophic levels. The accumulated organic matter found on a specified areas in a particular time is the standing biomass. The standing crop may vary at different times of the year. The amount of living matter in each of these trophic levels or in the constituent population is called standing crop. The high standing crop and biomass do not necessarily imply high productivity. The size of standing crop represents accumulated biomass, not the rate of production. Small organisms turn over rapidly, being eaten nearly as fast as they are produced, and therefore accumulate minimal biomass. The size of their standing crop has little relationship to their productivity (Smith, 1996).

Relationship between biodiversity and productivity

The hypothesis designated as "balance of nature," proposed by Hairston et al. (1960), triggered the interest of ecologists to explain the reasons behind the accu-mulation and retention of large biomass by the primary producers (green plants) as reflected by the vast green coverage in most parts of the world. Considering the close relationship of biodiversity with productivity, Odum (1971) opined that in low-nutrient environments, increase in biodiversity tends to enhance the pro-ductivity, but in high-nutrient environments, enhanced biological productivity in turn results in higher dominance and lower diversity. Carpenter et al. (1985) high-lighted the functional roles of fishes living on other small fish and planktons in the aquatic ecosystem in causing significant deviations in the rate of primary produc-tion, which is regulated by the nutrient inputs through bottom-up controls.

Concept of biodiversity, values and conservation

Traditionally, the term biodiversity has been used mainly to highlight the trend of depletion of the global living resources as a result of undesirable human activities and thereby has promoted to undertake necessary steps for protection and conservation of the biological world alongside paving the pathway for sustainable development. "Biodiversity" is defined as "variability among living organisms from all sources including inter phyla terrestrial, marine and other aquatic ecosystems and ecological complexes of which they are part: that includes diversity within species, between species and of ecosystems (UNCED, 1992; Ricklefs, 2004).

Interactions within, between and among various levels of biodiversity are the main intrinsic mechanisms to maintain the self-sustaining structural and functional attributes of biodiversity within the scale of time and space (Chakraborty, 2003, 2013). The survival of human being is entirely dependent on biodiversity for the following reasons.

(i) **Food**: Food of human beings is entirely (100%) derived from biodiversity; still human beings have not been able to culture or utilize not more than 20 species of animals, 30 species of fishes and 159 species of plants for the direct consumption as food.

(ii) **Medicine**: In our health care system, more than 70% of today's medicinesare based on natural product chemistry.

(iii) **Clothing:** Besides a few reyond fibers, all other fibers for clothing of human beings are derived from biodiversity.

(iv) **Shelter materials**: People residing at rural areas are entirely dependent on biodiversity for housing materials.

About 90% of Indian export market is dependent on biological world. Besides, biodiversity constitutes important raw materials for most of all biotechnological innovation and development. Conservation and sustainable use of biodiversity is a prerequisite for sustainable environmental management and development. Biodiversity constitutes resources upon which the present and future human society are dependent. Modern pace of development in the field of biotechnology has opened up new vistas for the bright future of human beings (Chakraborty, 2017, 2018; Meffeand Carrol, 1997).

Origin and patterns of biodiversity

There are five major causative agents which operate continuously to bring forth evolution viz. mutation, genetic recombination, genetic drift, reproductive isolation and natural selection. Through evolution, old species give rise to new species. Every genetic variation, from gene mutation to entire species, will disappear eventually. The distribution of spatially heterogeneous taxonomic diversity in the form of innumerable number of species belonging to a number of supra-specific taxa (genera, families, orders etc.), all over the globe is contemplated from the temporal perspective and the origins of such biodiversity are viewed on the evolutionary time scale of speciation and extinction. An array of ecological, biological, physical, chemical and geological events had their roles in giving origin and determining the distribution of a galaxy of biodiversity components across the globe.

Geological events like continental drift, plate tectonics and other such events have led to the splitting of Gondwana land into fragmented land masses of five continents with parallel environmental diversifications facilitating the evolution of a large number of species (Lyell, 1830). The wide range dispersion of landmasses promotes independent evolution of terrestrial and freshwater biota, within a continent after being facilitated by the large-scale gradients of environmental variables and resources, enabling each species to have optimal performance on a particular point and thereby resulting in an impressive diversity of organisms. As the diversity of living organisms has been distributed unevenly on the Earth, biogeographical processes might have had a major role in determining diversity patterns at the global level, which are reflected in the development of many similar patterns in taxonomic diversity across the world (Weiner, 1992; Whittaker, 1975). Besides, biodiversity becomes a natural form of capital, subject to the regulatory forces of the market and a potential source of considerable profit to countries possessing biodiversity components as "useful" natural set of species and genes that is used by the mankind for its own benefit, either by deriving from natural surroundings or through devising new technology like biotechnology.

In this context, not only ecological but also the economic valuation of biodiversity trigger powerful arguments in favor of conservation of biodiversity in this ecologically perturbed and changing world.

STANZA **Biological diversity, biodiversity, bio-complexity**:

The continuous and steady interactions among different living components of the world in relation to changing ecological conditions modify the biophysical environment to a considerable extent, accelerating the process of speciation and redefining the existing perception of biological diversity which is supposed to have evolved as the product of dynamic interactions among different levels of integration within the living world. Such activities of the biodiversity components for the alteration of the physical and chemical environment are mostly characterized by two major functional processes of ecosystems, such as the energy flows and cycling of matter, both of which impose a twofold influence of physico-chemical and biological dynamics. Such realization toward the concept of biodiversity results in a paradigm shift, contradicting the traditional belief to consider only the influence of the physico-chemical context upon the dynamics of the living world and not attaching that much importance on other interactions (Fisher, 1960).

The integrated approach encompasses both physico-chemical and biological influence leading to develop new concepts of functional ecology and biocomplexity. The term biocomplexity has recently emerged to interpret research outcomes of several functional interactions among different forms of biological components enjoying various levels of organizations in relation to their biological, chemical, physical and social environments. Biocomplexity being characterized by nonlinear, chaotic dynamics and interactions on different spatiotemporal scales helps in the integration of ecological, social and economic factors, deepening the human understanding of the living system in its entirety rather than in bits and pieces (Chakraborty, 2003; Soulé, 1985).

Biological diversity: a dynamic system

In the gamut of ecology, three major types of ecological processes involving the living and nonliving world operate and involve trophic relationships among different groups of organisms (food chains, food webs or trophic networks); dynamics of biogeochemical cycles; eco-biological processes for biological production (the capacity to produce living matter); accumulation and transfer of energy within an ecosystem. The biological diversity in an ecosystem functions at three levels of integration: (1) intraspecific diversity, that is the genetic variability brought down by biological heritage of populations where the species are able to respond to changes in the environment; (2) diversity among species (individually or in groups within trophic webs) with respect to their ecological functions (the nature and magnitude of the flow of matter and energy) contributed collectively to the dynamics of an ecosystem. Ecosystem diversity, in different time and spatial scales, is determined by several living and nonliving attributes such as species richness and diversity of niche in an ecozone. In addition, continuous and steady interactions among different biotic components and also with the prevailing nonliving ecological factors, biodiversity not only ensures the stability in ecosystem functioning but also determines and regulates the eco-geo-chemical cycles (fixation, storage, transfer, recycling of nutrients, etc.) and the hydrological cycle. In the ecological sense of the term, biological diversity results from dynamic interactions within and among the levels of organization of the living world, as well as with the physical and chemical environment.

Functional groups of biodiversity: complementarities and redundancies

It poses real challenge to determine the proportionate contribution of each species to sustain ecological processes. The term "functional groups" is often used to describe sets of species exerting a comparable effect upon a particular process or responding in a similar manner to changes in their external constraints. This may, for example, consist of the group of species that exploits the same category of food resources or else the group of species involved in major biogeochemical cycles (nitrogen, carbon etc.).

An ecosystem function may be provided by one single species or by a limited number of species in one particular system, while there may be a large number of species providing the same function in another ecosystem. "Functional redundancy" arises when several species occupying the same spatial niche provide similar functions, even though their relative importance may vary.

Role of species in ecosystem functioning

The functional contribution of different species toward flow of energy and cycling of matters in the process of functioning of ecosystems follows the dictates of the operating ecological principles for maintaining, recovering, regenerating and restoring of the respective ecosystems. Different ecosystems after being structured by different biological communities exhibit similarities in their functional process. Although each species has its own specific roles within an ecosystem, often different species are seen to display the same function. Various hypotheses have been proposed to explain the relationships between nature and the richness of species present in an ecosystem and their roles in the functioning of ecosystems. According to the hypothesis of diversity-stability, the productivity of an ecosystem and its capacity to sustain disturbances tend to increase steadily with the proliferation of the number of species in the system.

Such increase of species diversity leads to higher number of interspecific interactions facilitating more flow of energy in the trophic networks. Disruption of any part of such interactions (naturally or artificially) may cause either extinction or disappearance of one or more species, result in twofold development, collapse of the ecosystem dynamics or establishment of alternative pathways. The resilience stability of the disturbed ecosystem enables to cope with the changing ecological conditions and functions with the overlapping of different species in such a way that the disappearance of one species with its function can be compensated by others (Odum, 1971; Carpenter, et al., 1985).

The "rivet" hypothesis proceeds

The "rivet" hypothesis advocates the significant contribution in the functioning of ecosystem (Ehrlich and Ehrlich, 1981; Lawton, 1994; Walker, 1995). The capacity of an ecosystem to sustain the threats of ecological perturbation is by developing the power of absorption of the ecological changes, which start decreasing with the extinction or disappearance of certain species. Beyond a certain threshold, the ecosystem ultimately fails to endure the negative pressure on it resulting in a collapse as reflected by a significant change in ecosystem functioning. This hypothesis, besides upholding the concept of functional redundancy, simultaneously emphasizes the existence of some specialized functions. It can also be expressed that an ecological function hardly ceases unless and until all the species contributing to that function are eliminated from the ecosystem.

The hypothesis of "drivers and passengers"

The main message of this hypothesis is derived from the assumption that the functional roles of different species within an ecosystem vary from one another because of uneven distribution of ecological function among different species (Walker, 1992; MacDougall and Turkington, 2005). Many species are considered as superfluous (passengers), while some other drivers can contribute in different ways in maintaining the ecosystem as a whole. Species are categorized based on their functions in different conservation categories, such as keystone species, ecological engineers, umbrella species, flagship species, bioindicator species, and so on, and the presence or absence of which determines the stability of an ecosystem.

The idiosyncratic hypothesis

The main focus of this hypothesis is to lend support to the possibility that no relationship exists between the species diversity and their function in an ecosystem (Keddy, 1992; Lawton, 1994). Changes in the biological diversity result in the modification of the ecosystem functioning; the intensity, magnitude and direction of such modifications are very difficult to predict because of the unpredictability of the capability of each species to function which also varies from one area to another. Hutchinson, as an ardent supporter of theories of competition (competition controls the species abundance and resource availability), put forward his views by coining the phrase "plankton paradox" where so many species of phytoplankton successfully coexist in a proportionally simple ecological set-up disobeying the theory of competition and the limiting roles of deficiency of resources. These arguments were further strengthened by advocating the reasons behind these. Besides, he explained that the development of higher species richness is not because of the impact fluctuations in the environment parameters preventing the ecosystem from attaining a state of equilibrium over time but due to the coexistence of species in the community even in the nonequilibrium ecological state. However, such novel ideas initially received very feeble attention than they do deserve mainly because of the predominant paradigm of equilibrium theories.

Habitat ecology and its relevance to biodiversity

Ecological categories of distribution in different habitats

Ecological analyses of biodiversity for the purpose of comparing communities and ecosystems in respect of their distribution patterns are of several categories.

(1) **Species–area relations** wherein the number of species encountered is proportional to a power of the area sampled.
(2) **Alpha (α) diversity** which is the species within a community or habitat, comprising species richness and evenness.
(3) **Beta (ß) diversity** is the intercommunity diversity expressing the rate of species turnover per unit change in habitat.
(4) **Gamma ('Y) diversity** is the overall diversity at the landscape level, which includes both α and ß diversities.

Concept and definition of ecological niche

The concept of ecological niche has had a long history of development and interpretation in ecology. Grinnell (1917, 1928) was the first to coin the term "Niche" and highlighted it as the functional role and position of an organism in its community. Later, Elton (1927) regarded the niche as the fundamental unit of an organism or a species population in a community emphasizing its place in the biotic environment and its relations to food and enemies. It also highlights the status of the species in its community mostly determined by sizes and food habits (Leibold, 1995). Odum (1971) defined ecological niche as "the position or status of an organism within the biotic community and ecosystem" because of the structural adaptations, physiological responses, and specific behavior (inherited and learned) of the concerned organism.

The "habitat" of an organism is the place where it lives whereas the ecological niche includes not only the space occupied by an organism but also its functional roles in the community (its trophicposition) and its position in environmental gradients (temperature, pH, soil nutrients etc.) Three different types of ecological niche are:

(1) the spatial or habitat niche;
(2) the trophic niche;
(3) the multidimensional niche or hypervolume niche.

Spatial or habitat niche mainly adheres to the concept of habitat providing more emphasis on the physical space occupied by an organism. The concept of niche as put forward by Hutchinson (1957a, 1957b) relies more on the space rather than a microhabitat coordinating behavioral manifestations also. It is a multidimensional hyper volume enclosing the complete range of ecological conditions for the successful survivability of organisms. G.E. Hutchinson suggested that the niche could be visualized as a multidimensional space or hyper volume within which the environment permits an individual or a species to survive indefinitely and designated it as hyper volume niche (Hutchison 1958, 1965, 1978). Hutchinson (1965) moreover distinguished between the fundamental niche–the maximum abstractly hypervolume when the species is not constrained by competition or other limiting biotic interactions – and the realized niche, a smaller hypervolume occupied under particular biotic constraints. Connel (1978) suggested that both high and low levels of disturbances would lead to reduced diversity.

Hypothesis based on species abundance and resource gradients in ecological niche

Graphical plotting of species abundance against the sequence of occurrence of species along resource gradients resulted in the species abundance hypothesis (Whittaker, 1962, 1975), which in turn resulted in the origin of three more hypotheses based on the species abundance in relation to the resource gradients using Dominance Diversity Curves (Smith, 1996). The said hypotheses are as follows:

(1) **The random niche hypothesis:** This hypothesis views abundance as a random partitioning of resources distributed along a continuum, that is following a continuous gradient. It also considers an ecological niche as the amalgamation of several segments such as random, contiguous and nonoverlapping

segments, the length of each of which represents the abundance of a species, developing the proposition that greater the length, the more abundant is the species and shorter the length supports lesser abundance of species.

(2) **The niche preemption hypothesis**: This hypothesis, also named as the geometric distribution hypothesis, holds the view that the numbers of most abundant species are twice as numerous as the next abundant species, the abundance of which doubles in respect of the third species in the series. From these observations, it is inferred that most of the dominant species preempts half of the available niche space while the next dominant species preempts half of the remaining space and so on. In this type of niche partitioning, no overlapping of niche space takes place and is evident in the harsh environment, such as the desert ecosystem.

(3) **The log normal hypothesis:** Preston (1962) classified organisms on the basis of log arithmetic scales and for developing this hypothesis arithmetic scale is converted to geometric scale. All the species were organized into certain categories and each of these categories is named as octave. The first octave contains just half the numbers of species of the second octave and so on, and on plotting these data on the graph the x-axis highlights the rank of species whereas the y-axis depicts the number of species. A normal dominance diversity curve, high and flat in shape, is derived and designated as log-normal curve, based on which the property of the community can be described as hyperbolic, 's' shaped, straight line etc. This type of curve also depicts an undisturbed environment with the occurrence of only partial competition in the overlapped area.

Ecological guilds and ecological roles

Root (1967) defined ecological guild as a group of species that exploits the same class of environmental resource in a similar way. Smith (1996) defined ecological guild as a group of different species foraging or feeding in a similar habitat for exploiting or using environmental resources in a similar way. The study of biological diversity involves not only describing the great variety of biodiversity patterns on Earth from genes to ecosystems but also to find out what these diverse living entities are or what their function is.

Another aspect of functional diversity is the formulation of the "guild concept" which is a pattern of convergence. Guilds are functional groups of organisms whose members exploit environmental resources in a similar way. Species at the same tropic level that use approximately the same environmental resources are considered to be a guild of competing species. The nectar-feeding guild of birds, for example, is represented by hummingbirds (Trochilidae) in the new world tropics, by sunbirds (Nectariniidae) in the African and Asian tropics, by honeyeaters (Meliphagidae) in Australia and by honeycreepers (Drepanididae) in the Hawaii Islands. All are convergently similar in having a long thin beak that enables them to probe deep into flowers.

Difference between ecological guilds and niche

The concepts of guilds rest on functional manifestations of some species which are related based on their phylogeny and resource requirements. Niche denotes the functional roles of an individual species where guilds relate the functional roles of a group of species. Both the terms, niche and guilds are applied for potential competitors and partitioners. The members of a guild however exploit the resources together in such a way that minimizes niche overlap and competition. For example exploiting same resources lead to overlapping of niche and competition. But exploitation of resources takes place in different ways where the competition is minimized.

Ecological equivalents: Unrelated organisms occupying similar niches and habitats but in the different geographical regions may resemble each other morphologically and this is designated as ecological equivalents. These ecologically equivalent species may be taxonomically different, but they perform similar functions as a result of convergent evolution. Two species can be designated as ecological equivalent only when they occupy same or similar niche in different geographical areas as they are unable to permanently occupy the same niche in the same community. These two species are referred to as ecological equivalent. Asiatic lion (*Panthera leo parsica*) and African lion (*Panthera leo leo*) are examples of ecological equivalent.

Habitat fragmentation vis-a-vis habitat heterogeneity

Alteration of habitats by human activity is the greatest threat to the richness of life on Earth. The most visible form of habitat alteration is the destruction or removal of a habitat, but in habitat fragmentation, once continuous landscape gets divided into odd bits and pieces. A superficial view of habitat fragmentation portrays a large area of homogenous habitat being broken up into small pieces. At a landscape scale of analysis (a few kilometers across), the distribution of vegetation types typically corresponds to changes in elevation which reflect the temperature level and intensity of precipitation, gradients of sloping and other ecological aspects such as the amount of soil moisture and nutrients. This heterogeneity is vividly displayed in mountainous regions but also exists in different relatively flat landscapes including the river basins (Meffe and Carrol, 1997; Meffe et al., 2006).

Development of metapopulation and their roles

A group of conspecific populations occupying different habitats at the same time is known as metapopulation. Several natural disturbances such as fires, storms, floods etc. generate conditions which culminate in the creation of habitat heterogeneity in different landscapes such as forests and wetlands and beyond that also modify the physical environment. As a consequence of habitat fragmentation, disturbance-mediated patchiness, habitat quality for species varies spatially, and many species may be distributed as metapopulations, systems of local populations linked by dispersal. Metapopulations have important implications for patch dynamics and heterogeneity of ecological habitats (Halder and Chakraborty, 2015, 2019; Odum and Barret, 2005). When similar habitat patches are spatially separated across a reserve, individual species may have a metapopulation structure, with populations occurring in different suitable patches. The patch dynamics perspective assumes that the dispersal among similar successional patches is possible, countering local extinction processes (Picket et al., 1994; Hanski, 1999). Murphy et al. (1990) pointed out that the metapopulation perspective may be more critical for small biota, such as annual plants, invertebrates and small vertebrates than for the mega vertebrates championed as the umbrella species under which many other species are protected.

Ecology, paradigms complexity and metaphor

Complexity in the patterns, processes and scales for the function of an ecosystem has recently gained higher significance in ecology suggesting its status something more than just a scientific theory or hypothesis explaining the wealth of reality. In a complex ecological system having a wide range of diversities, multiple operating processes and development of different patterns pertaining to the interrelationships among the structural components, a multi-model approach with replaceable components allows for flexibility in the development of models and imparts triggering effects for the generation of theories or hypotheses. Complexity representing the inherent ingredients in the functional process of ecology has often been tackled by the researchers focusing mostly on simplifying the systems and also to make them acceptable for undertaking further studies.

Ecology has its uniqueness to deal with the intricacy of nature in the view of holism and individualism, but complexity offers a suite of metaphoric tools that harmonize these long-standing alternative views. The points pertaining to the interdependences and interrelationships among different fragmentary components or totality of ecosystem have been recognized as the central theme of complexity in ecology over the last century whereas the emergence of the concept has likewise been understood as central in complexity. Ecology has long been advocating for holism vis-a-vis individualism, whereas complexity endeavors a range of novel metaphoric tools each with distinct meanings harmonizing these long-standing alternative views (Odum, 1975, 1977, 1981; Pimm, 1984; Tilman, 1998).

Unfolding of environmental complexity representing the intricate relationships among different structural components of an ecosystem helps determine the causes of survivability of each organism, which lives in a matrix of space and time. Three levels of integration operate in ecology.

(1) The distribution and abundance of organisms;
(2) Ecology overlaps with environmental physiology and behavior in studies of individual organisms;

(3) Ecology intermingles into meteorology, geology, chemistry, physics, mathematics etc. to undertake research on different dimensions of biosphere and the whole-earth ecosystem.

The potentiality of immense cross-disciplinary approaches has been tracked as a major strength of complexity which, in ecology, is much more than a scientific theory and much more than an important empirical property of reality. Ecologists tend to emphasize certain "paradigms" that can be useful in conceptualizing biological patterns and processes and also to promote the advancement of ecology either in an attempt to make generalizations about nature, as a starting point for any scientific interpretation or to teach ecological concepts. This approach attaches more importance to tracing the historical pathways of the development of key ideas in ecology. Putting more stress on the increased appreciation of historical contributions in ecology has become a prerequisite to sustain scientific momentum by way of impeding the restructuring, resynthesis and recycling of old and existing ideas. The importance of paradigms lies in studying the evolution of ecological ideas and the development of ecological theories after being tested and accepted. The ecologists started examining various processes which attain paradigm status and thereby facilitate achieving ecological progress by erasing the impression of previous research outcomes (Graham et al., 2002).

The aforementioned discourses hardly throw any light on resolving the root causes of the interplay of ecology, complexity and metaphor but rather an overlap of scholarly interpretations of the complexity as an ongoing metaphoric dimension in ecology, keeping aside the polarizing tendencies that tend to deterge metaphor from science.

Conclusions

Advances in science because of the interplay of the iterative process of induction and deduction, prediction and testing significantly enhance scientific progress in biology and in ecology, which directly links data acquisition to well-posed hypotheses. The ecological studies with the prime objectives of understanding and analyzing the relationships of living organisms in the paradigm of environment involve four major scientific approaches, including (1) observation, scrutiny and investigation based on some queries; (2) substantiating the earlier ideas with generated research information; (3) undertaking of field surveys and experimental analysis to generate research information to evaluate the possible answers of research problems and (4) interpretation for drawing inferences of the ecological studies. Strong inference entails following a simple but rigorous protocol of experimental science, efficiently designed to falsify alternative hypotheses. While mathematics plays a key role in the study of ecology, ecological controversies are mostly biological in nature and will be resolved by biologists rather than mathematicians. The life of every organism is influenced by its interactions with the environment and with other organisms with which it shares its time and space (Chakraborty, 2021a, 2021b). An organism brings to these interactions a set of genetically based physical, physiological and behavioral features that shape their outcome. The prevalence of inductive approaches in biology in general and in ecology in particular is being reflected in the pursuit of harvesting and accumulating information of the present world, which has become more aggravated due to unprecedented technological breakthroughs generating unmanageable volumes and varieties of information pertaining to the interrelationships of organisms in respect of their surrounding environment from genes to ecosystem. Data and information derived from the research studies play great roles in harnessing the potential of empirical data to make more effective progress in the subject ecology, especially to tackle the pressing problems of humanity, in relation to their unhealth, disease and environmental dysfunction with the development of efficient theories, to explain complexity of ecological systems using integrated basic, simple, qualitative and quantitative principles. Similarly, so many models, hypothesis and theories have been devised to have a transparent and clearcut understanding of biodiversity from a theoretical perspective in ecology, which in turn accelerates the scientific progress, make the human beings more capable not only to address environmental challenges but also to overcome those threats. The subject ecology had its origin to cater to the needs of the naturalists to analyze and understand nature, which has been shaped by an array of interactions between man and nature in different phases of the onward march of human civilization during last two centuries, especially after the industrial revolution in the Europe followed by drastic changes in the land use patterns (unplanned urbanization, agricultural activities, deforestation, mining, etc.). In the next phase, life was considered as the central of all reality where materials were inveterated within life giving birth of the concept of "organicism" to achieve heuristic and conceptual distinction. Several anthropogenic activities during the last 15–20 years have caused drastic changes in natural ecosystem of this planet even to the point of collapse, permanent loss of innumerable number of species, deterioration of water quality, disruption of natural hydrologic and chemical cycles, wastage of tons of topsoil through massive soil erosion, destruction of genetic diversity and great sufferings of the climate of the planet. All those undesirable changes in the environment lead to cause depletion of biodiversity components which have been originated by the interactive processes in the pathways of evolution during the time span of several billion years.

The science of conservation biology being a rapidly developing discipline has become more involved in complex environmental policy issues and ecosystem management by continuous infusion of different disciplines of social, physical and life sciences. Many attempts to conserve biodiversity hinge on concepts of community organization that need careful thought and analysis (Levin, 1992, 1998, 2005; Levine and Rees, 2002; Meffe and Carrol, 1997; Meffe et al., 2006). Besides, conservation biology is required to be moulded with the economics, sociology and politics embodying the genetic basis of conservation with an emphasis on the losses of genetic diversity, demographic processes and regulation of populations, dynamics of populations and linking of population and landscape levels in conservation process. Summing up of all discussion it can be concluded that the subject ecology of the present time has been advancing strongly in three major areas.

First, communities and ecosystems, population and communities and their interlinkages through the interacting species driving the cycles of nutrients and flows of energy.

Second, modern evolutionary thinking is being combined with ecological studies to explain the process of evolution under the control of natural selection which have resulted not only in origin of new species but also the molding of the ecological patterns as reflected by differential behavioral manifestations of the organisms.

Third, conservation biology being a major arena in the ecological thoughts and applications has enhanced the need for ecological input in habitat management.

References

Allee, W. C. (1938). *The Social Life of Animals*. Norton, New York.

Allee, W. C., Emerson, A. E., Park, O., Park, T. and Schmidt, K. P. (1949). *Principles of Animal Ecology*. W. B. Saunders, Philadelphia, PA.

Allen, A. P., Gillooly, J. F. and Brown, J. H. (2005). Linking the global carbon cycle to individual metabolism. *Functional Ecology*, 19, 202–213.

Allen, T. and Starr, T. (1982). *Hierarchy: Perspective for Ecological Complexity*. University of Chicago Press, Chicago.

Anderson, T. R. (2013). *The Life of David Lack: Father of Evolutionary Ecology*. Oxford University Press, Oxford.

Arrhenius, S. (1889). Über die Reaktionsgeschwindigkeit bei der Inversion von Rohrzucker durch Säuren. *Zeitschrift für physikalische Chemie*, 4, 226–248.

Barrett, G. W. and Odum, E. P. (2000). The twenty first century: The world at carrying capacity. *Bioscience*, 50, 363–368.

Begon, M., Townsend, C. R. and Harper, J. L. (2006). *Ecology from Individuals to Ecosystems*. Blackwell Publishing, 1–738.

Birkhead, T. R., Wimpenny, J. and Montgomerie, B. (2014). *Ten Thousand Birds: Ornithology Since Darwin*. Princeton University Press, Princeton, NJ.

Breidbach, O. (2006). *Visions of Nature: The Art and Science of Ernst Haeckel*. Prestel, Munich, Germany.

Brown, J. H., Gillooly, J. F., Allen, A. P., Savage, V. M. and West, G. B. (2004). Toward a metabolic theory of ecology. *Ecology*, 85(7), 1771–1789.

Bulnheim, H. P. (1990). A century of marine zoological and ecological research around Helgoland Island. In *Ocean Sciences: Their History and Relation to Man*. Bundesamt für Seeschiffahrt und Hydrographie, Hamburg, Germany, 84–93.

Carpenter, S. R., Kitchel, J. F. and Hodgson, J. R. (1985). Cascading trophic interactions and lake productivity. *Bio Science*, 35, 634–639.

Carpenter, S. R., Walker, B., Anderies, J. M. and Abel, N. (2001). From metaphor to measurement: Resilience of what to what? *Ecosystems*, 4, 765–781.

Carson, R. (1962). *Silent Spring*. Houghton Mifflin, New York and Boston.

Carson, W. P. and Barrett, G. W. (1988). Succession in old-field plant communities: Effects of contrasting types of nutrient enrichment. *Ecology*, 69, 984–994.

Caswell, H. (1978). Predator mediated coexistence: A non-equilibrium model. *American Naturalist*, 112, 127–154.

Chakraborty, S. K. (2003). Biodiversity and conservation. In Mukhopadhyay, A. D. (Ed.) *Perspectives and Issues in Environmental Studies*. Vidyasagar University, Midnapore, India, 267–286.

Chakraborty, S. K. (2013). Interactions of environmental variables determining the biodiversity of coastal mangrove ecosystem of West Bengal, India. *The Ecoscan* (3), 251–265.

Chakraborty, S. K. (2017). *Ecological Services on Intertidal Benthic Fauna and the Sustenance of Coastal Wetlands Along the Midnapore (East) Coast, West Bengal, India.* Alteration and Remediation, Springer International Publishing AG Part of Springer Nature, Coastal Wetlands, 777–886.

Chakraborty, S. K. (2018). Bioinvasion and environmental perturbation: Synergistic impact on coastal mangrove ecosystems of West Bengal, India (Published in the book, *Impacts of Invasive Species on Coastal Environments: Coast in Crisis*, Makowski, C. and Finkl, C. Eds. and published by Springer International Publishing AG Part of Springer, Nature), 171–245.

Chakraborty, S. K. (2021a). Riverine ecology (volume 1): Eco-functionality of the physical environment of the rivers. *Springer Nature*, 1–566.

Chakraborty, S. K. (2021b). Riverine ecology (volume 2): Biodiversity conservation, conflicts and resolution. *Springer Nature*, 1–917.

Chapman, J. L. and Reiss, M. J. (1999). *Ecology: Principles and Applications*. Cambridge University Press, Cambridge, 1–330.

Charnov, E. L. (1976). Optimal foraging, the marginal value theorem. *Theoretical Population Biology*, 9, 129–136.

Chesson, P. (1998). Making sense of spatial models in ecology. In Bascompte, J. and Sole, R. V. (Eds.) *Modeling Spatiotemporal Dynamics in Ecology*. Springer, New York, 151–166.

Chew, M. K. (2006). Ending with Elton: Prelude to invasion biology. Dissertation. Arizona State University, Tempe, AZ.

Churchill, F. B. (1980). The modern evolutionary synthesis and the biogenetic law. In Mayr, E. and Provine, W. B. (Eds.) *The Evolutionary Synthesis*. Harvard University Press, Cambridge, MA, 112–122.

Clements, F. E. (1904). Studies on the vegetation of the state. III. The development and structure of vegetation. *Reports of the Botanical Survey of Nebraska*, 7, 1–175.

Clements, F. E. (1905). *Research Methods in Ecology*. University Publishing Co., Lincoln, NE.

Clements, F. E. (1916). *Plant Succession. Analysis of the Development of Vegetation.* Publication of the Carnegie Institute, Washington, DC, 242, 1512.

Clements, F. E. and Shelford, V. E. (1939). *Bioecology*. John Wiley, New York.

Clements, F. E., Weaver, J. E. and Hanson, H. C. (1929). *Plant Competition: An Analysis of Community Functions.* Carnegie Institute of Washington, Washington, DC.

Cody, M. L. and Diamond, J. M. Eds. (1975). *Ecology and Evolution of Communities.* Harvard University Press, Cambridge, MA.

Cohen, M. N., Malpass, R. S. and Klein, H. G. Eds. (1980). *Biosocial Mechanisms of Population Regulation.* Yale University Press, New Haven, CT.

Cole, L. C. (1951). Population cycles and random oscillations. *Journal of Wildlife Management*, 15, 233–252.

Cole, L. C. (1954a). The population consequences of life history phenomena. *Quarterly Review of Biology*, 29, 103–137. Reprinted in Real and Brown 1991: 238–272.

Cole, L. C. (1954b). Some features of random population cycles. *Journal of Wildlife Management*, 18, 2–24.

Connel, J. H. and Orias, E. (1964). The ecological regulation of species diversity. *American Naturalist*, 111, 1119–1144.

Connell, J. H. (1978). Diversity in tropical rain forests and coral reefs. *Science*, 199, 1302–1310.

Cooley, T. F., Greenwood, J. and Yorukoglu, M. (1995). *The Replacement Problems*. Publication from the Department of economics, Social science Centre, University of Western Ontario, Canada.

Costanza, R., D'Arge, R., De Groot, R., Farber, S., Grasso, M., Hannon, B., Limburg, K., Naeem, S., O'Neill, R. V., Paruelo, J., Raskin, R. G., Sutton, P. and Van Den Belt, M. (1997). The value of the world's ecosystem services and natural capital. *Nature*, 387(6630), 253–260. https://doi.org/10.1038/387253a0.

Costanza, R., Norton, B. G. and Haskell, B. D. (1999). *Ecosystem Health: New Goals for Environmental Management*. Island Press, Washington, DC.

Darwin, C. (1859). *On the Origin of Species by Means of Natural Selection, or the Preservation of Favoured Races in the Struggle for Life*. John Murray, London.

Di Gregorio, A. M. (2005). *From Here to Eternity: Ernst Haeckel and Scientific Faith*. Vandenhoeck and Ruprecht, Göttingen, Germany.

Dobzhansky, T. (1951). Evolution in the tropics. *American Scientist*, 38, 209–221.

Duncan, O. D. (1964). Social organization and the ecosystem. In Faris, R. E. L. (Ed.) *Handbook of Modern Sociology*. Rand McNally, Chicago, 37–82.

Egerton, F. N. (1973). Changing concepts of the balance of nature. *Quarterly Review of Biology*, 48, 322–350.

Egerton, F. N. (2011). History of ecological sciences, part 40: Darwin's evolutionary ecology. *ESA Bulletin*, 92, 351–374.

Egerton, F. N. (2013). History of ecological sciences, part 45: Ecological aspects of entomology during the 1800s. *ESA Bulletin*, 94, 36–88.

Egerton, F. N. (2014). History of ecological sciences, part 49: Formalizing animal ecology, 1870s to 1920s. *ESA Bulletin*, 96, 59–81.

Ehrlich, P. and Ehrlich, A. (1981). *Extinction: The Causes and Consequences of the Disappearance of Species*. Random House, New York.

Elton, C. S. (1927). *Animal Ecology* (New impression with additional notes. 1935.) Macmillan, New York.

Elton, C. S. (1942). *Voles, Mice and Limmings: Problems in Population Dynamics*. Clarendon Press, Oxford.

Elton, C. S. (1958). *The Ecology of Invasions of Animals and Plants*. Methuen, London, UK.

Elton, C. S. (1966). *The Pattern of Animal Communities*. Methuen, London.

Enquist, B. J., Brown, J. H. and West, G. B. (1998). Allometric scaling of plant energetic and population density. *Nature*, 395, 163–165.

Enquist, B. J., West, G. B. and Brown, J. H. (2009). Extensions and evaluations of a general quantitative theory of forest structure and dynamics. *Proceedings of National Academy of Science*, 106, 7046–7051.

Fagerstrom, T. (1987). On theory, data and mathematics in ecology. *Oikos*, 50, 258–261.

Fischer, R. A. (1930). *The Genetical Theory of Natural Selection*. Clarendon Press, Oxford.

Fisher, A. G. (1960). Latitudinal variations in organic diversity. *Evolution*, 14, 64–81.

Fretwell, S. D. (1975). The impact of Robert MacArthur on ecology. *Annual Review of Ecology and Systematics*, 6, 1–13.

Fuchsman, C. H. (1999). Alfred James Lotka (1880–1949), Statistician and demographer. *American National Biography*, 13, 937–938.

Gause, G. F. (1934a). Experimental analysis of Vito Volterra's mathematical theory of the struggle for existence. *Science*, 79, 16–17.

Gause, G. F. (1934b). *The Struggle for Existence*. Williams and Wilkins, Baltimore, MD, 1971. Dover Publications, New York.

Gillooly, J. F., Allen, A. P., West, G. B. and Brown, J. H. (2005). The rate of DNA evolution: Effects of body size and temperature on the molecular clock. *Proceedings of the National Academy of Sciences*, 102, 140–145.

Gillooly, J. F., Brown, J. H., West, G. B., Savage, V. M. and Charnov, E. L. (2001). Effects of size and temperature on metabolic rate. *Science*, 293, 2248–2251.

Gleason, H. A. (1926). The individualistic concept of the plant association. *Bulletin of the Torrey Botanical Club*, 53, 7–26.

Goodland, R. (1995). The concept of environmental sustainability. *Annual Review of Ecology and Systematics*, 26, 1–24.

Graham, M. H., Paul, K. D. and Hixon, M. A. (2002). Paradigms in ecology. *Past, Present, and Future Ecology*, 83(6), 1479–1480.

Gridgeman, N. T. (1973). Alfred James Lotka (1880–1949), demography, statistics. *Dictionary of Scientific Biography*, 8, 512.

Grime, J. P. (1993). Ecology sans frontier and research. *Oikos*, 68, 385–392.

Grinnell, J. (1917). The niche-relationships of the California thrasher. *Auk*, 34, 427–433.

Grinnell, J. (1924). Geography and evolution. *Ecology*, 5, 225–229.

Grinnell, J. (1928). Presence and absence of animals. *University of California Chronicles*, 30, 429–450.

Haeckel, E. H. P. A. (1866). *Generelle Morphologie der Organismen. Allgemeine Grundzüge der organischen Formen-Wissenschaft, mechanische Begründet durch die von Charles Darwin reformirte Descendenz-Theorie. Volume I: Allgemeine Anatomie der Organismen. 32 + 574 pages; volume II: Allgemeine Entwickelungsgeschichte der Organismen. 140 + 462 pages*. Georg Reimer, Berlin, Germany.

Haeckel, E. H. P. A. (1869). Uber Entwichelunge Gang 4. *Aufgabe de Zoologie Jemaische*, 5, 353–370.

Hairston, N. G. (1989). *Ecological Experiments. Purpose, Design, Execution*. Cambridge University Press, Cambridge, UK.

Hairston, N. G., Smith, F. E. and Slobodkin, L. B. (1960). Community structure, population control and competition. *American Naturalist*, 94 P, 421–425.

Halder Mallick, P. and Chakraborty, S. K. (2015). Does intra-site connectivity influence the dynamics of zooplankton metacommunity in fresh water habitats? *Turkish Journal of Fisheries and Aquatic Sciences*, 15, 661–675.

Halder Mallick, P. and Chakraborty, S. K. (2018). Forest, wetland and biodiversity: Revealing multi-faceted ecological services from ecorestoration of a degraded tropical landscape. *Ecohydrology and Hydrobiology*, 18(3), 278–296.

Hanski, I. (1999). *Metapopulation Ecology*. Oxford University Press, Oxford.

Harte, J. (2011). *Maximum Entropy and Ecology: A Theory of Abundance, Distribution and Energetics*. Oxford University Press, Oxford.

Harte, J., Smith, A. B. and Storch, D. (2009). Biodiversity scales from plots to biomes with a universal species – area curve. *Ecology Letters*, 12, 789–797.

Harte, J., Zillio, T., Conlisk, E. and Smith, A. B. (2008). Maximum entropy and the state-variable approach to macroecology. *Ecology*, 89, 2700–2711.

Holling, C. S. (1966). The strategy of building models of complex ecological systems. In Watt, K. E. F. (Ed.) *Systems Analysis in Ecology*. Academic Press, New York, 195–214.

Holling, C. S. (1973). Resilience and stability of ecological systems. *Annual Review of Ecology and Systematics*, 4, 1–23.

Hopwood, N. (2006). Pictures of evolution and charges of fraud: Ernst Haeckel's embryological illustrations. *Isis*, 97, 260–301.

Howard, L. O. and Fiske, W. F. (1911). The importation into the United States of the parasites of the gipsy moth and the brown-tail moth: A report of progress with some consideration of previous and concurrent efforts of this kind. *USDA Bureau of Entomology Bulletin*, 91, 1–345, 105–109 reprinted in Tamarin, 1978, 3135.

Hubbell, S. P. (2001). *The Unified Neutral Theory of Biodiversity and Biogeography*. Princeton University Press, Princeton.

Huston, M. A. (1979). A general hypothesis of species diversity. *The American Naturalist*, 113, 81–101.

Huston, M. A. (1994). *Biological Diversity: The Coexistence of Species on Changing Landscapes*. Cambridge University Press, Cambridge.

Hutchinson, G. E. (1957a). *A Treatise on Limnology. Volume 1. Geography, Physics and Chemistry*. John Wiley, New York.

Hutchinson, G. E. (1957b). Concluding remarks. *Cold Spring Harbor Symposia*, 22, 415–427.

Hutchinson, G. E. (1958). Concluding remarks. *Cold Spring Harbor Symposium of Quantitative Biology*, 22, 415–427.

Hutchinson, G. E. (1965). The niche: An abstractly inhabited hyper volume. In *The Ecological Theater and the Evolutionary Play*. Yale University Press, New Haven.

Hutchinson, G. E. (1978). *An Introduction to Population Ecology*. Yale University Press, New Haven, CT.

Israel, G. (1993). The emergence of biomathematics and the case of population dynamics: A revival of mechanical reductionism and Darwinism. *Science in Context*, 6(2), 469–509.

Jaynes, E. T. (1982). On the rationale of maximum-entropy methods. *Proceedings of the IEEE*, 70, 939–952.

Kaspari, M. (2008). Knowing your warblers: Thoughts on the 50th anniversary of MacArthur (1958). *ESA Bulletin*, 89, 448–458.

Kearney, M. R. and White, C. R. (2012). Testing metabolic theories. *The American Naturalist*, 180(5), 546–565.

Keddy, P. A. (1992). A pragmatic approach to functional ecology. *Functional Ecology*, 6, 621–626.

Kimler, W. C. (1986). Advantage, adaptiveness, and evolutionary ecology. *Journal of the History of Biology*, 19, 215–234.

Kingsland, S. E. (1982). The refractory model: The logistic curve and the history of population ecology. *Quarterly Review of Biology*, 57, 29–52.

Kingsland, S. E. (1985). *Modeling Nature: Episodes in the History of Population Ecology*. University of Chicago Press, Chicago, IL.

Kingsland, S. E. (1986). Mathematical figments, biological facts: Population ecology in the thirties. *Journal of the History of Biology*, 19, 235–256.

Kleiber, M. (1961). *The Fire of Life*. Willey, New York.

Kormondy, E. J. (2002). *Concepts of Ecology*. Prentice Hall of India Pvt. Ltd., India, 1–552.

Krausse, E. (1987). *Ernst Haeckel*. B. G. Teubner, Leipzig, Germany.

Krebs, C. J. (2008). *The Ecological World View*. CSIRO Publishing, Oxford, 1–574.

Krebs, C. J. (1994). *Ecology: The Experimental Analysis of Distribution and Abundances*. Harper Collins College Publishers, New York, 1–801.

Lack, D. L. (1954). *The Natural Regulation of Animal Numbers*. Clarendon Press, Oxford, UK.

Lack, D. L. (1966). *Population Studies of Birds*. Clarendon Press, Oxford, UK.

Lack, D. L. (1973). My life as an amateur ornithologist. *Ibis*, 115, 421–431.

Lawton, John H. (1994). What do species do in ecosystems? *Oikos*, 71(3), 367–374.

Leibold, M. A. (1995). The niche concept revisited: Mechanistic models and community context. *Ecology*, 76, 1371–1382.

Leibold, M. A. and Wootton, J. T. (2001). Introduction. In Elton, C. S. (Ed.) *Animal Ecology.* University of Chicago Press, Chicago, IL, xix–lvi.

Leigh, E. (1975). Population fluctuations and community structure. In van Dobben, W. H. and Lowe McConnell, R. H. (Eds.) *Unifying Concepts in Ecology*, Dr. W. Junk by Publishers, The Hague, 67–88.

Levin, S. A. (1992). The problem of pattern and scale in ecology. *Ecology*, 73, 1943–1967.

Levin, S. A. (1998). Ecosystems and the biosphere as complex adaptive systems. *Ecosystems*, 1, 431–436.

Levin, S. A. (2005). Self-organization and the emergence of complexity in ecological systems. *BioScience*, 55, 1075–1079.

Levine, J. and Rees, M. (2002). Coexistence and relative abundance in annual plant communities: The roles of competition and colonization. *American Naturalist*, 160, 452–467.

Levins, R. (1966). The strategy of model building in population biology. *American Scientist*, 54, 421–431.

Levins, R. (1968). *Evolution in Changing Environments.* Princeton University Press, Princeton, NJ.

Levins, R. (1985). *The Dialectical Biologist.* Harvard University Press, Cambridge, MA.

Lindemann, R. L. (1942). The trophic dynamic aspect of ecology. *Ecology*, 23, 399–418.

Lohff, B. (1990). The unknown wonders of the sea: Johannes Müller's research in marine biology. In *Ocean Sciences: Their History and Their Relation to Man.* Bundesamt für Seeschiffahrt und Hydrograpie, Hamburg, Germany, 141–148.

López-Urrutia, A., San Martin, E., Harris, R. P. and Irigoien, X. (2006). Scaling the metabolic balance of the oceans. *Proceedings of the National Academy of Sciences*, 103, 8739–8744.

Lotka, A. J. (1925). *Elements of Physical Biology.* Williams and Wilkins, Baltimore, 460.

Lovelock, J. E. (1979). *Gaia: A New Look at Life on Earth.* Oxford University Press, New York, 1988.

Lovelock, J. E. (1995). *The Ages of Gaia.* Oxford University Press, Oxford (2nd ed.).

Lyell, C. (1830). *Principles of Geology.* John Murray, London (1 vol).

MacArthur, R. H. (1955). Fluctuations of animal populations and a measure of community stability. *Ecology*, 36, 533–536.

MacArthur, R. H. (1957). On the relative abundance of bird species. *National Academy of Sciences (USA) Proceedings,* 43, 293–295.

MacArthur, R. H. (1958). Population ecology of some warblers of northeastern coniferous forests. *Ecology*, 39, 599–619.

MacArthur, R. H. (1968). The theory of the niche. In Lewontin, R. C. (Ed.) *Population Biology and Evolution.* Syracuse University Press, Syracuse, 159–176.

MacArthur, R. H. (1969). Patterns of communities in the tropics. *Biological Journal of the Linnean Society*, 1(1–2), 19–30.

MacArthur, R. H. (1972). *Geographical Ecology.* Harper and Row, New York.

MacArthur, R. H. and Levins, R. (1964). Competition, habitat selection, and character displacement in a patchy environment. *Proceedings of the National Academy of Sciences*, 51, 1207–1210.

MacArthur, R. H. and Levins, R. (1967). The limiting similarity, convergence, and divergence of coexisting species. *American Naturalist*, 101, 377–385.

MacArthur, R. H. and Pianka, E. R. (1966). On optimal use of a patchy environment. *American Naturalist*, 100, 603–609.

MacArthur, R. H. and Wilson, E. O. (1967). *The Theory of Island Biogeography.* Princeton University Press, Princeton, NJ.

MacFadyen, A. (1975). Some thoughts on the behaviour of ecologists. *Journal of Ecology*, 63, 379–391.

MacDougall, A. S. and Turkington, R. (2005). Are invasive species, the drivers or passengers indegraded ecosystems? *Ecology*, 86(1), 42–55.

May, R. M. (1973). *Stability and Complexity in Model Ecosystem*. Princeton University Press, Princeton, NJ.

May, R. M. (1981). The role of theory in ecology. *American Zoologist*, 21, 903–910.

May, R. M. (2004). Uses and abuses of mathematics in biology. *Science*, 303, 790–793.

Maynard Smith, J. (1964). Group selection and kin selection. *Nature,* 201, 1145–1147.

Maynard, Smith. J. (1972). *On Evolution*. Edinburgh University Press, Edinburgh.

Maynard Smith, J. and Slatkin, M. (1973). The stability of predator-prey systems. *Ecology*, 54, 384–391.

Meffe, G. K. and Carrol, C. R. (1997). *Principles of Conservation Biology*. Sinauer Associates, Inc., Sunderland, MA.

Meffe, G. K., Ehrenfeld, D. and Noss, R. F. (2006). Conservation biology at twenty. *Conservation Biology*, 20(3), 595–596.

MEC (Millennium Ecosystem Assessment) (2005). *Ecosystems and Human Well-Being Synthesis*. Island Press, Washington, DC.

Miller, G. T. and Spoolman, S. E. (2010). Environmental science. *Cengage Learning*, 1–545.

Molles, M. C. (2008). *Ecology Concepts and Applications*. McGraw Hill, Toronto.

Morowitz, H. J. (1968). *Energy Flow in Biology: Biological Organization as a Problem in Thermal Physics*.

Murdoch, W. W., Brigg, C. J., Nisbet, R. M., Gurney, W. S. C. and Stewart-Oaten, A. (1992). aggregation and stability in metapopulation models. *American Naturalist*, 140, 41–58.

Murphy, D. D., Freas, K. E. and Weis, S. B. (1990). An environment-metapopulation approach to population viability analysis for threatened invertebrates. *Conservation Biology*, 4(1), 41–51.

Naveh, Z. (2000). The total human ecosystem concept: Integrating ecology with economics. *Bioscience*, 50, 357–361.

Nicholson, A. J. and Bailey, V. A. (1935). The balance of nature. *Zoological Society of London Proceedings* (3), 551–598. Extracts in Real and Brown 1991, 125–156.

Odum, E. P. (1969). The strategy of ecosystem development. *Science*, 164, 262–270.

Odum, E. P. (1971). *Fundamentals of Ecology*. Saunders Company, USK, Philadelphia, 1–574.

Odum, E. P. (1975). *Ecology: The Link Between the Natural and Social Science*. Holt, Reinhart and Winston, New York.

Odum, E. P. (1977). The emergence of ecology as a new integrative discipline. *Science*, 195, 1289–1291.

Odum, E. P. and Barrett, G. W. (2005). *Fundamentals of Ecology*. Peter Marshall, 1–598.

Odum, H. T. (1981). *Energy Basis for Man and Nature*. McGraw Hill, New York.

Paine, R. T. (1966). Food web complexity and species diversity. *American Naturalist*, 100, 65–75.

Parker, G. A. (1984). Evolutionary stable strategies. In Krebs, J. R. and Davies, N. B. (Eds.) *Behavioral Ecology: An Evolutionary Approach*. Blackwell Scientific Publications, Oxford, 30–61.

Pasteur, L. (1862). Note remise au Ministere de I'Instruction publique et des cultes, sur sa demande, Avril 1862, In L'oeuvre de Pasteur, T.VII, p. 3.

Peters, R. H. (1991). *A Critique for Ecology*. Cambridge University Press, Cambridge.

Pianka, E. R. and Horn, H. S. (2005). Ecology's legacy from Robert MacArthur. In *Eco-Logical Paradigms Lost: Routes of Theory Change*. Elsevier Academic Press, Boston, MA, 213–232.

Picket, S. T. A. and White, P. S. (Eds.). (1985). *The Ecology of Natural Disturbances as Patch Dynamics*. Academic Press, New York.

Pickett, S. T. A., Kolasa, J. and Jones, C. G. (1994). *Ecological Understanding: The Nature of Theory and the Theory of Nature*. Academic Press, New York.

Pielou, E. C. (1981). The usefulness of ecological models: A stock-taking. *The Quarterly Review of Biology*, 56, 17–31.

Pimm, S. L. (1984). The complexity and stability of ecosystems. *Nature*, 307(5949), 321–326.

Pimm, S. L. (1991). *The Balance of Nature?* University of Chicago Press, Chicago.

Pimm, S. L., Lawton, J. H. and Cohen, J. E. (1991). Food web patterns and their consequences. *Nature*, 350, 669–674.

Preston, F. W. (1962). The canonical distribution of commonness and rarity, parts 1 and 2. *Ecology*, 43, 185–215.

Price, P. W. (1997). *Insect Ecology*. John Wiley and Sons, New York (3rd ed.).

Price, P. W. (2003). Historical views on distribution, abundance, and population dynamics. Chapter 2. In Price, P. W. (Ed.) *Macroevolutionary Theory on Macroecological Patterns*. Cambridge University Press, New York, 9–47.

Proctor, J. D. and Brendon, M. H. L. (2005). Ecology, complexity, and metaphor. *BioScience*, 55(12), 1065–1068.

Pyke, G. H. (1984). Optimal foraging theory: A critical review. *Annual Review of Ecology, Evolution, and Systematics*, 15, 523–575.

Qian, H. R. E. and White, P. S. (2004). The region effect on mesoscale plant species richness between eastern Asia and eastern North America. *Ecography*, 27, 129–136.

Richards, R. J. (2008). *The Tragic Sense of Life: Ernst Haeckel and the Struggle Over Evolutionary Thought*. University of Chicago Press, Chicago, IL.

Ricklefs, R. E. (1987). Community diversity: Relative roles of local andregional processes. *Science*, 235(4785), 167–171.

Ricklefs, R. E. (2004). A comprehensive frame work for global patterns in biodiversity. *Ecology Letters*, 7, 1–15.

Ricklefs, R. E. (2008). Disintegration of the ecological community. *American Naturalist*, 172, 741–750.

Ricklefs, R. E. and Miller, G. L. (1999). *Ecology*. W.H. Freeman and Company, New York, 1–822.

Ricklefs, R. E. and Schluter, D. (1993). *SpeciesDiversity: Historical and Geographical Patterns*. University of Chicago Press, Chicago.

Rinard, R. G. (1981). The problem of the organic individual: Ernst Haeckel and the development of the biogenetic law. *Journal of the History of Biology*, 14, 249–275.

Robinson, S. P., Downton, W. J. S. and Millhouse, J. A. (1983). Photosynthesis and ion content of leaves and isolated chloroplasts of salt-stressed spinach. *Plant Physiology*, 73, 238–242.

Root, R. B. (1967). The niche exploitation pattern of blue-gray gnatcatcher. *Ecological Monographs*, 37, 317–350.

Rosenzweig, M. L. (1995). *Species Diversity in Space and Time*. Cambridge University Press, Cambridge.

Roughgarden, J. (2009). Is there a general theory of community ecology? *Biology and Philosophy*, 24(4), 521–529.

Sanders, H. L. (1968). Marine benthic diversity: A comparative study. *American Naturalist*, 102, 243–282.

Savage, V. M., Gillooly, J. F., Brown, J. H., West, G. B. and Charnov, E. L. (2004). Effects of body size and temperature on population growth. *American Naturalist*, 163(3), 429–441.

Schwartz, M. (2018). The life and works of Louis Pasteur. *Journal of Applied Microbiology*, 91(4), 597–601.

Scudo, F. M. (1971). Vito Volterra and theoretical ecology. *Theoretical Population Biology*, 2, 1–23.

Scudo, F. M. (1984). The "golden age" of theoretical ecology: A conceptual appraisal. *Revue Européene des Sciences Sociales*, 22, 11–64.

Scudo, F. M. and Ziegler, J. R. Eds. (1978). *The Golden Age of Theoretical Ecology: 1923–1940: A Collection of Works*. Volterra, V., Kostitzin, V. A., Lotka, J. A. and Kolmogoroff, A. N. Eds. Springer-Verlag, Berlin, Germany.

Shelford, V. E. (1913). *Animal Communities in Temperate America*. Chicago University Press, Chicago.

Sibly, R. M., Brown, J. H. and Kodric-Brown, A. Eds. (2012). *Metabolic Ecology: A Scaling Approach*. Wiley-Blackwell, Oxford.

Simpson, G. G. (1964). Species density in north American recent mammals. *Systematic Zoology*, 13, 57–73.

Smit, P. (1967). Ernst Haeckel and his "Generelle Morphologie": An evaluation. *Janus*, 54, 236–252 + 2 plates.

Smith, J. M. and Price, G. R. (1973). The logic of animal conflict. *Nature*, 246, 15–18.

Smith, R. L. (1996). *Ecology and Field Biology*. Addison-Wesley Educational Publishers, Boston, MA, 1–740.

Soulé, M. E. (1985). What is conservation biology? *BioScience*, 35(11), 727–734.

Spatz, H. C. (1991). Circulation, metabolic rate, and body size in mammals. *Journal of Comparative Physiology*, 161, 231–236.

Stileng, P. (2002). *Ecology: Theories and Applications*. Prentice Hall, New Delhi, 1–403.

Strong, D. R., Simberlof, F. D., Abele, L. and Thistle, A. B. (1984). *Ecological Communities: Conceptual Issues and the Evidence*. Princeton University Press, Princeton, NJ.

Tamarin, R. H. (1977). Demography of the beach vole (Microtus breweri) and the meadow vole (M. pennsylvanicus) in southeastern Massachusetts. *Ecology*, 58, 1310–1321.

Tamarin, R. H. Ed. (1978). *Population Regulation*. Dowden, Hutchinson and Ross, Stroudsburg, PA.

Tansley, A. G. (1935). The use and abuse of vegetational concepts and terms. *Ecology*, 16, 284–307.

Thompson, W. R. (1939). Biological control and the theories of the interactions of populations. *Parasitology*, 31, 299–388.

Tilman, D. (1982). *Resource Competition and Community Structure*. Princeton University Press, Princeton, NJ.

Tilman, D. (1988). *Plant Strategies and the Dynamics and Structure of Plant Communities*. Princeton University Press, Princeton, NJ.

Tilman, D. (1994). Competition and biodiversity in spatially structured habitats. *Ecology*, 75(1), 2–16.

Tilman, D. and Pacala, S. (1993). The maintenance of species richness in ecological communities. In Ricklefs, R. E. and Schluter, D. (Eds.) *Species Diversity in Ecological Communities*. University of Chicago Press, Chicago, 13–25.

Turchin, P. (2003). *Complex Population Dynamics: A Theoretical Empirical Synthesis*. Princeton University Press, Princeton, NJ.

Tyndall, J. (1861). The Bakerian lecture on the absorption and radiation of heat by gases an vapours, and on the physical connection of radiation, absorption and conduction. *Philosophical Magazine*, 4, 1358–1363.

Ulanowicz, R. E. (1997). A hypothesis on the development of natural communities. *Journal of Theoretical Biology*, 85, 223–245.

UNCED (United Nations Conference on Environment and Development). (1992). *The Earth Summit*. The United Nations Convention on Biological Diversity, Rio de Janeiro, 3–14 June.

Urban, M. C. (2015). Accelerating extinction risk from climate change. *Science*, 348, 571–573.

Uschmann, G. (1972). Ernst Heinrich Philipp August Haeckel (1834–1919), zoology. *Dictionary of Scientific Biography*, 6, 6–11.

Volterra, E. (1976). Vito Volterra (1860–1940), mathematics, natural philosophy. *Dictionary of Scientific Biography*, 14, 85–88.

Volterra, V. (1926). Variation and fluctuations of the number of individuals in animal species living together. In Chapman, R. N. (Ed.) *Animal Ecology*. McGraw-Hill, New York, 409–448.

Walker, B. H. (1992). Biodiversity and ecological redundancy. *Conservation Biology*, 6, 18–23.

Walker, B. H. (1995). Conserving biological diversity through ecosystem resilience. *Conservation Biology*, 9, 1–7.

Wallace, A. R. (1823–1913) (1978). *Tropical Nature and Other Essays*. Macmillan, New York.

Watt, K. E. F. (1962). Use of mathematics in population ecology. *Annual Review of Entomology*, 7, 243–260.

Weiner, J. (1992). Physiological limits to sustainable energy budgets in birds and mammal. Ecological implications. *Trends in Ecology and Evolution*, 7, 109–116.

Weiner, J. (1995). Asymmetric competition in plant population. *Trends in Ecology and Evolution*, 5, 360–364.

West, G. B. and Brown, J. H. (2005). The origin of allometric scaling laws in biology from genomes to ecosystems: Towards a quantitative unifying theory of biological structure and organization. *Journal of Experimental Biology*, 208, 1575–1592.

West, G. B., Brown, J. H. and Enquist, B. J. (1997). A general model for the origin of allometric scaling laws in biology. *Science*, 276, 122–126.

Whittaker, E. T. (1941). Vito Volterra, 1860–1940. *Royal Society of London Obituary Notices of Fellows*, 3, 691–724.

Whittaker, R. H. (1962). Classification of natural communities. *Botanical Review*, 28, 1–239.

Whittaker, R. H. (1975). *Communities and Ecosystems*. MacMillanCompany, New York.

Williams, C. B. (1964). *Patterns in the Balance of Nature and Related Problems in Quantitative Ecology*. Academic Press, New York.

Wilson, E. O. and Hutchinson, G. E. (1989). Robert Helmer MacArthur, April 7, 1930 – November 1, 1972. *National Academy of Sciences Biographical Memoirs*, 58, 318–327.

Wilson, H. F. and Doner, M. H. (1937). *The Historical Development of Insect Classification*. John S. Swift, St. Louis, MI.

Printed in the United States
by Baker & Taylor Publisher Services